Capitalism and Commerce

Praise for

Capitalism and Commerce

"Making use of the literature of liberty, Younkins provides a very clear, concise, and accessible introduction to the conceptual foundations of capitalism and a free society."
—**Chris Matthew Sciabarra**, New York University

"Younkins's book is quite a *tour de force* through classical liberal views on production and exchange activities of people, as well as on some sweeping philosophical history. His views will appeal to, and be embraced by, individuals with classical liberal sensibilities."
—**Charles W. Baird**, California State University, Hayward

"Capitalism rests on a moral foundation, like the rest of civilization. Edward W. Younkins has done an extraordinary job of explicating that foundation, in an impressive and much-needed work."
—**Llewellyn H. Rockwell Jr.**, Ludwig von Mises Institute

"*Capitalism and Commerce* points out that what it takes to be successful in a capitalist society is being able to please others, and as a system, capitalism encourages moral behavior. It should be read by every journalist in America."   —**Gary Wolfram**, Hillsdale College

"[*Capitalism and Commerce*] is a powerful, scholarly antidote to all the shallow, politically-correct business bashing that is so prevalent in academe and the media."
—**Thomas J. DiLorenzo**, Loyola College of Maryland

"*Capitalism and Commerce* is far more than its altogether too modest subtitle *Conceptual Foundations of Free Enterprise* indicates. Yes, the book covers this topic with thoroughness, eloquence, and wisdom, but it also touches upon just about every question or criticism that anyone has ever made about the morality or practicality of free enterprise. . . . This book is a *tour de force* presentation of the case for economic freedom."
—**Walter Block**, Loyola University, New Orleans

Capitalism and Commerce

Conceptual Foundations of Free Enterprise

Edward W. Younkins

LEXINGTON BOOKS

A division of
ROWMAN & LITTLEFIELD PUBLISHERS, INC.
Lanham • Boulder • New York • Toronto • Plymouth, UK

LEXINGTON BOOKS

A division of Rowman & Littlefield Publishers, Inc.
A wholly owned subsidiary of The Rowman & Littlefield Publishing Group, Inc.
4501 Forbes Boulevard, Suite 200
Lanham, MD 20706

Estover Road
Plymouth PL6 7PY
United Kingdom

British Library Cataloguing in Publication Information Available

Library of Congress Cataloging-in-Publication Data

Younkins, Edward Wayne, 1948-
  Capitalism and commerce : conceptual foundations of free enterprise /
Edward W. Younkins.
      p. cm.
Includes bibliographical references and index.
  ISBN 0-7391-0380-6 (cloth : alk. paper)—ISBN 0-7391-0381-4 (pbk. :
alk. paper)
  1. Capitalism—Moral and ethical aspects. 2. Commerce—Moral and
ethical aspects. 3. Free enterprise—Moral and ethical aspects. I. Title.
  HB501 .Y68 2002
  330.12'2—dc21

                                                    2002009006

Printed in the United States of America

♾™ The paper used in this publication meets the minimum requirements of American
National Standard for Information Sciences—Permanence of Paper for Printed Library
Materials, ANSI/NISO Z39.48–1992.

For my parents, who taught me to love liberty, to accept responsibility, to respect reality, and to trust the judgment of my own mind.

Contents

Part IV: Governance

Part V: Obstacles to a Free Society

Part VI: In Retrospect and Prospect

Preface

Unless we can make the philosophic foundations of a free society once more a living intellectual issue, and its implementation a task which challenges the ingenuity and imagination of our liveliest minds, the prospects of freedom are indeed dark. But if we can regain the belief in the power of ideas that was the mark of liberalism at its best the battle is not lost.

—Friedrich A. Hayek

The survival and flourishing of business as an institution depends upon concepts and moral values that provide the foundations upon which a capitalistic society is constructed. These concepts and values include, but are not limited to: natural law, natural rights, individualism, personal responsibility, negative freedom, morality, freedom of association, civil society, the nature of true communities, the free market, private ownership, work, contract, the nature and responsibilities of the corporation, voluntary unionism, progress, entrepreneurship, technology, governance, justice, law, power, authority, constitutionalism, and pluralism.

In a world of change, the viability of the market economy is at stake unless those who live and participate within it possess a rational understanding and appreciation of its underlying concepts and values. Present and future participants in the business system need to have access to a "bank" of fundamental ideas that provide the groundwork for the free enterprise system—this book provides such a bank. Its purpose is to be a clear, consistent, and accessible introduction and guide for anyone wishing to pursue the study of the theoretical and moral foundations of capitalism.

Capitalism as defined in this book (i.e., uncompromising laissez-faire capitalism) involves that set of economic arrangements that could exist in a society in which the state's only function would be to prevent one person from using force or fraud against another person. Admittedly, I do not realistically expect to see such an economy in the near future. Rather, I offer it as an ideal for which we should strive since the morality of the capitalist system of rewards and punishments is consistent with the nature of human beings and the world.

This book embraces the major ideas and institutions that explain the essence and functions of commerce in a free society. The ideas are the philosophical concepts that have underpinned the idea of capitalism. The institutions include not only business associations, but also those legal and political institutions that have a major bearing on commercial enterprises. *Capitalism and Commerce* examines the conceptual foundations of business developed over centuries in a number of disciplines, including philosophy, economics, political science, law, history, and so on. This work introduces people to the idea of the free market as a moral institution with a theoretical framework rather than as simply a pragmatic means of efficient production. It is about freedom and the discovery of the type of society men require in order to engage in their own happiness-pursuing activities.

People who favor freedom and free markets are a diverse lot whose worldviews vary markedly. Advocates of capitalism differ in their arguments for a social system that maximizes individual freedom and in their views with respect to the nature of man and the universe. Fortunately, it is not necessary to first reach metaphysical or religious agreement in order to concur on the desirability of a system in which individuals do not use violence or fraud to injure others or to deprive others of their legitimately held possessions. Various proponents of capitalism agree that the proper role of the state is limited to protection of property and punishment of those who rob and cheat others.

It is anticipated that the theoretical principles discussed in this volume will be widely supported by those from various schools of thought including, but not limited to: (1) classical liberalism; (2) the Austrian School; (3) the Judeo-Christian perspective (also known as economic personalism); (4) the Virginia (Public Choice) School; (5) the Chicago School; (6) the Aristotelian or Human Flourishing School; and (7) Objectivism. Uniting these separate views is the need for freedom of the individual to choose how he wants to integrate himself into society through the use of his individual human potentialities. All agree that: (1) man's mind is competent to deal with reality; (2) it is morally proper for each person to strive for his personal flourishing and happiness; and (3) the only appropriate social system is one in which the initiation of physical force is forbidden.

Although I did not realize it at the time, this book had its origins in 1988 with a series of lectures and notes that I put together for my Conceptual Foundations of Business course as part of Wheeling Jesuit University's then new undergraduate major in Political and Economic Philosophy. Over the years, the notes were expanded and refined through study and reading of numerous volumes and articles from a variety of disciplines and through valuable discussions with my friends and colleagues.

By the mid-nineties I found myself writing essays and articles based on the same topics that I emphasized in my Conceptual Foundations of Business class. These have appeared in a number of journals such as *Ideas on Liberty* (formerly *The Freeman*), *The Social Critic*, *Journal of Markets and Morality*, *The Individual*, *The Free Radical*, *Free Life*, *Le Québécois Libre*, and *Liberty Free Press*. I have frequently used essays and articles to develop the ideas that appear in a more comprehensive manner in this book. Consequently, I would like to thank the editors of the aforementioned journals for permitting me to make use of previously published materials.

I have endeavored to be consistent in my writings and to make them accessible to a great number of readers by avoiding academic jargon and through the use of clear, nontechnical explanations of the ideas underlying the free market and limited government. My target audience is the educated layperson and the college student.

All of us are inevitably unknowledgeable in many complicated fields. Consequently, we do not try to function in those fields. However, every person works within or deals with the business system and therefore needs to understand its nature and foundations. Explaining the nature and underpinnings of business is the purpose of this book.

This work is mainly one of exposition. I make no claim to originality with respect to the major ideas that it presents. Because the volume is an exposition, I have freely used the ideas of countless others without detailed footnotes or other acknowledgment. This is unavoidable when one writes to educate others in a field to which many of the world's finest minds have contributed. However, at the end of each chapter I have included a list of recommended readings for those who wish to study a given topic in greater depth and detail. The recommended readings include those that support my free-market perspective, those that are in strong opposition to that view, and those that partially support it. A lot can be learned by reading and understanding your foes' writings as well as the works of those who hold mixed premises.

After a brief introduction, *Capitalism and Commerce* is divided into the following six sections: (1) Individuals, Communities, and the State; (2) Ownership; (3) Progress; (4) Governance; (5) Obstacles to a Free Society; and (6) In Retrospect and Prospect. The chapters are grouped in categories that make the most sense to me, but obviously some could easily have been placed in other groups. For example, the chapter on The Labor Union has been placed in the Ownership section because of the idea of voluntary unionism, but it could just as well been located within the Obstacles to a Free Society category due to the existence of coercive unions. In addition, the chapters do not have to be read in progression in order to be understood by the reader. Each chapter presents a self-contained treatment of the topic at hand that is consistent with the ideas presented in the rest of the book. Also, I've included a "Reader's Guide" to selected free-market-oriented organizations and periodicals for readers who may want the ideas presented in this book in greater depth and detail.

Over the last several years, many people have contributed importantly to this work by reading and commenting on all of it, various portions of it, or drafts of my essays containing ideas that appear in it. I am extremely grateful to the following individuals for their useful observations and suggestions: Charles W. Almond, Paul Anderton, Charles W. Baird, Doug Bandow, Walter Block, David Boaz, James Buchanan, Scott Carpenter, Tyler Cowen, Thomas J. DiLorenzo, Richard M. Ebeling, Kenneth G. Elzinga, Milton Friedman, Joseph S. Fulda, Sean Gabb, Stephen Grabill, Bettina Bien Greaves, Homayoun Hajiran, Stephen

Hicks, Robert Higgs, Beth Hoffman, John Hospers, Richard J. Klonoski, Yuval Levin, Spencer MacCallum, Tibor R. Machan, John E. Mansuy, Thomas G. Marx, Martin Masse, Robert W. McGee, Steve McGee, Thomas Michaud, Ron Nash, C. James Newlan, Michael Novak, Sid Parkinson, Lindsay Perigo, William H. Peterson, Karen M. Phillips, Richard Pomazal, Lawrence W. Reed, Sheldon Richman, Llewellyn Rockwell, Tom Rose, David Schatz, Chris Matthew Sciabarra, Fred Seddon, Rev. Robert Sirico, John Stossel, Jeffrey Tucker, Murray Weidenbaum, Walter E. Williams, and Gary Wolfram. Of course, inclusion in the above list does not indicate endorsement of this book or agreement with the ideas expressed within it. It does mean that each on this list has assisted me in some way with this current project. Most of all, I am indebted to my secretaries at Wheeling Jesuit University, Carla Cash and Carol Carroll, for their most capable and conscientious help in bringing this book to print.

Edward W. Younkins
Wheeling Jesuit University

Introduction

Capitalism and Morality

Capitalism is based on self-interest and self-esteem; it holds integrity and trustworthiness as cardinal virtues and makes them pay in the marketplace, thus demanding that men survive by . . . virtues, not . . . vices.

—Alan Greenspan

Few would deny that capitalism is the most productive and efficient economic system, especially after the collapse of Soviet Communism. But some critics still contend that capitalism is not a moral system. Yet, morality is impossible unless one has the freedom to choose between alternative actions without outside coercion. Choice delimits the sphere of morality. Because capitalism is based on freedom of choice, it allows for morality and character development— a key aspect of human flourishing. In addition, by permitting free market transactions, capitalism allows commerce to develop. Business in a free society not only requires, but also rewards, virtuous behavior by participants in the market.

Morality Requires Freedom

All human beings have natural rights either endowed by their Creator or inherent in their nature and have moral obligations to respect the rights of others. The purpose of natural rights is to protect individual autonomy and accountability. Natural rights impose a negative obligation—the obligation not to interfere with someone else's liberty. Being all ontologically equal and independent, no one ought to harm another with respect to his life, liberty, or possessions. It is illegitimate to use coercion against a man who does not first undertake the use of force. The role of government, as recognized by America's founders, is to protect man's natural rights through the use of force, but only in response, and only against those who initiate its use.

The natural right to political freedom is a social condition necessary for the possibility of moral action. This kind of freedom involves far more than simple democracy. It demands a protected private sphere within which an individual can pursue his freely chosen norms, actions, and ends without the arbitrary intervention of others. Natural rights, therefore, require a legal system that provides the necessary conditions for the possibility of self-actualization and morality.

There can be no morality without responsibility and no responsibility without self-determination. Responsible self-determination implies rationality, honesty, self-control, productiveness, and perseverance. In its absence, people will devalue liberty, qualities of character will diminish, and government institutions may take over and become the means for people to evade personal responsibility, to live off the efforts of others, and to force others to solve their problems.

Capitalism Makes Morality Possible

A social system such as capitalism is a system of relationships and cannot be moral or immoral in the sense that a person can be—only individuals can be moral agents. However, a social system can be moral in its effects if it promotes the possibility and likelihood of moral behavior of mindful human beings who act within it. It follows then, that because the formation of a social system is an act of men, there is a moral imperative to create the kind of political and economic system that permits the greatest possibility for self-determination and moral agency. Capitalism is that system.

Capitalism is itself only a means and leaves it to the individual to decide the types of goals to be pursued. The intellectual basis of capitalism is that the individual is free and has certain inviolable natural rights. Within a system of capitalism, the proper role of government is simply to enable people to pursue happiness on their own. Happiness cannot be given to people—they must attain it through their own efforts. The government cannot supply more than the prerequisite conditions.

No economic system can make good men or make men good. The best that an economic system can do is allow men to be good. Morality requires the freedom to be immoral. Capitalism, the system that maximizes this freedom, cannot guarantee a moral society; however, it is a necessary condition for one. Only when an individual has choice and bears responsibility for his actions can he be moral. Choice (i.e., free will) is the foundation of virtue. Morality involves choice and the use of practical reason in making that choice. Capitalism is consistent with the fundamental moral principles of life itself and, compared to other economic systems, is the most conducive to the use of man's free will, which makes moral behavior possible. Capitalism is the only social system that is in accord with the central role that practical reason plays in the moral lives of persons.

Character Development Requires Self-Direction

Human flourishing usually requires more than material wealth. However, prosperity is a crucial enabling condition that allows each individual the opportunity to develop his potential and find happiness through the cultivation of his talents, abilities, and virtues. Capitalism, the best system for wealth creation, permits individuals to spend less time on physical concerns thus giving them the time to turn to higher level pursuits of happiness such as education, love, creative and fulfilling work, character development, community building, etc.

Moreover, the highly individualized and self-directed nature of personal flourishing requires that practical reason be employed by a person confronting the particular and contingent facts of his concrete situation and determining at the time of action what is, in those circumstances, good and proper for him. Capitalism is the only system that protects and permits such conduct in the production and exchange of goods and services and therefore is a system defensible in terms of human flourishing.

Happiness is related to one's self-esteem that includes both a person's self-efficacy and self-respect. Self-respect, in turn, stems from a person's character development. By allowing for individual autonomy and self-determination, capitalism gives each person the chance to develop his character—the internal source of external behavior. Self-direction involves the use of one's reason and is a central necessary feature of human flourishing. Morality is a matter of character and the free exercise of will and judgment.

In order to flourish as a human being, a person must develop a good character—one of which he can be proud. This involves the cultivation of one's virtues—character traits that are morally and socially valued. A person has the ability to consciously deliberate when he faces ethical dilemmas. This deliberation includes the evaluation of alternative courses of action and the desires, ethical principles, and character traits that could be cultivated. This involves self-awareness, self-assessment, and self-regulation. The rational human life is characterized by the development and exercise of the moral virtues. One's virtues become more ingrained as he becomes more aware of their importance with respect to human flourishing and happiness.

The virtues are moral excellences—the lack of which lessens self-respect. In a free society an individual must develop and earn his personal character. When a person develops a good personal character he will be happier, more satisfied, and more self-actualized.

Business Rewards Virtuous Behavior

Commerce is concerned with providing goods and services that individuals perceive as being desirable or necessary in their lives. It follows that business is directly and fundamentally involved in the human pursuit of happiness. Business helps people to realize what they discern to be the good life.

When commerce is conducted within a capitalistic society, virtues are promoted. The pursuit of profit reflects the presence of many of the virtues. The free market rewards polite, accommodating, tolerant, open, honest, realistic, trustworthy, discerning, creative, fair-dealing businessmen. In the long run, profitable businesses tend to be populated by people who conduct the business in accordance with basic ethical principles calling for honesty, respect for persons and property, fidelity to commitments, justice, and fairness.

Business people have incentives to do well. Lying and cheating may ruin the company's image and reputation. Mistreating workers will lead to lessened productivity, absenteeism, grievances, and employee turnover. Unsafe working conditions will lead to higher wage demands. Misinforming customers or giving them less than they bargained for will lead to reduced sales. Ignoring product safety could lead to accidents, lawsuits, and decreased sales. Taking advantage of suppliers may result in shortages of material and possible shutdowns. Screening out potential employees because of race, gender, or other group characteristics means reducing the firm's chances of hiring the best workers. Excluding customers because of their group means losing sales to competitors. Ignoring all "stakeholder" demands can decrease long-run profitability—some expenditures for socially beneficial purposes are legitimate when they are expected to generate sufficient future benefits for the firm.

The Moral Responsibility of Businessmen

The moral responsibility of the directors, managers, and other employees of a corporation are to respect the natural rights of individuals. This involves the basic principle of noninitiation of physical force and includes: the obligation to honor a corporation's contracts with its managers, employees, customers, suppliers, and others; the duty not to engage in deception, fraud, force, threats, theft, or coercion against others; and the responsibility to honor representations made to the local community.

A businessman should be honest and just in his dealings with others—they should be identified and treated according to what they are, do, and freely agree to. For example, the most deserving employees should be promoted and the best bidders should be awarded contracts. In addition, a manager should not support government actions such as price supports, tariffs, quotas, and subsidies even though such policies may result in higher profits for his own company. To do so would involve coercion, one step removed. To support such natural-rights-violating actions would be to undermine the principles of the free society upon which business depends. When corporate leaders use the political process to protect themselves from competition and to receive taxpayer subsidies, they cease to be engaged in commercial activity.

Business Promotes Cooperation and Communication

Under capitalism business takes place by mutual agreement and for perceived mutual advantages. Voluntary exchange is a form of cooperation between buyers and sellers in which individuals can promote their own interests only by serving the interests of others. The most successful competitors are those who best cooperate with or satisfy others in society by discerning needs and wants imperceptible to others and the combination of resources that could meet those needs and wants. If a firm fails to take advantage of opportunities to create new products or services, it will lose profits to competitors. Competitors compel each other to cooperate more effectively with the buying public. Capitalism promotes businesses that are "other regarding" and tolerant of others. A free-market society also places a premium on communications and persuasion. It follows that one must establish a relationship of trust in order to persuade. Great rewards in the form of new products, new ideas, and expanded sales lie in searching for and trusting those who are different from us.

A Moral and Rational Defense

By protecting individual choice, capitalism not only generates enormous wealth but also creates an environment in which morality and virtue can flourish. In the end, capitalism is not only the most productive and efficient political and economic system, it is also the arrangement that best allows for and encourages personal flourishing, the use of one's reason, morality, and character development. Certainly, people can act morally or immorally in a capitalistic system just as they can in socialism, interventionism, etc. However, capitalism promotes a number of positive and morality promoting characteristics that are absent or weak in other systems.

Capitalism is a political and economic system in which an individual's rights to life, liberty, and property are protected by law. It is the system most able to make personal flourishing possible. By securing personal freedom, capitalism makes the successful pursuit of individual happiness more likely. A capitalist society can be viewed as a just society because all individuals are considered to be equal under the law.

Capitalism is derived from a worldview that holds that: (1) man's mind is competent to deal with reality; (2) it is morally proper for each person to strive for his personal flourishing and happiness; (3) the only appropriate social system is one in which the initiation of physical force is forbidden; and (4) it is not necessary to first reach metaphysical or religious agreement to agree on the desirability of an arrangement in which people do not use violence or fraud to injure others or deprive others of their legitimately held possessions. Capitalism is the only moral social system because it protects a man's primary means of survival and flourishing—his mind.

By permitting market transactions, capitalism allows for business to exist as a set of voluntary and organized human activities. Market exchange is a type of cooperation that increases one's ability to act on his own best judgments as to what will enhance his own well-being. Dealing with others by means of voluntary trade involves a relationship that is based on the mutual judgment that a particular exchange is to the advantage of each participant.

Commerce can be viewed as the social product of human concern with the intellectual and moral virtue of prudence—advancing one's own essential well-being. Prudence involves the critical evaluation of one's own interests. To be prudent is to apply intelligence to changing circumstances by acting in the right manner, at the right time, and for the right reasons. Commerce is a proper, morally justified area of human action in which businessmen are concerned with attaining economic well-being. Commercial interactions exist due to people's inability to provide for their own needs, wants, and desires. Businessmen succeed by producing wealth and by freely trading with others. For both the businessman and the customer, the other has instrumental value. Businessmen transform potential wealth into physical products and services by combining human innovations and discoveries with human labor and natural resources. Such wealth is primarily a product of the human mind. Through the use of intelligence, businessmen make possible physical goods, services, and enjoyment of life.

Recommended Reading

Acton, H. B. *The Morals of Markets*. London: Longman Group, 1971.

Barnard, Chester I. *The Functions of the Executive*. Cambridge, Mass.: Harvard University Press, 1938.

Berg, Ivar, ed. *The Business of America*. New York: Harcourt, Brace, & World, 1968.

Barry, Norman. *The Morality of Business Enterprise*. Aberdeen, U.K.: Aberdeen University Press, 1991.

Chesher, James E., and Tibor R. Machan. *The Business of Commerce*. Stanford, Calif.: Hoover Press, 1999.

Den Uyl, Douglas J. *The Virtue of Prudence*. New York: Peter Lang, 1991.

Elbing, A. O., and Carol Elbing. *The Value Issue in Business*. New York: McGraw-Hill, 1967.

Eells, Richard, and Clarence Walton. *Conceptual Foundations of Business*. Homewood, Ill.: Richard D. Irwin Inc., 1974.

Friedman, Milton. *Capitalism and Freedom*. Chicago: University of Chicago Press, 1962.

Hendrickson, Mark W., ed. *The Morality of Capitalism*. Irvington-on-Hudson, N.Y.: Foundation of Economic Education, 1992.

Machan, Tibor R. *The Main Debate: Communism versus Capitalism*. New York: Random House, 1987.

Machan, Tibor R., ed. *Commerce and Morality.* Totowa, N.J.: Rowman & Littlefield, 1988.

Machan, Tibor R. *Capitalism and Individualism.* New York: St. Martin's Press, 1990.

McGee, Robert W., ed. *Business Ethics and Common Sense.* Westport, Conn.: Quorum Books, 1992.

Novak, Michael. *The Spirit of Democratic Capitalism.* New York: Simon & Schuster, 1982.

Rand, Ayn. *Atlas Shrugged.* New York: Random House, 1957.

———. *Capitalism: The Unknown Ideal.* New York: New American Library, 1965.

Regan, Tom, ed. *Just Business: New Introductory Essays in Business Ethics.* New York: Random House, 1983.

Reisman, George. *Capitalism.* Ottawa, Ill.: Jameson Books, 1996.

Rogge, Benjamin A. *Can Capitalism Survive?* Indianapolis, Ind.: Liberty Press, 1979.

Selekman, Sylvia, and Benjamin Selekman. *Power and Morality in a Business Society.* New York: McGraw-Hill, 1959.

Shand, Alexander. *Free Market Morality: The Political Economy of the Austrian School.* London: Routledge, 1990.

Soloman, Robert C. *Ethics and Excellence.* New York: Oxford University Press, 1993.

Sommers, Christina, and Fred Sommers. *Vice and Virtue in Everyday Life.* New York: Harcourt Brace Jovanovich, 1993.

Walton, Clarence C. *Ethos and the Executive: Values in Managerial Decision-Making.* Englewood Cliffs, N.J.: Prentice-Hall, 1969.

PART I

INDIVIDUALS, COMMUNITIES, AND THE STATE

1

Individual Rights

The idea of natural right must be unknown as long as the idea of nature is unknown.
The discovery of nature is the work of philosophy. Where there is no philosophy,
there is no knowledge of natural rights as such.

—Leo Strauss

America was founded on the concept of rights; however, when many of its citizens speak of rights today, they mean something quite different from what was envisioned by Madison, Jefferson, Franklin, and Locke. These men shared the belief that individual rights were a fact of nature existing prior to, and independently of, any man-made laws. The purpose of the legislative process was not to create laws or additional rights of the legislators' own design but merely to proclaim and enforce men's natural rights while taking none of these rights from them. New conceptions of sovereignty and politics have recently become popular with the result that people have increasingly come to regard the government as the source of rights rather than as a defender of pre-existing individual rights. The assumption of this new view is that a right is not simply a freedom to do a certain thing but is the privilege of forcing others to take positive actions to provide some perceived entitlement. If this were true, a right would not be seen as a freedom but rather as a power.

Natural Rights Are Freedoms

To the founders, a right was a moral principle or imperative defining and sanctioning a man's freedom of action in a social context. Such a right represents a man's absolute power to seek an end. Under this process view of rights, the only duty imposed on others by such rights is the negative duty of forbearance—of not interfering with that to which a person has a right. If a person has a right to perform a certain activity, then others have the obligation not to interfere with that activity.

It follows that there are no group rights—only individual rights. Group rights are arbitrary and imply special interests. The state is not involved in the creation of rights—it mainly exists to protect an individual's natural rights. Concerned with protecting the self-directedness of individuals, rights are a metanormative concept that provides law with a moral underpinning.

Where do rights originate? Many believe that all humans are endowed with rights by God. Sovereignty, the source of rights, rests with the Creator. All human beings have natural rights inherent in their created nature and have moral obligations to respect the rights of others. Natural rights such as religious liberty, the right of self-directedness, the right to private property, and the right to economic initiative are founded in the nature of the person—each person having been made in the image of God.

Others say that certain moral rights are inherent in human nature and the human condition and are thought to be possessed by all persons because of their nature as rational beings. To flourish in accordance with human nature, a person must live intelligently. It follows that autonomy in the use of one's reason is a necessary, but not sufficient, condition of human flourishing. Respect for the self-directedness of each person is thus necessary because self-directedness is required for the flourishing of each individual.

The purpose of natural rights, also known as negative rights or liberty rights, is to protect individual autonomy and, for many, accountability to God. From the standpoint of interpersonal relations, each man is a self-owner with the inalienable rights of life, liberty, and the pursuit of happiness (which includes the right to private property). These protect a man's right to act freely to pursue his happiness. Rather than guarantee happiness, they leave us responsible for our lives and for the pursuit of our freely chosen goals. Natural rights impose a negative obligation—the obligation not to interfere with one's liberty. Being all equal and independent, no one ought to harm another with respect to his life, liberty, or possessions. It is illegitimate to use coercion against a man who does not first undertake the use of force. The role of government is to protect man's natural rights through the use of force, but only in retaliation, and only against those who initiate its use.

The natural right to freedom is a social condition necessary for the possibility of moral action. Freedom involves the idea of a protected private sphere within which an individual can pursue his freely chosen norms, actions, and ends without the intervention of arbitrary coercion. Natural rights, therefore, require a legal system which provides the necessary conditions for the possibility that individuals might self-actualize and pursue their own moral well-being.

There is a critical distinction between a person's right and the morality or immorality of the use of that right. Whereas political philosophy is concerned only with questions of rights and of the legitimate or illegitimate use of physical coercion in human relationships, personal ethics deal with the morality or immorality of the ways in which rights are exercised.

Individuals' natural rights do draw the lines that separate people, their properties, and their spheres of action. However, these rights also provide opportunities for community members to act virtuously toward one another. For example, under a system of natural rights, a person can withhold a claim (i.e., forgive a debt) against another person, express generosity, etc.

To be a natural right it must be possible for all persons to exercise the claimed right simultaneously without logical contradiction. Rights such as freedom of speech, freedom to own property, freedom of religion, and freedom of association are examples of natural rights. Each can be exercised by each person without denying that right to others. Whenever a right claimed by an individual imposes an obligation on another to perform a positive action, it is impossible for the alleged right to be exercised by each simultaneously without logical contradiction.

Natural rights are not only genuine rights, but they are timeless, possible to achieve, and require human action for their violation. In addition, it's possible for charity to exist within the realm of natural rights.

Welfare Rights Are Powers

During the 1960s, proponents of redistribution began to use the language of "rights" in their efforts: (1) to achieve a greater equalization of wealth; (2) to expand the role of government beyond its original conception; and (3) to allow recipients of government subsidies to think they are getting what they have earned or deserve. Welfare rights, also called positive rights, are rights to goods such as food, clothing, shelter, education, health care, a job, etc. Welfare rights are communal rights for the enforcement of which a coercive government is required.

This interventionist or positivist view of rights stems from the philosophy of legal positivism and asserts that the state can create and extinguish rights as long as it follows the rules of procedural due process. Under this alternative view, people can create rights through the government and are constantly revising their conceptions of rights. Positive rights are not derived from our natural rights.

A positive right of one person to food, health care, a job, education, and so on, imposes a duty on others to undertake positive actions to provide the entitlement and thus involves an expenditure of money, time, or effort. People have positive rights only at the expense of someone else's natural rights. Welfare rights are claims to the products of other persons' labor and involve demands for new forms of government compulsion. Rather than ensuring the procedural freedom of all individuals, they are, in fact, special privileges, conferred upon some persons at the expense of others.

The claim of welfare rights is meant to impose on some people the positive obligation to provide goods for others. However, neither needs nor demands create rights. If my need of a particular good establishes my right to it, then some other people have the involuntary obligation to provide me with the good at their expense. Other people are self-owners just as I am. I cannot morally force them to pay for my needs or wants. If others are forced to provide for me because of my welfare rights, then they are being used as a means to my welfare. The welfare rights idea is incompatible with the view of persons as ends in themselves. In addition, consistency requires that one man's rights not diminish the rights of others. For example, a government that simultaneously asserts the natural right to private property and then takes the property to fulfill welfare rights has adopted inconsistent principles.

Welfare rights are illegitimate rights—they change over time, are impossible to attain, and do not require human action for their violation. Furthermore, if there are welfare rights then it is impossible for a person to engage in charitable acts. I can't give a person something if it's his right to have it! A willingness to help others is a matter of personal choice—not a requirement imposed by the state.

Natural Rights Are Legitimate Rights

A legitimate right is not to a thing or to a given result—but to engage in an activity without the guarantee of success. For example, the right to property is not the power to have it taken from others, but simply to do something to attain it that does not violate the natural rights of others. This process conception of rights involves the legal ability of individuals to carry on certain processes without regard to the desirability of specific results as judged by other persons. The function of natural rights as metanormative principles is to protect the self-directedness and moral autonomy of individuals and thus secure the freedom under which individual happiness and moral well-being may be pursued.

When a person respects other individuals' rights, he sustains the conditions, which maximize the likelihood of improving his own life through voluntary exchange with others. It is in an individual's own interest to respect the freedom of others because freedom is a necessary condition for reasoned action. Each individual's reason spurs his production efforts, enhances his own life, and provides the means for him to offer something of value to others. Other individuals' provision of goods, services, innovations, theoretical and practical insights, and artistic creations can thus contribute toward one's own happiness and enjoyment of life.

A political and economic system that recognizes only (or mainly) negative rights is superior to systems that try to spell out extensive positive rights in addition to the negative ones. The minimal state allows individual community members to directly look out for and take care of people one knows personally. A system based on negative rights puts individual voluntarism, interpersonal attachments, and community goodwill at the core of political, social, and economic arrangements.

Recommended Reading

Finnis, John. *Natural Law and Natural Right.* Oxford: Oxford University Press, 1980.

Hart, H. L. A. "Are There Any Natural Rights?" *Philosophical Review* (October 1955).

Lomasky, Loren E. *Persons, Rights, and the Moral Community.* Oxford: Oxford University Press, 1987.

Machan, Tibor R. *Human Rights and Human Liberties.* Chicago: Nelson-Hall Co., 1975.

————. *Individuals and Their Rights*. LaSalle, Ill.: Open Court, 1989.

Miller, Fred D. *Nature, Justice, and Rights in Aristotle's Politics*. Oxford: Oxford University Press, 1995.

Nozick, Robert. *Anarchy, State, and Utopia*. New York: Basic Books, 1974.

Rasmussen, Douglas B. "Individual Rights and Human Flourishing." *Public Affairs Quarterly*. 3, 1989.

Rasmussen, Douglas B., and Douglas J. Den Uyl. *Liberty and Nature*. LaSalle, Ill.: Open Court, 1991.

Shue, Henry. *Basic Rights*. Princeton, N.J.: Princeton University Press, 1980.

Smith, Tara. *Moral Rights and Political Freedom*. Lanham, Md.: Rowman & Littlefield, 1995.

Spector, Horatio. *Autonomy and Rights*. Oxford: Clarendon Press, 1992.

Strauss, Leo. *Natural Rights and History*. Chicago: University of Chicago Press, 1953.

Sumner, L. W. *The Moral Foundations of Rights*. Oxford: Oxford University Press, 1987.

Tuck, Richard. *Natural Rights Theories: Their Origin and Development*. Cambridge: Cambridge University Press, 1979.

Veatch, Henry B. *Human Rights: Fact or Fancy*. Baton Rouge: Louisiana State University Press, 1985.

Zuckert, Michael. *Natural Rights and the New Republicanism*. Princeton, N.J.: Princeton University Press, 1994.

2

Individuals and Communities

A true community respects free persons; an inadequate or false community does not. . . . Unless he or she is injuring others, the only way in which a genuine community can approach a rational person is through rational and civil persuasion, not through coercion, force, or systematic oppression.

—Michael Novak

Individualism is the view that each person has moral significance and certain rights that are either of divine origin or inherent in human nature. Each person exists, perceives, experiences, thinks, and acts in and through his own body and therefore from unique points in time and space. It is the individual who thinks and has the capacity for original and creative rationality. Individuals' minds can interrelate, but thinking requires a specific, unique thinker. The individualist assumes responsibility for thinking for himself, for acting on his own thought, and for achieving his own happiness.

Freedom is the natural condition of the individual—each person from birth has the ability to think his own thoughts and control his own energies in his efforts to act according to these thoughts. Men are free to initiate their own purposive action when they are free from man-made restraints—when there is an absence of coercion by other individuals, groups of people, or the government. Freedom is not the ability to get what we desire. Other non-man-made obstacles such as lack of ability, intelligence, or resources may result in one's failure to attain his desires. Freedom means the absence of coercive constraints; however, it does not mean the absence of all constraints. For example, when one says that man is not "free" to fly, what is really being said is that man does not have the power to fly, given the laws of man's nature and the laws of the world. It follows that freedom is a necessary but not a sufficient condition for one's happiness. Individual happiness can be defined as the positive, conscious, and emotional experience that accompanies or derives from the use of one's individual human potentialities, including his talents, capabilities, and virtues. The sense of belonging to freely chosen communities is an important constituent of happiness. Although the individual is metaphysically primary (and communities are

secondary and derivative), communities are important because humans need to
belong to them in order to reach their potential for happiness. The social bonds
of affiliation are instrumentally valuable in the satisfaction of nonsocial wants
and desires and necessary for one's personal flourishing. A libertarian political
system, one that respects natural rights and allows for large amounts of individual freedom, best nourishes the formation of voluntary communities through
which people of common values choose to live by those values.

Genuine Communities Are Freely Chosen Communities

Assigning primary emphasis to the individual does not devalue social cooperation. Humans are not only distinct individuals but also social beings. Cooperative action affords growth possibilities and brings benefits which otherwise
would be unattainable by isolated individuals. Man's rationality allows him to
cooperate and communicate with others. In a free society, all cooperative social
ventures are entered voluntarily. In fact, individualism provides the best theoretical basis for a genuine community that is worthy of human life. Voluntary,
mutually beneficial relations among autonomous individuals are essential for the
attainment of authentic human communities. The uniqueness and worth of the
human person is affirmed when membership in a community is freely chosen by
the individuals that comprise it.

Individualism denies that a community or a society has an existence apart
from the individuals who make up that community or society. A community or
society is a collection of individuals—it is not some concrete thing or living
organism distinct from its members. To use an abstract term such as *community*
or *society* is to refer to certain persons sharing particular characteristics and related in specifiable ways. There is no such thing as the general will, collective
reason, or group welfare apart from, and other than, that possessed by each individual in a group. A community or a society is simply the association of persons
for cooperative action. Coordinated group action is a function of the self-
directed and self-initiated efforts of each person within the group.

Individualism and independence liberate interdependence. In a recent popular best-seller, Stephen Covey observes that interdependence is a choice that
only independent people can make. A positive, principle-centered, value-driven
person who organizes and executes his life priorities with integrity is capable of
building rich, enduring, and productive relationships with others. True independence of character empowers a person to act rather than be acted upon. Independence of character requires one to integrate certain principles (i.e., virtues)
such as integrity, courage, justice, honesty, fairness, and so on, into his nature.
Interdependent people combine their own efforts with the efforts of others to
achieve even greater success and happiness. They are self-reliant and capable
people who realize that more can be accomplished by working together than by
working alone. Interdependent persons choose to share themselves with, learn
from, understand, and love others and, therefore, have access to the resources

and potential of other human beings.

True Communities Respect the Primacy of Free Persons

The discrete individual person is the subject of value and the unit of social analysis. Each human being is an end in himself. Freedom, justice, virtue, dignity, and happiness all must be defined in terms of the individual; however, the pursuit of individual happiness will naturally and almost always occur in communities. Men have needs as individuals that cannot be met except through cooperation with other human beings—it is impossible to achieve human fulfillment in isolation. A true community respects free persons. Genuine communities arise when people are free to form voluntary associations to pursue their individual and mutual interests. Inherent in respect for the human person is respect for the reflectively chosen forms of association that persons create to pursue their common interests.

Individuals do not begin in a condition of isolation—to exist is to coexist. Birth, by nature, takes place within families, including parents, siblings, grandparents, aunts, uncles, cousins, etc. These family members, in turn, have numerous memberships in a variety of communities and voluntary associations. Men are unique, ontologically equal individuals who are not only born into a universal (i.e., human) community of shared mortality and accountability, but, because of their nature, also have potentialities which can only be realized through cooperation with other human beings. Equality involves the recognition of our common human capacity to be free to associate with those of our own choosing. Men are necessarily related to others and they can determine to a large measure the persons they will be affiliated with and the ways in which they will be associated. People are responsible for choosing, creating, and entering relationships that will enable them to flourish. If people are free, they will naturally form communities and voluntary associations, given their inherent need for belonging to communities. Communities arise when persons voluntarily unite together to search for and realize their essential being. When communities are freely chosen, the results are a sense of joint ownership, a coincidence of interest, and a sense of belonging on the part of the members. Community identification and involvement thus contribute toward the happiness of the individual participants.

In a free society, individuals tend to belong simultaneously to many different communities. To varying degrees, each person identifies with particular familial, religious, locational, occupational, professional, employment, ethnic, racial, cultural, social, political, or other communities. These communities are usually, but not necessarily, local and severely limited in size by the number of persons with whom an individual could have a personal acquaintance and relationship and share a recognizable common interest. Continuing technological advances in communications and transportation enhance people's ability to select the communities that best meet their needs and aspirations.

The Minimal State Allows True Communities to Flourish

The bonding together of citizens into voluntary communities and associations enables them to remain independent of the state. Life in freely chosen communities is better for the person than life as a dissociated individual in a large nation-state. Our skepticism of state power favors the placement of as many intermediate voluntary groups as possible between the state and the individual—these mediating institutions help individuals realize their objectives more freely and more completely. The principle of subsidiarity holds that the state should restrict its activities to those that individuals and private associations cannot effectively perform. Decisions are most wisely made by individuals and local agencies closest to the pertinent everyday realities, and by the next highest agencies only when beyond the capabilities of actors at lower levels. Subsidiarity allows free individuals to thrive in authentic concrete communities without the intervention of the state.

The purpose of the state is not to help people either materially or spiritually to pursue their visions of happiness—that is the role of individuals, communities, and voluntary associations. The proper function of the state is no more than to provide people with the enabling conditions for their own happiness-pursuing activities. This simply means preventing interference from others in such pursuit.

Whereas active state governments are inimical to the formation and operation of communities formed by voluntary participation, the generation of such communities is facilitated by the minimal state—one that operates within the constraints of liberal individualism. Rich and rewarding personal relationships based on voluntary cooperation and mutual assistance abound within minimalist, rights-based systems. The freedom of individuals is a necessary condition for the formation and vitality of true communities.

Recommended Reading

Beito, David. "Voluntary Associations and the Life of the City." *Humane Studies Review* (fall 1988).

Bellah , Robert N., et al. *Habits of the Heart: Individualism and Commitment in American Life.* Berkeley: University of California Press, 1985.

Berger, Peter L., and Richard John Neuhaus. *To Empower People.* Washington, D.C.: AEI Press, 1977.

Covey, Stephen T. *Seven Habits of Highly Effective People.* New York: Simon & Schuster, 1989.

Foldvary, Fred. *Public Goods and Private Communities.* Brookfield, Vt.: Edward Elgar, 1994.

Hiskes, Richard P. *Community without Coercion: Getting along in the Minimal State.* Newark: University of Delaware Press, 1982.

Hobhouse, L. T. *Liberalism.* New York: Oxford University Press, 1976.

Kelley, David. *Unrugged Individualism*. Poughkeepsie, N.Y.: Institute for Objectivist Studies, 1996.

Lomasky, Loren E. *Persons, Rights, and Moral Community*. New York: Oxford University Press, 1987.

Lukes, Steven. *Individualism*. London: Oxford University Press, 1973.

Machan, Tibor R. *Individuals and Their Rights*. LaSalle, Ill.: Open Court, 1989.

———. *Capitalism and Individualism*. New York: St. Martin's Press, 1990.

———. *Classical Individualism*. London: Routledge, 1998.

MacCallum, Spencer. *The Art of Community*. Menlo Park: Institute for Human Studies, 1970.

Marine, Brian John. *Individuals and Individuality*. Albany, N.Y.: SUNY Press, 1984.

Nisbet, Robert A. *The Quest for Community*. New York: Oxford University Press, 1953.

Norton, David. *Personal Destinies: A Philosophy of Shared Individualism*. Princeton, N.J.: Princeton University Press, 1976.

Novak, Michael. *This Hemisphere of Liberty*. Washington, D.C.: AEI Press, 1990.

Schmidt, Alvin J. *Fraternal Organizations*. Westport, Conn.: Greenwood Press, 1980.

Sherover, Charles M. *Time, Freedom, and the Common Good*. New York: University Press, 1990.

Tocqueville, Alexis de, and J. P. Mayer, eds. *Democracy in America*. Translated by George Lawrence. Garden City, N.Y.: Doubleday, 1969.

3

Civil Society

The happiness of individuals is the great end of civil society: for in what sense can a public enjoy any good, if its members considered apart, be unhappy?

—Adam Ferguson

Whereas the state, or political society, is based on coercion, civil society is based on voluntary participation. The state is the institutionalization of force with respect to its financing (e.g., taxation), the allowable activities of its citizens (e.g., regulation), or the forced participation of individuals (e.g., compulsory military service). In political society, someone else makes decisions about your life. In civil society, you make those decisions. Civil society is the sphere of cooperation, competition, and true charity.

Civil Society

David Boaz, in *Libertariansm: A Primer*, observes that civil society is made up of all the natural and voluntary associations in society, including families, churches, clubs, fraternal societies, neighborhood groups, charities, self-help groups, trade associations, unions, sole-proprietorships, partnerships, corporations, etc. Each association within civil society is created to achieve a specific purpose, but civil society as a whole has no intended purpose—it is the undesigned, spontaneously emerging result of all of the voluntary, purposive associations. Order in civil society results as the unintended by-product of the voluntary and mutually beneficial associations among the individuals in that society.

Communities emerge as individuals voluntarily relate to one another in an indefinite number of ways. A man needs to associate with others in order to flourish and fulfill his needs and desires. Oftentimes, engagement in communities leads to a sense of retrospective satisfaction in one's life. It follows that civil society is comprised of associations without being collectivist and is individualistic without being atomistic.

Civil society, the realm of freedom, is based on giving the widest possible discretion to the individual so that he has sovereignty over his own life in the pursuit of his happiness, as long as he respects the equal rights of others. It follows that political society should exist only to prevent force, fraud, and misrepresentation. As the state grows, civil society wanes. It is in civil society that men flourish and from civil society that prosperity, progress, and virtue flow.

The corporation has a primary position in the construction of the major alternative to the state—civil society. The corporation depends on investors for its financing. Its purpose is to provide goods and services in order to earn income for its investors, with fiduciary care for its invested capital. Sources of private capital and private wealth are crucial to the survival of freedom—the alternative is dependence on the state.

According to Michael Novak in *The Fire of Invention: Civil Society and the Future of the Corporation*, from the point of view of civil society, the corporation is an important social good for the following reasons: (1) It creates jobs; (2) It provides goods and services; (3) Through its profits it creates wealth that did not exist before; and (4) It is a private social instrument, independent of the state, for the moral and material support of other activities of civil society.

The corporation is a major supporter of many works of civil society, including charities, the arts, research, universities, etc. Of course, expenditures for such purposes are legitimate only when the stockholders have authorized them or when managers reasonably believe they will increase the firm's long-run profits.

In addition, corporations underpin the financial hopes of many Americans. Over half of the adult population owns corporations through mutual funds, pensions plans, etc.

Cooperation and Competition

Capitalism involves the voluntary exchange of goods and services between free and self-responsible individuals to their mutual benefit. With the advent of specialization of labor, people found it necessary to develop an exchange mechanism through which a producer of one item could exchange it for something he would produce less efficiently than another. Voluntarism ensures that both parties to an economic transaction will gain from it. Each person enters a free-market transaction because, in his own judgment, the result will be beneficial to him. Each party acquires something he values more in exchange for something he values less.

The free market, a key component of civil society, developed as men realized that they could accomplish more through cooperation than they could individually. Cooperation can actually enhance a person's individuality by increasing his chances of attaining his goals and flourishing as a human being.

In a world of scarce resources and self-interested individuals, each possessing the right to self-determination, it is essential for people to voluntarily cooperate with one another in order to attain their instrumental goals and pursue their needs for human interconnectedness. This implies the need for a minimal state, the rule of law, the division of labor, and a secure system of property rights.

Persons engaged in economic activity may be guilty of coercion, fraud, or theft in which one party will benefit at the other's expense. The proper role of the government under capitalism is to restrain and punish those who obstruct the practice of free exchange. In a free-market economy people are rewarded for serving others and are punished only for injuring others.

Capitalism is based on cooperation. Workers cooperate with their employers. Farmers cooperate with distributors and food processors. Manufacturers cooperate with distributors, both of whom are attempting to cooperate with consumers. Banks cooperate with individuals, firms, and families. Unions cooperate with corporations, etc.

Capitalism is inherently relational—it fosters human interdependence and a mutualistic outlook. Voluntary exchange is a form of cooperation between buyers and sellers in which individuals can only promote their own interests by furthering the interests of others. Limited by the rule of law, individuals and groups prosper only to the degree that they offer products or services for which people are willing to trade. The consumer is sovereign under capitalism. The only way for an individual or corporation to grow and remain economically successful is to continually satisfy consumers. This calls for an increasing regard for the interests, desires, tastes, and opinions of consumers. Failure to adjust one's actions to the consumers' wishes will result in losses and the shifting of resources to those who serve consumers better.

Under capitalism, successful competitors are those who cooperate with or satisfy others in society. Firms and individuals compete with one another in order to cooperate more effectively with the buying public. As a result, competition encourages invention, innovation, research, cost reductions, greater efficiency, and the development of new and better products and services.

The varieties of enterprise associations that exist are attempts to find better ways of attaining mutual purposes. Licensing agreements, joint ventures, outsourcing, and other forms of strategic partnering are common today. Even apparent competitors sometimes find it advantageous to cooperate with one another in their efforts to acquire needed resources or access to markets!

The profit-and-loss system in a voluntaristic society is just and moral. A person's wealth under capitalism depends upon his productive achievements and the choice of others to recognize them. Profits indicate that a businessman has served his fellowmen by using resources to produce a product or render a service at costs below the value people place upon the product or service. The firm making profits is using resources in a manner that satisfies what people want and need. Losses indicate that a businessman has failed to serve his fellowmen efficiently. Justice does not imply that everyone deserves some predetermined share of wealth, but that what people deserve varies according to their accomplishments, and that it is proper to observe those differences. As people recognize that rewards depend upon their efforts and outputs, their incentives to produce increase. Not only does profit provide risk takers with incentives, it also serves as a guide for allocating resources, provides a reward for efficiently serving other people, and serves as a measure of efficiency in the use of resources to satisfy customers.

True Charity

The goal should be to have no welfare state at all. Welfare is not only demeaning to its beneficiaries, government programs also diminish self-reliance, breed dependency, and reinforce social pathologies by creating unintended rewards for people to do the things they are trying to remedy (e.g., pay people to have children they can't support and encourage unemployment). Also, a system that tries to force acts of love, such as charity, violates the true nature of love and, as a result, creates injustice. The only way the state can "help" people is to give them wealth taken through taxation from someone else. Forcing people to be "charitable" makes them self-centered and resentful. When people are financially squeezed by the welfare state, they find their ability for private philanthropy to be greatly reduced. Only people who are allowed to keep what they have earned have the financial means to be benevolent and compassionate. The existence of government welfare brings red tape, diminishes the spirit of self-sacrifice, and fosters the unfortunate view that assistance to the poor is the state's job rather than private citizens' freely chosen obligations for charity.

Much of the need for the welfare state is caused by the government itself. For example, minimum wage laws create poverty by increasing unemployment, tariffs and quotas make consumer goods more expensive, and rent control promotes homelessness by supplying a disincentive to provide low-rental housing. In addition, regulations such as building codes, zoning requirements, and licensing laws have obstructed the development of small businesses that are crucial for raising people out of poverty through employment.

Even in the absence of government poverty-causing programs, there would still be unfortunate people such as the disabled, the illiterate, the sick, the unemployed, the mentally incompetent, the elderly, and single mothers of infant children. The welfare state is a poor substitute for personal local acts of charity that emphasize self-reliance and self-respect—qualities that tend to be missing when government welfare is viewed as positive "rights" to be asserted. Given that some type of charity is needed, private sector solutions are vastly preferable to governmental ones. Civil society allows for a variety of voluntary initiatives by family, friends, neighbors, churches, charitable organizations, unions, fraternal and friendly societies, and others, to help those in need. Voluntarism means doing away with coercion and relying on individual action, education, persuasion, and voluntary organizations based on generosity and neighborliness.

Individuals who give through private charities are aware of both the amount of their sacrifice and to a great extent, the actual use of their contributions. Private charity allows people to undertake ventures that the state either will not or cannot take on. People tend to give to private charities because they believe in the goals of the organization. Such sacrifices are made because individuals perceive value in their contributions. When a person donates his own resources he wants to receive value for his sacrifice. Charity may therefore be viewed as an exchange transaction in which both parties receive benefits. Recipients of charity must act in a manner that makes charitable acts desirable to the givers. They become happier when they choose to be committed to the happiness of others. Benevolence is a rational and self-interested virtue that enables men to gain pleasure by interrelating with others and helping them in the pursuit of their own happiness.

Self-respect and self-reliance are contributory to happiness. It follows that true charity encourages self-esteem in the recipients and emphasizes practical measures that help people to help themselves. When recipients of charity fight against adversity, take steps to help themselves, and gain self-esteem, the donor receives satisfaction and pleasure from the virtues of individuals he respects. It follows that charity, at the same time, can be both generous and self-interested. Also, because people do live in communities, are necessarily related to others, and consider the well-being of others to be important to them it is self-interested (in an enlightened sense) to consider the needs of others.

Reinvigorating Civil Society

In the past, families, neighborhoods, charities, churches, and other friendly societies taught and reinforced in their members the habits of self-responsibility, discipline, mutual support, and regard for the future. They fostered a sense of community and voluntarism, separate from, and independent of, state action. Our most serious challenge today is to re-create a vibrant civil society to solve the social problems that welfare statists have tried to solve with governmental action. A person who understands that he is a member of a free society tends to realize that its material and spiritual health needs his participation in its voluntary associations of good works and mutual help. In order to have a society of responsible and virtuous individuals, responsibility for virtue must be taken back from the state and returned to the individuals and associations that comprise civil society. Political society cannot mandate virtue, morality, and responsibility—it can only provide a framework for their possibility.

Government programs permit men to shift responsibility for the consequences of their actions to unwilling parties by disrupting the connection between cause and effect and crowd out private initiatives by enervating private citizens and breaking the bond between those in need and people who want to help. State programs teach that the roles of giving and organizing giving belong to the government rather than to individuals.

Social security has made people dependent on the state for their retirement income—politicians who pretend that it is in a trust fund spend citizens' forced payments currently. In civil society, people provide for their own retirement by investing in securities, savings accounts, and so on, that furnish the resources that create jobs and stimulate productivity and economic growth. The welfare state's transfer programs have made the poor dependent on the state—we need to eliminate programs that discourage self-responsibility and independence, destroy families and communities, and stand in the way of people who want to respond to problems around them. By forcing firms to act in prescribed ways, regulation limits the alternatives from which firms can choose and discover the best option available. Such intervention has prompted companies to make large investments in lobbying and influence-seeking activities—activities that result in the redistribution rather than the creation of wealth. A business performs its most vital functions when it is allowed to do what is was founded to do—hire people, provide goods and services, and generate wealth. Government regulation keeps firms from doing what they do best.

Recently (and ironically), government projects and programs have been started to restore civil society through state subsidization or coercive mandates. Such coercion cannot create true voluntary associations. Statists who support such projects believe only in the power of political society—they don't realize that the subsidized or mandated activity can be performed voluntarily through the private interaction of individuals and associations. They also don't understand that to propose that an activity not be performed coercively is not to oppose the activity but, simply, its coercion.

If civil society is to be revived, we must substitute voluntary cooperation for coercion and replace mandates with the rule of law. According to the *Cato Handbook for Congress*, Congress should:

- "before trying to institute a government program to solve a problem, investigate whether there is some other government program that is causing the problem . . . and, if such a program is identified, begin to reform or eliminate it;
- ask by what legal authority in the Constitution Congress undertakes an action . . . ;
- recognize that when government undertakes a program, it displaces the voluntary efforts of others and makes voluntary association in civil society appear redundant, with significant negative effects; and
- begin systematically to abolish or phase out those government programs that do what could be accomplished by voluntary associations in civil society . . . recognizing that accomplishment through free association is morally superior to coercive mandates, and almost always generates more efficient outcomes."

Every time taxes are raised, another regulation is passed, or another government program is adopted, we are acknowledging the inability of individuals to govern themselves. It follows that there is a moral imperative for us to reclaim our right to live in a civil society rather than to have bureaucrats and politicians "solve" our problems and run our lives.

Recommended Reading

Berger, Peter L. *To Empower People: From State to Civil Society*. Edited by Michael Novak. Contribution by Richard John Neuhaus. Washington, D.C.: Regnery Publishing, 1995.

Boaz, David. *Libertarianism: A Primer*. New York: Free Press, 1997.

Dionne, E. J., ed. *Community Works: The Revival of Civil Society in America*. Washington, D.C.: Brookings Institute, 1998.

Ehrenberg, John. *Civil Society: The Critical History of an Idea*. New York: New York University Press, 1999.

Eberly, Don E., ed. *Building a Community of Citizens: Civil Society in the 21st Century*. Lanham, Md.: University Press of America, 1994.

Eberly, Don E. *America's Promise: Civil Society and the Renewal of American Culture*. New York: Rowman & Littlefield, 1998.

Ferguson, Adam. *An Essay on the History of Civil Society, 1767*. New Brunswick, N.J.: Transaction Publishers, 1980.

Gellner, Ernest. *Conditions of Liberty: Civil Society and Its Rivals*. New York: Viking Press, 1994.

Green, David. *Reinventing Civil Society: The Rediscovery of Welfare without Politics*. London: Institute of Economic Affairs, 1993.

Hayek, F. A. *The Constitution of Liberty*. Chicago: University of Chicago Press, 1960.

Leef, George C. "The Virtues of Competition." *The Freeman* (July 1996).

Murray, Charles. *In Pursuit of Happiness and Good Government*. New York: Simon & Schuster, 1988.

Novak, Michael. *The Fire of Invention: Civil Society and the Future of the Corporation*. New York: Rowman & Littlefield, 1997.

Olasky, Marvin. *The Tragedy of American Compassion*. Washington, D.C.: Regnery Publishing, 1995.

———. *Renewing American Compassion*. New York: Free Press, 1996.

Seligman, Adam B. *The Idea of Civil Society*. Princeton, N.J.: Princeton University Press, 1995.

4

The Common Good

The common good is the sum of those conditions of social life which allows so-cial groups and their members relatively thorough and ready access to their own fulfillment.

—Vatican Council II

The idea of the common good has been one of the most vague and most difficult concepts to clarify in the history of man. For many, the common good has primacy over persons and thus takes precedence over self-interest. Some even reify the abstract concept of the common good, acting and speaking as if it has an existence of its own. When the common good of society is looked upon as something separate from and superior to the individual good of its members, there is a tendency for the common good to be interpreted as the good of the majority.

In politics, economics, and culture, the term is frequently employed when the speaker is encouraging others to make sacrifices "for the sake of the common good." The common good is often evoked in an economic context with reference to the poor and concern with equality and the distribution of wealth. Appeal to the common good is a device for inspiring people to attend to the conditions of the less fortunate.

Those who wish to impose their wills on their "subjects" also often use the expression *common good*. Advocates of socialist schemes tell us that we must join in because all human beings have a moral obligation to serve the common good rather than their own desires. We are told that it is the government that must provide for the common good because individuals cannot be trusted to voluntarily sacrifice for the common good. The result is the tribal notion of the common good as a vision aimed at or imposed by a ruler or a set of rulers. Exhibiting a disrespect for persons, political authorities frequently dictate the course of action to be undertaken to achieve the common good and set standards to gauge the extent of its realization.

Along with a number of faculty members from philosophy, political science, and economics, I regularly participate in the senior seminar for the majors in Political and Economic Philosophy at my university. At one session, several faculty members and students were engaging in a debate in which references were vaguely and frequently made to "the common good." One student bravely asked one of our political philosophy professors to define what exactly was meant by the common good, noting that our assorted professors commonly refer to common good but seldom define what they mean by that utterance. Stunned by the student's question and observation, the political philosophy professor exclaimed "Mr._____, if you don't know what the common good is, then you haven't learned a damn thing during the last four years!" Of course, the professor made no attempt to explicitly define the phrase. After several seconds of silence, I sensed no answer about to be provided to the student, so I decided to jump in to give the following inductive derivation and definition that I provide in my "Conceptual Foundations of Business" class.

Defining the Common Good

In order to discover what is in the common good of all men, I said, it is first necessary to determine what makes man man. We need to observe and specify the characteristics possessed by all men that differentiate them from other forms of life. Manness thus refers to the attributes that are the same in every instance of the species, man. Our first step is therefore to identify the essential distinguishing characteristics of men. We do this by inquiring about man's nature and the facts of his existence.

Man's distinctive nature is exhibited in his rational thinking, the process of abstraction and conceptualization that is necessary for his survival and self-actualization. Reason is man's faculty that perceives, identifies, and integrates the input that is received from the senses. Unlike plants and animals, man's unique nature is that he has no spontaneous and unthinking means of survival in the world. Men are living beings whose rational faculty sets them apart from all other living species. Man is a cognitive being who relies upon his reason as his means for obtaining objectively valid knowledge and as his basic tool of survival and fulfillment of his human capacities. To live as a human being, man must think, act, and create the conditions that his life requires to survive and prosper.

Freedom, a fundamental personal and social good, is another natural state of man's existence. Each person has the ability to think his own thoughts and control his own energies in his efforts to act according to those thoughts. Men are rational beings with free wills who have the ability to form their own life purposes, aims, and intentions. If a man is to maintain his life and fulfill his human potential, he must conceptualize the requirements of human survival and flourishing, face a multitude of choices and actions, and act in accordance with his rational conclusions. The right to liberty (and to life) is the right to the above process. Freedom is a necessary, but not a sufficient, condition for one's survival, moral well-being, and happiness.

Man's right to freedom can be logically derived from his nature. The object of the right to negative liberty is to allow people to live life as they choose, as long as their actions do not constitute an aggression against the freedom of others. Individuals are free to initiate their own purposive action when they are free from man-made restraints in the form of coercion by other individuals, groups of people, or the government. Because force is the means by which one's rights are violated, it follows that defended freedom is the fundamental common good. Whatever is alleged to be the common good must be good and must be universal. The common good must be that which is good for every human being. Liberty fulfills this requirement, because protected self-directedness is good for every person. The common good rests not in what men do when they are free, but rather in the fact that they are free. The common good consists in treating each person as an end and never solely as a means to an end. This simply means respecting the personal autonomy of each individual.

The common good of protected self-directedness can be possessed by all persons simultaneously. The commonness of the common good can be explained as its indivisible and nondiminishing availability to all members of the human community. Each person can possess the common good without his possession lessening in any way another person's possession of it. Each person can have the entire common good rather than simply a part of it. Because the common good is an intangible or nonphysical good, it can be shared by persons in such a manner that there is no restriction in the sharing of it. Any number of people can experience the common good and each person can possess it in total.

In contrast, when liberals and socialists (of whatever variant) speak of the common good, they are oftentimes actually referring to what are really material collective goods. This vision of the common good is something that, although possessed by all as a group, is actually divided up when distributed to various individuals. The distinguishing attribute of a collective good is that, as the number of sharers increases, each partaker actually possesses less of it. As each person possesses a collective good, the good becomes private and in no way can be viewed as common. Today's welfare-state liberals use the term *common good* for rhetorical purposes when they are advocating programs that actually distribute collective goods.

The Common Good Is Protected Individual Liberty

Each person has the right to be protected against all forms of external aggression initiated by private individuals or by the state. The proper role of the state is to protect the freedom that allows individuals to pursue happiness or the good that each defines for himself. The state ensures the common good when its functions are restricted to protecting the natural right to liberty and maintaining peace and order. The necessity of self-direction provides a rationale for a political and legal order that will not require that the autonomy of any individual will be sacrificed for that of any other. A minimal state only guarantees man the freedom to seek his own happiness as long as he does not trample the equivalent rights of others. A libertarian institutional framework is concerned with a person's outward conduct rather than with his virtuousness. A proper social system should not force a particular good on a man nor should it force him to seek the good—it should only maintain conditions of existence that leave him free to seek it. The legitimate purpose of the state is procedural in nature and simply involves the protection of our natural right to liberty.

To achieve the common good is to preserve the right and opportunity for every person to pursue the good as he sees fit. The common good is concerned with a man's ability to reflect upon his own actions and to make choices based on these reflections. The defense of individual rights allows for the development of institutions that nourish practical and voluntary cooperation without requiring previous agreement regarding final ends or personal desires. The essence of common good is to guarantee in all aspects of social life the benefits of voluntary participation and cooperation. The only way to ascertain if the common good is attained through cooperative effort is to observe whether or not each individual is cooperating voluntarily.

The purpose of the common good is to allow each and every individual's self-realization of his potentiality as a person. The common good is the set of conditions that permits people the opportunity to gain physical, spiritual, moral, cultural, and other goods for themselves through their own deliberations, judgments, choices, and actions.

Forced cooperation is contrary to the common good. Neither the goals of central planners nor of a majority deal with the common good. Mandatory participation may be for the good of the majority or of the central planners and their supporters, but not for all the individuals involved.

As I concluded my explanation, several students were nodding in agreement while the other professors sat in silence. Perhaps they were in awe of my uncommonly clear derivation of the common good. Or, conceivably, they might have been thinking, "Younkins, you've been teaching college for over half your life and you still haven't learned a damn thing!"

Recommended Reading

Aquinas, St. Thomas. "Common and Public Good." *Summa Theologica*. Translated and edited by Thomas Gilby. New York: McGraw Hill, 1963. Appendix 4.

Dickie, Robert B., and Leroy S. Rouner, eds. *Corporations and the Common Good*. Notre Dame, Ind.: University of Notre Dame Press, 1986.

Fortin, Ernest L. *Human Rights, Virtue, and the Common Good*. Edited by J. Brian Benestad. Lanham, Md.: Rowman & Littlefield, 1996.

Hancock, Curtis, and Anthony D. Simon, eds. *Freedom, Virtue, and the Common Good*. Introduction by Michael Novak. Notre Dame, Ind.: University of Notre Dame Press, 1995.

Hollenbach, David. "The Common Good Revisited." *Theological Studies* 50, 1989.

Maritain, Jacques. *The Person and the Common Good.* Translated by John J. Fitzgerald. New York: Charles Scribner's Sons, 1947.

Norton, David. *Personal Destinies: A Philosophy of Ethical Individualism.* Princeton, N.J.: Princeton University Press, 1976.

Novak, Michael. *Free Persons and the Common Good.* Lanham, Md.: Madison Books, 1989.

Rasmussen, Douglas B., and Douglas J. Den Uyl. *Liberty and Nature.* LaSalle, Ill.: Open Court, 1991.

Sherover, Charles M. *Time, Freedom, and the Common Good.* New York: New York University Press, 1990.

Simon, Yves. *A General Theory of Authority.* Notre Dame, Ind.: University of Notre Dame Press, 1980.

Udoidem, S. Iniobon. *Authority and the Common Good in Social and Political Philosophy.* Lanham, Md.: University Press of America, 1988.

Williams, Oliver F., and John Houck, eds. *The Common Good and U.S. Capitalism.* Lanham, Md.: University Press of America, 1987.

5

The State

The state is the great fictitious entity by which everyone seeks to live at the expense of everyone else.

—Frederic Bastiat

America was founded on the basis of an explicit philosophy of individual rights. The Founding Fathers held the view that government, while deriving its power from the consent of the governed, must be limited by the rights of the individual. The purpose of government was to maintain a framework of law and order within which individuals could pursue their own self-interest, controlled by the competitive marketplace. The legitimate role of the state is limited to protecting these natural rights through the use of force, but only in retaliation, and only against those who initiate its use. The state can be appropriately described as a purely defensive phenomenon that enables individuals to self-actualize and pursue their own freely chosen goals, responsibilities, values, actions, and their personal visions of happiness and the good.

A Limited Government Based on Constitutional Restraints

The framers believed in a higher law or natural law, over and above man-made law, which is the locus of ultimate authority of right and wrong. By deriving the authority of the state from God, the nature of legitimate political authority is seen as qualified and nonabsolute in its inception. Citizens retain inalienable rights, endowed in them by their Creator, upon which neither the state nor anyone else should trespass. Out of this emerges the idea of a government as a social institution set up voluntarily by men to defend their rights to individual action against anyone who violates or threatens them. Government is simply a man-made means to protect the arrangement between man and Creator in which man is free and self-responsible before God. In addition, men were viewed as flawed creatures—every human being sometimes sins. Rulers are not only finite in knowledge and ability but because of man's sinful nature may be corrupted by temptations of power. Therefore, no one should be trusted with too much power. An effective means of mitigating the effects of human sin in society is by decentralizing and dispersing power. Therefore, the Founding Fathers concluded that the combination of a free-market economy and a limited constitutional government would be an effective means to limit the abuse of power and impede its concentration into the hands of a few people. Their goal was to maximize voluntary exchanges while at the same time minimizing the use of coercive force.

It was John Locke who provided the philosophical basis for the makers of the Constitution who distrusted government while recognizing its necessity for a social order. Locke viewed human life as a gift from God and reasoned that the Creator of human life gives each person a right to use force to defend his life, a right to the product of his own labor, a right to defend his possessions, and a right to use his life as he desires. In the interest of efficiency, men transferred to government the right to use force in their own self-defense. Individual self-defense was thus replaced with organized self-defense. Government is a man-made institution that holds only such powers as it receives from individuals. Individuals did not and could not give the state any right to use force for any purpose other than self-defense. Because no individual has a right to interfere with the freedom of another, it follows that any attempt by the government to use force against a citizen for any reason other than self-defense of other citizens is an abuse of power and is an instance of the very thing that the state was organized to prevent. Therefore, a government should be restrained from improperly using its force against its citizens whether it is used for "humanitarian" purposes or for the benefit of those within the government itself. Government is organized by and operated for the benefit of the people but should be subject to a series of restraints that attempt to keep its power from being abused.

If individuals are to remain free there must be a legal system with the power to punish the violation of that freedom. Self-defense, a negative right, is the right of every person to defend his own life, liberty, or property. It follows that the powers of the state are logically limited to the nature of the rights of the individuals who transferred them to the state. The idea of a minimal state is thus based on a clear understanding of human nature, natural rights, and the requirements of reality. Equality before the law (i.e., political equality) is derived from the nature of the human person; however, because people are unequal in intelligence, motivation, ability, physical attributes, and so on, the result in a free society will be differing incomes, amounts of wealth, achievements, social statuses, etc. Inequality and diversity are intrinsic to the natural human order. Benevolence, compassion, charity, and virtue can only exist in a social system that recognizes that people are free and unequal.

The resulting constitutional government is based on skepticism toward the concentration of political power and is characterized by legal restraints imposed on power holders to ensure that individual rights will not be transgressed. Our constitutional government consists of: (1) a representative political system based on distribution of power at the local, state, and national levels; (2) the functional distribution of power between legislative, executive, and judicial branches; (3) a chronological distribution of power through frequent and periodic elections; and (4) a written constitution enforceable by courts through judicial review.

Freedom and the Pursuit of Happiness

The purpose of the state is not to help people either materially or spiritually to pursue their vision of happiness—that is the role of individuals, communities, and voluntary associations. The proper function of the state is no more than to provide people with the preconditions for their own happiness-pursuing activities. This simply means preventing interference from others in such pursuit.

Happiness is not something that can be given to people as wealth can be—they must achieve it through their own efforts. Happiness is the type of experience that accompanies or stems from the exercise of one's individualized human potentialities, including one's talents, abilities, and virtues. Happiness is that which we want for ourselves and for others. There is a major aspect of happiness that cannot be given by government or by anyone else. When people are in control of their actions and are free to face challenges, they tend to be happier. When the government attempts to supply happiness, it reduces individuals' control over their lives and deprives them of challenges and the chance to develop a sense of competence. People will be happiest if they are given freedom instead of money or goods. The good life, therefore, is the life spent in pursuit of the good life. Happiness requires the opportunity to build self-respect based on efficacious individual choice and action.

The state cannot govern a large number of people regarding the attainment of individual happiness because it is impossible to be personally knowledgeable of the moral character and other attributes of a large number of people. The state should therefore confine itself to matters that do not require personal knowledge about or by its citizens. The role of the state should be limited to protecting man's natural rights. The minimal state may be viewed as a defensive phenomenon with the purpose of providing only negative assistance.

The individual needs to be free in order to authentically follow his own particular inclinations and tastes. Freedom is also a necessary condition for the purpose of individual self-revision in which each person is able to judge, evaluate, and reflect, without constraint, on his past and present choices and commitments to decide if they really do represent his best interests. It is imperative that the state stay out of this self-deliberation process by adopting a politically laissez-faire attitude. This idea of neutral concern on the part of the state encourages us to adopt policies that enable all equally to determine and pursue their own conception of the good life.

Whereas active state governments are inimical to the formation and operation of communities formed by voluntary participation, the generation of such communities is fostered by the minimal state. Rich and rewarding personal relationships based on voluntary cooperation and mutual assistance abound within minimalist, rights-based systems. The freedom of individuals and the vitality of communities are thus intertwined.

The Common Good of the Political Community

The good of the individual person is inextricably related to the common good of the resulting political community. The common good of the political community involves the protection of each man's natural right to liberty through which he can self-actualize and freely pursue further duties and actions. Therefore, the legitimate purpose of the state, the protection of man's natural right to liberty, is procedural in nature and is the same as the promotion of the common good of the political community. In other words, the common good of the political community involves a set of social and legal conditions based on a man's natural rights.

The common good of the political community is not a single determinate goal that all men must attempt to achieve. Rather, it is the procedural implementation and protection of man's natural right to liberty. The natural right to liberty is a necessary precondition for the possibility of self-actualization and morality. There can be no morality without responsibility and no responsibility without self-determination. In order to provide the maximum self-determination for each individual the state should be limited to maintaining justice, police, and defense and to protecting life, liberty, and property.

Justice consists of equal treatment under social and legal conditions which include a set of known rules with respect to permissible and impermissible actions that may lead to unequal positions with no one knowing in advance what specific result the social and legal framework will have for any specific person. Inequalities are the inescapable consequences of uneven endowments and efforts. Principles of justice, by publicly defining man's natural rights, draw lines between persons. However, these lines, rather than preventing men from performing virtuous actions, actually enable men to freely recognize and fulfill one's obligations as a member of a community.

The Growth of Government

Until the early 1900s, the United States had a limited government; however, since the Great Depression, both attitudes toward government and the interpretation of the Constitution changed, resulting in an increasingly large government. When government goes beyond its legitimate limited role by gathering additional powers to itself, it invades other spheres and becomes interventionist and coercive. Any coerced exchange is not a free exchange—it is alien to and outside of the system of capitalism. Government initiatives such as minimum wage laws, rent control, zoning codes, international trade barriers such as tariffs and quotas, price supports, health and housing subsidies, bailouts of corporations, and other interventions negate the requisite pricing and allocating functions of the market, causing increased economic disorder. Every intervention of government into the free market other than to prohibit, prevent, and punish violations of man's natural rights not only violate God-given ethical principles but cause more problems to which interventionists respond with even more intervention.

There has been a slow but steady erosion in the protection the Constitution provides its citizens against arbitrary government power. This breakdown is largely due to changes in the prevailing attitude toward government—the fear of government power has been largely supplanted with the idea that discretionary government power should be used to attain "social" (i.e., distributive) justice. Consequences of the reduction of the constitutional limits on the use of governmental power include: the growth of government; the rise of a transfer society with its many opportunities for personal achievement through political activity; an undermining of self-reliance, market discipline, property rights, and the work ethic; the replacement of an ethic of freedom and responsibility with an ethic of dependence; and a decline in individual virtue, civil society, and economic welfare.

We need to return to the spiritual, political, and economic wisdom of our Founding Fathers. In their negative view toward government, all that a government should do is to establish and enforce standards of just conduct (i.e., general laws) under which free individuals will pursue their own goals and values.

Recommended Reading

Bandow, Doug. *The Politics of Plunder*. New Brunswick, N.J.: Transaction Publishing, 1990.

Bovard, James. *Lost Rights*. New York: St. Martin's Press, 1994.

———. *Freedom in Chains*. New York: St. Martin's Press, 1999.

Creveld, Martin van. *The Rise and Decline of the State*. Boston: Cambridge University Press, 1999.

Dorn, James A. "The Rise of Government and the Decline of Morality." *The Freeman* (March 1996).

Ebeling, Richard M. "The Free Market and Interventionist State." *IMPRIMIS* (August 1997).

Gierke, Otto von. *Political Theories of the Middle Age*. Translated by F. W. Maitland. Boston: Beacon Press, 1958.

Hayek, F. A. *The Road to Serfdom*. Chicago: University of Chicago Press, 1994.

Higgs, Robert. *Crisis and Leviathan*. New York: Oxford University Press, 1987.

Hoppe, Hans-Hermann. *Democracy: The God That Failed: The Economics and Politics of Monarchy, Democracy, and Natural Order*. New Brunswick, N.J.: Transaction Publishing Co., 2001.

Jasay, Anthony de. *The State*. Oxford: Basil Blackwell, 1985.

Krabbe, Hugo. *The Modern Idea of the State*. Translated with an introduction by George H. Sabine and Walter J. Shepard. New York: Appleton & Co., 1922.

Locke, John. *Two Treatises of Civil Government*. London: J. M. Dent & Sons, 1947.

MacIver, Robert. *The Modern State*. New York: Oxford University Press, 1926.

Mises, Ludwig von. *Omnipotent Government*. Spring Mills, Pa.: Libertarian Press, 1985.

Murray, Charles. *In Pursuit of Happiness and Good Government*. New York: Simon & Schuster, 1988.

Nock, Albert Jay. *Our Enemy, the State*. San Francisco: Fox & Wilkes, 1984.

Nozick, Robert. *Anarchy, State, and Utopia*. New York: Basic Books, 1974.

Rasmussen, Douglas B., and Douglas J. Den Uyl. *Liberty and Nature*. La Salle, Ill.: Open Court, 1991.

Richman, Sheldon. *Tethered Citizens: Time to Repeal the Welfare State*. Fairfax, Va.: Future of Freedom Foundation, 2001.

Roberts, Paul Craig, and Lawrence M. Stratton. *The Tyranny of Good Intentions*. New York: Prima, 2000.

Rothbard, Murray. *Man, Economy, and State*. Los Angeles: Nach, 1972.

Spencer, Herbert. *The Man versus the State*. Caldwell, Idaho: The Caxton Printers, 1969.

Weldon, T. D. *State and Morals*. New York: McGraw-Hill, 1947.

6

Personal Flourishing and Happiness

What is the Good for man? It must be the ultimate end or object of human life: something that is in itself completely satisfying. Happiness fits this description. But what is happiness? If we consider what the function of man is we find that happiness is a virtuous activity of the soul.

—Aristotle

An Aristotelian self-perfectionist approach to ethics can be shown to support the natural right to liberty which itself provides a solid foundation for a minimal state based on the principles of classical liberalism. This approach gives liberty moral significance by illustrating how the natural right to liberty is a social and political condition necessary for the possibility of personal flourishing—the ultimate moral standard in Aristotelian ethics interpreted as a natural-end ethics. A foundation is thus provided for a classical liberal political theory within the Aristotelian tradition.   Modern proponents of this approach include Douglas B. Rasmussen, Douglas J. Den Uyl, Tibor R. Machan, among others. The ideas presented in this chapter are heavily based on the work of these individuals.

Personal Flourishing

Personal flourishing (also known as human flourishing, self-actualization, moral well-being, etc.) involves the rational use of one's individual human potentialities, including talents, abilities, and virtues in the pursuit of his freely and rationally chosen values and goals. An action is considered to be proper if it leads to the flourishing of the person performing the action. Personal flourishing is, at the same time, a moral accomplishment and a fulfillment of human capacities, and it is one through being the other. Self-actualization is moral growth and vice-versa.

Not an abstraction, human flourishing is real and highly personal (i.e., agent relative) by nature, consists in the fulfillment of both a man's human nature and his unique potentialities, and is concerned with choices and actions that necessarily deal with the particular and the contingent. One man's self-realization is not the same as another's. What is called for in terms of concrete actions such as choice of career, education, friends, home, and others, varies from person to person. Personal flourishing becomes an actuality when one uses his practical reason to consider his unique needs, circumstances, capacities, and so on, to determine which concrete instantiations of human values, virtues, and goods will comprise his well-being. The idea of personal flourishing is inclusive and can encompass a wide variety of constitutive ends such as knowledge, the development of character traits, productive work, religious pursuits, community building, love, charitable activities, allegiance to persons and causes, self-efficacy, material well-being, pleasurable sensations, etc.

To flourish, a man must pursue goals that are both rational for him individually and also as a human being. Whereas the former will vary depending upon one's particular circumstances, the latter are common to man's distinctive nature—man has the unique capacity to live rationally. The use of reason is a necessary, but not a sufficient, condition for human flourishing. Living rationally (i.e., consciously) means dealing with the world conceptually. Living consciously implies respect for the facts of reality. The principle of living consciously is not affected by the degree of one's intelligence nor the extent of one's knowledge; rather, it is the acceptance and use of one's reason in the recognition and perception of reality and in his choice of values and actions to the best of his ability, whatever that ability may be. To pursue rational goals through rational means is the only way to cope successfully with reality and achieve one's goals. Although rationality is not always rewarded, the fact remains that it is through the use of one's mind that a man not only discovers the values required for personal flourishing, he also attains them. Values can be achieved in reality if a man recognizes and adheres to the reality of his unique personal endowments and contingent circumstances. Personal flourishing is positively related to a rational man's attempts to externalize his values and actualize his internal views of how things ought to be in the outside world. Practical reason can be used to choose, create, and integrate all the values, virtues, and goods that comprise personal flourishing.

Virtues and goods are the means to values and enable us to achieve human flourishing and happiness. The constituent virtues such as rationality, independence, integrity, justice, honesty, courage, trustworthiness, productiveness, benevolence, and pride (moral ambitiousness) must be applied, although differentially, by each person in the task of self-actualization—so must goods such as friendship, health, and knowledge. Not only do particular virtues and goods play larger roles in the lives of some men than others, there is also diversity in the concrete with respect to the objects and purposes of their application, the way in which they are applied, and the manner in which they are integrated with other virtues and goods. Choosing and making the proper response for the unique situation is the concern of moral living—one needs to use his practical reason at the time of action to consider concrete contingent circumstances to determine the correct application and balance of virtues and goods for himself. Although virtues and goods are not automatically rewarded, this does not alter the fact that they are rewarded. Personal flourishing is the reward of the virtues and goods and happiness is the goal and reward of personal flourishing.

The virtues can be viewed as contributory means to personal flourishing and happiness. Conventional goods also contribute to personal flourishing and happiness, but a case can be made that the virtues are more important because they control the value that other things in life have for you. The virtues can transform a man's life because they can transform his view of what happiness is. A person will continue to seek happiness, but his ideas of where to look for it and how he has to act to attain it can be reconfigured through virtue.

Because a large portion of an individual's potentialities can only be realized through association with other human beings, personal flourishing requires a life with others—family, friends, acquaintances, business associates, etc. These associations are instrumentally valuable in the satisfaction of nonsocial wants and desirable for a person's moral maturation, including the sense of meaning and value obtained from the realization of the consanguinity of living beings that accompanies such affiliations.

Men are necessarily related to others and they can determine to a great extent the persons they will be associated with and the ways in which they will be associated. Each person is responsible for choosing, creating, and entering relationships that enable him to flourish. Voluntary, mutually beneficial relations among autonomous individuals using their practical reason is necessary for attaining authentic human communities. Human sociality is also open to relationships with strangers, foreigners, and others with whom no common bonds are shared—except for the common bond of humanity.

A person's moral maturation requires a life with others. Charitable conduct can therefore be viewed as an expression of one's self-perfection. From this viewpoint, the obligation for charity is that the benefactor owes it to himself, not to the recipients. If a benefit is owed to another, rendering it is not a charitable act—charity must be freely given and directed toward those to whom we have no obligation. Charitable actions may be viewed as perfective of a person's capacity for cooperation and as a particular manifestation (i.e., giving to those in need) of that capacity. Kindness and benevolence, as a basic way of functioning is not an impulse or an obligation to others but a rational goal. Compassion is not charity and sentiment is not virtue. This nonaltruistic, noncommunitarian view of charity (and the other virtues) is grounded in a self-perfective framework under which persons can vary the type, amount, and object of their charity based on their contingent circumstances. Other contemporary concepts of charity rely on adherence to duty expressed as deontic rules or as the maximization of social welfare.

In *Unrugged Individualism*, David Kelley views benevolence as a commitment to achieving the values derivable from life with other people by (1) treating them as potential trading partners and (2) recognizing their humanity, independence, and individuality, and the harmony between their interests and ours. Benevolence means good will towards others. It involves a positive attitude toward people in general, a desire for their well-being, and a desire for peaceful and cooperative relationships with them. As an ethical principle, benevolence is not a matter of feeling, but rather a matter of acting on what we perceive. It is therefore possible to be benevolent even when one does not feel a positive emotion. Benevolence includes such traits as civility, sensitivity, kindness, sympathy, tolerance, generosity, and charity. Given that people live in society, and given that misfortune can affect any person, it is clearly in a person's self-interest (and crucial to his happiness) to live in a world in which people deal with one another in a spirit of helpfulness and mutual benevolence. Empathy is at the root of the virtue of benevolence. Empathy involves the knowledge of one's common humanity. The difference is perspectival—each person is a mind-body is his particular life circumstances.

According to Tibor Machan, generosity can lead to one's happiness because (1) it is a value to live in a society where people extend help to others and (2) giving help may be interpreted as a type of investment. Generosity is one of our means of pursuing our values—it is the importance we place on the well-being of others. Generosity involves the giving of something (i.e., an individual's time, effort, or property) as an expression of the giver's values, to an individual or group of individuals without the legal right to, or expectation of, specific immediate returns. As a virtue, generosity should be practiced at all stages of life; however, the extent and objects of your generosity will depend upon the stage of your productive life and other relevant circumstances. Because our lives are limited in time and we are limited in our resources and ability, we must discern and choose only a limited number of acts and objects to value through our generosity. However, a life that includes no acts of generosity is certainly morally deficient.

Happiness and Its Pursuit

Happiness can be defined as the positive conscious and emotional experience that accompanies or stems from achieving one's values and goals and exercising one's individual human potentialities, including talents, abilities, and virtues. In other words, happiness results from personal flourishing.

One's experience of happiness tends to correlate with a properly led life. A person's experience of happiness or unhappiness is an indicator or internal monitor of the objective status of one's pursuit of life and its values. The belief that one is flourishing is usually a product of a person taking rational and proper actions in his life. Of course, he may be mistaken and irrational and his activities may not be truly advancing his existence.

When people are properly happy, they are motivated to further act in a life-fulfilling manner. The joy found in one's flourishing helps to maintain and further a person's motivation to continue to engage in life-enhancing activities. There is a dynamic reinforcing interaction between the condition of factual flourishing and one's experience of flourishing (i.e., happiness). The better a man is at living, the more likely he will express happiness, love his life, and be inspired to live well.

The cognitive component of happiness is a judgmental process that consists of a positive evaluation of the conditions of one's life. This involves the judgment that one's life is measuring up favorably against his rational standards or expectations for it. The emotional aspect of happiness involves a feeling state regarding the preponderance of positive affect over negative affect. The affective side of happiness involves a man's sense of well-being (i.e., finding one's life or some portions of it fulfilling, rewarding, or satisfying).

Although happiness resists measurement, it is more important than anything that can be measured. Desired by all, happiness can be interpreted narrowly or comprehensively, foolishly or wisely, and may be either a conscious goal or an unconscious desire. The pursuit of happiness is something real, individualized, contingent, highly personal, diverse, and self-directed through the use of practical reason. Material wealth may provide the means of achieving happiness, just as it may represent the condition itself. Happiness is always being attained and is never totally attained—the pursuit of happiness is a goal that continues to the end of life with new contingencies, problems, and opportunities always arising. Happiness can be consistent with crisis, pain, grief, and struggle and is generally not possible without them.

Happiness in a comprehensive sense applies to one's life taken as a whole and thus arises from having a coherent, rationally chosen stance regarding the proper way to spend one's life. This is not the happiness we experience when we have obtained a particular goal or object. Rather, such metalevel happiness is evident through the holding of rational values with respect to the kind of life that is worth living and is characterized by a feeling of tranquility regarding the way one has lived and will continue to live his life. Metalevel happiness and object-level perturbation are compatible. Happiness at a metalevel provides a stable framework within which activity and striving are situated. A man who holds rational values and who selects ends and means consonant with the nature of existence and with the integrity of his own consciousness has achieved his values—not his existential values, but the philosophical values that are their precondition.

Metalevel happiness requires a proper perspective that comes from the serenity or peace of mind one gets from knowing that: (1) one is free to rationally choose among alternatives; (2) a person's potential for happiness is created in some particular way and with some particular nature which is not a matter of choice; and (3) nothing external can harm the core of one's self. Serenity requires wisdom, a sense of proportion, and the ability to deal with pain and emotions in a balanced and rational manner. Happiness means being serene in the face of the unchangeable, courageous before the changeable, and wise enough to determine which is which.

Many people attribute their happiness or unhappiness to the external events and conditions of their lives. It is likely that a person's perspective regarding the core of his existence has much more to do with his level of happiness than do any external circumstances. When something unfortunate (e.g., losing a job or loved one, suffering a physical injury or illness, etc.) happens to an individual who is basically disposed to be happy, he will certainly be sad or upset for a period of time (depending upon the gravity of the problem) but before long he will return to happiness as his overall state. On the other hand, when something positive (e.g., love, money, recognition or promotion at work, etc.) happens to a person who is disposed to unhappiness, he will be happy for a time but will very likely shortly become unhappy. Rather than evade negative experiences, happy people tend to take every feasible action to deal with the misfortune, and then shift their focus by placing positive aspects in the foreground and relegating negative ones to the background.

Metalevel happiness provides the confidence and peace of mind that enables us to enjoy our everyday pursuits (i.e., our passions). Whereas the serenity of metalevel happiness is unitary, our projects are many, diverse, and complex. Unlike metalevel tranquility that potentially can be the same for all, passions are different and unique for each person. Serenity results from the possession of a consistent and hierarchical system of beliefs, values, and emotions. Our passions involve our desires to satisfy, through action, the values to which we are committed. There are reciprocal and synergistic effects between one's metalevel happiness and happiness that is experienced when one has achieved or passionately attempted to achieve a particular goal.

Self-esteem (including self-efficacy and self-respect) is a necessary but not a sufficient condition of happiness. Self-esteem, the best predictor of happiness, is the disposition to experience oneself as competent to cope with the fundamental challenges of life and as worthy of happiness and success. A person of high self-esteem believes himself to be entitled to assert his needs and wants, achieve his values, and enjoy the fruits of his efforts. Self-esteem correlates with rationality, realism, independence, creativity, ability to manage change, willingness to admit and correct mistakes, purposeful and conscious living, intuitiveness, self-responsibility, self-acceptance, self-assertiveness, personal integrity, benevolence, and cooperativeness.

Self-Direction Requires a Minimal State

Self-direction (i.e., autonomy) involves the use of one's reason and is central and necessary for the possibility of attaining personal flourishing, self-esteem, and happiness. It is the only characteristic of personal flourishing that is both common to all acts of self-actualization and particular to each. Freedom in decision making and behavior is a necessary operating condition for the pursuit and achievement of human flourishing. Respect for individual autonomy is required because autonomy is essential to personal flourishing. This logically leads to the endorsement of the right of personal direction of one's life, including the use of his endowments, capacities, and energies.

These natural (i.e., negative) rights are metanormative principles concerned with protecting the self-directedness of individuals thus ensuring the freedom through which individuals can pursue their personal flourishing. The goal of the right to liberty is to secure the possibility of human flourishing by protecting the possibility of self-directedness. This is done by preventing encroachments upon the conditions under which human flourishing can occur. Natural rights impose a negative obligation—the obligation not to interfere with one's liberty. Natural rights, therefore, require a legal system that provides the necessary conditions for the possibility that individuals might self-actualize. It follows that the proper role of the government is to protect man's natural rights through the use of force, but only in response, and only against those who initiate its use. In order to provide the maximum self-determination for each person, the state should be limited to maintaining justice, police, and defense, and to protecting life, liberty, and property.

The negative right to liberty, as a basic metanormative principle, provides a context in which all the diverse forms of personal flourishing may coexist in an ethically compossible manner. This right can be accorded to every person with no one's authority over himself requiring that any other person experience a loss of authority over himself. Such a metanormative standard for social conduct favors no particular form of personal flourishing while concurrently providing a context within which diverse forms of personal flourishing can be pursued.

The necessity of self-direction for human flourishing provides a rationale for a political and legal order that will not require that the flourishing of any individual be sacrificed for that of any other nor use people for purposes for which they have not consented. A libertarian institutional framework only guarantees man the freedom to seek his moral well-being and happiness as long as he does not trample the equivalent rights of others. Such a system is not concerned with whether people achieve the good or conduct themselves virtuously. The minimal state is only concerned with a person's outward conduct rather than with the virtuousness of his inner state of being. Because rights are metanormative principles rather than normative ones, they cannot replace the role of the constituent virtues. A political and legal order based on the metanormative principle of the right to liberty allows people to act in ways that are not self-perfecting. Its purpose is not the direct and positive promotion of human flourishing—it is simply to allow persons to pursue their moral well-being on their own.

The good of the individual person is thus inextricably related to the common good of the political community that involves the protection of each man's natural right to liberty through which he can self-actualize and freely pursue further actions. Therefore, the legitimate purpose of the state, the protection of man's natural right to liberty, is procedural in nature and is the same as the promotion of the common good of the political community. In other words, the common good of the political community involves a set of social and legal conditions based on a man's natural rights.

It follows that the minimal state is only concerned with justice in a metanormative sense—not as a personal virtue. Whereas justice as a constituent virtue of one's personal flourishing involves an individual's specific contextual recognition and evaluation of people based on objective criteria, justice in a metanormative sense is only concerned with the peaceful and orderly coordination of activities of any possible person with any other. Justice as a normative principle is concerned with exclusive (i.e., selective) relationships and requires practical reason and discernment of differences of both circumstances and persons. On the other hand, justice as a metanormative principle is concerned with nonexclusive (i.e., open-ended and universal) relationships that do not assume a shared set of commitments or values. Although both types of justice are concerned with the social or interpersonal relationships, justice as a constituent virtue deals with others in much more specific and personal ways than when justice is considered as the foundation of a political order that is concerned with any person's relationship with any other human being. Therefore, metanormative justice (i.e., the basic right to liberty) provides the context for exclusive relationships to develop and for the possibility of personal flourishing and happiness.

Recommended Reading

Annas, Julia. *The Morality of Happiness*. New York: Oxford University Press, 1993.

———. "Virtue and Eudaimonism." *Social Philosophy and Policy* (winter 1998).

Branden, Nathaniel. *The Six Pillars of Self Esteem*. New York: Bantam Books, 1994.

Cooper, John. *Reason and Human Good in Aristotle*. Cambridge, Mass.: Harvard University Press, 1975.

Den Uyl, Douglas J. *The Virtue of Prudence*. New York: Peter Lang, 1991.

———. "The Right to Welfare and the Virtue of Charity." *Liberty for the Twenty-First Century*. Edited by Tibor R. Machan and Douglas B. Rasmussen. Lanham, Md.: Rowman & Littlefield, 1995.

Den Uyl, Douglas J., and Douglas B. Rasmussen. "Rights as Metanormative Principles." *Liberty for the Twenty-First Century*. Edited by Tibor R. Machan and Douglas B. Rasmussen. Lanham, Md.: Rowman & Littlefield, 1995.

Griffin, James. *Well-Being: Its Meaning, Measurement, and Moral Importance*. Oxford: Clarendon Press, 1986.

Hunt, Lester H. "Flourishing Egoism." *Social Philosophy and Policy* (winter 1999).

Hurka, Thomas. *Perfectionism*. New York: Oxford University Press, 1993.

Kelley, David. *Unrugged Individualism*. Poughkeepsie, N.Y.: Institute for Objectivist Studies, 1996.

Machan, Tibor R. *Human Rights and Human Liberties*. Chicago: Nelson-Hall, 1974.

———. *Generosity: Virtue in the Civil Society*. Washington, D.C.: Cato Institute, 1998.

Mack, Eric. "Moral Individualism: Agent Relativity and Deontic Restraints." *Social Philosophy and Policy* (autumn 1989).

McGill, V. J. *The Idea of Happiness*. New York: F.A. Praeger, 1967.

Miller, Fred D., Jr. *Nature, Justice, and Rights in Aristotle's "Politics."* Oxford: Clarendon Press, 1995.

Norton, David. *Personal Destinies*. Princeton, N.J.: Princeton University Press, 1976.

Rasmussen, Douglas B. "Community versus Liberty." *Liberty for the Twenty-First Century.* Edited by Tibor R. Machan and Douglas B. Rasmussen. Lanham, Md.: Rowman & Littlefield, 1995.

———. "Human Flourishing and the Appeal to Human Nature." *Social Philosophy and Policy* (winter 1999).

Rasmussen, Douglas B., and Douglas J. Den Uyl. *Liberalism Defended.* Cheltenham, U.K.: Edward Elgar, 1997.

———. *Liberty and Nature.* LaSalle, Ill.: Open Court, 1991.

Slote, Michael. *From Morality to Virtue.* New York: Oxford University Press, 1992.

Smith, Tara. *Viable Values: A Study of Life as the Root and Reward of Morality.* Lanham, Md.: Rowman & Littlefield, 2000.

Summer, L. W. *Welfare, Happiness, and Ethics.* Oxford: Clarendon Press, 1996.

Veatch, Henry B. *For an Ontology of Morals.* Evanston, Ill.: Northwestern University Press, 1971.

PART II

OWNERSHIP

7

Private Property

I shall endeavor to show how we might come to have a property in several parts of that which God gave to mankind in common, and that without any express compact of all the commoners.

—John Locke

The institution of private property is based on the natural human desire and right to survive and pursue one's vision of happiness. The idea of "freedom under the law" is rooted in the property-acquiring instinct and the need for safeguarding the possession of one's property. The body of law that has developed to protect ownership is based on the assumption that every rational man knows his interests best and should be permitted to pursue them. The right of private property is a moral and economic prerequisite for making the pursuit of individual excellence possible. There can be no morality without self-responsibility and self-determination, which, in turn, depend upon the existence of private property rights.

Private Property Rights: A Moral Concept

According to John Locke, the blending of an individual's labor with God's created universe produces private property. Private property results when something has been added by individual effort to transform previously unowned property. In Locke's view, individuals form societies in order to gain the strength to secure and defend their properties. It follows that the proper end of government is the preservation of property. Locke's main theme was that the ownership of private property is a natural right of every individual and that this right predated government. The inalienable rights of life, liberty, and the pursuit of happiness included in the Declaration of Independence are Lockean in nature and must be protected. Without protection of one's private property, other rights would have little meaning.

The Lockean approach is rooted in the idea that people own their own labor. Locke has implied that any man who has transformed an unowned resource owns the transformation that he has created. If a person owns what he has created from an unowned resource, he logically also owns whatever he or his agent creates from his property, which could then be sold for whatever price the market will yield. In other words, the voluntary transfer of justly acquired property is morally proper.

If men, who are at least partly material beings, have the right to life, then they have the right to maintain their lives with their own means and time as long as they do not infringe on the equal rights of others. Because human physical survival depends on the use of material objects, people have the right to determine the uses of these material objects.

All men are self-owners who have property in the free use of their time, abilities, and efforts. Each man has the moral right to control his own labor and to claim ownership of its fruits. The right to property is a natural right and shares the characteristics of any natural right. The hallmark of our free-market economy is that we have a moral right to property.

A distinction exists between innate and acquired property. A person possesses innate property as part of his own nature, along with the right to its control. Innate property refers to the productivity that is inherent in an individual's ability to work physically and mentally. Acquired property refers to things external to one's own person. It is not only the possession of material property, but the possession of scientific know-how, technical skills, and experience that determines the value of an individual in society.

Property may be viewed as mainly consisting of actions and knowledge rather than things. This idea is compatible with intellectual property such as patents and copyrights. This form of property does not refer to specific objects, but rather to the right of an inventor to build a mechanism or of an author to publish a work.

Property is best understood as a relationship between persons. One person has the right to exclude others from the current or future use of a certain resource. In addition, we have evolved from the idea of property as real assets to the idea of property as promises—stocks, bonds, mortgages, paper money, bank books, etc. These are symbols of ownership and do not refer to actual possession. Ownership of this type of property requires a specialized knowledge such as that possessed by accountants, bankers, lawyers, brokers, and managers who aid the owner in determining the best uses of his resources.

Knowledge is a type of property. Persons engaged in professions requiring long and advanced education have invested time, effort, and intelligence in a special kind of property, knowledge, and thus have a legitimate claim on the professional use of it.

Included in the concept of private property are the notions that an individual's work creates private property and that a person owns himself and therefore has property in the free use of his time, abilities, and efforts. Work requires the expenditure of time and energy. It is in work that we can find the foundations of profit, property, and corporations—all are justified in terms of the perfection of the human being. A property right in one's own person and in the resources that the person finds, transforms, and exchanges or gives, is a primary characteristic of free-market capitalism.

Private Property and Individual Freedom

Private property, the bedrock institution of capitalism, is essential for the preservation of individual freedom. When property rights are respected and protected, a person is able to keep and enjoy the product of his labor. In addition, human creativity and flourishing require property ownership by individuals. The free market requires that a person have the right to possess, use for consumption or further production, exchange for money or other property, dispose of, and restrict the access of others to his property. He may do whatever he wishes with his legitimately held possessions as long as he does not in so doing violate the natural rights of another person. In other words, individuals may possess, purchase, give away, and sell property (including their own labor) if they do not do so fraudulently, and they can do what they want with their property as long as they do not injure others.

Freedom is based on ownership. If it is possible for a man to own assets, it is also possible for him to have freedom of speech, religion, the press, etc. Private property increases individual freedom by dispersing ownership and control of property among a great number of people.

Inequality of abilities and property ownership is a manifestation of the human condition. Nevertheless, it should be realized that every person (even the poorest) owns his own life and should be free to engage in peaceful activities in his efforts to acquire property. However, there is no positive right guaranteeing that one will possess property and no positive duty for someone to create property and hand it over to someone else. There is only the negative duty of others not to coercively keep a person from engaging in peaceful actions in his attempts to acquire and keep property. Through the division of labor, each person is free to capitalize on natural inequalities in abilities, energy levels, motivations, and moral strengths in his efforts to manage his own life and pursue his own well-being. Property can legitimately be acquired by directly creating it or by creating something of value to another and freely trading with the other. A poor person's chances of becoming wealthy are maximized in a market economy.

A violation of a man's property rights is an expression of force against the man himself. The state should not use its coercive power to force a person to share his wealth with the less fortunate. True charity cannot be compelled.

Private Property Promotes Economic Performance

A system of well-defined, secure private property rights not only protects free-dom, it also promotes economic performance and progress. The rule of law protecting life and property is necessary for the development of a free society. When life and property are protected, social cooperation emerges and a nation of traders evolves into a capitalist economy. Voluntary exchange depends on private property—every trader is a property owner who is responsible for himself and his possessions and free to pursue his own good in his own way. A person's right to life, to the disposal of his time, and to the use of his abilities, derives from the fact that they are his own life, time, and abilities.

Wants and satisfaction vary greatly among individuals. Underlying our free-market system is the fact that each person seeks the greatest amount of satisfaction with the least amount of effort. Private property and free markets allow men to choose different occupations, products, lifestyles, and so on without interfering with the freedom of others to do the same. Because men possess a wide variety of abilities and talents, it follows that specialization increases productivity. By specializing and exchanging scarce economic goods with each other, each person is able to gain the maximum of satisfaction he seeks as limited by his creative capacities. Private property thus allows the widest possible amount of knowledge to be applied to the problem of scarcity as numerous individuals, possessing different combinations of abilities, apply their knowledge to the creation of goods and services.

Because all persons have greater respect for what they own than for what they hold in common, it follows that private ownership fosters wise stewardship. It is the "tragedy of the commons" that rivers, parks, beaches, lakes, and roads are all taken care of less well than private homes and businesses. Incentives explain why "publicly owned" resources and operations are outproduced by private enterprises and in a constant state of disrepair. Unowned natural resources such as grazing lands, timber tracts, and wildlife are quickly depleted. Similarly, unowned land, water, and air are frequently polluted.

The free market, as an impersonal mechanism, pressures individuals to satisfy the needs of others. Private property ownership encourages men to develop and use their resources in a way that is advantageous to others. Not only does such employment produce income but in a market economy the owner of resources such as capital and land can continue to enjoy their property only by employing it for the satisfaction of others' wants. The property owner cannot escape the costs of ownership and the need to act as a steward of his resources for the benefit of others. In a free society, the property needed for production and marketing can only be amassed and kept by an owner as long as he uses it as consumers want him to. The best way to hold and increase one's resources is to compete by catering to the customer's wishes—otherwise one is out of business. Consumers also compete with one another for available goods and services. Competition works to keep buyers and sellers honest in their business dealings and efficient in their use of scarce resources.

Private ownership makes men accountable for their actions. A person who harms another or damages another's property is responsible for the damages. People are responsible for the costs they impose on others and can profit from the positive things they do for others. Private property rights provide the link between the rational use of resources and the rewards or penalties of the decision makers. If a man owns property, all the costs and all the benefits accrue to him, so he seeks to make the best possible use of his resources.

Private ownership encourages owners to conserve for the future. The owner of property is an entrepreneur in the sense that he needs to predict future valuations that others will make and act accordingly. Whenever the estimated present value of using a resource in the future is greater than value of using the resource currently, the resource will be preserved for the future. Because property is transferable in a market economy, it follows that the market value of the resource will increase in expectation of the projected increased future value of the resource.

Under a system of well-defined, protected, and enforced property rights, the only economic transactions people engage in are positive-sum (i.e., wealth creating) ones in which both parties to the economic exchange believe they will benefit. After all, who would enter a one-sided bargain to his expected detriment?

Proper Role of the State

Contract law evolved to protect ownership and free trade. Business could not flourish if contracts were not usually fulfilled. One role of the state is to enforce performance. With the advent of specialization of labor, people found it necessary to develop an exchange mechanism through which a producer of one item could exchange it for something he would produce less efficiently than another. This type of bargaining relationship led to protection through the use of formal contracts. Property rights comprise the subject matter of all contracts. In addition to the above pragmatic basis for contract law, there is an ethical basis for requiring a man to keep his promise. Deceit is wrong. A man ought to do what he says he will do, especially when his word causes another, who relies on that word, to give a promise or take action. Private ownership would be precarious without a political system that protects property rights. The proper role of government under capitalism is therefore limited to protecting man's natural rights (including property rights) and enforcing contractual agreements—a breach of contract is an indirect use of force.

Private ownership circumscribes the power of the state. When a state controls all of the productive resources in society, it can suppress dissent, enforce conformity, and stifle democracy. However, in a system in which ownership is held by many individuals, power is more diffused, resulting in greater political and economic freedom for the individual.

The absence of property rights results in a zero-sum society—one in which a person can gain more wealth only by decreasing the wealth of others. In a collectivist society, people would simply take from each other—if everyone owned everything, trade would be impossible because every person's agreement would be needed for every transfer of property. People in such a society, either by themselves or through the use of government power, obtain wealth from others without their consent.

Contemporary Encroachments on Private Property

The private character of property is restricted today. Contemporary public encroachments on private property include, but are not limited to, the requirement to pay taxes on both real and personal property or face eventual loss of the property; land use control and zoning regulations; building codes; occupancy restrictions and facilities requirements on property used for economic gain; restrictions on the donative ability of the possessor of property to bequeath or transfer possessions (through the testator) upon his demise; rent controls; acreage quotas for farmers; government trade controls or quotas on international exchanges; the "right" of eminent domain; "open housing" legislation that takes away from the seller the right to choose his own customers; government grants of exclusive access to certain markets; price supports; price ceilings; minimum wage laws; maximum profit laws; rate regulations; controls over utilities, travel, housing, communications, insurance, interest, banking, and so on; taxation of individuals and businesses; unfunded employer mandates (such as family leave); and welfare transfers.

More and more the political process is being substituted for the market process and for private property. Government interference and the consequent loss of control over one's property constitute a direct assault on individual freedom. Control over property is the means for control over men. Government interferences impair an individual's freedom to realize his potentialities as he chooses and as his abilities allow. Today, government supremacy over individual property owners means that the state may permit individuals to temporarily hold title to its possessions and use them in limited ways at its discretion.

Because, as has often been said, human rights are property rights (and vice versa), it follows that all rights will become worthless if the state (or some person or group of persons) holds preemptive power over the property of the individual owner. Unfortunately, America has proceeded in the direction of subjugating property rights as the belief in the origin of rights has shifted from natural law to society and government.

Americans need to be reminded that the loss of property rights either preceded or accompanied the loss of other rights in totalitarian countries. A country without secure private property rights will ultimately be unable to defend any human rights at all. The person who is not allowed to own property becomes the property of someone else. The exercise of any right requires the use of property. People need a place to assemble and speak freely, materials to work on, etc.

All rights may be viewed as extensions or elaborations of property rights. There are no human rights that are separable from property rights. For example, the right of freedom of the press is dependent upon private property. The press cannot be free if the state owns all the printing presses, paper, and distribution systems. In addition, religion cannot be free if the government owns all the buildings and prints all the reading materials. Freedom of trade also presupposes property rights—without property rights individuals would simply take from each other. In our contemporary democratic society, government takes property without consent through the majority vote of people and the actions of the members of Congress and other government officials. Although considered to be "legal," actions such as government transfer programs can be deemed immoral since they violate individual rights.

The means of maintaining one's life is property and the loss of these means to the State results in the loss of the power of self-determination. When government acts to downplay the importance of property rights, the result will be the opposite—property rights will become more important to individuals. More and more will men realize that property rights are foundational to a free society—there can be no political or personal freedom without the right to use one's property as one sees fit.

Recommended Reading

Becker, Lawrence C. *Property Rights: Philosophic Foundations*. New York: Routledge, 1980.

Bethell, Tom. *The Noblest Triumph: Property and Prosperity through the Ages*. New York: St. Martin's Press, 1998.

DeLong, James V. *Property Matters*. New York: Free Press, 1997.

Demsetz, H. "Toward a Theory of Property Rights." *American Economic Review* (May 1967).

Dietze, Gottfreid. *In Defense of Property*. Chicago: Henry Regney Co., 1963.

Epstein, Richard A. *Takings: Private Property and the Power of Eminent Domain*. Cambridge, Mass.: Harvard University Press, 1989.

Epstein, Richard A., ed. *Private and Common Property*. New York: Garland Publishing, 2000.

———. *Constitutional Protection of Private Property and Freedom of Contract*. New York: Garland Publishing, 2000.

Hamilton, Walter. "Property According to Locke." *Yale Law Review* (March 1931).

Hoppe, Hans-Hermann. *The Economics and Ethics of Private Property*. Boston: Kluwer Academic Publishers, 1993.

Kramer, Matthew H. *John Locke and the Origin of Private Property*. Cambridge: Cambridge University Press, 1997.

Locke, John. *Of Civil Government*. Edited by Ernest Phys. London: J. M. Dent & Sons, 1943.

Miller, Fred Jr. "The Natural Right to Private Property." *The Libertarian Reader*. Edited by Tibor Machan. Totowa, N.J.: Rowman & Littlefield, 1982.

Nedelsky, Jennifer. *Private Property and the Limits of American Constitutionalism*. Chicago: University of Chicago Press, 1991.

Pipes, Richard. *Property and Freedom*. New York: Alfred A. Knopf, 1999.

Pombo, Richard, and Joseph Farah. *This Land Is Our Land: How to End the War on Private Property*. New York: St. Martins Press, 1996.

Rothbard, Murray N. *The Ethics of Liberty*. Atlantic Highlands, N.J.: Humanities Press, 1982.

Schlatter, Richard. *Private Property*. New Brunswick, N.J.: Rutgers University Press, 1951.

Waldron, Jeremy. *The Right to Private Property*. Oxford: Clarendon Press, 1988.

8

Contract

The logic of mutual gain from voluntary exchange is perfectly general . . . it does not create one set of rules for people who are rich and powerful and another set for those who are frail or meek. Instead, the law speaks about two hardy standbys in all contractual arrangements: A and B. These people are colorless, odorless, and timeless, of no known nationality, age, race, or sex. The patterns of social life are determined not by some powerful central authority but by the repetitive and independent decisions of thousands of separate individuals pursuing their self-interest.

—Richard Epstein

A contract is a binding agreement between two or more parties that usually results in some type of performance. Without doubt, trade and commerce could not thrive if freely made agreements were not normally carried out. Contract can be viewed as a method in which men bargaining with one another can make sure that their promises will last longer than their changeable states of mind. The law of contract provides a mechanism through which private individuals can, to a certain degree, predict, control, and stabilize the future. Contracts allow people to incur reciprocal responsibilities and commitments, to make promises others can rely on, to remove some uncertainty from life, and to establish reasonable expectations for future actions.

A function of the state, operating mainly through the court system, is to enforce performance by requiring the promisor to fulfill his bargain on penalty of fine or imprisonment or by awarding judgment against him for money damages when, without legal reason, he fails to perform. State compulsion has replaced private force, which was common in earlier time periods. State enforcement in concerns of bargain and promise can be viewed as one of the state's most important functions behind only peacekeeping and property defense. In essence, a breach of contract is an indirect use of force.

Contract Law's Pragmatic Basis

With the advent of specialization of labor, human beings created an exchange mechanism through which a man, who can produce something more efficiently than another, can exchange it for another item that he would create less efficiently than the other person. A person gives in order to receive, and this giving and receiving arrangement is frequently protected by a formal contract.

Frequently, one or both sides to an agreement are carried out at a later date. In order for an exchange to be arranged at one point in time, with performance to take place later, the parties, rather than simply rely on one another's honor to secure performance, normally depend upon a legally enforceable obligation to comply with the agreement.

The contract is integral to a market economy. Think of the variety of commitments that must be honored for any firm to operate. Each of these arrangements is usually defined by contract. If most of these contracts were not carried out according to their terms, commercial transactions would be impossible. Any commercial organization consists of numerous separate activities bound into an effective whole through a collection of contracts.

The idea that contracts are legally enforceable does not ensure performance, but does increase the probability of performance. When a party knows he may face legal action if he does not comply, he is more likely to complete his side of the bargain. In addition, if performance is not expected, the fact that a lawsuit may be brought may be sufficient to obtain an acceptable out-of-court settlement.

Contract liability is promissory liability. In a business society, where wealth largely consists of promises, it is of paramount importance to protect the interests of the individual promisees. Promises, in the form of contracts, have become a convention whereby people are able to realize their aims by creating expectations about one another's conduct.

The Moral Foundation of Contracts

In addition to the above pragmatic foundation for the law of contract, there is a moral basis for requiring a man to keep his promise. Deceit is wrong and should not be practiced. A man should do what he promises to do, particularly when his given word encourages another person, relying on that promise, to take action or make a promise to take action.

Morality, according to Immanuel Kant, requires that a man not make an exception of himself, and that he not follow rules or engages in practices that he could not recommend to all persons. As Kant puts it in his categorical imperative, "I ought never to act except in such a way that I can also will that my maxim become a universal law."

Consider the case in which a businessman is deciding whether or not he should break a contract. If he were to declare the principle of his action to be a universal law such as, "Always break contracts," or "Contract breaking is permissible," the act of breaking contracts would be self-defeating. The first assertion logically would result in a world in which people always breached their contracts and no one kept his word. Given the second maxim, people would never know whether or not a contract would be kept, and thus the purpose of both keeping a contract and breaking one would be defeated. Successful (i.e., to one's advantage) contract breaking is possible only when it is not made a universal law. Profitable contract breaking can only occur in a world in which contracts are normally honored. If contract breaking were universalized then business practice would become inconceivable and inexecutable. If a businessman were to advocate universal contract violation, his advocacy would be in vain. Therefore, applying Kant's categorical imperative, the businessman ought to keep the contract except, of course, in a case in which his promise was exacted by force or fraud. Fraud is implicit theft in that it involves the failure to fulfill a freely agreed-upon transfer of property.

The right of property includes the right to make contracts regarding that property. The right to contract is derivable from the right of private property. It follows that enforceable contracts are those in which the failure of one party to live up to the provisions of the contract implies the appropriation of property from the other party. Enforceable contracts are those supported by the authorization of legal coercion.

Contract's Legal Relatives

The underpinnings of contract law can be found in the law of torts (i.e., the law of private wrongs), and to a somewhat lesser degree, property law. The law of torts, which is based on the ideas of personal accountability, causation, and negligence, had previously granted remedies for deceit and trespass. Elements similar to deceit and trespass are present in a contract case in which a person attempts to perform some act for another and does it fraudulently or incompetently. Also, the concept of *assumpsit*, the complete failure to perform what a person had promised to do, was based on an analogy to tort law. In addition, in the still older law of property, we discover the phenomenon of an obligation, created by recorded and sealed deed, recognized in both religious and lay courts. We find here a situation in which a promisor conveys, by deed, a thing of value to the promisee.

The corporation logically grew out of the idea of contract. A voluntary association of human beings bound together in order to attain a purpose is the basis for the existence of a corporation. Corporateness is an inherent right common to all men and grounded in the principles of freedom of association and freedom to contract. Corporate stockholders, managers, and workers have a common interest in a corporation's survival and prosperity. The corporation can thus be viewed as a nexus for a set of contracting relationships among these and other individuals.

A corporation involves a set of bilateral and multilateral agreements with parties such as workers, unions, managers, stockholders, customers, bankers, suppliers, retailers, creditors, etc. These individuals enter into contracts with the firm in which they agree to trade value for value.

From Status to Contract

Contract law is a key component of a free society. Contracts involve a trade-off of flexibility for security and the voluntary assumption of mutual obligation and commitment. Through contract, a participant in civil society is differentiated from the atomistic individual.

Autonomous human beings have the rational ability and natural right to make their own life choices. A necessary condition of acting autonomously is the possibility of freely making mutually binding agreements. Autonomy thus requires freedom of contract. Better connections between persons can be made by contract, which works to mutual benefit, instead of through coercion, which does not.

Although a contract may appear to be the subordination of one man's will to another, the former gains more than he gives up, as does the latter. In a free society, the only transactions people engage in are positive-sum ones in which both parties believe they will benefit.

Historically, the rise of contract within Western civilization reflected the disintegration of a status-determined society. Contract became a tool of change and self-determination, an instrument of peace, and the only legitimate means of social integration in a free society. Progress depends on protected property rights and the confidence that contractual obligations will be honored.

Sir Henry Sumner Maine, the nineteenth-century legal historian, wrote that progressive societies exhibit a development from status-bound roles to those founded more and more on contractual freedom. Whereas a status system establishes obligations, conditions, and interrelations by birth, contract regards individuals as free and equal moral agents developing their own bonds with others. In a free society, there is high degree of social mobility and freedom to associate in response to current and expected future needs. Social arrangements are a result of the independent decisions of separate individuals pursuing their own interests, rather than by a central powerful authority such as the state or the Church.

In Western society, with the steady dissolution of castes, social classes, guilds, ethnic cultures, and so on, human resources have become more available to organizers in business and other associations. Organizers compete for the best managerial and nonmanagerial employees, and with the freedom of association present in the era of contracts, it is possible to create successful organizations despite some interference by the state.

Freedom to Contract Promotes Progress

In her 1998 book, *The Future and Its Enemies*, Virginia Postrel explains that, by treating individuals as free and equal generic units, contract permits people to create arrangements far beyond the plans of any grand designers. Only by treating individuals in this manner can overarching rules allow people to use their own knowledge, express their individuality, and take advantage of their own ideas by joining them and their property in various unanticipated ways. When people cannot make binding, enforceable commitments, dynamic progress is severely hampered. The idea of contract fosters progress by encouraging specialization and allowing an extended order to develop. Postrel also points out the especial importance of well-functioning legal systems when strangers interact in commercial and other situations. In addition, she notes that the goal of contract law is not to inspire legal suits but to settle or avoid them. Well-known rules that eliminate ambiguity make it more likely that promises will be kept.

In order to be invaluable to businessmen and other members of a free society, the contract must be a tool of virtually unlimited adaptability. To achieve this, the legal system must minimize the formality necessary for contractual transactions. It can do this by permitting freedom as to the form and content of contractual arrangements. Contracts have been rewritten through prior restraints (e.g., rent control, minimum wage laws, and interest rate ceilings) and subsequent nullification of contract terms. Legislators and judges should refrain from substituting their own judgments in cases where they believe there is unequal bargaining power or where they think that certain contracts are not in the "public interest." Contract sanctity is paramount. Such a free contract system encourages dynamic processes and technological achievements by permitting entrepreneurs to quickly and flexibly experiment with new ways of satisfying wants.

Recommended Reading

Buckley, F. H., ed. *The Fall and Rise of Freedom of Contract*. Durham, N.C.: Duke University Press, 1999.

Dimatteo, Larry A. *Contract Theory*. East Lansing: Michigan State University Press, 1998.

Epstein, Richard A. *Simple Rules for a Complex World*. Cambridge, Mass.: Harvard University Press, 1995.

Evers, Williamson M. "Toward a Reformulation of the Law of Contracts." *Journal of Libertarian Studies* (winter 1977).

Ferson, Merton. *The Rational Basis of Contracts*. Brooklyn, N.Y.: Foundation Press, 1949.

Fuller, Lon L., and Melvin Aron Eisenberg. *Basic Contract Law*. St. Paul, Minn.: The West Group, 1996.

Gilmore, Grant. *The Death of Contract*. Edited by Ronald K. L. Collins. Columbus: Ohio State University Press, 1995.

Hale, R. L. "Bargaining, Duress, and Economic Liberty." *Columbia Law Review* (July 1943).

Hillman, Robert A. *The Richness of Contract Law.* The Hague, The Netherlands: Kluwer Law International, 1996.

Llewellyn, K. N. "What Price Contract? Essays in Perspective." *Yale Law Journal* (March 1931).

Maine, Henry Summer. *Ancient Law.* Tucson: University of Arizona Press, 1986.

Radin, Max. "Contract Obligation and Human Will." *Columbia Law Review* (July 1943).

Scheiber, Harry N. *The State and Freedom of Contract.* Stanford, Calif.: Stanford University Press, 1998.

Slawson, W. David. *Binding Promises.* Princeton, N.J.: Princeton University Press, 1996.

Trebilcock, Michael J. *The Limits and Freedom of Contract.* Cambridge, Mass.: Harvard University Press, 1997.

9

Work

The dignity of labor is not based on its results, always vain and temporal, but on the fact that it permits the soul never to pause, always to ascend and to find its place in the very movement by which it flings itself forward, ever higher and further. If the mot d'ordre of Greek civilization was "Endure and abstain!" the slogan of our own, the civilization of labor, is "Work!"

—Adriano Tilgher

Included in the concept of private property are the notions that an individual's work creates private property and that a person owns himself and therefore has property in the free use of his time, abilities, and efforts. Work requires the expenditure of time and energy. Man is in control of his time and energy when he voluntarily and constructively works. Control of one's time and energy both reflects the meaning of freedom and constitutes the means by which a person exercises his freedom. Roughly one third of an average individual's adult life is devoted to working. It is in work that we can find the foundations of profit, property, corporations, and unions—all can be justified in terms of the perfection of the human being.

Throughout the Greco-Roman and Judeo-Christian eras up to about the eleventh century, there was an emphasis upon the life of the mind (i.e., contemplation and education) and, at best, only a grudging tolerance of manual labor and merchant labor. However, by the early Renaissance, all forms of work had become so highly valued that families took their family names from the type of work they performed (e.g., Miller, Smith, Cooper, Shoemaker, Miner, Wright). During the Renaissance and Reformation, work was accorded a much more honorable role and the active life was praised more than the life of thought. By the time of Thomas Aquinas in the thirteenth century, the Church had defined work as both an individual's natural right and duty. As respect for work grew so did respect for individual rights and liberty that needed to be protected from the power of the state. By the time of America's founding, there was a realization that the institutional framework required to protect individual rights and to ennoble work is one of capitalism including free markets, competition, private property, and limited government.

The Work Ethic and Its Critics

The Protestant Work Ethic contributed to the spirit and growth of capitalism. Protestants, especially Calvinists, believed that man was depraved and that salvation, consequently, must come only through Christ's work on the cross to pay the price for man's sinfulness. The Protestant Work Ethic came from the response of those saved, who, in gratitude for the great gift of God's salvation, wanted to apply the salvation through their obedience to God's commandments—one of which was to subdue the earth and be good stewards over it. As a result, men worked hard, were productive, and accumulated wealth. High living was forbidden because people had to account for the use of their possessions. Reinvestment naturally resulted, helping to stimulate the growth of capitalism. Through work, man served God. Planning, self-control, austerity, individualism, and devotion to occupations thereby pervaded the economic world. The Protestant Work Ethic stressed the sacred nature of property, the virtue of hard work, and the importance of independence, thrift, and accumulation.

The Protestant Work Ethic not only added a dimension of nobility to work, it also viewed every productive job as a calling—something that a man is meant to do. A calling is unique to the individual, requires the specific talent to do the job, and is accompanied by the enjoyment and sense of accomplishment, satisfaction, and renewed energy that its performance gives to the called person. When a man has a calling, he tends to have greater respect for what he does.

Christianity raised work to participation in the creative work of God. People began to search for what the Creator intended for them to do with the unique resources He endowed in each of them. Every person has talents that allow for productivity that God wants each individual to cultivate and treat as gifts. God did not make the world complete but to be completed. Work was thus viewed as a way to cocreate with God and cooperate with Him in bringing creation to its perfection.

Today, when people hear the term *work ethic* they think of a broad philosophy encompassing a variety of beliefs, meanings, and dimensions, including, but not limited to, the following: (1) Men have a religious and moral obligation to fill their lives with hard work and live an ascetic existence; (2) Men should amass wealth through honest labor and keep it through thrift, frugality, and wise investments; (3) Men are expected to work long hours, with little or no time devoted to leisure or recreation; (4) Workers should be extremely productive and produce a large quantity of goods and services; (5) Workers should be proud of their work and perform their functions to the best of their ability; (6) Workers should be loyal and committed to their company, their profession, and their work group; (7) Employees should be achievement-oriented, constantly striving for advancement; and (8) Workers should be dependable with an attendance record of low absenteeism and tardiness.

There has been an assault on the work ethic and work itself during the last century. As the intensity of religious belief has waned during this period, there has been a corresponding decline in the belief in the dignity of work. Replacing these beliefs has been a hedonistic elevation of leisure, play, and free time.

The image of productive persons has been constantly denigrated by authors, educators, media journalists, politicians, and other intellectuals. Not only do they attack the producer, his integrated thinking, the value of his product, and his individual rights (including his property rights), they also attempt to expropriate his profits for their own chosen projects. Work is portrayed as distasteful and as something to be avoided. In addition, the worker is depicted as a victim of capitalists, corporations, and employers who seek to exploit and reduce the worth of the worker.

Attempts have been made to place barriers in front of men who want to work. Unions try to limit work hours and the productive output of each laborer. Minimum wage laws cause unemployment by pricing low-skilled workers out of jobs. Maximum hour laws either restrict the hours that a person can work or punish employers who have to pay a premium for overtime. Children are kept from working by child labor laws even if such work is agreeable to the child's parents or legal guardian. Compulsory school attendance and prolonged schooling have kept many young people out of the job market. Social security and other retirement programs keep older citizens off the job market. Laws that encourage or mandate unionization and exclusive representation protect unions from competition and diminish the economic freedom of employers and union workers who may prefer to bargain independently or as a member of another union and workers who are not members of the protected union. Unions often (1) impose limits on supervisory personnel performing production work and on employees doing work outside of an employee's classification, (2) require a minimum number of workers on a given job, and (3) bargain for rules limiting the use of labor-saving machinery and methods. Occupational licensing laws, through education requirements, examinations, and license fees, create barriers to entry in many professions. Government jobs programs reduce economic freedom and employment opportunities. The jobs created by such programs are financed by diverting resources from the private sector. Such jobs tend to be deficient because they don't meet legitimate customer demands and cause unemployment through their crowding out effect. Laws that made it more difficult and costly to close down or relocate a plant deprive employees and business owners of their freedom to decide for themselves and place the immobile firm at a competitive disadvantage compared to new firm. Immigration laws diminish people's ability to change employment or look for jobs in another country. In addition, both federal and state governments tax workers and employers and subsidize those who don't work. Then there is John Dewey's legacy, "progressive" education, which emphasizes "socialization" rather than cognition and efficacy and breaks the link between education and work by treating education as merely an end in itself. Rather than teach "socialization," educators need to encourage independent, individual judgment and to provide the reasoning skills and factual knowledge that a rational man will need when he enters the world of work.

Work Is Essential for Human Flourishing and Happiness

The war against work is also a war against individual fulfillment and freedom. Work is at the root of a meaningful life, the path to individual independence, and a necessity for human survival and flourishing. It is also the distinctive means by which men concretize their identity as rational, goal-directed beings. Productive work is the process by which man controls his existence by acquiring knowledge and translating or objectifying his ideas and values into physical form. Work is a synthesizing activity, involving both cognitive and physical aspects, that permits the actualization of specifically human abilities and desires. Work is needed not only for sustenance but also for one's psychological and spiritual well-being—it is the means through which a man can maintain an active mind, attain purposes, and follow a goal-directed path throughout his lifetime. Productive work can serve as an integrating standard of one's life.

Because men must work for their material well-being, employment is a major factor in most people's lives. Men, as conscious beings, depend upon their volitional efforts and logically reasoned choices to survive and flourish. Work is integral to a man's flourishing and happiness—the positive conscious and emotional experience that accompanies or stems from achieving one's values and goals and exercising one's individual potentialities, including talents, abilities, and virtues. Each worker is a rational being who is naturally motivated to pursue his own happiness, able to discern opportunities and barriers to his happiness, and cognizant that his happiness is, for the most part, dependent upon his own efforts. Each rational person understands that reality requires him to live intelligently in order to live a meaningful life. There is an inextricable link between reason, self-interest, productive work, goal achievement, human flourishing, and happiness. Without these, the only alternative would be consumptive altruism.

Work is a concrete expression of rationality. Every productive human endeavor originates with mental effort and involves the translation of thought into a definite material form. Every creative work and discovery contributes to human existence by increasing man's understanding of reality or by making human life longer, more secure, or more pleasurable.

Productiveness comprises an important existential content of virtuousness and is a responsibility of every moral person. At issue is not your field of work, the level to which you rise, or how much you accomplish. Because people differ with respect to their intelligence, talents, and circumstances, the moral issue becomes how you address your work given your facticity, including your potentialities and concrete circumstances.

A productive life not only builds character, it also requires virtuous work habits and adherence to basic ethical norms. There are many virtues associated with work, including perseverance, patience, conscientiousness, self-control, obedience, cooperation, longanimity, constancy, honesty, integrity, fairness, and justice. Virtuous workers are energetic, productive workers who: (1) think objectively, rationally, and logically; (2) focus on reality; (3) ask clear, pertinent questions and listen carefully; (4) use time efficiently and effectively; (5) search for facts in their total context before judging; (6) organize their lives and work toward worthwhile endeavors; (7) set value-producing goals and strive to accomplish them.

Those who do not respect the value of work tend to be unemployed, often lack any sense of ethics, and are more likely to turn to a life of crime. This is evidenced by the increase in crime that accompanied the assault on work during the current century.

Work and Freedom

There is an inseparable connection between meaningful work and individual freedom. In a free society, no worker is forced to stay in a job when he is free to accept another that he finds more appealing. Both the right to quit and the right to dismiss are based on voluntarism. In a free society, all employment contracts embody the perceived mutual advantage of both the employer and the employee who freely agree to have an economic relationship with one another. Although the bargaining power of the parties may vary over time and location, neither the employer nor the worker has an inherent advantage over the other. In fact, they are equal and autonomous with respect to the most critical and core aspect of work—the freedom to accept or reject an employment contract. It is only the state's legal intervention that can artificially and arbitrarily favor either the employer or the employee. A truly voluntary relationship fosters peaceful cooperation between the worker and the company and can turn a job into a source of one's happiness. When a person works to attain his personal goals through his freely chosen job he will gain a sense of personal worth. He will also gain self-respect by not being dependent on other people for his sustenance.

For maximum freedom to exist, those who are able to work must work. If they fail to do so, both they and those who support them lose some of their freedom. Both dependence and slavery are demeaning. The state does not have the right to either sanction idleness or to force people to work either for their own benefit or for the benefit of others. People differ with respect to the amount of time they want to work, the kind of work they want to do, the standard of living they want to achieve, the amount of recreation they want to experience, and the amount of education they want to receive. These should be individual decisions reached voluntarily and cooperatively with other involved parties. Neither the state nor any other group or person can determine these types of personal choices. Although work (and other activities) is natural for man, there are no normative standards regarding how much of each activity a man is to do.

Employment Ethics Means Respecting Natural Rights

It is the employer who has the facilities, wants certain functions performed, has the job to offer, and is willing to pay for its performance. The employee furnishes the desired skills and receives a mutually agreed-upon payment for supplying them in an agreed-upon time period. The essence of the employment relationship is a voluntary agreement of exchange in which each party desires to gain something. Each party is morally and legally obligated to honor the terms of the agreement once the offer has been accepted. In a free society, the employer and employee are independent moral agents each acting in his own best interest without deception, coercion, or fraud. Employees have the basic individual rights of free choice—one can choose to accept or reject the offer or make a counteroffer, but once the terms are consented to, the worker is required to honor them. If a prospective worker does not like the deal that is being offered, he has numerous options such as taking steps to gain more education involving skills that are more in demand, move to other geographical areas or industries, join a union, etc. With the workers' freedom come both more opportunities and more risks. The employer is also a risk taker—paying wages to employees before any profits are made.

Although workers do not have an inherent moral right to health and safety protection, they can bargain to make such concessions a condition of the employment contract. Likewise, the employer does not have a duty to provide such protection although he can offer to make health and safety conditions part of the contract. If workers knowingly agree to work under risky health or safety conditions, they will have no basis for complaints in the event of resulting sickness or harm. Of course, because the employer's primary concern is with the profitability of the company, he should be concerned with employer morale, safety, health, and productivity because the workers are vital to the company's profits. Employers who ignore such concerns do so to their own detriment and experience high employee turnover, grievances, absenteeism, tardiness, and low morale.

Because work is multidimensional, the employer has to consider many factors other than who is the "most qualified" on paper. Depending upon the circumstances, attributes such as personality, sex, race, looks, height and weight, etc., may be relevant considerations. Because the manager's primary concern is the well-being of the company, he ought to hire the applicant who he believes is most likely to do the best job in the particular circumstance of his business.

No one has a right to a job in a free society because this would mean that another party would have the duty to provide him with the job. Rather, the right to work simply means that a man has the right to apply for work as part of his pursuit of happiness, without the interference of others. An employer does not owe a job to anyone, let alone to any one in particular. If an employer does not hire someone based on grounds other than lack of qualifications, he has not violated the prospective worker's rights. However, he may be morally at fault depending upon the circumstances. For example, it would be morally acceptable not to hire a black for a specific position if the manager believed that in doing so it would be damaging to the business (e.g., in a Chinese restaurant). However, the manager would be morally deficient if he were categorically prejudiced, not considering individuals from a certain group without reference to the nature of the particular job and the probable impact on the business itself. Unjust discrimination is a violation of business ethics but not a violation of rights.

In a free society, job security exists only to the degree that there is a demand for the job, which means to the degree that there are customers for the product or service that the job helps to produce. Logically, to the extent that one man's job is made secure, another person's job or opportunity to pursue one is jeopardized. To depend upon job security from a labor union or legislation would shift responsibility from one man's life to others.

There is nothing wrong with noncoercive unions or with the union's members agreeing to go out on strike. However, the company has no moral obligation to rehire the workers. When workers refuse to work, except in the case when the employer fails to meet his side of the bargain or has used deception or coercion, there is a breach of the employment contract and therefore the strike is the same as resigning. Given this, the strikers may not use force or threats to keep others from working in their place.

Recommended Reading

Anthony, P. D. *The Ideology of Work*. London: Tavistock Publications, 1977.

Applebaum, Herbert. *Work in Market and Industrial Societies*. Albany, N.Y.: SUNY Press, 1984.

———. *The Concept of Work*. Albany, N.Y.: SUNY Press, 1992.

———. *The American Work Ethic and the Changing Work Force*. Westport, Conn.: Greenwood Publishing Group, 1998.

Bell, Daniel. *Work and Its Discontents*. Boston: Beacon Press, 1956.

Byrne, Edmund F. *Work, Inc.: A Philosophical Inquiry*. Philadelphia: Temple University Press, 1990.

Cabot, Richard C. *What Men Live By: Work, Play, Love, Worship*. Boston: Houghton Mifflin, 1914.

Clark, Dennis. *Work and the Human Spirit*. New York: Sheed and Ward, 1967.

De Grazia, Sebastian. *Of Time, Work and Leisure*. New York: Twentieth Century Fund, 1962.

De Man, Henri. *Joy in Work*. Translated by Eden Paul and Cedar Paul. London: George Allen & Unwin, 1929.

Friedmann, George. *The Anatomy of Work: Labor, Leisure, and the Implications of Automation*. New York: Free Press of Glencoe, 1961.

Hall, Richard H. *Dimensions of Work*. Beverly Hills, Calif.: Sage Publications, 1986.

Herzberg, Frederick. *Work and the Nature of Man*. New York: World Publishing Co., 1966.

Marshall, Paul, et al. *Labour of Love: Essays on Work*. Toronto: Wedge Publishing, 1980.

Meilaender, Gilbert C., ed. *Working: Its Meaning and Its Limits*. South Bend, Ind.: University of Notre Dame Press, 2000.

Miller, Gale. *Its a Living: Work in Modern Society*. New York: St. Martin's Press, 1981.

Novak, Michael. *The Catholic Ethic and the Spirit of Capitalism*. New York: Free Press, 1993.

———. *Business as a Calling: Work and the Examined Life*. New York: Free Press, 1996.

Oldham, Joseph. *Work in Modern Society*. London: SCM Press, 1950.

Pahl, R. E. *On Work: Historical, Comparative, and Theoretical Approaches*. New York: Basil Blackwell, 1988.

Roethlisberger, E. J., and W. J. Dickson. *Management and the Worker*. Cambridge, Mass.: Harvard University Press, 1939.

Simon, Yves. *Work, Society, and Culture*. Edited by Virkan Kuic. New York: Fordham University Press, 1971.

Tilgher, Adriano. *Work: What It Has Meant to Men through the Ages*. New York: Harcourt Brace, 1930.

Tucker, Jeffrey. "The Moral Obligations of Workers." *The Freeman* (May 1997).

Watson, Tony. *Sociology, Work and Industry*. London: Routledge & Kegan Paul, 1987.

Weber, Max. *The Protestant Ethic and the Rise of Capitalism*. New York: Charles Scribner's Sons, 1930.

10

The Labor Union

Trade unions in a free society embody the right of working men, shared with every other member of society, to join together in the pursuit of common interests. As a private association of men, the trade union enjoys a status no different from that occupied by any other private association. . . . Violent, coercive, or fraudulent acts, on the theory of the free society, are as vicious and antisocial when performed by trade unions as they are when committed by the Ku Klux Klan.

—Sylvester Petro

Many individuals in society applaud the virtues of unionism. Embedded in our culture is the idea that unions are legitimate institutions that played a key role in American economic and social progress and that, without unions, the United States would have fallen into labor chaos and class warfare between workers and capitalists. Unions are given credit for raising the standard of living of workers, instituting democracy at the workplace, promoting social justice, and protecting helpless workers who were powerless when pitted against the giants of industry.

This chapter takes a close look at the character, functions, and ideological underpinning of unions in an effort to get at their true nature. It explains that, although unions claim to be organized against employers, they are fundamentally organized against other workers. This chapter views unions as cartels of workers who collude to raise their wages above free-market levels. Also analyzed are the ideas of labor's disadvantage and exploitation, notions derived from socialism, that provide the ideological foundation of unionism.

During the years 1932-1935, Congress passed Acts that empowered unions by instituting a legal framework for labor relations that discarded common law rules of property, contract, and tort that applied equally to all parties, replacing them with a coercive framework heavily favoring the worker over the employer. This chapter explains why this New Deal decision was one of the biggest mistakes in American history.

The chapter concludes by explaining how free-market philosophy is consistent with voluntary unionism but against coercive unionism. Legitimate unions are shown to be those that limit themselves to means of raising wages and improving working conditions that do not violate the rights of others.

The Nature and Methods of Unions

A labor union is an organization of workers in an industry, trade, or profession with the goal of achieving a monopoly of employees therein in order to have the ability to determine the working conditions for its employees. The main function of unions is to protect union members from the consequences of a competitive market—in a free society union employees would be in competition against other employees in the labor market. Labor unions are able to attain higher than market wages by restricting the supply of labor through the exclusion of nonmembers from access to competition for available jobs.

Contrary to popular belief, employers and employees are not competitors—their relationship is essentially one of cooperation and mutual benefit. Although there is occasional and sporadic conflict between employees and employers (e.g., during contract negotiations and grievance proceedings), unions are basically organized against other workers. Unions align with management in their efforts to reduce the supply of labor available to firms. When a company agrees that a given union will be the exclusive bargaining agent for its workers, competing workers who are unorganized or not members of that particular union are excluded from bidding for productive employment.

A union's goal is to organize *all* competing workers in a given industry, trade, or profession. This is true because if only a portion of the workers are organized, thereby receiving higher wages, the employer with union workers will likely lose business to nonunionized competitors with lower labor costs and hence able to sell at lower prices. The threat from competing workers in the free market would lead to the collapse of unionism in that industry, trade, or profession.

The only way that unions can attain their purposes is through the coercive power of government. Unions are state-protected monopolies or legal cartels. Labor legislation grants union employees the privilege to command higher wages than they could earn in a competitive market. Legislation excludes nonunion workers whenever greater than 50 percent of workers in a plant, industry, or profession select a particular union to be their exclusive bargaining agent. Labor legislation is intended to improve the union's well-being and protect the jobs and wages of one group of workers by restricting the opportunities of other workers.

The unemployed nonunionized workers are not allowed to compete and thereby bring down the higher than free-market wages of the privileged union workers. Those excluded from higher paying union jobs are forced to compete for work in the free labor market. Their addition to the existing supply of free-market labor further drives down wage rates in nonunionized occupations. To add insult to injury, those excluded from higher paying union jobs are restricted by the floor instituted by minimum wage laws that frequently prevent employment at the reduced market wage rate that would have prevailed in the nonorganized sector in the absence of such legislation. The effect of both the minimum wage and the union wage is to raise wages above the market level, which, in turn, results in unemployment.

Legislation that mandates unionization decreases the economic freedom of both employers and workers. A firm may prefer to ignore a union, just as workers may prefer to deal individually with the employer.

Most harmed by unionism are the workers excluded from union membership. There is a redistribution of wealth in the form of higher wages to union workers at the expense of lower wages to free-market workers. Of course, the union must have a coexisting free labor market to absorb those excluded from union membership. The employers in a nonunionized sector are essentially granted a subsidy by the state in the form of lower-priced employees. Also hurt are consumers of goods and services produced by union workers. Higher union wage costs are passed on to consumers in the form of higher prices than would have existed in a free market. The wealth transfer affected by unions is accomplished involuntarily through coercion and intimidation.

The failure of union-determined wages to adjust to competitive market conditions leads to both unemployment and a distorted allocation of labor resources. An unregulated labor market would be the most conducive to employers' and workers' economic well-being and pursuit of happiness—men should be free to contract with whomever they want and to have as wide a range of labor market choices as possible as long as they don't infringe on the equal rights of others.

The law precludes the development of a market for representational employment services that prospective employees would pay for. Workers are not permitted to decide which of several unions is best for them as individuals or if it is better for the worker to represent himself in labor negotiations. Labor law grants a union the legal right to be the exclusive bargaining agent for all the workers in a bargaining unit even though some of them may not want to be represented. Unions are associations of individuals who are required to accept the representation of particular union officials for an indefinite period of time based on a majority vote in an election in which they may not have even taken part. There is no provision for periodic reelections, although there does exist a provision to allow for a decertification vote. If the union is decertified, those who still want union representation are not permitted to have it. Also, if the vote is in favor of keeping the union, those against it will still be required to recognize it as their representative unless, of course, they decide to terminate their employment.

Any worker owns his own labor services and has the right to withhold them if he doesn't like the compensation package. It follows that if each worker has this right, then a group of workers can exercise this right simultaneously. However, not only is a strike a collective withholding of labor services by employees who do not like the compensation package offered by the employer, it is also an attempt to close down the employer by denying his firm access to replacement workers, suppliers, and customers through violence or threat of violence on the picket line or elsewhere.

Mass picketing, even if is peaceful, can be intimidating. At the very minimum it is an implicit threat to those crossing the picket line. In essence, picketing is a form of trespass against the common law property right of the struck company to continue to do business. Picketing is illegitimate because its purpose is to coerce and physically prevent suppliers, customers, competing laborers (scabs), and others from doing business with the strike target.

Employees do not have property rights to their jobs unless their contract specifies to the contrary. It follows that there is no basic right for any employee, or group of employees, to prevent other workers from employment with the struck firm. Employees own their labor services, but they don't own their jobs. Every worker, both union and nonunion alike, owns his own labor services and has the right to accept any terms of employment he is offered. Nonemployed competing workers have every bit as much a right to compete for jobs—both union members and replacement workers have the same job-related natural rights. If voluntary association and mutual consent are the legitimate foundations of employment, it is immoral, and should be illegal, for one group to forcibly prevent another from competing for jobs.

If employers were forbidden to hire permanent replacement workers, they could not impose any long-term costs on the striking employees. The ability or inability to find permanent replacement workers willing to work at the wage being offered gives firms and unions reliable market-based feedback with respect to the reasonableness of their offers and demands.

In an economic strike, one over compensation and working conditions, the employer may legally hire permanent replacement workers—in an economic strike, striking workers have the first claim on any job that a replacement worker later leaves. In an unfair labor practices strike, one over alleged illegal acts such as discrimination or refusal to bargain with a certified exclusive bargaining agent, the employer is legally permitted to hire temporary replacement workers. Upon the settlement of an unfair labor practices strike, the striking workers must be given the chance to assume the jobs being performed by the replacement workers.

Union Ideology Is Derived from Socialism

Union ideology is based on the following ideas: (1) Employees and employers are natural enemies; (2) The employers possess enormous advantages in this relationship; (3) Under capitalism, competition drives the employer to use his power advantage to exploit and abuse his workers; (4) The owners of property (i.e., the capitalists) are only entitled to the return for that which they produce with their own labor; (5) Only labor produces the surplus over costs from which profits derive; (6) The wage system under capitalism is unjust; (7) Taking away the product of a worker's labor leads to alienation of the worker; (8) Whenever there is a need to compete, profits depend on lower costs, which mean wages are cut or workers lose their jobs altogether; (9) Employers oppress workers by reducing wages, laying workers off, speeding up the work process, lengthening hours, and so on; (10) All workers are members of a single class; (11) There is a class struggle between capitalists (including managers) and laborers; (12) Workers cannot get their just rewards in an open market; and (13) Protection from abuse and exploitation lies in strong unionism and collective bargaining which the government can provide only by granting worker organizations special privileges at the expense of the common law rights of employers, nonunion employers, and antiunion employees.

Analyzing the preceding list of ideas leads one to conclude that union ideology is based on the socialist vision of injustice in general and Marx's labor theory of value in particular. Clarence B. Carson in *Organized against Whom? The Labor Union in America* explains that unionism is a derivative ideology from socialism—unionism's ideas of collectivism, class-consciousness, and class struggle all originate in socialism. Carson further observes that both socialism and unions are religion-like in nature. Socialism is religion-like because of its vision of creating a Heaven on earth (utopia). Socialism is both a substitute for religion and religion-like. Carson compares unionism with faith in God—both are ideas in which we believe in or do not believe in. He also points out the missionary character of unions' organizing work with respect to converting people to unionism. Unions are historical and theoretical offshoots of the socialist movement and have goals (i.e. higher pay, better working conditions, grievance settling, etc.) that are ethical in character—they claim that their members have been wronged and that they can only obtain justice by banding together. Consequently, unions claim special political immunities and privileges on the grounds that they are right and that justice requires their activities. Union political activity has as its proposed end the establishment of conditions under which workers can successfully make their ethical claims, thus establishing their vision of Heaven on earth. Carson argues that if unions are religious or at least quasi-religious institutions, then Congress should have been prohibited from empowering unions as it did in the 1930s. He explains that Congress transgressed the prohibitions against establishing religion when it gave unions special privileges, special standing before the government, the right to have a monopoly, and the protection and support of the government.

The Demise of Common Law Employment Rights

Before the Norris-La Guardia and National Labor Relations Acts (NLRA) in the 1930s, the employment relationship consisted of voluntary exchange contracts between employers and employees. A return to the common law of contracts, property rights, and tort would permit each person to decide if he wanted to contract with or join any union for representation services. Under such an arrangement there would be competitors among labor organizations and the possibility of having workers represented by a variety of unions and other workers having no representatives. Instead, they would bargain for themselves as individuals.

Before these acts, an employer had the common law right to fight the unionization of his company. The employer could enter into "yellow dog contracts" with the employees in which the two parties would agree not to have a union—one reason for such contracts was the desire of the employees to avoid the loss of work and wages that would occur during strikes. Because these agreements were voluntary, they must have been to the mutual benefit of both parties. In addition, before the 1930s, the employer was free to attempt to persuade workers that unionization would not be to their benefit. Also, in his efforts to gain loyalty to his firm, the employer could refuse to hire workers who wanted to engage in union-related activity. The employer also had the common law right to establish a company union. Then, of course, the company always had the right to voluntarily agree to hire workers who belonged to a specific union.

Unions were subject to the antitrust laws before Norris-La Guardia—not so thereafter. The National Labor Relations Act then destroyed the common law right of an employee to join a union of his own choosing or to represent himself. After such New Deal legislation, unions operated with the help of laws and court decisions to force employees to join them to gain a monopoly of particular jobs. Unions were free to use violence (picketing) against competing workers and intimidation against the employers through the strike.

After a union has been certified as an exclusive bargaining agent, it is presumed to have majority support indefinitely (unless there is a decertification election) even if all the workers who originally chose it are no longer with the company. Section 8(a) 3 of the National Labor Relations Act empowers unions with monopoly bargaining privileges to agree with employers that all workers represented by the unions must join the union or at least pay union dues. Section 14(b) of the Act permits states to forbid such arrangements. Twenty-one right-to-work states have chosen to do so by banning all forms of union security. In these states workers can be forced to have a union (selected by majority vote) represent them, but they cannot be forced to join or pay dues to any unions. However, in the twenty-nine other states, security clauses are permitted. In these states, workers who do not want to be represented by a union (but are forced to because of monopoly representation) may be compelled to pay for the unwanted representation or be fired. Nonunion (i.e., union-free) workers who don't want to become members of a union may be forced to pay dues (or their equivalent) as a requirement of their employment.

If a union security agreement specifies a union shop then the worker must join the union after a probationary period. However, if it specifies an agency shop, the worker does not have to join the union but must pay dues or their equivalent. In an agency shop, workers do not have to become members, but they all must pay dues or "service fees" to the unions that represent them. Unions employ a free-rider argument to justify this coercion. They argue that, without the imposition of forced dues, some workers would choose to receive the benefits of union representation but not pay for them. The goal of compulsory union dues is apparently to prevent free riders. Of course, if a union simply represented those who wanted it, there would be no free-rider problem. The union's free-rider problem stems from section 9-A of the National Labor Relations Act that requires that a certified union be the exclusive representative that bargains with the employer for all workers, both union and non-union. Unions that have gained monopoly bargaining privileges by majority vote must represent all workers, whether those workers want it to or not. The unions created the free-rider problem themselves when they persuaded the authors of the NLRA to permit monopoly bargaining. They now use monopoly bargaining as an excuse for forced dues!

By empowering labor unions the government did away with the old common law rules of contract, property, and tort that applied equally to all involved parties. They were replaced with a coercive legal framework designed to help labor union leaders attain their goals. As a result, common law courts were replaced by administrative tribunals (e.g., the National Labor Relations Board) which could be relied upon to implement prounion policies. The government thus promoted unions by failing to apply laws of equal applicability to unions and employers alike, used its power to support unions, and allowed unions to use force in pursuit of their ends.

Labor in a Free Market

Every person in a free-market economy is free to accept the best offer that he receives. Whereas competition among workers makes certain that no one is overpaid, competition among employers ensures that no one is underpaid. In a free market, labor would be treated the same as any other factor of production. If employers would combine to pay less than the market rate, other businessmen would come to the market and offer more to laborers, ultimately bringing wage rates up to the marginal productivity of labor. A free-market order allocates to each worker the fruits of his labor.

The sale of a private citizen's labor is not a concern of the state. In the absence of government interference, each worker earns what he is worth and every person seeking work will be able to find a job. The cure for widespread unemployment is to repeal the laws that prevent workers from competing for higher paying jobs or from taking lower paying jobs. Each person looking for work should be permitted to accept a job at the highest wage he can get—the cure for unemployment is free competition for jobs. In addition, the appropriate relationship between wage rates and prices can only result in a free market. Also, involuntary unemployment cannot occur in a free society. In a free market the terms must be agreeable to both parties. If no agreement is made, unemployment will result. However, this is voluntary unemployment, because one party has decided not to accept the other party's offer.

When the market is not allowed to operate freely, unemployment will occur. If unions are granted monopolistic power they will be in a position to demand benefits greater than they could get in a free market. In addition, it is more moral to let people work for less than a minimum wage then force them to be unemployed as a consequence of the state's conception of what a minimum wage should be. It is certainly better for men to work for less than the minimum wage than forcing them to be dependents of the state. Minimum wage laws have the same restrictive effects as compulsory and exclusive unionism—both destroy the natural rights of individuals to voluntarily bid for jobs.

In a free society, labor unions would simply be voluntary groups attempting to promote their members' interests without the benefit of special immunities and privileges. There can be no moral objection to workers forming a voluntary, private association to represent them in employment negotiations. Such combinations of labor are morally permissible as long as the group does not interfere with the equal rights of others. It follows that labor law in a free society should protect the rights of the individual worker instead of "rights" of unions as organizations.

This involves freedom of contract whereby some workers would choose to join a particular union, some would choose to belong to other unions, and others would rather deal with the employers individually and directly. Most labor legislation attempts to replace private agreements and contracts with government edicts that protect the rights of one group of workers while denying the rights of others. If a right cannot be exercised simultaneously by all persons in the same manner, it fails to be a natural right. It follows that the only employment rights that can be held and exercised by all individuals in the same way and at the same time is the right to make and accept or reject employment-related offers to and from others.

Voluntary, competitive unions would not be as powerful as those granted monopoly status but power is not necessarily to the advantage of the employees. There should be no place for coercive labor unions within our legal system. Voluntary unions do all they can to raise their members' wages and working conditions except violate the rights of other people by initiating violence against them. Voluntary unions restrict themselves to legitimate activities such as mass walkouts and boycotts. Coercive unions are those which do all they can do promote their members' welfare both by legitimate, non-rights-violative behavior as well as by the use of physical brutality aimed at nonaggressing individuals. It follows that public policy should defend voluntary unions and eliminate coercive ones.

Recommended Reading

Baird, Charles W. "Freedom and American Labor Relations Law: 1946-1996." *The Freeman* (May 1996).

———."Labor Law Reform: Lessons from History." *CATO Journal* (spring/summer 1990).

———."Toward Equality and Justice in Labor Markets." *The Journal of Social, Political, and Economic Studies* (summer 1995).

Barbash, Jack. *The Practice of Unionism*. New York: Harper & Bros., 1956.

Block, Walter. "Labor Relations, Unions, and Collective Bargaining: A Political Economic Analyses." *The Journal of Social, Political, and Economic Studies* (winter 1991).

Booth, Alison L. *The Economics of the Trade Union*. Cambridge: Cambridge University Press, 1995.

Carson, Clarence B. *Organized against Whom? The Labor Union in America*. Alexandria, Va.: Western Goals, 1983.

Dickman, Howard. *Industrial Democracy in America: Ideological Origins of Na-*

tional Labor Relations Policy. LaSalle, Ill.: Open Court, 1987.

DiLorenzo, Thomas J. "Government's Assault on the Freedom to Work." *The Freeman* (September 1991).

Dulles, Foster R. *Labor in America*. New York: Thomas Y. Crowell, 1960.

Dunlop, John T., and Walter Galenson , eds. *Labor in the Twentieth Century*. New York: Academic Press, 1978.

Epstein, Richard A. "A Common Law for Labor Relations: A Critique of the New Deal Labor Legislation." *The Yale Law Review* (July 1983).

Freeman, Richard B., and James L. Medoff. *What Do Unions Do?* New York: Basic Books, 1984.

Galenson, Walter. *The American Labor Movement, 1955-1995*. Westport, Conn.: Greenwood Press, 1996.

Hoxie, Robert. *Trade Unionism in the United States*. New York: Appleton-Century-Croft, 1924.

Hutt, W. H. *The Theory of Collective Bargaining 1930-1975*. Washington, D.C.: Cato Institute, 1974.

Leef, George. "Workers and Unions—How about Freedom of Contract?" *The Freeman* (December 1992).

Lindblom, Charles E. *Unions and Capitalism*. New Haven, Conn.: Yale University Press, 1949.

Perlman, Mark. *Labor Union Theories in America: Background and Development*. Evanston, Ill.: Row, Peterson & Co., 1958.

Perlman, Selig. *The History of Trade Unionism in the United States*. New York: Augustus M. Kelley, 1950.

Petro, Sylvester. *The Labor Policy of the Free Society*. New York: Ronald Press, 1957.

Raybach, Joseph G. *History of American Labor*. New York: Free Press, 1966.

Reynolds, Morgan O. *Power and Privilege: Labor Unions in America*. New York: Universe Books, 1984.

Richberg, Donald R. *Labor Union Monopoly, a Clear and Present Danger*. Chicago: H. Regnery Co., 1957.

Scoville, John W. *Labor Monopolies or Freedom*. New York: Arno Press, 1972.

Seidman, J. *Union Rights and Union Duties*. New York: Harcourt Brace, 1943.

Taft, Philip. *The Structure and Government of Labor Unions*. Cambridge, Mass.: Harvard University Press, 1954.

Tannenbaum, Frank A. *Philosophy of Labor*. New York: Alfred A. Knopf, 1951.

Troy, Leo. *Beyond Unions and Collective Bargaining*. Armonk, N.Y.: M. E. Sharpe, 1999.

11

The Corporation

But the most highly developed and usefully employed means of voluntary cooperation is the corporation, for in a corporation an individual may join the group as an owner or as an employee or as both. By its very nature and the rules that govern it, a corporation provides easy ways for persons to join and to leave, as owners or as employees. By utilizing the corporate form, the group can acquire a size needed to initiate and accomplish modern-sized jobs, a task to which no other form of voluntary association lends itself as readily. And by corporate organization, the group can best ensure a continuity of existence.

—Roger M. Blough

The idea of corporate social responsibility emerged as an issue in the early twentieth century, when corporations were criticized for being too large, too powerful, antisocial, and for engaging in anticompetitive practices. Some business leaders, acting either out of paternalism or from a sense of charity, began to use their private wealth for community and social purposes. A shift from individual philanthropy to corporate philanthropy evolved when community needs seemingly outpaced the resources of even the wealthiest individuals.

In addition, the concept of corporate social responsibility can be traced to actions taken and pronouncements made by American business leaders as strategic responses to antibusiness sentiments that developed during the late 1800s and early 1900s. The goal of these business leaders was to promote corporations as forces for the social good and thereby lessen the threat of government intervention and regulation. For example, the writings of Carnegie and other intellectual defenders of business espoused the charity and steward-ship principles and argued that although a corporation must pursue profits, its wealth should be used for the benefit of the community.

Consequently, the stewardship principle was used to urge managers to view themselves as trustees of the public interest. Accordingly, managers should act in the interest of *all* those who can influence or are influenced by a firm's actions, not just stockholders and directors, but employees, officers, creditors, customers, suppliers, communities, competitors, government, and society in general.

Although the intended purpose of undertaking socially responsible actions and issuing moral pronouncements was to appease reformers calling for legislation to control businesses, the actual result was to strengthen the power of the adversaries of business by acknowledging the social nature of the corporation. The idea of corporate social responsibility gained wide acceptance over the subsequent years as diverse groups and social activists used the concept as a rallying cry in their demands for changes in the purposes of American businesses. Increasingly, managers were urged to view themselves as trustees of the public interest who should act in the interest of *all* those who could influence or be influenced by a company's actions.

Academicians and other corporate critics, realizing the need for a "moral sanction" to underpin the idea of corporate social responsibility, began proclaiming the doctrine that corporations are possessions and servants of society that are created through the permission of the state, which itself owes its existence to society. Consequently, managers have been told that they should weigh and balance the multiple claims and interests of conflicting stakeholder groups throughout society. By so removing management decisions from their connections to the search for profit and the enhancement of stockholder value, managers have been assigned the impossible task of balancing competing claims of a variety of stakeholders.

This chapter challenges what Robert Hessen has called "concession theory"—the belief that corporations are common property and creatures of society that require state permission for their existence and that are obliged to serve the "public interest." The tenets of a more realistic and compelling theory are presented. This opposing theory, Hessen's "inherence theory," rests on the principles of choice, consent, voluntary association, contractual authorization, and individual rights (including property rights).

The Corporation as Common Property: A Flawed Doctrine

Many advocates of corporate social responsibility emphasize the social nature of the corporation that they contend exists as the result of a highly implicit and flexible contract with society that determines its duties and rights. They portray the corporation as responsible to and subject to the will of society (i.e., the people). Both the state and the law are viewed as creatures of society. Because, from this perspective, corporations are created by the government that, in turn, owes its existence to society, it follows that corporations are actually made by society and are responsible to the public to serve whatever is deemed to be in the public interest or for the common good. (It is interesting to note that when corporate critics refer to the public interest or the common good, they are frequently actually referring to the interest or the good of some individual or group of individuals intent on imposing their own views or goals upon others.) Because the corporation only exists because of social permission, "society" is said to be able to legitimately demand that a corporation perform certain activities that the owners and managers do not wish to perform. During the twentieth century, "society" has been reassessing its expectations of corporations and has pressured them to balance profit making with social responsibility. Social crusaders believe that corporations should be socially responsible both out of gratitude for their existence and a moral sense of reciprocation for benefits received from society, including the purchase of their goods and services and the access to, and use of, public goods. In essence, the corporation is viewed as more like common property than as private property. Some critics even propose that the corporation be brought under government control to ensure the common good.

From this erroneous point of view, the corporation is a fictitious person. The state controls its birth and its death, and corporate powers are exercised as a matter of concession and privilege rather than of right. The corporation is a purely artificial creature of the state, strictly accountable for the limited functions that it is granted. As a legal entity, distinct from its owners, the corporation, through its charter, gains privileges that the government confers. Thus, corporateness is conferred by public act rather than through private agreements and, as a result, the corporation is highly vulnerable to regulation by the state. If corporations are created by the state, then the state can tell them what to do. This theory holds that corporations owe their existence and gain their authority from the government, which itself acquires its authority from the people. It follows that corporations are created for the benefit of society and must therefore serve the public interest. Under this flawed view, corporations are creatures of the law, established by the government, and endowed with special legal privileges, including the most important one—limited liability.

Proponents of this view tend to suffer from the misconception that a society has a concrete existence apart from the individuals that comprise that society. To use an abstract term such as *society* is simply to refer to a collection of individuals with innumerable projects, needs, and wants of their own. There is no such thing as the general will or group welfare apart from the wills and welfare possessed by each individual in society. A corporation cannot be created by, and responsible to, an abstraction. A corporation is created by, owned by, and operated by a freely constituted group of individuals. The state merely recognizes and records the formation of corporations—it does not bring them into existence. This action by the state in no way binds the corporation to the service of the public interest.

The Corporation Properly Understood: Private Property and Voluntary Association

A corporation is a community of people voluntarily working together for common and/or compatible goals and having, in varying degrees, shared values and concerns. It follows that people tend to join, stay, and succeed with one corporation rather than another because of the extent of their agreement with the goals and values of the corporation's stockholders, directors, officers, and employees.

According to inherence theory, a corporation, man's voluntary approach to achieving economic competence, is created through the exercise of individual rights (i.e., freedom of association and freedom of contract). Men have an inherent right to form a corporation by contract for their own benefit and in their mutual self-interest. Based upon a consciousness of common interests, the corporation is an association of individuals who engage in a particular type of contractual relationship with one another in order to pursue common business objectives, is governed by rules of the individuals' own making, and is said to be able to assert rights and assume obligations. When rights and obligations are imputed to a corporation, what is really being referred to are the rights and obligations of its members who create and sustain it (i.e., the stockholders, directors, officers, employees, etc.).

Corporations are properly viewed as voluntary associations and as private property. Arising from individual contracts, corporations are not the creation of the state—the state simply recognizes and records their creation in a similar fashion as it does with births, marriages, sales of real estate, etc. The corporate charter is merely the articles of incorporation which are not related to state authority and do not obligate the corporation to serve the public interest. Because corporations are not created by the state, the government has no authority to tell them what to do.

The state grants a charter as a legal technicality and neither creates nor changes the essence of these voluntary associations whose success depends upon the social bonds that unite their members and upon the human need for group membership. The state may choose to recognize these units but in so doing it simply acknowledges that which already exists. Corporateness is a right common to all persons. The corporation is an association of human beings bound together in order to achieve a purpose. Positive law alone cannot provide the community of purpose necessary for a corporation to exist. In fact, the equivalent of a corporation frequently exists in the absence of legal action.

The corporation's contract with society is a fiction. Corporations are expressions of individual freedom, do not derive their power from society, and need only respect individuals' natural rights and adhere to government regulations.

The unique features of the corporation can be explained in terms of its contractual origins rather than as special privileges. For example, limited liability is not a privilege that is guaranteed to a corporation—a would-be creditor can decline credit to a corporation unless one or more of its stockholders assume personal liability for the obligation. Limited liability is therefore the product of a contract between shareholders and creditors who find the provision acceptable.

Stakeholder Theory as a Management Strategy

As a management strategy, stakeholder theory has merit and holds that effective corporate managers pay attention to those individuals and groups who are vital to the survival and success of the firm—shareholders, employees, suppliers, customers, the local community, etc. In this context, stakeholder theory only describes an approach for improving corporate profits—it suggests no moral social responsibility for corporations.

Socially responsible actions may be acceptable when the manager undertakes them in anticipation of effects that, in the long run, will be beneficial to business. A socially responsible investment should have a direct business purpose, involve cost-benefit analysis, and be expected to generate sufficient future net tangible benefits for the firm and its shareholders. The question is not whether an activity is in the interest of a firm, but whether it is enough in its interest to justify the expenditure.

Socially responsible actions and expenditures should be linked to business goals, thus tying in with the company's need to attract loyal customers, productive employees, and enthusiastic investors. Socially responsible activities can serve both the company's interests and those of the beneficiaries. For example, a firm's advertising and corporate philanthropy can be closely related. Linking charitable contributions in direct and measurable ways to the company's products or services helps to increase sales to customers whose social values affect their purchasing decisions. In addition, donations to causes that improve the community can be used to attract skilled workers. Donations can also be given to research or educational programs that have obvious connections to the firm's economic interest. Company-sponsored employee volunteer programs not only can help others, but also can attract good employees, build their character, create a sense of teamwork and corporation mission, and improve their performance.

John M. Hood's *The Heroic Enterprise* provides specific illustrations of how companies can and do serve society through the pursuit of profits. Sponsoring wellness, safety, and health promotion programs for employees can save money in lower health, accident, and life insurance premiums. Providing childcare, family leave, flextime, job sharing, employee assistance programs (e.g., counseling), and opportunities for telecommuting not only benefit the firm but also its workers and their families. When a company humanely and effectively uses outplacement services for employees who are laid off due to strategic rightsizing, the result is not only a savings in severance payments, but also good public relations and maintenance of employee morale and productivity. Also, making profits can be in line with the social interest of rebuilding distressed communities, especially if the communities are viewed as underserved markets. By helping to renovate inner cities, making them safer and training their residents, firms can serve their own interests as well as those of the urban population. Earning the trust of consumers and community leaders can lead to long-term profitability.

Stakeholder Theory: A Flawed Ethical Theory

Anthony Buono and Lawrence Nichols as "any identifiable group or individual who can affect or is affected by organizational performance in terms of its products, policies, and work processes" have vaguely and broadly defined the term *stakeholder*. Stakeholder theory becomes problematic when it is viewed as an ethical theory. Proponents of stakeholder theory as an ethical theory attempt to base their argument on Kant's principle of respect for persons. For example, according to Evan and Freeman, each stakeholder group has a right to be treated as an end in itself and not as a means to some other end and, therefore, must participate in determining the future direction of the firm in which it has a stake. In other words, the corporation should be managed for the benefit of its stakeholders and the groups must participate in decisions that affect their welfare. Such participation is indirect with managers having the surrogate duty to represent the stakeholders' interests. Managers are said to have a fiduciary relationship to stakeholders and must act in the interests of the stakeholders as their agent.

These stakeholder theorists misinterpret Kant's principle. What he actually said was that every human being is entitled to be treated not "merely" as a means but also as an end in him. To regard persons as ends is to recognize which is autonomous moral agents that are the same as respecting individuals' natural rights to pursue their own goals and to associate with those of their own choosing according to mutually agreeable terms. Respecting the autonomy of stakeholders does not imply that they are entitled to a say in corporate decisions nor that the firm should be conducted in their interests. It merely means dealing with them in freely bargained transactions without the use of force or fraud. No stakeholder should be forced to associate with the company without his consent.

When viewed as an ethical theory, stakeholder (or constituency) theory erroneously suggests that corporations are possessions and servants of larger society. As a result, managers have been told that they should treat all stakeholders as having equally important interests. This leaves managers wondering how to weigh and balance the multiple claims and interests of conflicting stakeholders.

By removing management decisions from their connections to the commercial search for profit and the enhancement of shareholder value, managers would be in the impossible situation of balancing competing claims of a variety of stakeholders. Without the explicit goal of returning the highest value to stockholders, managers would find themselves in the position of having to make essentially political rather than business decisions.

True Corporate Responsibility: Respect for Natural Rights

The social responsibility of the corporation, through its directors, managers, and other employees, is simply to respect the natural rights of individuals. Individuals in a corporation have the legally enforceable responsibility or duty to respect the moral agency, space, or autonomy of persons. This involves the basic principle of the noninitiation of physical force and includes: the obligation to honor a corporation's contracts with its managers, employees, customers, suppliers, and others; duties not to engage in deception, fraud, force, threats, theft, or coercion against others; and the responsibility to honor representations made to the local community.

Respect for contracts implies respect for individual rights. Beyond respecting the rights born of specific individual contractual agreements, obeying the law, and adhering to the minimalist principle of noninjury, a corporation and its managers are not ethically required to be socially responsible.

Customers, employers, suppliers, and others autonomously negotiate for and agree to contract with the corporation. If managers were to break an agreement with the shareholders to maximize profits in order to give one or more groups more benefits than they freely agreed upon, they would not only be violating the rights of the owners, but also would not be respecting the autonomy of individuals within other groups. Corporations and their managers are obligated to respect the rights of individuals within each group, but the rights are limited to the rights of parties in market transactions. The social responsibility of corporations is limited to respecting the natural rights of all individual parties.

The corporation is a species of private property created by individuals through the exercise of their natural rights, and its managers are responsible to the owners rather than to society or to the government. The responsibility of a corporation and its managers is to engage in open and free competition without deception and fraud. This simply means respecting the individual or natural rights of persons. To attempt to promote corporate social responsibility, except for stockholder-favored projects and for those expected to be in the best long-run interests of the owners, amounts to a moral wrong.

Managers Are Agents of the Stockholders

In an individualistic society all contracts are entered into voluntarily. Each person is free to associate with others for their own mutually agreeable purposes. The corporation is a form of property created by individuals in the exercise of their natural rights. The corporation is thus the result of a contract between individuals who wish to combine their resources and, if desired, delegate a portion of the authority and responsibility for managing and using these resources. Managers therefore have the obligation to use the shareholders' money for specifically authorized shareholder purposes that can range from the pursuit of profit to the expenditure of funds for social purposes. If managers use this money for activities not authorized by the shareholders, they would be guilty of spending others' money without their consent, failing in their contractual obligation to the owners and, therefore, violating the rights of the shareholders. Owners have a property right in the corporation and a correlative right to engage in profit making if so desired. It follows that those who act in their behalf (i.e., the managers) have a duty to carry out the wishes of the owners, who usually invest to make a profit.

Managers are employees of the shareholders and have a contractual and hence moral responsibility to fulfill the wishes of the shareholders. As a corporate executive, the manager is an agent of the owners of the corporation and has a fiduciary responsibility to them. Corporate social responsibility may be permitted within the limits of prior contractual agreements with the shareholders. This occurs when individuals organize corporations for reasons other than, or in addition to, profit. Also, socially responsible actions such as charitable contributions may be acceptable when the manager makes these in anticipation of effects that, in the long run, will be beneficial to business.

As an individual, a manager may have other obligations that he should voluntarily assume by using his own money, time, and resources—not those of his employers. However, when functioning in his corporate capacity, he has a duty not to divert corporate funds from stockholders' authorized purposes. Discontented shareholders may theoretically bring suit against the directors and managers when they spend the shareholders' money on unauthorized social responsibility projects that are not in the owners' interest. However, it is more likely that they will vote against such directors, attempt to remove the managers, or simply sell their shares.

Stockholders Are the Only True Stakeholders

According to stockholder theory, the obligation of a corporation and its managers to its stockholders is fiduciary. Stakeholder theory implies a multi-fiduciary approach that is inconsistent with free markets, property rights, and the moral view that there is a special fiduciary obligation owed by management to the stockholders. Because stockholders hire managers to serve their interests, managers are responsible to the stockholders. It follows that managers do not have the right or obligation to spend the stockholders' money in ways that have not been sanctioned by the owners no matter what social benefits may occur by doing so. Corporations are simply arrangements whereby stockholders advance money to managers to use for specific ends. Managers are limited by their agency relationship to exclusively serve the objectives outlined by their stockholder principals. Expenditures for socially beneficial purposes are only legitimate when they have been specifically authorized by the stockholders or when managers believe they will increase the firm's long-run profitability, perhaps through the creation of goodwill.

Stockholders are the only true stakeholders. One must invest in a corporation to actually have a stake in it. Other so-called stakeholder groups, with the possible exception of employees, have no stake or interest in the success of any specific corporation as long as the corporation is able to fulfill the freely contracted obligations it has with the stakeholder group. They may be concerned about how corporations affect them, but to actually have a stake in a particular firm requires one to care about its success and this normally requires a financial investment.

. Recommended Reading

Bainbridge, Stephen M. "In Defense of the Shareholder Wealth Maximization Norm: A Reply to Professor Green." *Washington and Lee Law Review* (fall 1993).

Bander, Edward J., ed. *The Corporation in a Democratic Society.* New York: H. W. Wilson Co., 1975.

Berle, Adolph A. Jr., and Gardiner C. Means. *The Modern Corporation and Private Property.* New York: Harcourt, Brace and World, 1968.

Blough, Roger M. *Free Man and the Corporation.* New York: McGraw-Hill, 1959.

Bork, Robert H. *Capitalism and the Corporate Executive.* Washington, D.C.: AEI Press, 1977.

Bowen, Howard R. *Social Responsibilities of the Businessman.* New York: Harper & Bros., 1953.

Buono, Anthony F., and Laurence T. Nichols. "Stockholder and Stakeholder Interpretations of Business' Social Role." *Business Ethics.* Edited by W. Michael Hoffman and Jennifer Mills More. New York: McGraw-Hill, 1990.

Clarkson, Max, ed. *The Corporation and Its Stakeholders: Classic and Contemporary Readings.* Toronto: University of Toronto Press, 1998.

Cortenraad, Wouter H. F. M. *The Corporate Paradox: Economic Realities of the Corporate Form.* Dordrecht, The Netherlands: Kluwer Academic Publishers, 1999.

Crane, Edward H. "Corporate Giving: The Case for Enlightened Self-Interest." *The Freeman* (November 1991).

Den Uyl, Douglas. *The New Crusaders.* Bowling Green, Ohio: Social Philosophy and Policy Center, 1984.

Evan, William M., and R. Edward Freeman. "A Stakeholder Theory of the Modern Corporation: Kantian Capitalism." *Ethical Theory and Business.* Edited by Tom L. Beauchamp and Norman E. Bowie. Englewood Cliffs, N.J.: Prentice-Hall, 1993.

Drucker, Peter F. *Concept of the Corporation.* New York: John Day Company, 1946.

Friedman, Milton. *Capitalism and Freedom.* Chicago: University of Chicago Press, 1962.

Handlin, Oscar, and Mary F. Handlin. "Origins of the American Business Corporation." *Journal of Economic History* (May 1945).

Hessen, Robert. "A New Concept of Corporation." *The Hastings Law Journal* (May 1979).

Hessen, Robert. *In Defense of the Corporation.* Stanford, Calif.: Hoover Institution Press, 1979.

Hood, John M. *The Heroic Enterprise.* New York: Free Press, 1996.

Jacoby, Neil H. *Corporate Power and Social Responsibility.* New York:

Macmillan, 1973.

Jones, Thomas M. "Corporate Social Responsibility Revisited, Redefined." *California Management Review* (spring 1980).

Kaysen, Carl, ed. *The American Corporation Today.* New York: Oxford University Press, 1996.

Kuhn, James W. *Beyond Success: Corporations and Their Critics in the 1990s.* Contribution by Donald W. Shriver. New York: Oxford University Press, 1991.

Levitt, Theodore. "The Danger of Social Responsibility." *Harvard Business Review* (Sept.-Oct.,1958).

Makower, Joel. *Beyond the Bottom Line: Putting Social Responsibility to Work for Your Business and the World.* New York: Touchstone Books, 1995.

Mason, Edward S., ed. *The Corporation in Modern Society.* Cambridge, Mass.: Harvard University Press, 1959.

McCord, David. "The Modern Corporation—Twenty Years After." *University of Chicago Law Review* (summer 1952).

Novak, Michael. *Toward a Theology of the Corporation.* Washington, D.C.: AEI Press, 1981.

———. *The Fire of Invention: Civil Society and the Future of the Corporation.* Lanham, Md.: Rowman & Littlefield, 1997.

Novak, Michael, and John W. Cooper, eds. *The Corporation: A Theological Inquiry.* Washington, D.C.: AEI Press, 1981.

Romano, Roberta. *The Genius of American Corporate Law.* Washington, D.C.: AEI Press, 1993.

Shaw, Bill, and Frederick R. Post. "A Moral Basis for Corporate Philosophy." *Journal of Business Ethics* (December 1993).

Svendsen, Ann. *The Stakeholder Strategy: Profiting from Collaborative Business Relationships.* San Francisco: Berrett-Koehler Publishers, 1998.

Walton, Clarence C. *Corporate Social Responsibilities.* Belmont, Calif.: Wadsworth Publishing Co., 1967.

Weiner, Joseph L. "The Berle-Dodd Dialogue on the Concept of the Corporation." *Columbia Law Review* (December 1964).

Williams, Oliver F., and John W. Houck, eds. *The Judeo-Christian Vision and the Modern Corporation.* South Bend, Ind.: University of Notre Dame Press, 1982.

12

Business

The calling of business is to support the reality and reputation of capitalism, democracy, and moral purpose everywhere, and not in any way to undermine them.

—Michael Novak

A sense of suspicion and grudging tolerance looms over business. America is culturally prejudiced against commerce. Anticapitalist ideas have had a dramatic impact in this country. Business and businessmen have been maligned as dishonest, unfair, greedy, insensitive, underhanded, evil, and morally deficient. Negative images have been promulgated for centuries by intellectuals, the Church, socialists, popular culture, storytellers, aristocrats, Supreme Court justices, historians, and others. The focus of business on profit and its preoccupation with prosperity and earthly happiness have been declaimed as immoral.

Certainly, there are bad businessmen just as there are bad men in other walks of life. Businessmen don't always act virtuously. Capitalism is simply a socioeconomic mechanism that permits individuals to act morally or immorally. Capitalism is, without doubt, much better than its image. Its economic freedom is consistent with underlying moral principles of life itself. Capitalism relies on a system of rewards and punishments that minimize coercion, prejudice, and irrationality in human relations. Business in a free society rewards businessmen who are honest, trustworthy, understanding, self-reliant, rational, and hard working. Whereas practices such as lying, deception, fraud, and theft might lead to short-term gains, such practices would certainly lead to ruin in the long run.

The term *society* refers to voluntary interactions among consenting human beings. The market is a process of social cooperation, employing a division of labor, where people specialize in a variety of tasks in expectation of demand for the goods and services they produce. The business realm is thus a cooperative system of value-seeking individuals who produce and trade for mutual advantage.

Businessmen must be committed to reality. After scientists and engineers uncover new knowledge, it is the task of the businessman to determine how to use that knowledge. Rational thinking is the cause of wealth production. The businessman searches for opportunities and combines land, labor, and capital to create wealth. The market creates benefits in the form of new and better products and lower prices. A businessman benefits only by offering goods and services that others are willing to buy. If he does not cater to the desires of others, he will not prosper. He enables others to attain what they want and to pursue their visions of happiness. The businessman is an appropriate symbol of a free society. Capitalism inspires business behavior that is prudent, diligent, prescient, innovative, imaginative, and virtuous. The successful businessman must be a risk-taking man of ideas and moral action.

The Nature of Man and the World

Reality lies outside the human mind and is what the mind focuses on in man's efforts to discern and discover the principles related to the operation of the physical world. People need to understand the nature of man and the world and the nature of human action in order to determine how to act. The order of nature is not invented by man. Rather, he uses his unique attribute, reason, to apprehend the order by which he is bound.

All things have a nature, including man. A natural order exists in the universe. What is called natural law is found in the nature of things. Reason brings these laws into our knowledge by observing and contemplating the underlying order and regularities of the world.

Man's distinctive characteristic is his rationality. Because he can choose and can recognize cause and effect, he is a morally responsible being. Without free will, he could not be held accountable for his actions. When an individual realizes he is responsible for the actions he takes, he is more likely to use his mind to anticipate the consequences of his actions.

In economics, politics, and other areas, there are principles and laws written into the nature of things. Because man is a being with a particular nature, a specific type of society is required for his proper functioning as a human being.

Work is built into the human condition. Men must transform parts of their natural environment into consumable forms in order to survive and prosper. Wealth has to be produced by men. Nature provides the raw materials, but man must use his mind to uncover the knowledge of how to use them and must use his physical abilities to convert them into usable form.

A man must obtain what he requires, if he is to maintain his life. Either he or someone else must produce the things that he requires. There is an innate inequality of men with respect to their capacities to perform different kinds of work. Human beings are born unequal with regard to their intellectual and physical abilities. Division of labor is a logical outcome of man's rational reaction to countless natural conditions.

Every person is born an individual with respect to his mind and body. Each one has inborn differences based on his brain structure and physical endowments. Each person has peculiar aptitudes, which can be recognized, developed, and used. Each person has his own mental faculty, distinctive set of drives, ways of thinking, emotional makeup, and the like. Because each person is distinctive, people differ in their preferred ways of pursuing their happiness.

A free society leaves each individual free to think, to act on his thoughts, and to enjoy the rewards of his actions. Business in a free society permits one to perform a specialized task, at which one excels, while gaining the benefits of others performing tasks at which they excel. Because talents vary from one person to another, they can create and enjoy more if they specialize in production and then exchange with others.

No two persons can value anything in exactly the same way. The market is the means by which free men attempt to satisfy their varying individual values. The free market is a spontaneous order that coordinates countless diverse values, abilities, and bits of information. Business, a necessary response to human needs, is the economy. It is the sector which makes possible our material abundance and well-being.

Scientists discover nature's laws. Engineers use these laws to develop new product ideas. In turn, the businessman takes the theoretical achievements of the scientists and engineers and turns them into reality. The businessman takes scientific discoveries into his factories and transforms them into products that meet men's needs and increase the pleasure of their existence.

The Role of Business

Free enterprise is the natural, voluntary collaboration of individuals exchanging the products of their minds, creativity, abilities, and energy. Free enterprise thus involves all of us. It is what unobstructed individuals do to maintain their lives. As long as activity is peaceful it should be permitted. It follows that, from this perspective, every person is as much a businessman as individuals usually identified as such. Every individual who engages in gainful employment in exchange for pay participates in business. He trades his time, energy, and efforts in order to receive remuneration that he can use to satisfy his needs and attain his desires.

Business is the way people in a free society organize their economic activities by producing and marketing goods and services in response to the voluntary actions of people in the marketplace who either purchase or abstain from purchasing. Commerce makes it possible for people to pursue their desires and achieve prosperity through trade with others. Business is the method by which a man can voluntarily offer to exchange what he possesses for what he desires. It is the most effective means by which a person can pursue his vision of happiness in accordance with the natural law principle of natural rights. It follows that a legitimate businessman does not profit through force, fraud, deception, or other immoral means.

Each person values things subjectively in accordance with his unique attributes and individual judgments. Businesses develop to meet the diverse and numerous wants of distinct persons. In a free society, a business endures only as long as it pleases enough individual customers. A businessman thus earns his wealth and serves himself only when he first addresses the well being of others. The free market coordinates the skills and activities of disparate individuals with varying goals and diverse values. The successful businessman serves others as those others want to be served and not as he thinks they should want to be served.

Business involves everyone who engages in trading what he creates and owns (i.e., his ideas, goods, and services) to others who consider what they have to be less desirable than the exchange items offered in return. People part only with what they value less for what they value more. It is a myth that in an exchange, what one gains the other party must lose. In a voluntary exchange, both participants must expect to gain or no exchange will take place.

To be successful, a businessman must objectively perceive reality and rationally process and evaluate information. He must detect information gaps between consumer wants and needs and the potential of a new but as yet undeveloped product or service to meet those wants and needs. The businessman must anticipate new markets and consumers' future wants and needs, learn from competitors' successes and failures, accumulate capital for his projects, acquire the needed resources, coordinate numerous activities and employee skills, and take risks by trading present and known values for resources that only promise a potential future value for him. Profit is payment for the businessman's thought, vision, initiative, determination, and efficiency.

Businessmen aim to produce a profit by selling at the highest price the market will permit while buying at the lowest prices the market will yield. They profit by doing the best they can in creating goods and services that consumers desire. The role of business is to produce the best possible goods, services, and ideas at the lowest possible cost so as to maximize the firm's profits. The businessman earns profits by using as little as possible to provide customers with as much as possible. Profit is made by creating wealth and trading with others.

Human flourishing involves the creation, acquisition, and use of wealth in fulfilling activities. It is the practical insights and reason of individual human beings as producers and consumers that are needed, not only in the production and attainment of wealth, but also in the pursuit of each person's unique vision of his happiness.

Business, as a calling, is related to the flourishing of the individual. Innumerable individuals have satisfied their needs, actualized their potentialities, and attained their goals in the realm of business. It follows that the businessman's activities are morally proper and worthy goals.

The intellectual and moral virtue of prudence is concerned with the intelligent living of one's life. If a person is to be prudent about his life, he must attend to his total well-being. Prudence thus involves the intelligent pursuit of profit, prosperity, and commercial success. Business can be viewed as the social product of human concern with prudence—advancing one's own essential well-being and that of his loved ones. To be prudent is to apply intelligence to changing circumstances by acting in the right manner, at the right time, and for the right reasons. Commerce is a proper, morally justified area of human action in which businessmen are concerned with obtaining economic well-being. Businessmen transform potential wealth into physical products and services by combining human innovations and discoveries with human labor and natural resources. Through the use of intelligence, businessmen make possible physical goods, services, and enjoyment of life. In a way, businessmen are specialists in the virtue of prudence. They provide people with power over their lives by supplying goods and services that can reduce their labor and increase the time available to pursue other chosen activities. Businessmen help their fellowmen pursue their unique visions of happiness.

The core of business is wealth creation. Its essential nature involves the production of value for trade. Professional businessmen are specialists in voluntary exchange. In a firm, managers are employed to add to the net worth of the company. They are not typically hired to carry on programs of social reform. The businessman provides business competence for a price. People normally invest to increase their wealth and the businessman furnishes the skills to meet this goal.

Business *qua* business serves those who wish to trade and does not make use of coercion. It is the entry of the state into the business realm that leads to coercive monopolies and unfair advantages. Unlike business, the state relies on coercive power rather than on voluntary agreement. When a failed or faltering business is rescued by a government handout, it is no longer a business. Likewise, when a businessman obtains his results outside the market framework by receiving special privileges (e.g., subsidies or monopolistic advantages) granted by the government, he forfeits his status as a businessman.

A firm's economic power is derived from its ability to produce material values and offer them for sale. Unlike political power, which depends on physical force, economic power relies on voluntary choices. A company is powerless when it fails to provide things that people want to purchase. The only leverage the businessman has is the quality of his products and his ability to persuade.

Sometimes businesses lobby government for special privileges such as bailouts, price supports, subsidized loans, trade protection, resource privileges, grants of monopoly, etc. A moral business would succeed or fail on its own without any government assistance. If a moral businessman makes a mistake, he is prepared to suffer the consequences. If he fails, he takes the loss. A moral businessman profits only if he satisfies the needs of people by offering better products or services or at a lower price than do others. When practiced properly, business is a noble and virtuous pursuit.

The free market supplies the individual with a host of competing decentralized alternatives. Competition, a moral expression of freedom, permits people to make choices and act upon them and leads to new and better products and services, higher wages, more jobs, and a higher standard of living. Competition is a natural phenomenon through which firms strive to efficiently use resources and vie to satisfy human wants. Competitors succeed when they offer goods and services that consumers value and are willing to buy. Fortunately, when competitors fail under a free market, this does not mean that we also have a failed economy. Unsuccessful businesses simply have to make way for the successful ones and for new competitors willing to enter the market. The free market rewards businessmen unequally but equitably according to consumers' evaluations of their products and services.

Image Versus Reality

Throughout history Western culture has at best been ambivalent and oftentimes has been disdainful regarding the moral merits of business. Of those engaged in various professions, businessmen have been the most denounced, vilified, and misunderstood. The hostility toward gains and contempt for commerce can be traced to cultural inheritances from the days of the Greek philosophers who emphasized the essentially vulgar characteristics of retail trade.

Plato consigned the trader to the lowest level in his ideal society. He ranked men from the bottom up beginning with workers, tradesmen, and artisans whose function it was to provide life's necessities. Warriors were assigned a higher status and philosophers were at the top. Plato valued rational ability over courage and declared that the philosophers should rule. Contemplation constituted the worthy life. Plato's otherworldly dualism denigrates man's corporeal nature and assigns the intellectual and spiritual dimensions of man to a higher level. The mind is thus held to be morally and ontologically superior to the body. Although Aristotle disagreed with Plato's otherworldliness and on many other philosophical issues, he agreed with him that intellectual contemplation was man's highest activity.

Much later, the eighteenth-century German philosopher, Immanuel Kant, taught that if a person acts in order to gain benefits, the act has no moral value. It follows that since the goal of business is to make profits, then business cannot be said to have moral worth. In essence, Kant removed prudence from the province of morality, thus debarring business from any chance for respect.

The avowal of self-interest renders the businessman and the business system suspect. Once business had been deprived of its moral standing, it was not long before people began questioning and renouncing as evil its inherent profit motive and means of seeking wealth through capitalizing on people's earthly desires. It is impossible to separate business from its goals.

The views of the above philosophers were only the beginning. There has been an almost universal bias against business and the businessman on the part of intellectuals, historians, writers of fiction and nonfiction, filmmakers, socialists, the popular culture, the Church, cartoonists, and others. To this day television, radio, newspapers, magazines, books, and plays tend to portray the businessman as evil, greedy, crooked, and immoral. Even business ethics texts typically say that self-interested behavior leads to immoral actions and caution businessmen to restrain their self-interested behavior. It is no wonder that business activities are regarded with cynicism by the public at large when what they are exposed to are largely unfavorable, untrue, and incomplete images of business. The public image of business includes many villains but only a handful of heroes.

In truth, businessmen are as good or as bad as the average man. Businessmen do not always behave morally. Some lie, cheat, and act irresponsibly or with impunity, but in the long run such behavior is certainly unwise. Capitalism rewards business behavior that is honest, civil, fair, compassionate, diligent, prudent, and heroic. In a free society, people in business are neither better nor worse than those in other professions. There are good and bad in all walks of life and certainly no justification to believe that all business people are evil. Moral principles that are valid for all people are equally valid for those in business.

Hostile public opinion may result from the absence of adequate and true information and the presence of misinformation regarding business. Most businessmen earn their rewards by personal ability and free trade in a free market. Business is essentially decent but corruptible. Business provides earthly well-being. Business supplies a rational and humane system of rewards in exchange for individuals' productive efforts. Wealth is the result of a creative process. The primary purpose of business is not to help mankind by producing and selling goods and services. Businesses do benefit others but this is only a secondary consequence of their actions. Although businesses thrive from satisfying customers, their primary purpose is to generate profits for their owners who want to be happy and live well. In a free economy, people can advance their own lives by pleasing customers who through their voluntary actions determine the distribution of rewards. The moral justification for business profits is the right to private property. Men must be permitted to act to ensure their own survival and pursue their own flourishing. Living well involves all that makes us human. To survive and thrive on earth requires a concern for one's material well-being. Material prosperity enables a man to cultivate his mind and spirit, to seek wisdom, and to develop his character. Business is a natural moral consequence of this concern and an essential activity of what is required to live a full life. When people are criticized for acting selfishly, they are oftentimes being derided for exercising their right to pursue their own happiness.

So-called intellectuals, those who deal with ideas expressed in words, disproportionately oppose capitalism and business. These social critics report, interpret, analyze, and comment on public affairs. They include scholars, professors, journalists, literary critics, novelists, playwrights, filmmakers, television newsmen, political staffers and speechwriters, and others who see part of their function as observing, finding faults, and proposing societal changes. Unlike the man in the street who tends to be ambivalent toward business, most intellectuals take great joy in maligning business and verbalizing anticapitalist viewpoints. They look down on businessmen and wonder why they did not choose to use their talents to achieve social goals.

Businessmen appear materialistic, unreflective, and mundane to the intellectual. Intellectuals are also apt to think of wealth as a finite quantity and to view it as stolen if made and as underserved if inherited. They also see business proficiency as in opposition to the moral tradition of duty, which says that we must sacrifice selflessly and serve others. The doctrine of altruism says if a person possesses something needed by another, he must surrender it or be guilty of theft. Strong believers in Marx's labor theory of value, most intellectuals perceive the relationship between employer and employee as one of exploiter to victim. To the business moralist, success in the market often looks like exploitation. The businessman is also frequently blamed for depressions and recessions. Intellectuals also like to promote the idea that political crusaders and humanitarians, rather than businessmen, are responsible for America's well-being.

Intellectuals have a hard time giving the market its due credit. After all, in their minds the market system does not appear to be fair to the intellectuals themselves. They were the most valued, rewarded, and successful in school where standards differ from those in the free market. Whereas schools reward intellectual achievements and verbal ability, the market rewards business skills and character traits such as honesty, friendliness, rationality, practicality, realism, creativity, self-reliance, hard work, etc. They therefore resent the capitalist system in which they are not held in as much esteem as when they were in school and are not rewarded financially as well as many businessmen. Intellectuals are predisposed to perceive the market as too disorderly and to prefer rewards to be centrally distributed like they were in their schooldays.

Many novels, films, plays, and television programs are not representative of the real business world. These media have often been unflattering in their depiction of business and capitalism, have attacked business for destroying an old communal order based on equality, and have lamented the businessman's preoccupation with material success and the domination of large organizations in people's lives. The businessman has been depicted with hostility and derision and has been portrayed as materialistic, greedy, miserly, villainous, corrupt, unethical, hypocritical, insecure, insensitive, anticultural, exploitative, smaller-than-life, depersonalized mechanized, repressive of emotions, and subservient to the system.

A small percentage of our society's fictional works have characterized the businessmen in a more favorable light by emphasizing: the possibilities of life in a free society; the inherent ethical nature of capitalism and the good businessman; the strength, courage, integrity, and self-sufficiency of the hardworking businessman; and the entrepreneur as wealth creator and promoter of human progress. A few positive images do exist, but more are needed in order to illustrate the value of free enterprise, innovation, and personal initiative. People should be shown the positive and honorable qualities of business, businessmen, and careers in business.

Business Is a Noble Calling

Although businessmen represent one of the leadership groups in society, they tend to feel uneasy, self-conscious, and even guilty about their positions. After all, Western culture has frequently derided and criticized the free enterprise system and generally holds business in low esteem. Although the benefits of business are welcomed, there has been a general predilection for people to begrudge productivity and those who cause it. As a result, many businessmen believe that if they are to earn respect, they must do so by doing more than performing well in business. Many attempt to prove their value by "giving back" to education, the arts, the community, etc. There is a tendency to defend their profession by pointing to socially responsible activities such as charity and philanthropy or to external consequences of their commercial activities such as jobs created or taxes paid to the government.

The goal of many business critics appears to bring down the more able to the level of the less able and to make the producers feel unearned guilt for their accomplishments. This envy can be viewed as an egalitarian outcry against the reality of individual differences in abilities, attainments, and rewards. These critics appear to be opposed to the departure of business and the free market from their unattainable ideals of egalitarianism and collectivism. They also do not like the fact that capitalism permits moral pluralism. Many social critics would prefer a universal ethical code imposed by fiat or at least by consensus.

Most professionals are viewed mainly in terms of services provided and only secondarily in terms of their profits. Businessmen, on the other hand, are primarily perceived in terms of their profits. Many people do not seem to understand that to be a businessman is to serve others. Businesses must satisfy their customers if they are to survive. Service is a prerequisite of profit. Businessmen create goods and services for themselves and others. Every product and service that sustains and improves human lives is made possible by the world's creators. Businessmen should take pride in their achievements and their virtues of rational thought and productive work that make them possible. Business is a noble calling. There is no justified reason for an honest businessman to be ashamed of his profession or to feel guilty about his earnings.

Too many misconceptions and misstatements have been disseminated about business. Business has rarely been treated fairly or accurately. We need to proclaim the truth about business. Many Americans are uninformed about the workings of business, the free-market system, and the nature of government powers. They have not been taught the concepts underpinning free enterprise. Many do not realize that the American economy has moved away from capitalism and, thus, they frequently blame capitalism and businessmen for faults of the "mixed economy." Each of us needs to do our part in words and deeds to improve the image of business and the businessman. Our goal should be to match the image of free enterprise with its reality.

Recommended Reading

Berg, Ivar, ed. *The Business of America*. New York: Harcourt, Brace, & World, 1968.

Blough, Roger. *Free Man and the Corporation*. New York: McGraw Hill, 1959.

Chamberlain, John. *The Enterprising Americans: A Business History of the United States*. New York: Harper and Row, 1963.

Cheit, Earl, ed. *The Business Establishment*. New York: John Wiley & Sons, 1964.

Chesher, James E., and Tibor R. Machan. *The Business of Commerce*. Stanford, Calif.: Hoover Press, 1999.

Cochran, Thomas C. *Basic History of American Business*. Princeton, N.J.: D. Van Nostrand Co., 1959.

DeGeorge, Richard T., and Joseph A. Pichler, eds. *Ethics, Free Enterprise, and Public Policy*. New York: Oxford University Press, 1978.

Den Uyl, Douglas J. *The Virtue of Prudence*. New York: Peter Lang, 1991.

Diamond, Sigmund. *The Reputation of the American Businessman*. Cambridge, Mass.: Harvard University Press, 1955.

Eells, Richard, and Clarence Walton. *Conceptual Foundations of Business*. Homewood, Ill.: Richard D. Irwin, 1974.

Elbing, A. O., and Carol Elbing. *The Value Issue in Business*. New York: McGraw Hill, 1967.

Fukuyama, Francis. *Trust: The Social Virtues and the Creation of Prosperity*. New York: Free Press, 1995.

Garrett, Garet. "Business," *Civilization in the United States: An Inquiry by Thirty Americans*. Edited by Harold E. Stearns. New York: Harcourt Brace, 1922.

Glover, J. D. *The Attack on Big Business*. Boston: Harvard University Press, 1954.

Greiner, Donna, and Theodore B. Kinni. *Ayn Rand and Business*. New York: Texere, 2001.

Hood, John M. *The Heroic Enterprise*. New York: Free Press, 1996.

Lavoie, Donald. *Rivalry and Competition*. London: Oxford University Press, 1959.

Lichter, S. Robert, Linda S. Lichter, and Stanley Rothman. *Video Villains: The TV Businessmen 1955-1986*. Washington, D.C.: Center for Media and Public Affairs, 1987.

Lichter, S. Robert, Linda S. Lichter, and Daniel Amundson. *Does Hollywood Hate Business or Money?* Washington, D.C.: Center for Media and Public Affairs, 1994.

McVeagh, John. *Tradeful Merchants: The Portrayal of the Capitalist in Literature*. London: Routledge & Kegan Paul, 1981.

Miller, William, ed. *Men in Business*. Cambridge, Mass.: Harvard University Press, 1952.

Novak, Michael. *Business as a Calling*. New York: Free Press, 1996.

O'Toole, James. *The Executive's Compass*. New York: Oxford University Press, 1993.

Rand, Ayn. *Atlas Shrugged*. New York: Random House, 1957.

————. *Why Businessmen Need Philosophy*. Edited by Richard E. Ralston. Marina del Rey, Calif.: Ayn Rand Institute Press, 1999.

Sternberg, Elaine. *Just Business*. New York: Oxford University Press, 2000.

Sutton, Francis X, Seymour E. Harris, Carl Kayson, and James Tobin. *The American Business Creed.* New York: Schocken Books, 1962.

Walton, Clarence C. *Business and Social Progress.* New York: Praeger Publishers, 1970.

Walton, Scott D. *American Business and Its Environment.* New York: Macmillan Co., 1966.

Warner, W. Lloyd, and Norman H. Martin, eds. *Industrial Man: Businessmen and Business Organizations.* New York: Harper and Brothers, 1959.

Watson, Charles E. "The Meaning of Service in Business." *Business Horizons* (January-February 1992).

Watts, Emily Stipes. *The Businessman in American Literature.* Athens: University of Georgia Press, 1982.

Weaver, Henry Grady. *The Mainspring of Human Progress.* Irvington-on-Hudson, N.Y.: Foundation for Economic Education, 1984.

Worthy, James C. *Big Business and Free Men.* New York: Harper and Brothers, 1959.

PART III

PROGRESS

13

Entrepreneurship

The sight of an achievement was the greatest gift a human being could offer to others.

—Dagny Taggart in Ayn
Rand's novel *Atlas
Shrugged*

There exists a widespread hostility within society to entrepreneurs and entrepreneurship. This is due, to a certain degree, to envy on the part of those who are less competent, less visionary, less creative, and less successful than others. In the past, entrepreneurs such as Rockefeller, Vanderbilt, and Carnegie were maligned and vilified for being innovative and focused businessmen with uncommon vision and an unrelenting work ethic who helped advance the standard of living of all Americans. Bill Gates, Sam Walton, and Ken Iverson are among their modern day counterparts. Attacks on such great enterprisers tend to come from less-efficient and envious rivals who attempt to achieve through the political process what they failed to accomplish in the marketplace.

It is a fact of human existence that some individuals are more capable than others, that some individuals are harder workers than others, and that some individuals are better at creating wealth than others. Envy is an egalitarian outcry against the claimed metaphysical injustice of the existence of individual differences in abilities, accomplishments, and monetary outcomes. There will always be inequalities among people. Differences between people simply exist. The idea of justice does not apply to conditions built into the nature of life—justice is a concept that only pertains to other-directed human actions.

Perhaps the envious will be less likely to disparage the wealth creator once they have learned: (1) the true nature of the entrepreneur's work; (2) the fact that there is no fixed quantity of economic benefits; (3) that the entrepreneur does not profit at the expense of his customers; (4) that the larger the entrepreneur's profit, the better off individuals in society must be; (5) that the existence of differences in human talents is neither just nor unjust—it just is; (6) that individuals possess the free will to use or not use the abilities that nature has endowed them with; (7) that economic equality is incompatible with nature; and (8) that each person should be allowed to use his aptitudes to their fullest in the pursuit of his conception of happiness.

Entrepreneurs Are Wealth Creators

Wealth, in the form of goods and services, is created when individuals recombine and rearrange the resources that comprise the world. Wealth increases when someone conceives and produces a more valuable configuration of the earth's substances. Although resources or raw materials are finite, the human mind, through ingenuity and creativity, is able to continually increase the wealth of the world. Profits are a person's reward for wealth creation.

It is the existence of unremitting change in human activities that summons entrepreneurs in their search for profits. A critical ability for a successful entrepreneur is to make appropriate predictions regarding the uncertain future. Because accurate knowledge of the future is a valuable asset, the entrepreneur is willing to invest time and money in information gathering and dissemination.

Every one of us makes predictions about an uncertain future and we all make our life decisions in terms of our assessment of that future. However, some individuals are so capable at forecasting the future that they specialize in that activity by becoming entrepreneurs. The entrepreneur predicts, responds to, and creates change regarding the discovery of new resource sources, new consumer desires, and new technological opportunities. He seeks profit by creating new products and services, new businesses, new production methods, etc. The successful entrepreneur correctly anticipates consumer preferences and efficiently uses resources to meet these preferences. The goal of an entrepreneur is to know the consumer's future wants before the consumer knows them.

Markets create incentives to search for opportunities that a person's singular knowledge provides to him. No individual has perfect knowledge of the earth's resources and their potential uses. Profits result when a man reduces imperfections in knowledge by discerning and producing a more valuable arrangement of things. An entrepreneur is concerned with opportunities that are not perceived as such by others.

The potential for profits motivates men to discover and use new information before it becomes widely known to others. Profit opportunities always await alert individuals with creative ideas. Attentive people reinterpret the world in order to grasp and act upon profit opportunities that have eluded others. Ultimately, wealth is a product of intelligence and creative vision. Foresight, envisioning the potential of some product, service, process, technology, or market, precedes action.

An entrepreneurial insight is checked against reality through its incremental development as knowledge and experience are amassed. New ideas are refined, changed, refocused, improved, and expanded through incremental experimentation and the constant search for betterment.

The successful entrepreneur realizes that knowledge and opportunities are constantly changing, highly local, and individuated. Information exists as dispersed bits of knowledge possessed by various individuals throughout society. This information consists of both scientific knowledge and the disarrayed knowledge pertaining to the particular conditions of time and space.

Although the wealth creator can experience luck and serendipity, he does not rely on them. Profits and losses are not the results of totally random processes. Entrepreneurs do not randomly choose their projects. Rather, they seek out knowledge by constantly asking questions, looking for patterns, making novel connections, imagining possibilities, and projecting the future.

Regardless of a person's metaphysically given natural endowments, it takes great effort and choice to actualize one's potential. Reality requires that valuable goods and services be created. Although ability (especially intellectual ability) is crucial, it is not sufficient. The entrepreneur must be a man of ideas and a man of action who can implement appropriate ideas, often in the face of adversities.

A person's actions are motivated from within. An inspired individual may seek to attain his goals and values, to better the conditions of his life, to accomplish something outstanding, etc. Whatever his incentives, he must be committed to action, reality, and the need to transform ideas into concrete form. An entrepreneur attains wealth and his other objectives by providing people with goods and services that further flourishing on earth. Entrepreneurs are specialists in prudence—the virtue of rationally applying one's talents to the goal of living well.

A wealth creator tends to be a person of superior ability who pursues his goals relentlessly even in the face of obstacles, opposition, setbacks, and failures. To be a self-driven doer, one must expend both mental and physical effort. He must persist in the face of adversity, confront the unknown, face challenges, risk and learn from failure, have confidence in his capacity to deal with the world, and take practical rational steps in the pursuit of his goals. The successful entrepreneur tends to be a visionary, competent, independent, action-oriented, passionate, confident, and virtuous person who use reason to focus his enthusiasm on reality in his efforts to attain his goals.

We Live in a Positive-Sum World

A zero-sum game is one in which the winner's earnings come solely from the loser's losses. In a zero-sum world, if one person profits then someone must lose because there is only a fixed amount to go around. We must always come up with a sum of zero when we add together all the changes in the economic wealth of all individuals, because one person can only prosper at the expense of others. In such a static world, economic activity merely redistributes existing wealth.

Fortunately, we do not live in a zero-sum world. Individuals' subjective valuations determine the economic value of things. Personal valuations of a marketable good can have different values for a given person in different situations and at different times. In addition, the same item can have dissimilar values for various individuals in the identical situation and at the same time. In a free exchange both parties benefit or they would not make the exchange. Exchange in a free market is a positive-sum game involving mutual accommodation.

Entrepreneurs create wealth by offering what is perceived to be a more valuable combination of resources than the combination that existed previously. Profits are an entrepreneur's reward for increasing the wealth of individuals in society. The entrepreneur does not profit at the expense of others. Rather, he gains because the product of his actions is judged to be worth more than what existed before his undertaking.

Discovery and Justice

In *Discovery, Capitalism, and Distributive Justice,* Israel Kirzner makes the case that once the role of discovery is comprehended, the notion that the entrepreneur is entitled to the profit he has created can be seen to apply to the normative evaluation of capitalist distribution. He argues that entrepreneurial discovery is the originative act upon which all production depends.

Before a profit opportunity is discovered, it cannot be said to have existed in any economically intelligible and meaningful sense. The discoverer, who creates an opportunity and brings something into existence, is justly entitled to it.

Kirzner explains that the act of mixing labor with a previously unowned part of nature has to be preceded by the originative act of discovering that such an act would be worthwhile. Therefore, the attainment of acquisition cannot be said to diminish what is available to others, because prior to the discovery, the possession wasn't available to anyone. The discovery of the possibility actually created it.

Obstacles to the Entrepreneur

The wealth of certain individuals and groups is tied to the status quo. The discovery of new products, services, and processes means that some established products, services, and technologies will be valued less. As a result, firms tied to the past may find their products, services, and methods becoming obsolete and may even experience business failure.

The government often responds to politically influential interests by acting against progress in order to preserve the status quo. The greatest enemy of the entrepreneur is government intervention in the form of regulation, paperwork, taxes, high interest rates, occupational licensing fees, government-conferred monopolies, etc. Such obstacles actively discourage innovative activity and risk-taking and arrest the wealth-creating process. In addition, information is lost when price signals are stifled by price ceilings, rent controls, minimum wage laws, etc. The entrepreneur requires accurate information regarding incomplete or mistaken market responses in order to know which actions should be taken.

When the government protects some against failure, it actually increases the overall costs of failure by imposing it on others. If the government did not protect unsuccessful businesses, then the loss of wealth experienced by them would be accompanied by a transfer of resources to those who would put them to more valuable uses. Allowing some businesses to fail and others to begin would provide an incentive to redirect capital into more productive and profitable uses. Economic failure cannot be avoided if we are to experience economic progress. If an individual is responsible for his losses then the market will work to permit the adoption of appropriate behavior. Profits and losses are inherent in the human condition.

Protecting Market Entrepreneurs

Profit opportunities are best discovered and pursued within a legal framework that permits individuals an interest in discovering them. The entrepreneur requires the freedom and flexibility to adapt to individuated conditions by acting in accordance with his best judgment. It is necessary to protect the ability of all people to enter the market without restraints and favors perpetuated by the state.

Political entrepreneurs seek and receive help from the state and, therefore, are not true entrepreneurs. Market entrepreneurs do not request nor obtain such assistance. They are the only true entrepreneurs. A successful market entrepreneur accepts the responsibility of using his own judgment, uses his mind to create material values, is honest in his dealing with others and with reality, risks failure and loss, persists in the face of adversity, is alert for information regarding previously unrecognized needs and ways of meeting them, and earn profits as his reward for increasing the wealth of individuals in society. Unlike the political entrepreneur, the market entrepreneur relies on the market mechanism to sort out the successful from the unsuccessful entrepreneurs.

Recommended Reading

Berger, Brigitte, ed. *The Culture of Entrepreneurship*. Oakland, Calif.: Institute for Contemporary Studies, 1991.

Case, John. *From the Ground Up: The Resurgence of American Entrepreneurship*. New York: Simon & Schuster, 1992.

Collins, James C. *Built to Last: Successful Habits of Visionary Companies*. Contribution by Jerry L. Porras. New York: Harpercollins, 1994.

Drucker, Peter. *Innovation and Entrepreneurship*. New York: Harperbusiness, 1993.

Folsom, Burton W. *The Myth of the Robber Barons*. Herndon, Va.: Young America's Foundation, 1996.

———. *Empire Builders: How Michigan Entrepreneurs Helped Make America Great*. Travers City, Mich.: Rhodes & Easton, 1998.

Gunderson, Gerald. *The Wealth Creators: An Entrepreneurial History of the United States*. New York: Plume, 1989.

Jennings, Reg, Charles Cox, and Cary L. Cooper. *Business Elites: The Psychology of Entrepreneurs and Intrapreneurs*. New York: Van Nostrand Reinhold, 1994.

Josephson, Matthew. *The Robber Barons*. San Diego, Calif.: Harcourt Brace, 1962.

Kanter, Rosabeth Moss. *The Change Masters: Innovation and Entrepreneurship in the American Corporations*. New York: Simon & Schuster, 1985.

Kizner, Israel M. *Competition and Entrepreneurship*. Chicago: University of Chicago Press, 1978.

———. *Discovery and the Capitalist Process*. Chicago: University of Chicago Press, 1985.

———. *Discovery, Capitalism, and Distributive Justice*. Hagerstown, Md.: Basil Blackwell, 1987.

Locke, Edwin A. *The Prime Movers: Traits of the Great Wealth Creators*. New York: AMACOM, 2000.

Martin, Michael J. C. *Managing Innovation and Entrepreneurship in Technology-Based Firms*. New York: John Wiley & Sons, 1994.

Miner, John B. *The 4 Routes to Entrepreneurial Success*. San Francisco: Berrett-Koehler Publishers, 1996.

———. *A Psychological Typology of Successful Entrepreneurs*. Westport, Conn.: Greenwood Publishing Group, 1997.

Peterson, William H. "Entrepreneurship, the Possible Dream." *The Freeman* (November 1985).

Pile, Robert B. *Top Entrepreneurs and Their Businesses*. Minneapolis, Minn.: Oliver Press, 1993.

Roberts, Edward B. *Entrepreneurs in High Technology*. Oxford: Oxford University Press, 1991.

Shefsky, Lloyd E. *Entrepreneurs Are Made, Not Born*. New York: McGraw-Hill, 1996.

Sobel, Robert. *The Entrepreneurs: Exploration within the American Business Tradition*. New York: Weybright & Talley, 1974.

14

Technology

The form of made things is always subject to change in response to their real or perceived shortcomings, their failures to function properly. This principle governs all inventors, innovators, and engineers. And there follows a corollary: Since nothing is perfect, and indeed, since even our ideas of perfection are not static, everything is subject to change over time. There can be no such thing as a "perfected" artifact; the future perfect can only be a tense, not a thing.

—Henry Petroski

Technology is an attempt to develop means for the evermore effective realization of individuals' chosen values. Technology, a prerequisite for the survival of humans, is one of the foremost ways in which people impress their ideas and values on the world. Learning and embracing technology is important because it situates learners as participants in the process, provides them with theoretical and practical contexts for their actions, and requires them to reflect about the technological process, its products, and its potential and expected impacts on the natural world and its inhabitants. A classical liberal political framework would provide the freedom required for human progress and economic dynamism. Privatization of federal research and development is one key step toward the establishment of such a framework. In turn, as federal R & D is reduced, federal technology transfer activities will also decline.

Technology and Progress

The purpose of technological advancement has been to make life easier through the creation of new products, services, and production methods. These advances improve people's standard of living, increase their leisure time, help to eliminate poverty, and lead to a greater variety of products. New technologies enhance people's lives both as producers and consumers. By making life easier, safer, and more prosperous, technological progress permits persons more time to spend on higher-level concerns such as character development, love, religion, and the perfection of one's soul.

If people resisted technological change, they would be expressing their satisfaction with existing levels of disease, hunger, and privation. In addition, without experimentation and change, human existence would be boring—human fulfillment is dependent on novelty, surprise, and creativity. Advancing means progressing—taking steps toward a goal, an objective, or a better place.

An innovative idea by one man not only contributes to the progress of others but also creates conditions permitting people to advance even further. Ideas interact in unexpected ways and innovations are frequently used in unforeseen applications. Innovations are based on developing new combinations of ideas, testing them, finding their deficiencies, and trying potentially better combinations. Technological progress thus involves a series of stages consisting of experimentation, competition, errors, and feedback.

Innovations do not simply replace other products. Rather, they develop new and expanded markets of their own. In addition, new technology does not cause a net increase in unemployment nor make labor obsolete. While technology does both create and destroy jobs, on balance it is a net creator of jobs. Certainly some workers lose their jobs due to technological advances. On the other hand, increases in productivity due to new technology typically result in higher profits that are reinvested. This reinvestment leads to the creation of more jobs although frequently of a different type than the original jobs lost.

New technology may require the development of new skills and/or the need to move to a new location, but it does not cause greater overall unemployment. As technological advancements increase labor's productivity, the demand for labor will tend to rise, which, in turn, creates more job opportunities.

Workers tend to benefit from technological advances. As labor's productivity increases, wages also tend to rise. In addition, the increase in labor productivity raises the potential of some unemployed workers, whose marginal costs previously exceeded their marginal productivity, past the point of their employability, thus creating additional jobs. Finally, wage earners, as consumers, will gain from the decrease in product prices that tends to result from the increase in productivity and output.

Historically, there have only been three periods of great progress—the Golden Age of Greece, the Renaissance, and the Industrial Revolution. Since the Renaissance, modern culture has been oriented toward the future, creation by design, innovation, and technological progress. The flourishing of human thought and accomplishment during these three periods was fostered by the exalted status of the individual. Individualism was most thoroughly evidenced in nineteenth century America. The Industrial Revolution, America, and capitalism were the result of the ideas of individual rights, private property, freedom, and limited government. It is only in a society where individual action is allowed that the power of the human mind can be unleashed.

Freedom Promotes Technological Progress

There is a reciprocal relationship between technology and freedom. A free market unhampered by government intervention is the most fertile environment for technological and economic progress. Freedom is a practical necessity for progress in an unpredictable, uncertain, and risky world. Freedom encourages profit seeking and innovation that, in turn, result in greater productivity and employment. In a free society, entrepreneurs are constantly searching for new technologies that make human labor more productive. Technology furthers a free society by providing new opportunities to communicate, work, compete, and deal with others across social and physical barriers.

Science and technology underpin economic prosperity. Investments in research and development that yield new technologies increase long-term productivity and high-paid job growth. Technologies such as the electric motor, the internal combustion engine, and fluorescent and incandescent lighting have had an enormous effect on the way we live and work today. Emerging technologies such as cryogenics, photovoltaics, aerogels, fuel cells, radio-wave lighting, shape-memory metals, quantum chips, biochips, microelectromechanical system (MEMS), and the Internet may have great effects on the way we live in the future. In the past, the wheel and the steam engine enhanced and complemented human physical powers. Today, innovations such as the microprocessor amplify human intellectual capabilities.

When legislators pass laws that restrict or forbid the use of technology, they grant a privilege to noninnovative firms and their workers at the expense of firms who would have used the new technology and the workers who would have had different, and often better jobs, that the increased productivity would have ultimately created. Efforts to prevent the use of new technology stifles the development of new firms, products, and jobs because the required resources are invested in inefficient protected technological processes leading to higher costs and prices and lower real incomes. Technology-watching firms attempt to persuade the government to act on their behalf by passing laws and mandating financial penalties.

Calls for protectionism come from firms that have not modernized their production processes and thus are unable to compete with more efficient, lower-cost companies. Both mandated compensation to displaced laborers and restrictions on the use of technology will reduce the profits of the firms affected, thereby reducing capital accumulation and its reinvestment that would have led to an eventual increase in the level of employment.

Friends and Enemies of Progress

Virginia Postrel's 1998 book, *The Future and Its Enemies*, defies conventional political boundaries of left and right and liberal and conservative to divide the world into dynamists and stasists. The book's thesis is that the most useful and pertinent intellectual vision is about those who welcome the future and those who want to stop, turn back, or regulate change.

According to Postrel, dynamists prefer an open-ended society where creativity and enterprise, operating under general and predictable rules, generate progress in unpredictable ways. Dynamists appreciate evolutionary processes such as market competition, playful experimentation, scientific inquiry, and technological innovation. A dynamist is one who works creatively across barriers and obstacles and in areas once thought to be disparate to construct combinations based on the free play of imagination and discovery. Dynamists seek progress, rather than perfection, through trial and error, feedback loops, incremental improvement, diversity, and choice. They are learners, experimenters, risk takers, and entrepreneurs who understand the importance of local knowledge and evolved solutions to complex problems. Not surprisingly, dynamists are frequently attracted to biological metaphors as symbols of unpredictable change and growth, variety, experimentation, feedback, and adaptation.

Stasists have an aversion to change and either abhor progress or want to control it according to their own vision. Stasists include those who long for the good old days, technophobes, technocrats, supporters of big government programs, and individuals whose investments or jobs are in jeopardy due to some specific innovation. They may come from the left (unionists, environmentalists, Luddites, etc.) or from the right (religious traditionalists, nativists, etc.). Stasists on the left want to regulate the market and the development of technology. Those on the right loathe change and have protectionist economic leanings.

Of course, not all change is for the good. The desirability of a given change is subject to rational assessment. What is required is a libertarian institutional framework that guarantees man the freedom to seek his material and moral well-being as long as he does not infringe upon the equal rights of others. Only then will a person be able to use his rationality and free will to choose, create, and integrate all the values, virtues, and goods that can lead to his well-being. This, naturally, includes the rational evaluation, choice, and use of technology and innovations.

Privatizing Federal Research and Development

Science and technology fare better under free markets than under central planning. Not only is the individual better than the government at gaining knowledge, private property and private enterprise are able to reward human ingenuity. There is no evidence that innovations come from government bureaucracies. Private entrepreneurs can accomplish what government planners often say can't be done. Because the engine of innovation and productivity is investment in the private sector, it follows that we should favor an economic climate that rewards private investment in research and development and promotes the effective and innovative use of technology by private firms.

We need to reallocate the responsibility for technological innovation away from the state and into the hands of private technology makers and consumers. Currently, some 700 scientific and technological research labs are owned or supported by the federal government. Recently, they have expanded their scope beyond basic R & D to provide services that compete with private-sector scientific, testing, and energy firms. The result has been a government subsidy for federal facilities to perform fee-based scientific analyses in addition to exploration of basic science. Privatization would end subsidies to major industries (e.g., petroleum and aerospace), which would then have to pay for research currently funded by taxpayers. Privatization would also free labs from the constraints of the federal budget process, cumbersome procurement and civil service rules, and the inability to sell their outputs at market prices.

The government increases federal funding for technologies that it favors thus eliminating the incentive for private R & D. The case for federal funding of research is that R & D is desirable and that the private sector will conduct too little of it because of market failures resulting from firms desiring to be free riders who would rely on others' research rather than undertaking scientific and technological research projects. Consequently, the argument goes, there will be an underinvestment in R & D.

There is no evidence that government will triumph or that markets will fail. In the public sector, research funds are awarded based on political factors thus becoming a form of "pork barrel" spending. Politicians, facing the impossible job of assigning priorities to a myriad of research projects, tend to choose those with the greatest number of supporters or those helping their local constituencies. On the other hand, private sector scientists and entrepreneurs are guided by price signals and choose research projects that, if successful, would be the most profitable and the most likely to meet human needs. Markets and price signals permit superior targeting of research projects and resources. Private firms can earn large rewards by solving important problems. In addition, the private sector's superior ability to select and use R & D resources will have a positive effect on the rate of technological progress over the years.

Privatization is overdue for federal research facilities. The task of linking research with human needs is not suitable for a political bureaucracy. Privatizing federal R & D labs (e.g., National Aeronautics and Space Administration [NASA], United States Department of Agriculture [USDA], Department of Energy [DOE], United States Geological Survey [USGS], and National Institute of Standards and Technology [NIST]) would give more control of research to users.

The existence of NASA, a taxpayer-funded monopolist of space transportation, historically has stifled the development of a private space transportation industry. The use of communication satellites was the first successful commercial space activity. A nascent commercial space activity is the use of land remote sensing satellites to produce images useful in cartography, oil exploration, private-citizen monitoring of governments, etc. In addition, private firms have rented lab space and modules inside NASA's space shuttles for scientific experiments and the processing of materials in microgravity. Space is a commercial frontier as evidenced by its potential uses, including: (1) the use of space as a waste-disposal site; (2) private-sector operation of reusable launch vehicles; (3) commerical passenger-carrying space transportation vehicles (e.g., space tourism in Low-Earth-Orbit), (4) use of the U.S. portion of the International Space Station as platforms for developing new products and services; (5) the establishment of hotels, labs, or factories in Low-Earth-Orbit; (6) in-orbit use of the Shuttle fleets, external tanks as habitable environment for lab space and other activities; and (7) the generation of low-cost electrical power using orbiting microwave or optical "mirrors" or satellites outfitted with large photo voltaic cell arrays.

Recognizing the need to back the government out of civilian space activities and to allow imaginative private sector ideas to flourish, Congress passed the Commercial Space Act of 1998. This step toward privitization: (1) allows the Federal Aviation Administration (FAA) to license the launch and landing of reusable launch vehicles and commercial payloads; (2) mandates the use of commercial launch services for most government payloads; (3) requires government to purchase space science data from private companies; (4) requires NASA to study commerical possibilities for the International Space Station and further privatization of the Space Shuttle; and (5) streamlines licensing requirements for remote sensing satellites.

As a symbol of freedom and adventure, space is also a romantic frontier. The 1999 film, *October Sky*, based on Homer Hickam's biographical novel, *Rocket Boys*, illustrates the excitement, motivation, and sense of personal potential and achievement that can result when private individuals set out on their own to conquer the final frontier. Just after Sputnik I was launched on October 5, 1957, three boys from a poor dying mining town in southern West Virginia decide that they are not about to turn over outer space to the Communists. Over a three-year period, Hickam and his friends learn a great deal about rocketry, successfully launch numerous rockets in front of large supportive crowds, and eventually win the National Science Fair.

NASA, a government bureaucracy founded in 1958, has little reason to develop inexpensive space transportation. Whereas entrepreneurs are rewarded when they cut costs, public managers are rewarded when they increase the size and scope of their programs and increase their budgets. In addition, public managers avoid risk by inflating their costs—errors could lead Congress to cut NASA's budget.

Unlike the trial and error approaches of private entrepreneurs, NASA's program is run as a centralized bureaucracy. After carefully studying all of its options and considering the political aspects of the program, bureaucrats choose the one best approach to an opportunity or a problem and massively fund the program until it works.

The aeronautics industry would benefit from privatizing NASA labs by having more control over R & D. Firms could commission proprietary research that would not have to be shared with competitors. Each center could be sold to a consortium of firms, to an employee-owned corporation, or to an independent entity.

The energy, aviation, construction, biomedical, and other industries would be able to exert more control over R & D with the privatization of DOE labs. Cost recovery and profits would occur through user fees. Whereas the responsibility for the design and manufacture of nuclear weapons and environmental clean-up could be transferred to the Department of Defense (DOD), other labs could be sold to the highest private bidder or through employee buyouts. Similar privatization schemes could be carried out with USGS, USDA, and NIST labs.

Taxpayers would be the major beneficiaries of the privatization of federal labs. Proceeds from the sale of the labs could help lower the national debt or balance the budget. The agencies previously operating the labs would subsequently have lower annual budgets. Also, labs transferred to the private sector would pay corporate income taxes.

Reducing Federal Technology Transfer Activities

With the passage of the Stevenson-Wydler Innovation Act of 1980 and the Federal Technology Transfer Act of 1986, all federal labs were required to develop programs for transferring technology to the private sector and to state and local governments. President Reagan supported this second act because he believed that investments in R & D for federal programs were not returning sufficient dividends to taxpayers in terms of new products, processes, and jobs. This legislation was amended in 1996 by Public Law 104-113 that created incentives and encouraged the commercialization of technology created in federal labs. A National Technology Transfer Center (NTTC) was established in 1989 by Congress to provide American firms and individuals with access to federal R & D to better enable them to compete in the international marketplace. In addition, the government, rather redundantly, has six Regional Technology Transfer Centers (RTTCs) to help U.S. firms improve their competitiveness by assisting them in the location, assessment, acquisition, and utilization of technologies and scientific and engineering expertise within the federal government.

The use of federal R & D results have been meager—studies have indicated that only about 10 percent of federally owned patents have ever been used. A major factor in successful technology transfer is a perceived market for the technology. Because R & D in federal labs is undertaken to meet an agency's mission, decisions reflect public sector rather than commercial needs. Consequently, technology transfer depends upon "technology push" rather than "market pull."

Federal labs were created to perform the R & D necessary to meet government needs, which normally are not consistent with the demands of the marketplace. It is no wonder that federal technology transfer activities have not met with much success. Ultimately, the privatization of federal labs will lead to the reduction and elimination of federal technology transfer activities. Privatization will transfer resources out of the hands of stasist government bureaucrats and scientists and into the hands of private-sector dynamists who are more likely to foster economic prosperity, technological progress, and cultural innovation.

Recommended Reading

Bolland, Eric J., and Charles W. Hofer. *Future Firms: How America's High Technology Companies Work.* New York: Oxford University Press, 1998.

Cetron, Marvin. *Probable Tomorrows: How Science and Technology Will Transform Our Lives in the Next Twenty Years.* Contribution by Owen Davis. New York: St. Martin's Press, 1997.

Cohen, Linda R., Roger G. Noll, et al. *The Technology Pork Barrel.* Washington, D.C.: Brookings' Institute, 1991.

Cowan, Ruth Schwartz. *A Social History of American Technology.* New York: Oxford University Press, 1996.

Cross, Gary S., and Rick Szostak. *Technology and American Society: A History.* Englewood Cliffs, N.J.: Prentice Hall, 1995.

Dasgupta, Subrata. Technology *and Creavitity.* New York: Oxford University Press, 1996.

D'Souza, Dinesh. *The Virtue of Prosperity: Finding Values in a Age of Techno-Affluence.* New York: Free Press, 2000.

Gump, David P. *Space Enterprises: Beyond NASA.* New York: Praeger, 1990.

Krogh, George von, Kazuo Ichijo, and Ikujiro Nonaka. *Enabling Knowledge Creation: How to Unlock the Mystery of Tacit Knowledge and Release the Power of Innovation.* New York: Oxford University Press, 2000.

McLucas, John L. *Space Commerce.* Cambridge, Mass.: Harvard University Press, 1991.

Mokyr, Joel. *The Lever of Riches: Technological Creativity and Economic Progress.* New York: Oxford University Press, 1990.

Pearson, Ian, and Chris Winter. *Where's It Going.* London: Thames & Hudson, 2000.

Postrel, Virginia. *The Future and Its Enemies.* New York: Free Press, 1998.

Rothschild, Michael L. *Bionomics: The Inevitability of Capitalism.* New York: H. Holt, 1990.

Snyder, Carl. *Capitalism the Creator.* New York: Macmillan Co., 1940.

Stehr, Nico. *Knowledge Societies.* London: Sage, 1994.

Sullivan, Neil F. *Technology Transfer: Making the Most of Your Intellectual Property.* Cambridge: Cambridge University Press, 1995.

Teich, Albert H., ed. *Technology and the Future.* Boston: Bedford Books, 1999.

Teitelman, Robert. *Profits of Science: The American Marriage of Business and Technology.* New York: Basic Books, 1994.

Toffler, Alvin. *Powershift: Knowledge, Wealth, and Violence at the Edge of the 21st Century.* New York: Bantam Books, 1991.

Volti, Rudi. *Society and Technological Change.* New York: Worth Publishing, 1995.

Winner, Langdon. *The Whale and the Reactor: A Search for Limits in an Age of High Technology.* Chicago: University of Chicago Press, 1988.

PART IV

GOVERNANCE

15

Justice

Justice is a habit whereby a man renders to each one his due with constant and perpetual will.

—Justinian's *Corpus Juris Civilis*

Justice is a concept that applies only to other-directed human actions. The question of justice and injustice only arises when there are multiple individuals and some practical considerations regarding their situations and/or interactions with one another. In one sense, it is a concrete, objective, and recognizable principle (i.e., respect for individual rights) that provide the foundation for a free society. Justice, in such a metanormative context, means to respect free choice. In turn, to be just and moral in a normative sense (i.e., as a central, social virtue of human flourishing) requires respect for individual free choice. Only free persons can be just and moral persons. Metanormative justice provides a criterion for law and for the possibility of individual morality and normative justice.

The idea of justice has been debated for thousands of years. The first section of this chapter briefly surveys the conceptual foundations of Western notions of justice. Next, two dominant theories of justice in America in the twentieth century are compared and contrasted. These are John Rawls' end-state (or distributive justice) theory and Robert Nozick's entitlement (or process) theory. Finally, a set of principles of metanormative justice congruent with the possibility of human flourishing and morality in a free society is presented.

Western Ideas of Justice

Western concepts of justice are derived from Greco-Roman philosophical traditions and the teachings of Christ. From Greco-Roman traditions comes the ancient maxim, "to live honestly, to hurt no one, to give everyone his due."

In ancient Greece, justice was believed to be derived from the order of society—a good society fostered justice, and justice fostered a good society. For Plato (428-348 B.C.) and his contemporaries, justice was seen as the paramount virtue with respect to our relations with others. According to Plato, justice is the bond that holds a society together. Both individualism and personal rights had little to do with the Platonic conception of justice that appeals even today to collectivists who emphasize the social context of justice. Followers of Platonic justice tend to place their faith in the state. Karl Popper has even gone so far as to claim that Plato's conception of justice is identical with that adopted by modern totalitarianism.

According to Aristotle (384-322 B.C.), justice is voluntary—a man acts justly or unjustly whenever he performs his acts voluntarily. He explains that justice is the virtue through which each person enjoys his own possessions in accordance with rightful and just laws—not those that legalize theft and redistribute property from some individuals to others. Natural and universal justice should precede and form the basis for law. Such justice is superior to state-dictated justice that is special and limited to the needs of the government. Justice, in the tradition of Aristotle, means treating individuals in accordance with their deserts, treating equals equally, and treating unequals unequally.

The Roman contribution to the concept of justice was the notion of law as an aggregation of personal rights. Justice was seen as an abiding disposition to give every man his right. No longer viewed as a function of society as a whole, justice became the concern of the legal aspect of society—it became specialized in an institutional function protecting personal rights, rather than as the social concern of all citizens.

The ancient idea of commutative (i.e., reciprocal) justice involves the exchange of things profitable for things profitable. As I supply a benefit for you, I also receive one from you. A contract of exchange is an act of voluntary commutative justice in which each person obtains something of greater value to him than that which he gives in return. The purpose of commutative justice is to preserve equality of rights between individuals. The idea that each person, minding his own business, should receive rewards that are appropriate to his work implies both freedom and responsibility. Through Roman law, this doctrine of justice passed into European legal codes and ultimately into English and American law.

In Western theology, the biblical Book of Job embodies the idea that each man has God-given rights. Justice is the right of all and certain things are owed to a man simply because he exists as a man. Our political traditions have interpreted these to be life, liberty, and the right to pursue happiness. Such justice is to be achieved, not through the dictatorship of man, but through the rule of law. Without justice, the rule of men, rather than law, attains power. Without objective law, the individual is at the mercy of rulers and their agents. The rule of law means that the state must be bound by fixed and predictable rules and that the same laws govern all people.

Implicit in the phrase "to each his own" are the beliefs that: (1) man has a distinct, constant nature; (2) justice in the natural order consists of the consistent application of truth; (3) the universe operates as constructed; and (4) man has free will and is fallible. Given the nature of man and the universe, it is just to respect the right of each human being to make his own noncoercive free choices in his search for truth, justice, and happiness.

Augustine (354-430) interpreted the eternal law as the divine reason and will of God that commands the observance of the natural order of things. He called a person's proper understanding of the universe's eternal principles natural law. Justice, for Augustine, precedes the state and is eternal. Laws that are not just are not laws at all—the moral force of a law depends on the extent of its justice. Natural justice must precede law and form the basis of law thereon. For Augustine, the primary relationship in justice is between a person and God.

Thomas Aquinas (1225-1274) defined the virtue of justice as a consistent and lasting resolve to render to everyone his due. He viewed justice as certain rectitude of mind, whereby a man does what he ought to do in the circumstances confronting him. Aquinas agreed with Augustine in that laws framed by man can be either just or unjust.

Aquinas believed it was just for market prices to fluctuate to reflect need, scarcity, and cost. He also maintained that a seller should be liable for defects in the goods he sold because otherwise the buyer will have paid too much for what he received. This would be a violation of commutative justice that has the purpose of preserving equality of rights between individuals (e.g., between the value of an item purchased and the price paid for it, between the wages paid by an employer and the work performed by the employee, etc.).

According to Hobbes (1588-1679), there exists both an immortal God and a mortal God, the State, which he called the Leviathan. Hobbes maintained that the omnipotent state was the center of both secular and spiritual power. From the Hobbesian view, the state can create, confirm, and take away rights. It follows that, for Hobbes, justice is that which is meted out by the power of the state. Because Hobbes defines law as a command of the sovereign, it follows that where there is no sovereign, there is no law.

For John Locke (1632-1704), the concept of justice is a major underlying theme throughout his political thought as a whole. For Locke, natural justice sets the limits and provides the direction for civic justice via the concept of natural rights. Moreover, at its most basic level, Locke's theory of justice is a natural law theory even more than a natural rights theory. Whereas individual rights are inalienable, they are nevertheless based upon, and limited by, the law of nature. According to Locke, justice is inconceivable without personal property—where there is no property, there is no justice. The essence of Lockean justice is the security of each person's personal possessions as a right based on the law of nature.

Jeremy Bentham (1748-1832) expounded a utilitarian idea of justice called legal positivism or legal realism that stands in opposition to the classical and Christian understanding of justice and law. To the legal positivist, laws are no more than commands of human beings. For the positivist, there is no necessary relationship between law and morality or between descriptive law and normative law. The only source of justice recognized by positivists is the sovereign state.

John Stuart Mill (1806-1873) said that it was inconsistent with justice to be partial. The public good is promoted when justice is impartially administered because it is to each person's benefit that no injustice be done to him, so it is also to his benefit that the principle that makes him secure should not be violated for other men, because such a violation would weaken his own security. Justice requires rule by known general principles of conduct, which apply without exception, to all regardless of status or wealth, in an unknown number of future instances. It follows that all citizens should have equal access to legal recourse in the event of an attack on their life, property, or freedom.

Justice: The Contemporary Debate

The U.S. Constitution is a fundamental document defining the American concept of justice. Strongly influenced by John Locke, some of the constitution's major assumptions are: (1) An individual has a natural right to liberty and his own free pursuit of happiness; (2) Government is a contract among the governed; (3) Laws must depend on the consent of the governed; (4) Justice is most likely to be achieved when government is through the consent of the governed; (5) Representative government is necessary for justice; and (6) The individual must be protected against the potential power of government.

In the Constitution, equality was not equated with justice. The framers believed that justice exists when all interactions among people are based on voluntary exchange. To them, it was the process of interactions, not the outcomes, which mattered. Today, however, a new idea of justice (often called social justice) equates justice with equality. This view is used to call for a process of enforced equalization and to make envy an acceptable emotion. Under this new concept of justice, an individual is free to exercise his rights as long as such exercise does not violate state-created superior or equal rights of others or the common good as defined by the state. The demand for equality, if fully recognized and implemented, would mean the end of a free society and would result in treating people unequally because the state would have to treat individuals differently in order to make up for their excess or deficiency of ability, motivation, and other attributes. The notion of social justice is used to foster social reform through state intervention and economic planning, devices which require the sacrifice of the moral ideas of individual freedom, individual responsibility, and voluntary cooperation.

The most widely discussed theory of distributive justice during the past three decades has been proposed by John Rawls. In lieu of the concept of the state of nature, Rawls introduced the methodological concept of an "original position," a hypothetical and counterfactual condition which requires us to visualize the negotiators of the basic terms of political association conducting their negotiations behind a "veil of ignorance" while having no knowledge of their individual life conditions, including their talents, intelligence, sex, race, class, religion, wealth, conception of the good, etc. According to Rawls, to be fair in selecting the principles of justice, the possibility of bias must be removed. Fairness in Rawls' theory requires the more favored to agree to the type of distributive rule they would prefer if they were not more favored.

Rawls thus argues that the principles that should govern the basic structure of a just or well-ordered society are principles that would be selected by rational individuals in specially constructed, imaginary circumstances called the original position. For Rawls, a society is well ordered when (1) its members know and agree to the same principles of social justice and (2) the basic institutions of society generally satisfy and are widely known to satisfy these principles. Rawls argues that if we are to justify the use of the coercive power of the state over individuals, it ought to be in terms of reasons that all can accept or should accept.

Rawls proposes that persons in an original position will or should agree that all social primary goods (e.g., basic liberties such as political freedom and freedom of choice in occupations, opportunity, income, wealth, and the bases of self-respect) are to be distributed equally unless an unequal distribution of any or all of these goods is to the advantage of the least favored. Rawls thus depicts justice as an issue of fairness, focusing on the distribution of resources, and permitting an unequal distribution only to the extent that the weakest members of society benefit from that inequality. To Rawls, this justifies the coercive limitation of unjust resources and therefore redistribution where it would improve the situation of the disadvantaged. For Rawls, even if an inequality does not harm the least well off, it is unjust if it leaves them no better off than before. This emphasizes a redistributionist type of justice and a defeasible presumption in favor of equality in the distribution of primary goods such as wealth and income. Rawls' assumption that equality is desirable puts the burden of justification on those who support some type of inequality.

According to Rawls' difference principle, an inequality can be advantageous to the person who gets the smaller share because inequalities can constitute incentives which increase the size of the pie to be shared, so that the smaller piece may be larger in absolute terms than an equal share of the smaller pie that would have existed in the absence of such incentives. The difference principle collapses to strict equality under conditions where differences in income and other rewards have no effect on the incentives of individuals. However, in the real world currently and in the foreseeable future, greater rewards bring forth greater productive effort, thus increasing the total wealth of the economy and, under the difference principle, the wealth of the least advantaged.

A practical implication of the difference principle is that society must redistribute income up to the point where the wealth of the representative poorest individual (an abstraction) is maximized. In other words, "society" should tax and redistribute the wealth of the more advantaged up to the point where their incentives to produce more disappear.

Rawls recognizes that by allowing at least some greater level of rewards to accrue to the skilled and motivated, the poor will be better off than they would have been with a totally equal distribution of income. He also realizes that redistribution cannot go as far as his ethical preference for equality would recommend without making everyone (including the poor) worse off. At some point, impairing individuals' economic incentives would reduce the total wealth in society.

Rawls argues for inheritance taxes on the basis that an unregulated transfer of wealth from people to their children would result in the entrenchment of wealth in particular segments of society. According to Rawls, individuals who are not fortunate enough to have wealthy parents do not merit worse starting points and, consequently, worse life prospects than those who were so fortunate. Ignoring the right that people have to bequeath wealth to whomever they want, Rawls contends that society should equalize the prospects of the least well off by taxing the undeserved inherited gain of children of rich persons, and using the tax proceeds to aid the least well off.

Rawls describes his theory as political rather than metaphysical—it is political in the sense that it does not depend on any of the metaphysical assumptions that are disputed among reasonable citizens in a pluralistic society. Rawls argues that democracy is required by justice, because as a procedure it complies with the tenets of justice in that it assigns everyone equal and extensive rights and liberties and because of its propensity to produce just results. For Rawls, the function of justice is to ensure that disagreements are resolved on the basis of prior agreement instead of through force. Thus, even if there are disagreements about the justice of particular laws and policies, there should minimally be agreement with respect to the procedures used to resolve these conflicts. Rawls renounces what he refers to as liberal equality (i.e., political equality and a market economy tempered by interventionist government efforts aimed at furthering equality of opportunity). He finds liberal equality insufficient because it seeks to ameliorate only those inequalities stemming from differences in social and historical circumstances, thereby permitting real differences in individual ability and effort to emerge as the causes of economic success. Rawls believes there is no more good reason to allow the distribution of wealth and income to be determined by the possession of natural endowments than by social and historical factors. Rawls contends that individuals do not deserve the genetic assets they are born with. He explains that, from a moral perspective, the level of effort people are willing to put forth is, to a great extent, influenced by their natural endowments. Consequently, those who are more productive due to their greater natural abilities have no moral right to greater rewards, because the abilities and motivation that make up their work cannot be morally considered to be their own. In effect, Rawls' difference principle is an agreement to consider the distribution of natural talents as a common asset and to share in the fruits of this distribution, no matter what it ends up being. In this view an individual's natural endowments are not considered to be his own property, but rather the property of society.

Rawls contends that underserved inequalities call for redress in order to produce genuine (i.e., fair) equality of opportunity instead of procedural (i.e., formal) equality of opportunity. Rather than having all play by the same rules or being judged by the same standards, Rawls wants to provide everyone with equal prospects of success from equal individual efforts. Rawls' idea of fairness requires that the state have the power to control outcomes and to supercede the preferences of individual citizens.

What makes Rawls' idea of justice so important is that he systematically expresses a vision that had already underpinned a great deal of social policy, legal theory, and even international relations. The goal of Rawls' conception of justice is to put certain segments of society in the position that they would have been in except for some undeserved and unfortunate circumstances.

The Rawlsian idea that one's own status, endowments, and wealth are unearned is especially potent when it is combined with (1) the Kantian notion that there is no virtue in pursuing one's own personal flourishing and/or (2) the guilt felt by those who are ashamed to live in material abundance while others in the world suffer. Kant advocated abject selflessness and held that an action is moral only if a person performs it out of a sense of duty without regard to any personal goal, desire, motive, or interest—if a person acts to derive benefit, his action is amoral. Furthermore, Kant would even maintain that no moral credit would accrue to a person who gains pleasure from his charitable activities even though he did not seek such pleasure. In addition, so-called political guilt can be defined as the belief that one belongs to a group of people that has unjustly or unduly fortunate circumstances, endowments, or privileges. Allan Levite has explained that those who regret their good fortunes are drawn to egalitarian political ideologies that promise to remove the social or economic inequality that is the source of their guilt. Such people wish to level society in a manner that will alleviate their own guilt feelings. They believe that only the state is powerful enough to redistribute resources thereby relieving their political guilt. The state's promise to provide for the poor relieves guilt-ridden people of the stigma of "privilege" that they feel they bear by making it appear as though their resources and employment roles were granted by official state permission, instead of being the result of privilege or chance.

Rawls focuses on how goods are distributed among persons "representative" of various positions in society, but ignores which individuals have which goods and how they gained possession of them. Critics of Rawls argue that people hold an entitlement to what they produce or have legitimately acquired and therefore should be protected from Rawls' proposed redistributionist policies. They hold that the difference principle involves unacceptable infringements on liberty in that redistributive taxation to the poor requires the immoral takings of just holdings. Rawls' opponents contend that whether a given income or wealth distribution is just or unjust depends solely on the manner in which that distribution came about, not on the pattern of the distribution itself.

Another criticism is that fairness is not the proper standard of justice—the world is inherently unfair and thus "unjust." Nature does not produce a state of equality. No two people possess the same mental or physical attributes—some are smarter, more talented, better looking, etc. People have the free will to either use or not use the talents that nature has endowed them with. It follows that economic equality is a goal that is incompatible with nature. True justice is attained when people's lives and property are secure and they are free to own property, order its direction, determine the purpose to which their bodies are put, engage in consensual transactions and relationships with others, and freely pursue their conception of happiness.

Rawls also fails to recognize that talents are not a common pool. The aptitudes that one person enjoys in no way lessens the number and magnitude of abilities that are available to another. My talent is not acquired at your expense. Rawls is rebelling against reality, nature, and the existence of human talent. A natural fact, such as the existence of one's talents, is neither just nor unjust—it just is. So why should those "favored by nature" be made to pay for what is not a moral problem or an injustice and is not of his or her own making?

Finally, Rawls' theory can be challenged on the grounds that he is confusing justice with prudence—the virtue of advancing one's own well-being. To be prudent is to apply intelligence to changing circumstances. Rawls' maxi-min strategy appears to be a rational construction of prudence rather than of justice. A prudent man in the "original position" might choose a social structure under which he would be "least worse off" if things went badly for him. Such a choice could be called prudent, but certainly not just.

Robert Nozick has provided the most persuasive and comprehensive case against Rawlsian justice by arguing for a theory based on the principle that all human beings have absolute rights to their person and to the fruits of their labor. Nozick compares and contrasts two systems of justice: (1) his own entitlement theory, which is based on the historical process of acquiring and transferring resources; and (2) end-state or time-slice theory, which is based on the current distribution of resources. Rawls' difference principle is of the latter type.

Nozick's entitlement theory holds that a distribution is just if it results through just acquisition from the state of nature or through voluntary transfer via trade, gift, or bequest from a prior just distribution. Nozick proposes that: (1) a person who acquires a holding in accordance with the principle of justice in acquisition is entitled to that holding; (2) a person who acquires a holding in accordance with the principle of justice in transfer, from someone else entitled to the holding, is entitled to the holding; and (3) no one is entitled to a holding except by (repeated) application of 1 and 2.

The principle of justice in acquisition states that an acquisition is just if the item is previously unowned and the acquisition leaves enough to meet the needs of others. The principle of justice in transfer is meant to protect voluntary contracts while ruling out theft, fraud, etc. In other words, a holding is just if it has been acquired through a legitimate transfer from someone who acquired it through a legitimate transfer or through original acquisition.

Nozick also proposed the principle of rectification of injustice in holdings. Although difficult to accomplish in some cases, an honest effort must be made to identify the origins of illegitimate holdings and to remedy the situation by compensating the victims of theft, fraud, and intimidation.

Nozick takes his lead from the Lockean notion that each person owns himself and that by mixing one's labor with the material world, one can establish ownership of a portion of the material world. Nozick explains that what is significant about mixing one's labor with the material world is that in so doing a person tends to increase the value of a portion of the external world. He reasons that in such instances, self-ownership can bring about ownership of a part of the physical world. According to Nozick, the Lockean Proviso means: (1) that previously unowned property becomes owned by anyone who improves it; (2) that an acquisition is just if and only if the position of others after the acquisition is no worse than their position was when the acquisition was unowned or owned in common.

For Nozick, the right not to have others interfere in one's life is fundamental—any coercion is illegitimate. Persons are viewed as having natural rights that are prior to society and which must be respected if we are to treat individuals as ends in themselves and not merely means in the endeavors of others. Kant's categorical imperative provides a foundation for Nozick's principle of transfer. Individuals should be treated as ends and never simply as means. A person's autonomy should always be respected. Only the individual person can legitimately decide what to do with his talents, abilities, and the products of his talents and abilities.

Nozick's idea of process equality means equal treatment before the law. The U.S. Constitution reflects this view in its due process and equal protection clauses. According to this perspective, all individuals should be identically subject to universal rules of just conduct and the state should not grant special privileges or impose special burdens upon any individual or group of individuals.

Nozick refers to the contrary view of equality as end-state equality. From this perspective equality among people is increased when the differences between their incomes, level of wealth, or standards of living are decreased.

The second idea of equality is incompatible with the first. When the state interferes with the process of voluntary exchange to bring about more equality in the end-state sense, the state must treat individuals with unequal voluntary exchange outcomes unequally. In other words, the state would discriminate against those with better voluntary exchange outcomes in favor of those with worse voluntary exchange outcomes.

The process and end-state (i.e., distributive) theories of justice are irreconcilable. Because people have unequal endowments, the free market will inevitably lead to unjust, in the second sense, results. Coercive transfers that are unjust in the first sense can only remedy this "injustice."

Nozick advocates a system in which the role of the government is limited to the protection of property rights. This view rules out taxation for purposes other than raising the money needed to protect property rights. Nozick explains that any taxation of the income from selling the products of exercising one's talents involves the forced partial ownership by others of people and their actions and work.

Nozick argues that if we can determine that a specific person is entitled to a specific piece of property, then it is apparent that people with such claims can justly transfer property to whomever they see fit such as their spouses, children, favored charitable organizations, etc. As long as the transfer is voluntary, Nozick contends that there is no need for "society" to worry about how the representative least well off person is affected. It follows that inheritance taxes are not legitimate according to Nozick's theory.

Principles of Justice

Den Uyl and Rasmussen distinguish between metanormative justice and justice as a constituent virtue of one's personal flourishing. Metanormative justice is concerned with the orderly and peaceful coordination of any person with any other. This type of justice deals with nonexclusive, universal, and open-ended relationships, thus providing the foundation of a political order and the context for exclusive relationships to develop and for the possibility of personal flourishing and happiness. Justice as a normative principle and constituent virtue involves a person's contextual recognition and evaluation of others based on objective criteria. Normative justice is concerned with selective (i.e., exclusive) relationships and requires practical reason and discernment of differences of both persons and situations. Justice as a constituent virtue deals with individuals in more specific and personal ways than does justice in a metanormative sense. Not all character failings or immoral behaviors are crimes. The question of how persons ought to act (i.e., normative justice) and the question of how society ought to be structured (i.e., metanormative justice) are separate and distinct investigations. The principles of justice discussed below deal solely with justice in the latter sense (i.e., in the sense of the social structure that should be adopted).

Nature has its own imperatives. An argument can be made that the world is governed by principles or laws that dictate how society ought to be structured in much the same way that natural laws dictate how bridges or buildings should be constructed. Given the nature of man and the world, if we want persons to be able to pursue happiness, peace, and prosperity while living with one another, then we should adopt and respect a social structure that accords each person a moral space over which he has freedom to act and within which no one else may rightfully interfere. The idea of natural rights defines this moral space. The idea of natural rights can be used to create a legal system that makes it possible for individuals to pursue happiness and carry on a virtuous life.

It follows that the fundamental principle of justice is respect for free and nonaggressive choice. Both justice and morality require respect for individual free choice. A state that restricts freedom of choice violates the basic principle of justice. Justice means that a person must be accountable for his own actions, entitled to the reward of his labor, and responsible for the consequences of his wrongdoings. Freedom not only means that the individual has both the opportunity and freedom of choice, it also means that he must bear the consequences of his actions.

Justice and injustice do not depend on positive law. Justice, a broader concept than law, provides a criterion for man-made laws. A just law is one that is based on, and not contradictory to, natural rights. Injustice involves the violation of natural rights and includes murder, assault, theft, kidnapping, enslavement, rape, fraud, etc. If the behavior generating a specific distribution of wealth or income defies rules prohibiting force, theft, or fraud, then the behavior and the distribution are unjust. No particular way of distributing goods can be said to be just or unjust apart from the free choices individuals make. Any distribution of benefits and costs is just if it results from persons freely choosing to exchange with one another.

The law serves justice when it is used to restore the peace when a person's rights have been violated. However, the law can misuse its power by itself violating people's rights either for its own purposes or to further the ends of some third party. A law is applied justly if it is applied impartially and consistently. Injustice occurs when like cases are not treated in the same manner. The law should treat similar cases alike unless there is some material, relevant difference. Laws can be unjust—so can the administration of the law. Mercy with respect to the application of the law is at odds with justice. If mercy is just, then every criminal ought to be set free.

Metanormative justice is concerned with individual rights. The right of private property is a person's right to acquire, possess, use, and dispose of scarce resources, including his own body. Resources may be employed in any manner that does not interfere with other individuals' use of their resources.

Whereas most property rights are freely alienable (i.e., transferable) a case can be made that the right to acquire one's person is inalienable. A claim that a right is inalienable is different from a claim that it is nonforfeitable. It is possible to forfeit one's rights because of some wrongdoing. Because control of one's body cannot be transferred, it can be argued that the right to control one's body likewise cannot be transferred. For example, a person who "sells" himself into slavery would still have control over his actions and would have to willfully act to comply with the "owner's" orders. Put another way, a person's moral agency cannot be transferred to another person and if that faculty cannot be transferred, then neither can the ownership of that faculty. Because he retains his moral agency, a slave can be held accountable for his actions.

All those who endorse a classical liberal conception of justice do not hold the idea that some rights are inalienable. This is because to maintain that a right is inalienable is to limit individuals' freedom to contract. Many classical liberals hold that persons should be able to pursue happiness by voluntarily exchanging any of their rights.

The right of first possession stipulates that property rights to unowned resources are acquired by being the first to claim, control, and improve them. In addition, the right of freedom of contract specifies that a rightholder's assent is needed to transfer alienable property rights both while one is alive and through the use of a will upon one's demise. It is unjust to violate the above rights through force or fraud.

The right of reparation (or restitution) demands that a person who violates the rights that define metanormative justice must compensate the victim of the rights violation for the harm produced by the injustice. If necessary, such payment may be collected by force. Reparationists oppose violence against people except for self-defense and to educe restitution from criminals and tortfeasers. Criminals and tortfeasers lose their right to self-defense to some degree and do not get their self-defense rights back until they have paid for their crimes and torts by compensating their victims. In addition to condoning violence against a criminal to stop him from committing a crime, restitutionists condone the use of violence (e.g., imprisonment and forced work) against criminals and tortfeasers to compel them to make reparation. According to the principle of strict proportionality, the amount of restoration should be limited to that which is necessary to fully compensate the victim—there should not be overcompensation or undercompensation.

A special case of commutative justice, the obligation of making restitution involves the returning of something stolen (or if not possible, its value), the restoration or repair of something destroyed or damaged, compensation for an injury that has been unjustly inflicted, etc. Restitution is called for in cases of theft, fraud in contracts, the culpable nonpayment of debts, the nonreturning or excessive delay in returning borrowed items, the failure to reveal defects in items sold, deceit with respect to the quality of an item sold, etc.

Like reparationists, retributionists condone violence for self-defense and to force a criminal or tortfeasor to compensate his victim. However, retributionists also condone the use of force to punish a criminal for his crime.

Neither reparationists nor retributionists espouse utilitarian objectives such as rehabilitation or deterrence, both of which can be sought without concern for justice. Instead, their focus is on personal responsibility, just compensation, and for retributionists, deserved punishment. Justice depends on desert, and desert is a matter of past performance, rather than of future possibilities. Of course, there is the problem of trying to objectify the subjective value of just restitution and, for retributionists, the degree of deserved punishment. It is easy to generalize that the level of a punishment should fit the severity of the crime (i.e., punishment must be proportionate to desert), but it is much more difficult to obtain agreement on the appropriate punishment for a particular crime.

The right of self-defense allows the proportionate use of force against those who threaten to violate another's rights. Normal self-defense is allowed when the commitment of a rights violation is impending. Extended self-defense is permitted when a person has indicated, by past rights violations or other proven prior conduct, to be a threat to violate rights in the future. Whereas restitutionists would tend to argue for life imprisonment for convicted murderers on the basis of extended self-defense, retributionists would argue for life sentences (and some for capital punishment) on the basis of deserved punishment.

Metanormative justice is a concept that can be used to evaluate the propriety of the use of force. The principles of metanormative justice presented in this chapter can be debated, refined, and then used to critically evaluate, validate, and correct human laws that are coercively enforced.

Recommended Reading

Alejandro, Roberto. *The Limits of Rawlsian Justice*. Baltimore, Md.: Johns Hopkins University Press, 1998.

Aquinas, St. Thomas. *Philosophical Texts*. Fair Lawn, N.J.: Oxford University Press, 1960.

Aristotle, "*Nichomachean Ethics*." Book V in *Selections*. New York: Charles Scribner's Sons, 1957.

Augustine, St. *The City of God*. Garden City, N.Y.: Doubleday and Co., 1958.

Barnett, Randy. *The Structure of Liberty*. New York: Oxford University Press, 1992.

Barry, Brian. *Justice & Impartiality*. Oxford: Oxford University Press, 1996.

Bentham, Jeremy. *Introduction to the Principles of Moral and Legislation*. New York: Hofner Publishing Co., 1948.

Den Uyl, Douglas J., and Douglas B. Rassmussen. "Rights as Metanormative Principles." *Liberty for the 21st Century*. Edited by Tibor R. Machan and Douglas B. Rassmussen. Lanham, Md.: Rowman & Littlefield, 1995.

Hobbes, Thomas. *Leviathan*. New York: Liberal Arts Press, 1958.

Kirzner, Israel M. *Discovery, Capitalism, and Distributive Justice*. Hagerstown, Md.: Basil Blackwell, 1989.

Laserson, Max M. "Power and Justice: Hobbes versus Job." *Judaism* 2 (January 1953): 50-59.

Levite, Allan E. *Guilt, Blame, and Politics*. San Francisco: Stanyan Press, 1998.

Locke, John. *Two Treatises of Government*. Cambridge: Cambridge University Press, 1963.

Mill, John Stuart. *Principles of Political Economy*. New York: Kelley, 1979.

Miller, Fred D. Jr. *Nature, Justice, and Rights in Aristotle's Politics*. Oxford: Oxford University Press, 1996.

Nash, Ronald H. *Freedom, Justice, and the State*. Lanham, Md.: University Press of America, 1980.

Nozick, Robert. *Anarchy, Utopia, and State*. New York: Basic Books, 1974.

Plato. *The Republic of Plato*. Edited by F. M. Conford. Fair Lawn, N.J.: Oxford University Press, 1945.

Pope, Marvin. *Job: A New Translation with Introduction and Commentary*. New York: Doubleday, 1973.

Popper, Karl. *The Open Society and Its Enemies*, vol. 1, chap. 6. New York: Harper Torchbook, 1963.

Posner, Richard A. *The Economics of Justice*. Boston: Harvard University Press, 1983.

Raemer, John E. *Theories of Distributive Justice*. Boston: Harvard University Press, 1998.

Rawls, John. *A Theory of Justice*. Boston, Mass.: Harvard University Press, 1971.

———. *Political Liberalism*. New York: Columbia University Press, 1993.

Sowell, Thomas. *The Quest for Cosmic Justice*. New York: Free Press, 1999.

Sunstein, Cass R. *Free Markets and Social Justice*. Oxford: Oxford University Press, 1996.

16

Law

Every human law has just so much of the nature of law as it is derived from the law of nature. But if in any point it departs from the law of nature, it is no longer a law but a perversion of the law.

—St. Thomas Aquinas

There ought to be, and many times are, a close nexus between man-made law and justice—law should aim at justice. Laws should be the objective expressions of the nature of reality rather than merely the subjective prejudices or whims of some person, group of people, or society as a whole. Natural law is objective because it is inherent in the nature of the entity to which it relates. The content of natural law is accessible to human reason. For example, it is easily understood that because each man has a natural right to survive, flourish, and pursue his own happiness, no other man or group of men should attempt to deprive him of a chosen value or action through the initiation or threat of force.

Historically, socially emergent ideas of legal principles, oftentimes in accord with the nature of reality, occurred prior to their adoption by political authorities. Voluntary forms of governance through customary private laws preexisted state law and effectively ordered human affairs. Law arose as a spontaneous order— something to be discovered rather than enacted. Law is an evolutionary systemic process involving the experiences of a vast number of people.

The cherished American ideal of the rule of law embodies the notion that every person is bound by rules, including those in government. The rule of law requires that people should be governed by accepted rules, rather than by the arbitrary decisions of rulers. These rules should be general and abstract, known and certain, and apply equally to all individuals.

Constitutional governments are based on a previous commitment to freedom under the rule of law. The essential attribute of constitutionalism is a legal limitation on government. Under constitutionalism, rulers are not above the law, government power is divided with laws enacted by one body and administered by another, and an independent judiciary exists to ensure that laws are administered objectively. An efficient and effective constitution allows government to function to protect the lives and liberties of citizens without violating the rights of some to provide gain to others.

Nonstatist customary and privately produced laws continue to exist today. Members of many voluntary associations prefer to operate under rules of their own choice and making rather than relying on those of a coercive government.

The Evolution of Law

The idea of law includes fundamental rules of behavior, as well as institutions and devices for changing, clarifying, refining, and applying the rules. Law is a natural outcome of people living and working together. If people are to live among others, there must be a way to resolve the inevitable disputes. Law can be seen as the activity of subjecting human conduct to the governance of rules.

The evolution of law began before history was recorded with laws built up one by one as disputes were settled. In fact, the development of rules in society predates both courts and the written law. For thousands of years, customary and private legal systems alone ordered human activities. The power of customary law is found in the fact that it is reflected in the conduct of people toward one another. The further a society moves away from customary and private law systems, the greater the need for laws coercively enforced by the state.

The law is essentially discovered, not made. Law is a systemic discovery process involving the historical experiences of successive generations. Law reflects and embodies the experiences of all men who have ever lived.

Customary law involves spontaneously evolved rules emerging through dispute adjudication. Customary law provides a rather reliable process for discovering the natural law, because a spontaneously evolved and voluntarily followed custom is more likely to result in mutual advantages to the involved parties than a rule imposed by a powerful group. Natural law is the immutable standard to which man-made laws must correspond in order to be legitimate. Natural law is the general body of rules of right conduct and justice common to all men. Analogously, a common law system in which law arises via judicial precedent is better than a system in which courts and judges merely apply positive laws enacted by a legislative body.

Anglo-Saxon customary law involved a group of individuals, often referred to as a bohr, pledging surety for each of its members. In such an arrangement, each person secured his property claims by freely accepting an obligation to respect the property rights of others, who were expected to reciprocate. The group would back up this pledge of surety by paying the fines of its members if they were found guilty of violating customary law. The surety group had financial incentives to police its members and exclude those who frequently and flagrantly engaged in undesirable behavior. Individuals would deal cooperatively with those known to be trustworthy while refusing to interact with those known to be untrustworthy. These solidarity rules evolved spontaneously as individuals utilized ostracism instead of violence. There is a certain timeless appeal to such reciprocal agreements. Modern parallels to these reciprocal voluntary agreements can be found in insurance agencies, credit card companies, and credit bureaus. Insurance agencies spread risks through the combining of assets. Credit card companies stand behind the actions and claims of their members. In addition, credit bureaus attest to the financial standing of their members.

Additional institutional arrangements easily evolve in such a cooperative social order. When a charge is disputed, nonviolent means of resolving conflicts and clarifying property rights emerge. For example, the dispute resolution process could be handled through the appointment of a mutually acceptable arbitrator or mediator. If the loser pays restitution, he may be permitted to rejoin the group. The coercive power of a central authority is not required in such a voluntary social arrangement.

Anglo-Saxon courts (moots) were assemblies of common men and neighbors. Operating similar to surety groups, their jurisdiction depended upon the consent of the parties. The moots passed judgment according to customary law.

In the late Middle Ages, the Law Merchant, a far-reaching system of private mercantile law that operated through reputation, credit, and economic embargo, regulated commercial transactions throughout Europe. This system of voluntary law emerged in response to the need for common standards to govern international trade. Members formed their own Europe-wide court system and legal order. They relied on credit reports for enforcement and the fact that those declining to submit to the system's rules and decisions would have great difficulty finding other merchants to do business with. Merchants who did not adhere to the Law Merchant standards found themselves ostracized from the community of reciprocal commercial relationships.

Bruce Benson has concluded that customary legal systems tend to share the following basic characteristics: (1) a strong concern for individual rights; (2) laws enforced by victims backed by reciprocal agreements; (3) standard adjudication procedures established to avoid violence; (4) offenses treated as torts punishable through economic restitution; (5) strong incentives for the guilty to submit to the prescribed punishments due to the threat of social ostracism; and (6) legal change by means of an evolutionary process of developing customs and norms.

States amassed enough power to claim monopoly in law relatively recently and only after a long battle with competing legal systems. State law gained dominance in the competition among medieval European legal systems such as Canon law, the Law Merchant, feudal (manorial) law, etc. State law forged ahead in part to the state's success in military conquests. In addition, the state's power to tax allowed it to subsidize its legal services. Royal law absorbed the functions of the Law Merchant by adopting its precedents and enforcing them at lower prices. Royal law, and eventually state law, wielded greater coercive power than competing legal systems which depended on reciprocity and trust.

The state was able to lower its costs and legitimize its claims as the monopoly source of law by establishing courts backed by the threat of violence.

Citizens in a given geographical area began to view the sovereign as the sole legitimate source of law. Eventually, the state formulated and imposed its own laws in addition to claiming to be the source of existing customary laws. Early codes of kings were mainly codifications of customary law.

The influence of Christianity provided the throne with a godly character thus enabling kings to assert a divine mandate. When kings reformed royal law to absorb portions of the Church's Canon law, the state's legal system gained the strength and aura of ecclesiastical law.

Before the Norman Conquest in 1066, governance and law in England were extremely decentralized. William the Conqueror greatly contributed to the destruction of competing legal systems by completing the centralization of royal power that had been begun by Alfred the Great in the ninth century. William and his successors worked to bring competing legal systems under royal control in order to levy fines and surcharges that would accrue to the king. By 1200, royal law dominated the legal order of England and other countries in Europe.

In retrospect, most modern nation-states evolved from nonstatist extortionist institutions. There was a natural progression as tribal war chiefs became kings and kingdoms developed into nations. The coercive state is thus seen as the source of all law. The existence of coercive institutions and rules stifles the growth of voluntary trust relationships. In addition, the motivation for honoring commitments shifts to the avoidance of punishment from the sovereign state.

Still, competing legal and governance systems have continued to exist. In fact, multiple systems have been more common than unitary systems. For example, in the American West, before federal power had reached the territories, disputes were resolved by private courts. Throughout its history, America has been the home of wagon trains, cattlemen's associations, mining camps, clubs, churches, unions, trade associations, private communities, alternative dispute resolution arrangements (i.e., arbitration and mediation), etc. Polycentric law naturally fills the voids that appear when state laws are found to be lacking. For example, informal customary norms are currently effectively regulating the Internet. Systems of private and customary law rely on individual motivation and market mechanisms, rather than the state's monopoly of power, to provide the incentives to cooperate and maintain order.

Natural Law

Conventionalists maintain that law and justice are merely man-made conventions and that no action can be deemed to be right or wrong unless a particular populace, through its customs or positive laws, declares that it is right or wrong. Positivists espouse relativism and subjectivism with respect to what is proper or improper.

Natural law opposes the idea that moral law is relative, subjective, and changeable. Natural law provides a criterion by which positive laws can be judged. If the law of the state runs counter to natural law, it is held to be unjust. Positive law and normative justice are not synonymous. If justice is pertinent, then natural law is pertinent.

Natural law derives from the nature of man and the world. It is discoverable through the use of reason in accord with nature, eternal and unchangeable, and applicable to all persons. Natural law theory supports universally shared moral principles and norms that raise man above relativism and subjectivism.

Because natural law can be derived from what is inherent in human nature, it would be valid even if God did not exist. Thomas Aquinas has explained that there exists a system of moral beliefs accessible to human reason and independent of divine revelation. Man has a particular nature involving specific natural needs and the ability to use reason to recognize what is good for man in accordance with those needs.

Although natural law is essential to Christianity, Christianity is not essential to natural law. Natural law is in agreement with God's will, not because of divine revelation, but because the nature of man and the world mirror God's will. A person does not have to be a Christian to understand the conditions and framework of human existence and social life, although believers in the Divine will avow that the conditions and framework are of God's creation. In creating each existent, God implanted the law of its nature within it. The law of nature, as dictated by God, is superior in obligation to all other laws. To believe in the natural law is to believe that there are moral standards that transcend the customs, practices, and laws of any given community. Positive law can be viewed as the system of rules created by humans in their attempts to put natural law into practice.

The Rule of Law

Law is the activity of subjecting human behavior to the governance of rules. The rule of law is concerned with regularizing the use of power. Whereas society is a spontaneous order, the state is a protective agent with the monopoly role of enforcing the rules of the game. Because the monopoly on coercion belongs to the government, it is imperative that this power not be misused. Under the rule of law, everyone is bound by rules, including the government.

As explained by Hayek in his various works, the rule of law requires law to be: (1) general and abstract, (2) known and certain, and (3) equally applicable to all people. The rule of law also necessitates independent judges unmotivated by political considerations and protection of a private domain of action and property.

In a free society each person has a recognized private sphere, a protected realm which government authority cannot encroach upon. The purpose of law is to preserve freedom and moral agency.

The rule of law is a metalegal principle. Similar to natural law theory, it provides a benchmark against which laws can be evaluated. From this perspective, law is about the discovery of the rules of just conduct. For example, the history of common law has been one of attempting to discover general rules that will foster a smoothly functioning social order. There is a large amount of natural law precedent embodied in the common law.

The rule of law ensures that judges decide disputes in terms of existing known and general rules and not according to the perceived desirability of particular outcomes. The purpose of the judge is to maintain an order, not to attain some specific result or direct society's resources to particular persons or uses. His function is to ascertain, articulate, and refine the rules of justice that will permit the preservation of the social order. A judge is not to issue edicts—he is only to rule when a dispute is brought to him. Once law has drawn the boundaries of individual discretion, courts should not second-guess individual use of that discretion. Judges should carry out the law—not change the law.

Distributive (i.e., social) justice is irreconcilable with the rule of law. The rule of law only establishes the rules for the social game. These rules of justice conduct are applicable to an as yet unknown and indeterminate number of persons, cases, and instances. These rules have no reference to particular persons, places, or objects. In short, such laws do not try to designate who will be winners or losers or what the society that emerges from these rules will look like.

Hayek has distinguished between two different kinds of laws. The first involves man's attempts to discover and express clearly what the general rules of justice really are. Here the law is essentially discovered, not made. These laws apply to all, including the leaders. Power should be divided with laws made by one body and administered by another. Also, an independent judiciary is required to make certain that laws are administered fairly. Those who administer the law should have little or no discretion. The second type of law involves rules dealing with the internal operation of the organization. These administrative measures are devised to run the internal operations of the government. Essentially, these commands tell civil servants how to carry out their duties regarding the running of the bureaucratic public sector.

There has been a tendency for the law-finding function of the government to be confused with its administrative functions. A great deal of what we think of as law today is really administrative legislation meant to direct the internal operations of the government, rather than to preserve justice. In other words, the organizational rules of authorities are mistakenly given the same status as general rules of justice.

As the distinction between administrative commands and rules of justice became blurred, the restraints on government power have weakened. This led to the false impression that our elected officials possess and should possess as much power in deciding the rules of justice as it has in the formulation and execution of administrative proposals. It is no wonder that many of our elected officials think they are "running the country."

Hayek saw the problem as stemming from the fact that the power of conducting the government and the power of discovering the rules of just conduct are combined in the same representative bodies. As a result, over the years, legislation has increasingly included directives commanding people how to act with the goal of attaining specific outcomes. During the last half century, the rule of law has been displaced with what has been termed *social justice*.

In addition, the rule of law is further weakened when legislative and judicial power is delegated to unelected government bureaucrats. Starting in the 1930s, Congress began passing general laws, leaving the details up to administrative agencies. These agencies enforce and interpret their own rules and regulations that, although they have the force of law, have not been ratified by the constitutional lawmaking authority.

Pluralism and Constitutionalism

Pluralism and constitutionalism share skepticism toward the concentration of power. Whereas power is the force by which one can compel others to obey, authority is the right to direct and command (i.e., to be obeyed). Authority requests and requires power. Authority is restricted to assigned areas. Given the corruptible nature of human beings, there is a tendency for power to overflow its bounds. Power exercised without authority is a threat to freedom.

Authority would be necessary even if society solely consisted of saints and wise men. Authority is necessary to ensure unity of action within an organization. Legitimate activities call authority into being. It is the creation of a position or an office, not one's appointment to it, that represents the authentic investiture of authority. Authority goes with an office, is impersonal, and is essentially independent of the person who exercises it.

Power is an instrument of control. It is exercised legitimately when it is employed to discharge effectively the functions of the office. If power exceeds the means appropriate to these functions, it becomes illegitimate.

Pluralism, both the cause and effect of freedom, involves multiplicity, diversity and, oftentimes, conflict. Pluralism requires tolerance, voluntarism, and a combination of individualism and voluntary associationism. The aim of pluralism is a wide diffusion of power. Its structure is the voluntary groups working between the national government and individual citizens. When power is diffused into many bodies, imbalances of power are prevented and the individual is protected from the tyranny of the one, the few, or the many.

Pluralism is concerned with the distribution of authority and functions among the various sectors of society (i.e., the economic, political, and moral-cultural sectors) and among the various types of groupings within each of these sectors. A free society favors processes and devices that disperse decision-making power, thus enhancing the possibility for the use of individual freedom.

It was not until the medieval period, well after the fall of the Roman Empire, that circumstances favorable for pluralism were present. This was a time when authority was challenged and threatened (e.g., church and state, pope and emperor, emperor and king, king and baron, lord and vassal, etc.).

Only when men were forced to create new associations to perform functions once carried out by a powerful central authority did pluralism come into existence. Pluralism thus fostered individual freedom, responsibility, and creativity and encouraged the development and growth of new forms of association to meet human needs.

Constitutional governments are distinguished by specific restraints that try to ensure that power is not abused. By dividing power, a constitution provides a system of restraints upon government action. A constitution is a set of fixed written rules that limit the exercise of political power. The systematic use of written constitutions as fundamental and paramount law, enforceable in courts on behalf of citizens whose rights were encroached upon by these rulers, did not emerge until the end of the eighteenth century.

The impetus behind constitutional government was a desire for justice and the idea underlying restraints is of a higher natural law limiting the operations of the state. As an instrument, the Constitution is a grant of powers. The doctrine of enumerated powers, the cornerstone of the Constitution, held that the government had only those powers that the people have given it. It follows that the Constitution can also be viewed as a symbol of the reserved rights of the American people. The belief that the legitimate governmental authority originates with the people is derived from the American political theory of the consent of the government.

Constitutional arrangements for protection of individual liberty presume a prior commitment to liberty under the rule of law. These American political traditions presuppose certain convictions about human nature. Because men are not angels, and because men are to govern other men, controls on the government are necessary. The idea of constitutional government also recognizes the natural rights of individuals and the moral responsibility of each citizen as a person. The American Constitution is thus designed to maximize each individual's equal right to pursue his own peaceful goals and experience the benefits and responsibilities of private ownership.

The American constitutional political system is based on a territorial distribution of power, the distribution of power among agencies with functionally differentiated realms of authority, a chronological distribution of power through periodic and frequent elections, and a written constitution enforceable by courts. With respect to the territorial distribution of power, portions of power are vested in state governments as opposed to the national government. Also, both national and state governments are populated by representatives of people from various geographical locations. Functionally, the constitution proposes that there are different types of governmental powers and that these powers should not be concentrated in just one body of government officials. The American solution has been to separate then into these kinds of power: executive, legislative, and judicial. Laws should be made by one body and administered by another. An independent judiciary is necessary to make sure the laws are administered fairly and objectively. In addition, pluralism provides a functional distribution of authority and additional restraints on power by maintaining many voluntary power centers throughout society. The chronological distribution of power places limits on the tenure of office.

In addition, the party system, the free press, and voluntary associations aid in holding government officials accountable. Politicians are kept responsible, not only through periodic elections, but through constant publicity of their actions and discussions and through citizens' rights to associate together and to petition the government. The eternal vigilance of the people is an important check on the power of the government.

Since the 1930s, the federal government has assumed many powers not assigned by the people and not enumerated in the Constitution. Most post-New Deal elected and appointed officials seem to have forgotten that authority limits the exercise of power to certain areas and to certain people who have a legitimate right to use it. For example, the courts have transformed contract and tort law from devices for the private ordering of affairs into vehicles of public policy in which the faultless can be held liable because "someone must pay" or because the judge believes the law to be wrong or wants to achieve certain outcomes.

Recommended Reading

Arendt, Hannah. "Authority in the Twentieth Century." *Review of Politics* (October 1956).

Barnett, Randy. *The Structure of Liberty.* Oxford: Clarendon Press, 1998.

Bell, Tom W. "Polycentric Law." *Humane Studies Review* 7, no. 1 (winter 1991-1992).

Benson, Bruce L. *The Enterprise of Law.* San Francisco: Pacific Research Institute, 1990.

Berman, Harold J. *Law and Revolution: The Formation of Western Legal Traditions.* Cambridge, Mass.: Harvard University Press, 1983.

Buckle, Stephen. *Natural Law and the Theory of Property.* Oxford: Oxford University Press, 1991.

Corwin, E. S. "The Higher Law. " *Background of American Constitutional Law.* New York: Great Seal Books, 1928.

Dahl, Robert A. *Pluralistic Democracy in the United States: Conflict and Consent.* Chicago: Rand McNally, 1967.

Finnis, John. *Natural Law and Natural Rights.* Oxford: Clarendon Press, 1980.

Fuller, Lon. *The Morality of Law.* New Haven, Conn.: Yale University Press, 1964.

Hart, H. L. A. *The Concept of Law.* Oxford: Oxford University Press, 1961.

Hayek, F. A. *The Constitution of Liberty.* Chicago: University of Chicago Press, 1960.

———. *Law, Legislation and Liberty.* Chicago: University of Chicago Press, 1973.

Jovenel, Bertrand de. *On Power: Its Nature and the History of Its Growth*. New York: Viking Press, 1949.

Kariel, Henry S. *The Decline of American Pluralism*. Stanford, Calif.: Stanford University Press, 1961.

Krabbe, H. *The Modern Idea of the State*. New York: Appleton, 1922.

Kurland, Philip B., and Ralph Lerner, eds. *The Founders' Constitution*. Chicago: University of Chicago Press, 1987.

Lee, Dwight R. "The Political Economy of the U.S. Constitution." *The Freeman* (February 1987).

Leoni, Bruno. *Freedom and the Law*. Indianapolis, Ind.: Liberty Fund, 1991.

Locke, John. *Essays on the Law of Nature*. Edited by W. von Leyden. Oxford: Clarendon Press, 1952.

Lutz, Donald. *The Origins of American Constitutionalism*. Baton Rouge: Louisiana State University Press, 1988.

McElroy, Wendy. "The Non-Absurdity of Natural Law." *The Freeman* (February 1988).

McIlwain, Charles H. *Constitutionalism: Ancient and Modern*. Ithaca, N.Y.: Cornell University Press, 1940.

Novak, Michael. *On Two Wings: Humble Faith and Common Sense at the American Founding*. San Francisco: Encounter Books, 2002.

Oppenheiner, Franz. *The State: Its History and Development Viewed Sociologically*. Translated by John Gitterman. Indianapolis, Ind.: Bobbs-Merrill, 1914.

Pangle, Thomas L. *The Spirit of Modern Republicanism: The Moral Vision of the American Founders and the Philosophy of Locke*. Chicago: University of Chicago Press, 1988.

Pound, Roscoe. *The Development of Constitutional Guarantees of Liberty*. New Haven, Conn.: Yale University Press, 1957.

Simon, Yves. *Nature and Functions of Authority*. Milwaukee, Wis.: Marquette University Press, 1940.

Spiro, Herbert J. *Government by Constitution: The Political System of Democracy*. New York: Random House, 1959.

Sutherland, Arthur E. *Constitutionalism in America: Origin and Evolution of Its Fundamental Ideas*. Waltham, Mass.: Blaisdell Publishing, 1965.

Weber, Max. *The Theory of Social and Economic Organization*. Translated by A. M. Henderson and Talcott Parsons. New York: Oxford University Press, 1947.

17

Corporate Governance

A business corporation is organized and carried on primarily for the profit of shareholders. The powers of directors are to be employed for that end. The discretion of the directors is to be exercised in the choice of the means to attain that end, and does not extend to a change in the end itself, and to the reduction of profits or the non-distribution of profits among shareholders in order to devote them to other purposes.

—*The Michigan Supreme Court in Dodge v. Ford (1919)*

Governance is the exercise of authority that involves not solely the right to direct but also to lead and to control within an organization. Two problems exist regardless of whether the organization operates within political society or within civil society: (1) How to accumulate the power and authority required to achieve the purposes of the association; and (2) How to limit the power and authority to specified areas rather than to allow it to overflow into areas that are not its concern. Although the same problems need to be addressed, governance within enterprise associations such as corporations is not at all like governance within a governmental body. Commercial activity conducted by corporations and by other forms of business is fundamentally different from the types of activity conducted by coercive governments.

Political Governance Requires Restraints of Power

Constitutional governments are characterized by specific restraints established by law and imposed on power holders to ensure that citizens' rights will not be transgressed. Constitutionalism embodies the principle that the government is organized by and operated on behalf of the people, but subject to a series of restraints to keep power from being abused. By dividing power, constitutionalism provides a system of restraints upon coercive state action.

The basic idea underpinning restraints rests on the notion of a law higher than positive man-made law, and thus limiting the operation of the state. Natural law provides a criterion by which positive laws are judged. Another basic principle underlying the idea of limited government is that legitimate governments always rest on the consent of the governed.

What America has developed from the above ideas are: (1) A political system with a central-local distribution of power; (2) Subordinate distributions of power among agencies with functionally defined realms of authority; (3) A chronological distribution of power through periodic and regular elections; and (4) A written constitution enforceable by the courts limiting the exercise of political power. As detailed by Jane Jacobs, such restraints are appropriate for a system based on ideas such as force, taking and dispensing, obedience and discipline, hierarchy, tradition, loyalty and exclusivity, trust only of insiders, deception for the sake of the assignment, vengeance, ostentatiousness, etc.

The Mistaken Call for Corporate Constitutionalism

Reformers have mistakenly called for constitutionalism, a principle of public government, to be applied to the operation of the private corporation. Their fear is that freedom, without the existence of constitutional restraints, may lead to corporate absolutism in the economic sphere. According to critics, the concentration of the control of property in the hands of a few managers, no matter how dispersed the actual stock ownership may be, threatens the idea of pluralism. What has resulted has been a call for the development of means by which the powers of these "private governments" can be moderated regarding those both inside and outside of the firm.

There has been a recent demand for due process in corporations. Critics argue that when a corporation has the power to affect a great many lives, it should be subject to the same constraints under the Constitution that apply to the government. Some have advocated the control of corporation by external agencies (e.g., federal chartering). Others have recommended control through internal institutional devices such as: (1) stakeholder directors on the board; (2) social audits; (3) the preparation of community impact analyses; (4) the implementation of plant closing restrictions; (5) full-time, outside professional directors; (6) ethics committees; and (7) separating the board chair (external) from the president (internal).

Some critics maintain that corporations, because of their size, special legal status, and economic, political, and social impacts, have as much public power as do states and, therefore, as "private governments" should be federally chartered, constitutionally limited, and held to higher levels of social responsibility than noncorporate firms. They argue that modern corporations represent large concentrations of power and have the potential to effect great changes in society. In other words, social responsibility arises from social power. Because corporations can affect the interests of others, they must be concerned with social responsibility. Advocates of corporate democracy theory even go so far as to call for restraints on the control of shareholders and managers so that the corporation can be run as a democracy in the interests of all of its constituents. Reformers have failed to recognize that commerce is essentially different from government and that methods appropriate to government are not germane to commercial enterprises. Jane Jacobs has explained that, unlike coercive governments, commerce is based on ideas such as trade, voluntary agreements, honesty, openness to strangers, competition, inventiveness, efficiency, initiative and enterprise, thriftiness, dissent for the sake of the job, etc.

Corporations Are Voluntary Associations

A corporation, man's voluntary approach to achieving economic competence, is created through the exercise of individual rights (i.e., freedom of association and freedom of contract). Men have an inherent right to form a corporation by contract for their own benefit and in their mutual self-interest. Based upon a consciousness of common interests, the corporation is an association of individuals who engage in a particular type of contractual relationship with one another in order to pursue common business objectives, is governed by rules of the individuals' own making, and is said to be able to assert rights and assume obligations. When rights and obligations are imputed to a corporation, what is really being referred to are the rights and obligations of its members who create and sustain it (i.e., the stockholders, directors, officers, employees, etc.).

Corporations are properly viewed as voluntary associations and as private property. Arising from individual contracts, corporations are not the creation of the state—the state simply recognizes and records their creation in a similar fashion as it does with births, marriages, sales of real estate, etc. The corporate charter is merely the articles of incorporation which are not related to state authority and do not obligate the corporation to serve the public interest. Because corporations are not created by the state, the government has no authority to tell them what to do.

The state grants a charter as a legal technicality and neither creates nor changes the essence of these voluntary associations whose success depends upon the social bonds that unite their members and upon the human need for group membership. The state may choose to recognize these units but in so doing it simply acknowledges that which already exists. Corporateness is a right common to all persons. The corporation is an association of human beings bound together in order to achieve a purpose. Positive law alone cannot provide the community of purpose necessary for a corporation to exist. In fact, the equivalent of a corporation frequently exists in the absence of legal action.

Corporate Governance Requires the Freedom to Create and to Execute

Michael Novak observes in *The Fire of Invention: Civil Society and the Future of the Corporation* that corporations are nothing like states. In government, executive power is feared and thus checked—in the corporation it is desired and therefore fostered. Because a corporation is not a political community, checks and balances are not appropriate to it. In a corporation the whole idea is to accomplish certain goals and to create something new. In government the point is to keep leaders from doing anything beyond their stated powers. In corporations we value swift action. Contrariwise, in government we desire judiciousness and deliberation. Institutions should be fundamentally understood and judged in terms of their purpose or essential aim.

Investors who have an idea, combine their resources, and attempt to create new wealth create corporations. The corporation can only survive and prosper if it meets the needs of its customers and the purposes of its investors, including the provision of goods or services at a profit along with fiduciary care for resources invested in it.

A corporation is created to attain specific purposes. It follows that the problem of corporate governance is not to check power—it is to summon up and channel power toward the accomplishment of organizational objectives. No one should desire a "separation of powers" within a corporation. Executives must be permitted to execute.

With respect to corporate governance, owners are in sufficient control via the buying and selling of shares and other actions. Discontented shareholders may theoretically bring suit against the directors and managers when they spend the shareholders' money on unauthorized projects that are not in the owners' interest or engage in other *ultra vires* acts. However, it is more likely that they will vote against such directors, remove the managers, or simply sell their shares.

In a publicly owned corporation, the owners may be located all over the world. However, it is more probable that a large percentage of the shares of any major firm will be owned by particular mutual funds and pension plans, who act as proxies for a large number of individuals. The relationships between shareholders and corporate managers and shareholders and money managers are principal-agent relationships. The growth of mutual funds and pension plans means broader stock ownership and stronger pressure on behalf of stockholders to keep managers in line. Because directors of mutual funds and pension plans want to invest in highly profitable firms, there is a powerful motivation for corporate directors and managers to continue to work hard and creatively. Money managers, as agents of the absentee-owner shareholders, can vote a CEO out of office by taking control of the board of directors of his company or can sell the stock of companies from which they no longer expect competitive returns.

We are in an era of fiduciary capitalism in which there is a concentration of ownership in the hands of a relatively small number of decision makers.

However, legal ownership is still widely dispersed and the fiduciary duty of the money managers of mutual funds and pension plans gives them the responsibility to exercise the powers of ownership. The fiduciary standard requires that the fiduciary take only those actions that a prudent person would take regarding the management of the resources entrusted to the fiduciary. In discharging their fiduciary duty, money managers purchase securities and vote proxies. In essence, they exercise ownership rights, although on behalf of their beneficiaries.

The idea of the morality of the principal-agent relationship is certainly not new. For example, consider the Biblical Parable of the Talents in which the master entrusted assets to three servants and then departed the country, thereby creating a situation involving the separation of ownership and control. Two of the servants invested the assets, were very productive, and therefore were rewarded when the master returned. The third buried the assets, returned them without even earning any interest on them, and was punished. This story clearly illustrates the idea that separating control from ownership does not strip the owner of his rights. Today, we've simply added the idea of the fiduciary responsibility of the mutual fund or pension plan manager as a middleman, between the owners and the managers of a corporation.

Corporations Do Not Possess the Power of Coercion

Not only would constitutional measures reduce the efficiency and effectiveness of corporations, some (e.g., proposals for stakeholder and outside directors) would also ensure directors with relatively little relevant experience. More importantly, these measures would restrict the rights of private property owners. Ethically, a corporation's "power" is irrelevant. Unlike governments, they do not enjoy the power of coercion. The idea of a private government is oxymoronic. Only the state can force people to do things through its political, military, and police power. When a business offers a quid pro quo to its potential customers, employees, and others, it simply adds to their existing set of options—this in no way constitutes an exercise of power. Therefore, only governments should be constitutionally limited by legal restraints imposed on power holders to keep power from being abused.

What about the possibility of the abuse of power by individual managers over employees within a corporation? Certainly, corporations need to give authority to command others and provide the means necessary to gain obedience to these commands. Authority, the right to be obeyed by others, requires power. In a firm, authority and power should be restricted to assigned legitimate areas. Power exercised without authority is illegitimate. Surely, any well-run firm will have internal due process policies and procedures to provide some assurance of nonarbitrariness by requiring those who exercise authority to justify their actions. In a free society, if management's order is not agreeable to a worker who believes it to be arbitrary or not within the manager's legitimate sphere of authority the worker can choose to: (1) initiate the firm's due process procedures; (2) practice constancy by ignoring the manager's overstepping of his authority by looking toward longer-run goals; or (3) terminate his relationship with the company.

Recommended Reading

Berle, Adolph A. Jr. *Economic Power and the Free Society*. New York: Fund for the Republic, 1957.

Berle, Adolph, and Gardiner Means. *The Modern Corporation and Private Property*. New York: Harcourt & Brace, 1967.

Blair, Margaret H. *Ownership and Control: Rethinking Corporate Governance for the Twenty-First Century*. Washington, D.C.: Brookings Institute, 1995.

Brown, Courtney C. *Putting the Corporate Board to Work*. New York: Macmillan, 1976.

Demb, Ada F., Friedrich Neubauer, and Franz-Friedrich Neubauer. *The Corporate Board: Confronting the Paradoxes*. New York: Oxford University Press, 1992.

Den Uyl, Douglas. *The New Crusaders*. Bowling Green, Ohio: Social Philosophy and Policy Center, 1984.

Eells, Richard. *The Government of Corporations*. New York: Free Press, 1962.

Hessen, Robert. *In Defense of the Corporation*. Stanford, Calif.: Hoover Institution Press, 1979.

Hood, John M. *The Heroic Enterprise*. New York: Free Press, 1996.

Jacobs, Jane. *Systems of Survival: A Dialogue on the Moral Foundations of Commerce and Politics*. New York: Random House, 1992.

Johnson, Joseph. *No Man Can Serve Two Masters: Shareholders versus Stockholders in the Governance of Companies*. London: Social Affairs Unit, 1998.

Kaufman, Allen. *Managers vs. Owners: The Struggle for Corporate Control in American Democracy*. New York: Oxford University Press, 1995.

Keasey, Kevin, and Mike Wright, eds. *Corporate Governance: Responsibilities, Risks, and Remuneration*. London: John Wiley and Son, 1997.

Kochan, Nicholas, and Michel Syrett. *New Directions in Corporate Governance*. London: Business International Limited, 1991.

Kristol, Irving. "On Corporate Capitalism in America." *The Public Interest* (fall 1975).

Lawriwsky, Michael L. *Corporate Structure and Performance: The Role of Owners, Managers, and Markets*. New York: St. Martin's Press, 1984.

Manne, Henry G. *The Modern Corporation and Social Responsibility*. Washington, D.C.: American Enterprise Institute, 1972.

Monks, Robert, and Nell Minnow. *Power and Accountability*. New York: Harper Collins, 1991.

Nader, Ralph, and Mark Green, eds. *Corporate Power in America*. New York: Grossman Publishers, 1973.

Nader, Ralph, Mark Green, and Joel Seligman. *Taming the Giant Corporation*.

New York: W. W. Norton, 1976.

Novak, Michael. *The Fire of Invention: Civil Society and the Future of the Corporation*. New York: Rowman & Littlefield, 1997.

Prentice, D. D. *Contemporary Issues in Corporate Governance*. Edited by P. R. J. Holland. New York: Oxford University Press, 1993.

Rappaport, Alfred. *Creating Shareholder Value: A Guide for Managers and Investors*. New York: Free Press, 1997.

Roe, Mark J., and Margaret M. Blair, eds. *Employees and Corporate Governance*. Washington, D.C.: Brookings Institute, 1999.

Scott, John. *Corporate Business and Capitalist Classes*. New York: Oxford University Press, 1997.

Sternberg, Elaine. *Corporate Governance: Accountability in the Marketplace*. London: Institute of Economic Affairs, 1998.

Williamson, Oliver. *Markets and Hierarchies*. New York: Free Press, 1975.

PART V

OBSTACLES TO A
FREE SOCIETY

18

Collectivist Thinkers

*It is in the light of our beliefs about the ultimate nature of reality that we formu-
late our conceptions of right and wrong; and it is in the light of our conceptions
of right and wrong that we frame our conduct, not only in the relations of private
life, but also in the sphere of politics and economics. So far from being irrelevant,
our metaphysical beliefs are the final determining factor in all our actions.*

—Aldous Huxley

America was intentionally created based on the following fundamental philosophical ideas: (1) The material world is an orderly, intelligible, natural domain that is
open to man's mind; (2) Man's rational mind is able to attain an objective knowledge of reality that is necessary for the pursuit of one's happiness—a man is able
to acquire knowledge based on evidence provided by the senses; (3) The good life
is one of personal self-actualization—each person should strive to attain his own
happiness through his own independent thoughts and efforts; (4) Each man has
inalienable natural rights to his own life, liberty, and the pursuit of his own happiness; (5) A government with limited power is needed in order to secure these rights.
  The founding fathers' advocacy of rights, reason, freedom, individualism, capitalism, and the minimal state was based on the writings of Aristotle, Aquinas, Locke,
and Adam Smith, among others. America, the Industrial Revolution, and the growth
of capitalism were all products of the thought of these individuals.
  Today, the founding fathers' fundamental ideas have been rejected by a great
many intellectuals who ascribe to the ideas of positive rights, an activist government, skepticism, subjectivism, relativism, and pragmatism. The assault against the
ideas championed by America's founding fathers has been led by a number of
philosophers ranging from Plato to Dewey. At the time of the Declaration of
Independence, Aristotle's ideas were generally thought to be superior to Plato's.
Since then, a number of thinkers have rediscovered and built on Plato's ideas with
devastating consequences for the idea of a free society. The purpose of this chapter
is to explain the basic ideas of these collectivist thinkers so that supporters of a free
society will be able to identify their enemies' errors and thus have the ammunition
to argue persuasively for a free society and against a collective one.

Plato's Attack on the Open Society

Plato (427-347 B.C.) held that the world is made up of two opposed dimensions—true reality (i.e., the intelligible) and the material world (i.e., the sensible). True reality is a set of universal ideas that are the "essential forms," "absolute essences," or "disembodied abstractions," which represent and contain all the qualities that the particular members of classes of material objects have in common.

There is an absolute form, essence, or idea, which is the true nature and reality shared by particular members of a class. Ideas are nonmaterial existents in another dimension separate from man's mind and from any of their corporeal embodiments.

Plato explains that sensible things of the world cannot be known with any certainty because they are in a continual state of impermanence and change. Objects of sense cannot be known for at the very instant the observer approaches they will have already changed. From this, he concluded that there is nothing real and stable in the sense world.

Change is everywhere—things in the world are always transforming. Yet, change is contradictory and contradictions are unknowable and unintelligible. Plato surmises that the world of particulars is unknowable; yet, he is convinced that knowledge must be possible.

For Plato, the Ideas that we contemplate always transcend the things of which we have sensible experience. These Universals are immutable, noncontradictory, eternal, have identity, and are knowable. Knowable implies real to Plato.

Plato explains that we really never see "manness," we only see individual men. To be a man is never identical with the particular person whom we experience with our senses. Because individual men are simply particular manifestations of the Idea, manness, they are not actually real. All individual men are essentially the same Idea in a variety of instantiations. Individual men come and go but the essence of what it means to be a man stays the same.

Plato argues that the existence of universal ideas in human minds demands the existence of a supramundane world of pure essences that are stable, real, and eternal. These Ideas exist as real entities apart from the world of sense. Plato argues that Universals are real and that they exist in another dimension of reality. This is the essence of Plato's two-world metaphysical and epistemological dualism.

Plato says that we necessarily have to know the Universals first. (He failed to realize that we acquire our universal ideas from sensible objects via a process of abstraction.) Plato contends that only by already knowing the Universals can we group the particulars. For him, all knowledge is deduction.

He alleges that men's souls must have had a preexistence in a former life in the world of Ideas. The soul knew these concepts before its entrapment in a physical body and can remember these Ideas when contact is made with actual things through the senses. When the soul encounters a copy of an Idea in the sense world, a process of reminiscence is set in motion, making a man curious and spurring him on in his efforts to know reality. The objects of sense are but faint changing imitations of the eternal, unchanging Ideas.

Particulars are shadows or reflections of Universals that somehow participate in the Universals. Plato offers no literal explanation of participation. Somehow the Universals project out or shine forth into the emptiness of space thus casting shadows or reflections of themselves and causing the particulars of the sensible world to come into existence.

According to Plato, the soul is born with knowledge that it forgets when it is imprisoned in the body. Knowledge is thus buried in the mind (or soul). Encounters with particulars activate the soul's knowledge of Universals. When one's memory is jolted, he is prompted to turn inward in order to look upward to find the Forms. True reality cannot be known by logic or reason, it can only be known through mystical experience (i.e., intuition and revelation).

Plato maintains that the soul must have come from the world of Forms. This can be criticized on Plato's own terms. Whereas Forms are Universals, the soul is a particular. How can a particular soul exist in a world of Universals? Only "soulness" should be there. In addition, if the soul actually had a previous existence, shouldn't the awakening of the innate universal ideas revive the memory of the soul's previous existence itself?

Plato observes that only a select few, who have been endowed with the innate capacity to contemplate, are able to master the path to true knowledge. The few who are attuned to true reality are by natural right the rulers of the vast majority of men. Plato calls for a benevolent despotism of the select few who are willing to live the life of the mind and to ignore the pleasures of the material world.

Plato's metaphysical and epistemological dualism is also an ethical dualism of good and evil, right and wrong. There is a moral conflict between the world of the senses and the world of the intellect. To attain happiness one needs to turn away from the material world and its inclinations and instead attend to the contemplation of timeless, changeless Ideas.

The soul, which understands that happiness consists in the world of Ideas, is never satisfied with the knowledge of inferior degrees. Because the higher world is better, it is moral to turn to the better world. The highest form of love, according to Plato, is the love of wisdom that is only found in the higher world of Forms beyond this world. It follows that the soul wants to escape from the bodily world to rise to the world of Forms to be with the highest degree of knowledge. Plato is thus espousing an otherworldly egoism—self-denial and sacrifice in this world in order to obtain salvation and the highest values in the higher world. Plato's Ideas are endowed with real existence in a world superior to the world that we see. It follows that the citizens of Plato's state should concern themselves with the transcendent world and not give in to the inclinations of sense and passion.

Plato explains that not only should a man shun the pleasures of the sense world in the name of loyalty to a higher dimension, he should also deny his individuality in the name of unity with the collective. An individual man is just a particular shadow cast by the Universal manness. It follows that all men make up one unity and that no one person is an autonomous reality. In politics, this leads Plato to collectivism. The individual is simply a fragment, whereas the group (the collective) is a higher manifestation on earth of the Universal manness. It is closer to the whole. Collectivism is a higher and closer development toward the Universal manness. The individual is thus subservient to the group. Since the needs of the whole take precedence, the individual should put aside his own interests for the needs of the whole.

This leads to Plato's advocacy of a life of self-sacrificial service to the community, the standard of value in society. Through his efforts to extinguish his own individuality, each person will become one with the community and live only to serve its welfare.

Plato's organic theory envisages an omnipotent state that is more real than the individuals who live within it. This state is to be ruled by a special elite of philosophers who have the ability to escape (as far as is possible in this world) the domain of sense experiences and rise to the contemplation of universal Ideas. For Plato, the criterion of morality is the interest of the state and the proper life is one of selflessness and renunciation.

On earth you are to obey the state (i.e., the philosopher-kings) that teach you to eschew the bodily world and purify the soul through self-sacrifice. If you do this, then you are rewarded in the higher world—egoism is put off until then.

Rousseau's "General Will"

The belief that man, by nature, is good was espoused by the French philosopher, Jean Jacques Rousseau (1712-1778). He believed that people in the state of nature were innocent and at their best and that they were corrupted by the unnaturalness of civilization. In the state of nature, people lived entirely for themselves, possessed an absolute independence, and were content.

According to Rousseau, in the state of nature, people tended to be isolated, war was absent, and their desires were minimal and circumscribed (i.e., commensurate with their basic survival needs). People did not have the drive to acquire more possessions. There was plenty to go around, an absence of reliance on others, and no real need for extensive social interaction. However, there did exist an unreflective sympathy and general compassion toward others that was indiscriminate and not based on merits.

In the state of nature egoism was absent and compassion was present. Rousseau saw compassion for the undeserving in particular and for mankind in general to be the greatest of the virtues. He regarded contempt of another, which could lead to hurt feelings, as a vice and as always bad. Rousseau wanted no one's feelings to be hurt. He felt that a proper society had no place for blame, criticism, judgment, comparison with others, and the distinction of worth among men. He said it was wrong to recognize distinctions because this makes people unequal. It was worse to be affronted than to be injured. What mattered to Rousseau was a person's good intentions rather than his achievements or outer appearances.

Rousseau proclaimed the natural goodness of man and believed that one man by nature is just as good as any other. For Rousseau, a man could be just without virtue and good without effort. According to Rousseau, man in the state of nature was free, wise, and good and the laws of nature were benevolent. It follows that it was civilization that enslaved and corrupted man and made him unnatural. Because in the order of nature all men were equal, it also follows that distinction and differentiation among men are the products of culture and civilization. Because man is by nature a saint, it must be the corrupting influence of society that is responsible for the misconduct of the individual.

The fundamental problem for Rousseau is not nature or man but instead is social institutions. Rousseau's view is that society corrupts the pure individual. Arguing that men are not inherently constrained by human nature, Rousseau claims that men are limited and corrupted by social arrangements. Conceiving of freedom as an absolute, independent of any natural limitations, Rousseau disavows the world of nature and its inherent laws, constraints, and regulations.

Rousseau assigned primacy to instinct, emotion, intuition, feelings, and passion. He believed that these could provide better insights into what is good and real than could reason. Rousseau thus minimized reason and differences in the moral worth of individuals. He failed to realize that freedom is meaningless in the absence of reason. He did not grasp that reason connects the moral subject to the world of values.

Rousseau observed that although life was peaceful in the state of nature, people were unfulfilled. They needed to interact in order to find actualization. According to Rousseau, evil, greed, and selfishness emerged as human society began to develop. As people formed social institutions, they developed vices. One such institution was private property that encouraged avarice and self-interest. Rousseau viewed private property as a destructive, impulsive, and egotistical institution that rewarded greed and luck. Civil society thus was born when people began fencing off their property, claiming that it was theirs, and finding that other people agreed with them.

Depravity is due to the corruption of man's essence by civilization. For Rousseau, civil society resulted from the degeneration of a basically good state of nature. Man's problems arose because of civil society. He believed that the state of nature changed because it was internally unstable. For example, because talents were not distributed equally among persons, the balance that existed in the state of nature was disturbed and with inequality came conflicting interests. The more talented, able, and intelligent people brought about advances in science, technology, commerce, and so on. Because people simply are born with certain natural endowments, a person cannot be praised for having talent or blamed for not having it. Rousseau saw talent as naturally leading to achievement. Inequality developed as some people produced more and earned more. He failed to acknowledge the importance of motivation, industry, and volitional use of one's reason and other potentialities.

People were no longer isolated and began to depend on each other. Those who just happen to have talents create new products and the desire for them. Buyers and sellers depend on each other but these dependencies are unequal because of the existence of a pyramid of ability. Rousseau contends that, as a result, the talented acquire property and become ambitious. All, including those without talent, become competitive, rivalrous, jealous, power-hungry, prestige seeking, and desirous for superiority over others. Civil society transforms men from isolated beings with limited wants into the warlike creatures found in a Hobbesian state of nature. For Rousseau, civil society is a state of war.

Rousseau maintains that people did not have the right to rise above subsistence without everyone's consent. Everything changed as civil society developed, but permission was not given for things to change. He contends that it is wrong to change the condition of all without asking. Rousseau is distressed that some people become relatively poorer without having lost anything. Not only are their feelings hurt, their right to stagnate has been violated. The poor, weak, and indolent did not want to change, but things around them changed, forcing them to steal or receive subsistence from the rich.

Rousseau thought private property to be the source of social ills. He considered that private ownership of property tended to corrupt men and destroy their character and regarded the man without property (i.e., the noble savage) to be the freest. Although he did not actually support the abolition of private property, he believed that private property should be minimal and should be distributed equally among the members of the society.

Rousseau anticipated the need for the state to minimize private property. He wanted the property of the state to be as great and powerful as possible, and that of the citizens to be as small and weak as possible. With private property being so limited, the state would need to apply very little force in order to lead the people.

Rousseau says that it is impossible to go back to the state of primitive natural man. He says that men need to be governed as they now are and that any future change in human nature will come later as a result of re-education to indoctrinate individuals to believe that the public interest is their personal interest.

Rousseau advocates a new corrective social contract as a blueprint through which a proper society can be built. He says that we should seek unanimous agreement with respect to a new social contract that eliminates the problem of dependence on one another while permitting each person to obey only himself and to remain as free as before. He declares that this can be accomplished through total alienation of each associate to the whole community. He calls for a total merger in which each individual gives up his right to control his life in exchange for an equal voice in setting the ground rules of society. Rousseau appeals to people to surrender their individual rights to a new moral and collective body with one will.

The public person formed by social contract, the republic, has a will he calls the "general will." What it wills is the true interest of what everyone wants whether they realize it or not. When you are forced to obey it, you really are obeying yourself, the true and free you.

According to Rousseau's theory of social contract, people leave an anarchic state of nature by voluntarily transferring their personal rights to the community in return for security of life and property. He argues that people should form a society to which they would completely surrender themselves. By giving up their rights, they actually create a new entity in the form of a public person that would be directed by a general will. When people join the community, they are voluntarily agreeing to comply with the general will of the community.

The idea of the general will is at the heart of Rousseau's philosophy. The general will is not the will of the majority. Rather, it is the will of the political organism that he sees as an entity with a life of its own. The general will is an additional will, somehow distinct from and other than any individual will or group of individual wills. The general will is, by some means, endowed with goodness and wisdom surpassing the beneficence and wisdom of any person or collection of persons. Society is coordinated and unified by the general will.

Rousseau believed that this general will actually exist and that it demands the unqualified obedience of every individual. He held that there is only one general will and, consequently, only one supreme good and a single overriding goal toward which a community must aim. The general will is always a force of the good and the just. It is independent, totally sovereign, infallible, and inviolable.

The result is that all powers, persons, and their rights are under the control and direction of the entire community. This means that no one can do anything without the consent of all. Everyone is totally dependent on everybody for all aspects of their lives. Such universal dependency eliminates the possibility of independent individual achievement. In addition, when the individual joins society in order to escape death or starvation, he can be a sacrificial victim ready to give up his life for others. Life is a gift made conditional by the state.

All power is transferred to a central authority or sovereign that is the total community. Major decisions are made by a vote by all in what Rousseau calls a plebiscite that is something like a town meeting without the benefit of debate. A legislator proposes laws but does not decide on them. The legislator is a person or an intellectual elite body that works out carefully worded alternatives, brings people together, and has people vote with the results binding on all. The authority of the legislator derives from his superior insight, charisma, virtue, and mysticism. The legislator words the propositions of the plebiscite so that the "right" decision will result. The right decisions are those that change human nature. The unlimited power of the state is made to appear legitimate by the apparent consent of the majority.

Between plebiscites, the government (i.e., the bureaucracy) governs by decree. The government interprets the laws and settles each case based on the perceived merits. Both executive and judicial, the government is a bureaucracy with huge discretionary powers. The legislator is over and above this bureaucracy. In a total democracy, the real government is the bureaucracy that applies the law to day-to-day situations.

Rousseau was an advocate of the ancient idea of the omnipotence of the law-giver. Rulers are in some way attuned to the dictates of the general will and able to incorporate these dictates into specific laws. No one can challenge these laws because their source is the wise and beneficent general will. Rousseau permits no disobedience of the general will once its decisions have been made. Man's will must be subordinated and he must abide by the general will even though he thinks he disagrees with it. The person who "disagrees" with the general will must be mistaken.

According to Rousseau, each person wants to be good and therefore would want to obey the general will. It follows that when a person disagrees with the general will, he would actually be acting contrary to his own basic desires and that it would be proper to use force to attain his agreement with the general will. The general will reflects the real will of each member of society. By definition, the general will is always right. The general will is the overriding good to which each person is willing to sacrifice all other goods, including all particular private wills.

The "good citizen" assigns to society's laws a goodness and wisdom exceeding his own goodness and wisdom. It is therefore quite possible to have a conflict between what a person thinks that he wills and that which he truly wills. The good citizen is able to identify his own will with the general will.

If the general will is supreme, then citizens are free only to obey in equal servitude. People who refuse to comply with the general will can be forced to comply. If people want to be good, the rulers can make them be good. Rousseau thus viewed the political community as the proper means for liberating men from their mistaken perceptions and from the conflicts and corruptions of society.

Rousseau's idea of the general will is related to the organic concept of the state as not merely real but more real than the individuals who live within its bounds. What matters is the whole of which the individual is a part. The individual person and his own ideas, values, and goals mean nothing. By regarding human beings as means to higher ends, rather than an end in themselves, Rousseau greatly contributed to the intellectual collectivization of man. It was a small step to Hegel's contention that the general will is the will of the state and that the state is the earthly manifestation of the Absolute. Furthermore, there was an easy transition from Hegel's political philosophy to the totalitarian systems of Marx and Hitler.

Rulers who followed Rousseau's philosophy were able to demonstrate a vibrant but deceptive humanitarianism. They expressed love for humanity while at the same time crushing those who disagreed with the general will. For example, during the French Revolution, individuals like Robespierre were given enormous power to express the general will. Of course, dictators like Robespierre turned the general will into an expression of their own wills. Likewise, today when politicians refer to the good or aim of society, they are almost always referring to the good or aim of an individual or collection of individuals who want to impose their own vision upon others.

Rousseau maintained that the state must control all schooling because the objective of schooling is to develop citizens who want only what the community (i.e., the general will) wants. Because mankind was infinitely perfectible, human beings' human failings could be eradicated by education.

Rousseau wants to mold and socialize the individual through universal public education. He wants to make men more docile and to believe that when they are obeying the law they are only obeying themselves. According to Rousseau, obeying the law is always in one's own interest—the interest of one's higher self, not the self who wants to be made an exception.

In Rousseau's educational system, a child would explore nature and its requirements in order to learn what he needs to know. The child would have a tutor who would secretly devise situations in which nature would teach what the tutor wants it to teach. Believing he was free, the student would equate his will, with his mentor's will. This would serve to condition him to equate his own true will with the general will.

Kant's Epistemological Dualism and Self-Sacrificial Ethics

The major philosophical problem as seen by Immanuel Kant (1724-1804) was to save science by answering skeptic David Hume (1711-1776), who declared that man's mind was only a collection of perceptions in which there are no causal connections. Hume argued that all knowledge is from experience and that we are incapable of experiencing causality. He explained that causality, as well as entities, are only true by association and customary belief. Causality is simply man's habit of associating things together because of experiencing them together in the past. Necessary connections between objects or events are not implied by experiences of priority, contiguity, and constant conjunction.

Hume contended that experience does not give us necessity or mustness. He said that things are contingently true, but that they could be otherwise. We can imagine them being different than what we have experienced in the past. Just because something occurred in a certain way in the past does not mean that it has to occur in the same way in the future. Without necessity, our knowledge about the world is merely contingent. We cannot say with certainty that there are objects, identity, causality, order, and other laws of reality. Hume's conclusion was that we are forced to be skeptics. Science is thus wiped out at its foundation because science deals with causal connections.

Kant wanted to limit Hume's skepticism and rescue science from it. As we shall see, Kant's solution is to argue that order is the mind's contribution to the way we experience the world. The mind supplies order and structure to empirical stimuli. The human mind receives sensory stimuli and organizes, structures, and synthesizes them to give us our perceptual experiences. The mind has an inescapable set of innate and subjective processing and ordering powers and devices through which it structures or filters what it receives from reality. The world that men perceive and act in is thus a product of mechanisms inherent in the structure of human consciousness.

There are two main questions with respect to knowledge: (1) What can man know? and (2) How does man know? Regarding the first question, Kant states that you can know your experiences—the world as it appears to you. To answer the second question Kant contends that man's mind determines how reality appears to him. Consciousness is structured so that it controls the content of what man perceives and conceives. Notice Kant's trick. He has switched or substituted the how for the what. How man perceives and conceives, in essence, replaces the content of what he knows. Man's means of perceiving and thinking becomes the content of his perceiving and thinking and true reality is adjudged to be unknowable and out of bounds. Men are cut off from reality.

Kant says that we don't need more content (i.e., sense data) from the world. Rather, what we need to do is to organize, structure, and synthesize the disintegrated world of David Hume. Kant declares that consciousness makes synthesis necessary and possible by performing the synthesis itself. The mind processes discrete sense data before it reaches a man's perceived level of awareness. The necessity we see in reality is put there by consciousness through its own processes. The idea that the mind creates necessary relationships is what he called his Copernican Revolution in epistemology. Instead of the mind corresponding to reality, the world must conform to the mind's rules. For Kant, the mind's role is no longer to identify but instead to create necessary connections. Preconscious, automatic, non-volitional processes built into the mind impose order and create relationships. As a result, our experiences will always be orderly, structured, and systematic.

How does Kant attempt to prove his radical new theory? He begins by distinguishing between analytic a priori knowledge and synthetic a posteriori knowledge. Analytic judgments are made when the predicate of a proposition is known through the analysis of the subject. A priori means independent of experience. Analytic a priori truths are logical, necessary, and certain but tell us in nothing about the sense world. Synthetic a posteriori knowledge tells us about the world but does not give us necessity or causality. Such knowledge is from sense experience and is therefore contingent knowledge that we can imagine being different. Knowledge about the world is only contingently possible rather than necessary. Experience does not give us necessity or mustness. The empirical method (i.e., observation) tells us about the world by bringing together a subject and a predicate, but does not supply us with necessary truths.

In order to save science, Kant needed to create a method to establish mustness and necessity and to validate truth. What he needed was synthetic a priori truths—necessary and factual truths about the world.

Analytic a priori knowledge gives us certainty without facts and synthetic a posteriori knowledge gives us facts without certainty. Realizing man's need for certainty about the world of objects, Kant sets out to prove the existence of synthetic a priori knowledge.

He states that if there is certainty it must be a priori and therefore must be supplied by consciousness. He postulates that we have a problem of synthesis rather than of content and that necessity comes from consciousness. He therefore takes a look at sense experiences and asks if there are any things that are always there. If there are things that are always there, they must be there and must be provided by consciousness. Are there necessary ways to perceive the world and what are they and are there necessary ways to conceive the world and what are they? These ways need to be deduced—we can't experience them because they are prior to experience. We need to find the mind's contribution to each of the above. If we can find necessity in experience it must be from the subjective world and be mind contributed.

At the perceptual level, we find space and/or time to always be present in our experiences. Space and time are always a person's form of outer experience (extrospection) and time is always a person's form of inner experience (introspection). Space and time are necessary issues of form rather than of content and are not derived from sense experience. Kant concludes that space and time are a necessary part of the way we perceive the world because they are provided by man's mind that imposes them on a world of fleeting sensations. Men always have experiences here and now and recall them there and then. Space and time are therefore inborn elements of one's sensing power. The senses furnish the raw materials of knowledge and the mind arranges knowledge according to its own nature. Space and time are necessary inescapable, subjective a priori mental forms that organize and condition the perception of things.

Kant next turns to the conceptual level where he derives the categories that guide the synthesis of sensory fragments into wholes. Recognizing that he has already proven that space and time are necessary forms of perceiving, Kant asks if space and time require certain categories of conceptualization. He reasons that the fundamental categories must be observed in the kind of judgments that the human mind is capable of making.

What do space and time presuppose? They presuppose the existence of objects. Kant proposes that all perception and all thought presupposes the existence of mental categories. One's awareness of the world comes from synthesizing categories providing apprehension of things. With respect to intellection proper, Kant derives categories such as entity, causality, quantity, quality, etc.

Through reason, logic, and science, Kant explains that the mind is able to know things as they appear, but it cannot obtain knowledge of reality. For Kant, the world consists of two opposing realms—true reality (the noumenal realm) and the world of appearances (the phenomenal realm) that is a creation of man's consciousness. Kant declares that the world that we can know is mind constructed and that any necessary order is in the subjective world. We don't know what is in the objective world. Kant's epistemological dualism leads to abject skepticism. Knowledge of the noumenal world is not possible. According to Kant, the mind creates the phenomenal world but cannot know the noumenal world, the world in itself. This leads one to ask how Kant knows that the noumenal world even exists, if it can't be known. For Kant, belief in the noumenal world must be an act of faith. Reality is out of bounds. Metaphysical knowledge is impossible. Such knowledge is denied by Kant in order to make room for faith.

Kant's social subjectivism holds that it is the consciousness of mankind taken as a whole group, rather than the consciousness of the individual, that creates the world of appearances. The mental structure that is common to all persons is superior to the idiosyncratic knowledge of a given particular imperfect human being.

Each person, as a member of the same species, has the same processing apparatus (i.e., categories or filters) in his consciousness and consequently constructs the world in the same way. If an individual sees things differently from the majority, he must be wrong due to some deformity or deficiency in the categories or filters in his own consciousness. For Kant, "objectivity" means collective subjectivism. Truth is mass agreement. This proposition is the result of switching man's attention from the objective to the subjective and ultimately to the collective subjective. Truth, to the degree that it can be established in the phenomenal world, is to be decided by the majority. Men can know the phenomenal realm, a totally internal world, because they create it themselves.

According to Kant, the mind can get beyond sense experience only through postulates that are based on a nonrational faith. These postulates are that a man has free will, the soul is immortal, and God exists. Kant has limited science to the phenomenal realm in order to open the noumenal realm to faith and intuition.

With respect to moral judgments, Kant maintains that each individual feels or intuits a sense of rightness or duty. Because the objective, absolute, eternal moral order of being to which a man ought to conform is beyond the world of appearances, reason is incapable of determining what is moral or immoral. Kant thus made true morality exempt from reason by shifting morality from the sphere of reason to the domain of intuition, feelings, or faith.

Kant's moral philosophy was influenced by Rousseau's political philosophy. Whereas in politics Rousseau distinguished between the general will and the particular will, Kant in ethics differentiated between the rational will of the individual and the desires of the individual. Kant wants a person to follow the rational will by willing for himself what he would will for others. For Kant, who was unconcerned with particular desires, the essential self is the general self. As Rousseau's moral disciple, Kant saw disinterest as the general interest. Whereas Rousseau calls for man to obey the general will, Kant tells him to obey the universal moral law. It can be said that Kant learned to honor "man" from Rousseau.

In effect, Kant says that we have an a priori moral concept in our minds that controls the form but not the content of our judgments. Each person has an inner voice (perhaps our conscience), the source of moral laws, that tells us what our duties (i.e., moral obligations) are. Somehow a person's noumenal self breaks into his phenomenal self to divulge what he ought or ought not to do.

Kant asserts that a man should act solely for duty's sake even though an action conflicts with his inclinations and desires. Because of a man's selfishness, depravity, and weaknesses, he needs a principle to enable him to go beyond his self will and thereby obey a will that is universally valid. Such a principle, the categorical imperative, demands that a man behave in a certain way (i.e., from a sense of duty) regardless of his desires or inclinations. This principle requires that a moral judgment be universalizable without contradiction for all mankind.

For Kant, moral worth has nothing to do with success in the modern world. It is faith that reveals the real essence of man as an abstract self that attains self-expression by legislating universal moral laws for itself and obeying such laws regardless of the consequence.

In order to accommodate duty, Kant had to deny the idea of happiness. Selfless and lifelong obedience to duty, without any expectation of reward, is required for moral value. Moral action is an end in itself rather than a means to an end. Kant observes that a man cannot be certain that no portion of desire is subconsciously motivating him. Thus, the closest a man can get to Kantian morality is when his desires conflict with his duty and he acts contrary to his desires. Dutiful sacrifice, giving up that which you value (i.e., your own happiness) in favor of that which you don't value is the hallmark of a virtuous man.

For Kant, if a man's senses and/or reason are involved in knowing an object, the object contemplated is unreal. Likewise, if a man's desires (including a man's interest in being moral) are part of the motivation for an action, the action itself is nonmoral. An action must be done from a sense of duty, not for any selfish reason.

For example, you may like helping people and thus do so. Kant would say that there would be no moral credit in that situation even if it were in line with your duty. If you want to do something good for someone, you must do it but you can't be sure you did it for the right reason. You can only be sure if the action was totally against your desire! Only if you don't want to do an action can you be certain you are acting from duty and are thus being moral.

Kant wants to extirpate self-interest from morality. Thus, self-sacrifice and self-denial are essential for man's duties. To be moral, a man must not get any satisfaction from an action. Morality is an end in itself. A person can have morality or a person can have happiness but he can't have both.

Kant's philosophy constitutes an all-out attack on the mind's ability to know reality. Man's mind is denied access to the noumenal world. In addition, regarding knowledge of the phenomenal world, Kant says that the individual must yield to the perceptions of the majority. This certainly leads to skepticism but, additionally, it negates the value of the individual self. The mind is the self and to sacrifice the mind is to sacrifice the self. If the mind cannot know reality, a person cannot form values, make judgments, discern the good, or act to achieve the results of his thinking.

Whereas Kant argued that an individual gains value from selfless sacrifice, his followers maintained that society is omnipotent and must be obeyed, that people must be subservient to society, and that people gain value from selfless service to the collective, the race, the working class, etc. Various versions of secular altruism have named other persons as the beneficiaries of self-sacrifice. Hegel called for self-sacrifice to the architects for world history. The proletariat was the proper recipients of sacrifice for Marx. For the Nazis, it was the master race. Bentham and Mill called for the sacrifice of the minority to the majority.

Kant believed that man's categories were universal and unchangeable. For Kant, there is one universal collective. His followers break the collective into subgroups. Each little collective is said to create its own reality. Marx claimed that the categories differed among economic subgroups. Multiculturalists believe that groups create their own reality based on race, gender, ethnicity, sexual preference, etc. Because each group has its own reality, it is impossible to discuss, judge, and negotiate. The result is tribal warfare, continual strife, and political lobbying to get the state to use its coercive power on behalf of the favored group.

Hegel's State as the Divine Idea on Earth

Kant's ideas largely constitute the starting point of Hegel's (1770-1831) thinking, which, in turn, provides a metaphysical framework for Marxian thought. It is in Hegel's philosophy that we find the full expression of the concept of the state as superior to the individual.

Hegel declares that reality is a systematic progression of clashing contradictions—thesis, antithesis, and synthesis. An idealist in metaphysics, he maintains the underlying reality of the universe is the nonmaterial, divine, dynamic, cosmic mind

(God, the Spirit, Idea, World Reason, the Absolute, etc.) whose nature it is to evolve constantly, thereby unfolding itself in a series of stages. In one of these stages, the Spirit externalizes itself in the form of the material world, taking on the appearance of numerous seemingly distinct and autonomous individuals. The finite is real only in the sense that it is a phase in the self-development of the Absolute. Nature is thus conceived as a coherent whole and external manifestation of World Reason that is progressively revealed in time and space. Individual minds and actions are all phases or parts of the Divine Mind—they constitute steps in its self-actualization. Not a transcendent being, Hegel's God is an Absolute that is immanent in reality.

According to Hegel, God as mind, is everything but is unaware of his own identity. God, for Hegel, is not omniscient. This God is driven by need to discover his identity. Unknowledgeable of his own infinitude, God creates the apparent objective world in his search for his own nature. God thus struggles to get past this illusion of otherness. The Absolute (i.e., the primacy of consciousness cosmic spirit) creates the objective world that is in fact a surface appearance. Tensions occur and a dialectical process follows through which truth (i.e., the oneness of all apparent things) is sought.

The Spirit must progressively actualize itself until it reaches its full development—the key to which is the interplay between opposites. The Absolute finds expression in nature through a process of contradiction. All ideas contain their own contradictions, which, rather than being obstacles to truth, are in fact the very means for achieving truth. These contradictions exist for the imperfectly reflecting human mind. Hegel explains that both the assertion and negation of a statement may be viewed as true if they are understood as imperfect expressions of a higher proposition (synthesis) that contains all that is essential in both of these, embodying it in a fuller entity. This is an ongoing process. The final truth about reality will contain no distinctions of any kind. Everything will be one.

Hegel understood the world as process rather than as made up of entities. He believed that we need to get below the appearance of things (i.e., to get to the essence) in order to really know them. The essence negates the appearance. The key is to look for tensions and the contradictions that are apparent and inherent to each stage of the process.

For Hegel, the State is the highest embodiment of the Divine Idea on earth and the chief means used by the Absolute in manifesting itself as it unfolds towards its perfect fulfillment. Hegel argued that the State is the highest form of social existence and the end product of the development of mankind, from family to civil society to lower forms of political groupings.

The State is a superorganic whole made up of individuals grouped into local communities, voluntary associations, etc. These parts have no meaning except in relation to the State, which is an end in itself. The State can demand that its parts be sacrificed to its interests. Each man is subordinate to the ethical whole—if the State claims one's life then the individual must surrender it. Because everything is ultimately one, the collective has primacy over the individual. Hegel's State has no room for the idea of individual rights or a liberal theory of the State; instead it provides an ethical underpinning for totalitarianism. The State is an independent, self-sustaining, superorganism made up of men and having a purpose and will of its own.

Because men across different groupings (nations) disagree in their moral feelings, each State rightly legislates its own moral code—true morality is expressed in and through the laws of the State that must be obeyed by the citizens of that State but not by the members of other States. The State expresses the universal will and therefore the true will of every individual within it. Obedience to the will of the State is the only way for a man to be true to his rational self, because the State is the true self of the individual. Freedom, the right to act rationally, consists in acting in conformity with the orders of the government. The State has supreme right against the individual whose highest duty is to submerge himself into the State. Hegel calls for an antidemocratic authoritarian State that has absolute right over its component members precisely in order to attain maximal freedom.

In any particular era, one State may become the preferred vehicle of the Absolute. This favored State can be recognized by its dominant position in the world arena. That nation has absolute right over all the others, including the right to launch wars. For Hegel, wars among nations are unavoidable and healthy representations of the evolution of the Absolute. The nation that wins the wars during a particular period is the one preferred by God. This position is not a permanent one. Each victorious, conquering nation comes closer to the ideal State than the one defeated—each represents a more perfect incarnation of World Reason.

The form of Hegel's collectivism is nationalism rather than the majority or mankind as a whole (i.e., a World State). Pitting one nation against another makes possible the even more perfect realization of the Universal Idea. Hegel argues that a World State would not have a contradiction and thus a resulting synthesis would be impossible. However, a World State would have a contradiction in anarchy with a potential resulting synthesis of freely chosen voluntary communities and associations.

Marx's Dictatorship of the Proletarian Majority

Marx (1818-1883) accepted Hegel's ideas in modified form contending that the Absolute, rather than being God, is nature (matter) unfolding itself in an endless process of dialectical development. Marx replaced Hegel's Spirit with matter and economic interests. By substituting economic forces for the Absolute as the definer of history, Marx thereby secularized Hegel's theory. In addition, he replaced Hegel's warring states with the class struggle and Hegel's monarchy with the dictatorship of the proletariat. By proclaiming that the Absolute is simply a reflection of matter, Marx uses the dialectic as the ruling force in the evolution of history. Social events are thus rooted in, and determined by, matter. Historical phenomena such as culture, philosophy, politics, and religion are determined by economic factors such as the method of production. At each stage of history, the class that controls the means of production controls society. Not a static situation, each mode of production generates an opposing movement.

Marx liked the Hegelian idea that moral ideals are realized in the march of history, but wanted to seek the ideal in the real itself. Marx learned the dialectical method, through which one looks for contradictions, from Hegel, but transformed Hegel's dialectical idealism into dialectical materialism. He thereby switched the focus from Hegel's vertical transcendence to his own emphasis on horizontal transcendence. Marx was a materialist who repudiated Hegel's doctrine of the primacy of consciousness (i.e., thought) and who believed that the nature of thought is determined by the material reality of that which it reflects.

The pivotal person in this transition was Ludwig Feuerbach who taught that men were mistaken when they gave away their humanity to a "God illusion." He said that people were attributing to God all the good and admirable traits of man, thereby leaving men impoverished and alienated. For Feuerbach, God (and religion) is the projection into the heavens of man's deepest longings. The individual man, realizing that he himself is not perfect, combines all the virtues and perfections of all the people and projects a composite figure into the heavens and calls it God. Feuerbach proclaims that this is mistaken and that all the purported perfections of God are already in the species man as a whole. Declaring that man is a species being who lives for the species, he states that if such a being believes in a transcendent God then he necessarily feels alienated from his true essence. Feuerbach tells us that we can reclaim our essence by calling back this projection from the sky and instead turn to worshipping mankind (i.e., ourselves) in the collective. He says that Hegel was teaching us to love the wrong thing and thus to hate ourselves.

Feuerbach proclaimed that Hegel's philosophy was a fantastic imagining and that the truth was actually anthropological with man's essence existing in his productive work. In order to reclaim man's essence, men would need to change the conditions under which they worked. This could be done by shifting people's love from God to mankind and by taking part in work communally for the benefit of all of mankind.

Marx was attracted to Feuerbach's idea of the sensible and concrete goal of making actual the humanity that is within us and on earth. Marx focused on actions taken to change the material world and the conditions under which we work. Whereas Feuerbach saw man enriching God and degrading and alienating man by making Him the creator (or grand producer), Marx more particularly saw the enrichment of the capitalist and the impoverishment and alienation of the workers as mankind's greatest problem. Marx's goal was to overcome the duality between owner and nonowner and to transcend and end economic classes, the source of the conflict.

Marx believed that a society preceded recorded human history in which men experienced no sense of alienation because there was no alienated production. Under a system of primitive communism, the necessary product was produced for the whole tribe, the division of labor was absent, and the worker actualized himself as a species being.

By some means, men entered into patterns of alienated production and the accumulation of private property. Men began to appropriate the products of other people's labor for their own purposes. The products a man produced confronted him as things apart from him and thus he was alienated from his work. Alienation, a parting or estrangement with something, occurs when products are taken by employers as well as when products are transferred to fellow workers when a job is broken up into specialties and workers separated into rigid categories. Man is non-alienated when he sees the whole product. Man is alienated from the product of his labor when the capitalist appropriates it. The wage earner is thus alienated from the product of his labor. He is alienated from himself by private property that sets him against others and separates him from his social nature. Man's life forces are taken from him under the system of alienated labor.

For Marx, the division of labor is forced labor. Contrary to man's real essence, the division of labor is what is wrong with the world. It is the division of labor that creates class differences and suppresses the unity of the human race (i.e., the species). Marx, like Rousseau, argued that the longing for private property led to the division of labor, which, in time, gave rise to the existence of separate social classes based on economic differences.

Marx saw the essential nature of man as a species being who labors cooperatively. He argues that language is a social product and that, in time, language is the creator of reason (i.e., consciousness). Reason, for Marx, is a social product! The social whole is the locus of reason and the essence of man's reason is collective. According to Marx, man's potentialities are those of the entire species. Thus, whenever man acts, he does so as a surrogate for the whole species. As a proxy or stand-in for humanity, a person's individual self is simply a manifestation of a fundamental underlying universal self. Only by activating the potentialities of the species can an individual find his fulfillment. It follows that truly human work is nonalienated labor through which a person has the opportunity to actualize the whole spectrum of human potentialities just as he has a mind to. Marx thus denies the legitimacy of the idea of the division of labor by saying that a person need not and should not be anything specific with respect to his work.

Alienated individuals are portrayed as worthless, degraded, and without dignity. There can be no self-esteem in a market economy. Marx says that a person can only truly fulfill himself when he acts as a species being. It is only when a man's explicit, honest, and direct motive is to produce for mankind that he can fulfill his true self, his species self. Influenced by Kant, Marx argued that a man loses his moral worth when he produces efficiently for the market. The fact that he is specializing for his own benefit indicates that he is not pursuing the ethics of the whole species. Marx thus echoes Kant's conflict between the desire to benefit and succeed and the pursuit of one's moral worth. A person's motive is what counts in the moral sphere. A man's true self is his universal self. Marx agreed with Kant's notion that man has a deeply concealed essence. Marx thus sees man as having two selves—a fragmented, alienated, greedy, success-seeking self and his universal species self. Marx's ultimate goal is to overcome, through revolution, the separation of man from his true self caused by the modern world of work. He wants to put man in a position in which he can engage in any kind of work that he wants to. His goal is to end alienation by reuniting man's life with his essence. He wants men to realize that only when they all achieve do any of them achieve. For Marx, the purpose of work is the development of man as a collective (i.e., of the species man). Marx believes that in communism, man will become reunited with his species essence—his abstract, communal essence. At that time, the full potential of human life will be released. Marx's goal is a future society in time and space that would permit a full, harmonious, and perfect human existence.

Marx states that the sole and permanent cause of history is the change from one mode of economic production to another. He even views consciousness as a derivative of economic factors. For Marx, consciousness is a by-product of the material forces of production. The individual's mind is shaped by his tools and by organization of the workplace.

According to Marx's doctrine of historical materialism (called dialectical materialism by some later writers), the laws of history are based exclusively on the material (i.e., economic) conditions of life. Marx considers the economic factor the key to the evolution and interpretation of all human history. Marx thus adapted the Hegelian dialectic to a materialist theory of human society.

For Marx, all history is explained in terms of the nature and development of the factors of production, including both the material forces of production and the social relations of production. The material forces of production, which Marx assumes to tend to grow, include technology, factories, machinery, and so on. The social relations of production include all the rules directing men in their use of the material forces of production. The social relations of productions include answers to questions such as: Who owns? Who gives orders? Who takes orders? etc. It is the material forces of production that lead to the social relations of production. The social relations of production equal what Marx terms the base of society, the rules governing a man's access to the means of production. These social relations of production comprise what we would call civil society.

Changes in the forces of production and the relations of production altered society's economic structure resulting in mankind's fall from the age of communal property and primitive communism. A social superstructure forms around the economic structure to justify and enshrine it. This superstructure is determined by the base of society and is made up of all the laws, philosophies, religions, moral codes, ideologies, politics, educational institutions, books, and other aspects of culture. As the material forces of production change, there is tension between them and the old social relations of production. Eventually, a massive revolutionary change takes place, resulting in new social relations. In turn, the social superstructure changes in response to the changes in the base of society.

According to Marx, the forces of production via the social superstructure have produced two separate forms of social consciousness—one for the owners and one for the nonowners. After a while, the social superstructure lags behind and becomes archaic, resulting in a reactionary false consciousness. Marx explains that some people want to preserve the social superstructure (i.e., capitalism) despite the fact that new forces of production render it ready for change. Of course, there are some insightful progressives, like Marx himself, who understand the changes that need to be made! Although the forces of production are evolving, the advanced productive energy is constrained by the old social superstructure. Tension between the change agents for the future and those supporting the old social superstructure will lead to revolution and the overthrow of the old social superstructure and its replacement with a new one to justify the new economic structure. Numerous incremental and quantitative changes and tensions accumulate until a sudden and radical qualitative change takes place via a revolutionary process.

People, who are aware of the new forces of production, those being exploited by the old social superstructure, develop a class consciousness and rise up to overthrow the old superstructure. Marx explains that worker exploitation is the catalyst for the objective conditions necessary for the defeat of the capitalist social superstructure. At that point, a dictatorship of the proletariat will take control of the state in order to eradicate capitalism. For Marx, the state is an instrument of social control used by the members of one class to suppress the members of another class. The state recognizes the rights of the possessing class in order to exploit the non-possessing class. It follows that the proletariat must use the state to destroy the remnants of capitalism and its ideology. After the demise of capitalism, there will be no more need for a state because only one class, the proletariat, will then exist.

Whereas Kant had taken the mind's structure as a given, Marx contends that all men do not have the same method of thinking—humanity can be split into contending groups, each with its own distinct mode of consciousness and competing with one another in its efforts to define reality. Each group thus creates its own truth. There is a different truth and a different logic for each type of person. Marx thus pluralized Kant's social subjectivism by proclaiming that each rival economic class has its own way of defining the truth.

The labor theory of value is a key concept in Marxian ideology. Marx held that the value of commodities is determined by the amount of labor used in making them. Labor power is the only commodity capable of generating surplus value. The source of profit is the difference between the value of the labor sold by the worker and the value of the commodity that was produced through his labor. Workers are systematically exploited because the difference accrues to the capitalist. The worker is cheated because the employer, rather than paying him the full value of his labor, keeps the profit for himself. The employer does this by paying less to the worker than the valued added by his labor. Capitalists pay laborers enough for their sustenance, appropriate the surplus value, and reinvest it in more capital. As capital becomes greater in proportion to labor, the source of the surplus value is reduced, and the workers are forced to work longer, harder, or for reduced pay rates. Ironically, whereas the capitalist's goal is to gain surplus value, he undermines the very source of surplus value by exploiting the workers.

Marx distinguishes between production for use and production for exchange. He explains that it is unnatural to produce for exchange rather than for use. Whereas a product has use value, a commodity, which is made for sale or trade, combines use value with exchange value. Exchange value is found in the social relations of production. When one produces for use he is fulfilling his species unity. Contrariwise, with respect to commodity production, one produces for the market, destroys the joy found in creation, breaks up the original unity of the production process, no longer controls his product, and becomes competitive and alienated. All commodity production necessitates a sacrifice of labor under alienating circumstances.

Marx explains that social institutions should conform to a given mode of production. Revolution is inevitable when they fail to do so. He argues that the contradictions inherent in a capitalistic society will lead to a class struggle between economic groups that will ultimately result in a classless society. Unlike Hegel, Marx is only concerned with one triad—capital, labor, and the classless society.

As the objective conditions for revolution come into being, the proletariat develops a class consciousness or awareness of their circumstances and exploitation by the capitalists. The proletariat wants a classless society and economic equality, rather than just equality under the law. By acting for all men, like Hegel's hero in history, they will seize the state and eliminate private property, the division of labor, and class barriers. The state as the representative for the dominant class will deteriorate and will simply become an administrative body for all. Alienation will end under communism where the purpose of work will be seen as the production of the species man, our essential being. Man will no longer be separated from man—he will be totally social.

For Marx, history can only be understood as a succession of class struggles in which primitive communism gave way to slavery, slavery to feudalism, feudalism to capitalism, with capitalism yielding to socialism and eventually communism. Only then will class divisions and alienation end and will man be reunited with his essence.

Marx argues that this revolution is not just another step in the dialectical process because the oppressed group is so massive that they become representative of humanity. In addition, their suffering is so harsh and intense that they embody the essence of all human suffering and thus desire to end all of mankind's pain and hardships. Because the revolution is different from all others, there will be an end to the process. The victory of the proletariat means the extinction of class societies and the end of class struggles.

Marx argues that under capitalism the proletariat has gradually absorbed all social groups except for a small contingent of capitalists. The victory of the proletariat will thus be a win for almost everyone in society (except the capitalists). Class conflict will end and class divisions will have been eliminated once the proletarian victory has been achieved. The spirit of true community can only be established gradually by abolishing the causes of selfishness and by a long process of education.

Between the overthrow of the capitalistic system (and the bourgeois state) and the rise of a new society in which the individual functions as a cell within a living body, Marx calls for the interim rule of the dictatorship of the proletariat. During this proletarian stage of socialism, the proletarian majority will use the state in behalf of the overwhelming mass of the people. After capitalism has been conquered, there will be no further need for the state. Marx contends that soon this form of state will itself disappear as selfishness, force, and coercion vanish from human relations. Marx did not accept Hegel's idealization of the state. Rather, he longed for its eventual and gradual atrophy, with its function falling into disuse in a fully socialized society that guarantees the highest possible degree of happiness for everyone.

As the exchange economy crumbles, the move to communism takes place. Goods and services will be moved from the exchange system to the social dividend system and will be distributed to citizens according to need. The Hobbesian struggle of "all against all" will disappear because there will be plenty of goods and services to go around and no need for competition or theft. With no need for force, there will be no need for the state to keep order and security.

Marx thought that man was only rational as a species. Rationality was not an inherent characteristic of the individual whose decisions were chaotic and based on what he called product fetishes. Because it is only society or the group as a whole that can think rationally, Marx called for economic decisions to be made by a rational group of central economic planners. Marx's assumed ever-expanding forces of production called for the policy of conscious collectivist planning for the production of goods and services for the use of society as a whole.

Marx condemns capitalism because it is alienating; he does not view it as necessarily unjust. Only if one's direct motive is to produce for the species, instead of for himself, can a man truly fulfill his real self. He says that we are fortunate because there are latent and inherent problems or contradictions in capitalism that will lead to a revolution of the proletariat and the overthrow of capitalism. These conditions include the increasing misery of the proletariat as capitalists try to get more out of their workers, declining profits, and periodic and deepening crises and business cycles.

Marx's humanistic doctrines supplied a flexible philosophical basis for many of the reigns of terror experienced during the twentieth century. The implication of his idea of the communal nature of man is that the individualist who diverges from this doctrine is branded as being against human nature. His tenets of historical materialism, class consciousness, and the collective nature of thought and rationality lead to polylogism and group warfare. To these are added his convictions that production for gain and trade is inhuman and alienating, that the division of labor is malignant, that a person's need constitutes a claim, and that private property in the means of production must be abolished. Given all of the above, there will always be some group of intellectuals who "know" what is best for everyone and who are ready to use force to enforce their convictions. Of course, they want to employ some other oppressed class to battle for these changes.

Marx fails to explain how a communist society could abandon the specialization of labor that made the wealth and productivity of modern society possible while concurrently retaining modern production methods. In addition, he did not grasp the illogic of his labor theory of value. He did not comprehend that the value of labor stems from the value of the laborer's product that is determined by supply and demand. He had it backwards. The value of the product is not determined by the value of the labor. He also failed to see man as an entity with a specific nature. According to Marx's concept of human nature, man had both an essential nature as a human being and an historical nature that developed and evolved. With respect to this historical nature, Marx viewed man as a process to be changed. He also envisioned a changeable world that, having been constrained for centuries, would progressively become less constrained and ultimately unconstrained in some future time when there will be abundance, no alienation, no state, no egoism, no psychological insecurity, production for use, and no production for profit. In short, everything will be public and the individual will become fully socialized.

Chris Matthew Sciabarra has observed that Marx's Utopian view of the world is essentially an acontextual, ahistorical quest for human ideals with no understanding of the limits or nature of reason. Marx's historical materialism presumes a kind of synoptic knowledge on the movement of history that is invalid because it drops the real context of human conduct. Marx's problem arises when he steps into the future to evaluate the present from an imagined future vantage point that holds as one of its premises the possibility of "total knowledge" which enables the proletariat to plan the society with virtually no deleterious unintended consequences.

Marx assumes the information required by future planners will be available despite the fact that these planners will have destroyed the mechanisms (i.e., the price system), which permits such information to be generated and socially traded. Marx is projecting that the same kinds of knowledge will be available to a future generation of planners in the absence of the context that makes such knowledge possible and specific to a particular time and place.

Marx is placing himself outside the very historical process that he analyzes. It is as though he is permitting himself privileged access to information about a future that is ontologically and epistemologically impossible. Marx's flawed vision presumes a total and omniscient grasp of history, the possibility of godlike planning and control, and a mastery of the many resources, tacit practices, and consequence of social action.

Dewey's Pragmatism and Activism

American pragmatism represents an activist development of Kant and Hegel's idealism. As a theory of mutable truth, pragmatism claims that ideas are true insofar as they are useful in a specific situation—what works today in one case may not work tomorrow in another case. The standard of moral truth is expediency. Ethical ideas are accepted as long as they continue to work. According to John Dewey's (1859-1952) social pragmatism, what is true is that which works for a society (not for an individual) through the promotion of the public good. Dewey advocates a relativistic, secularized form of altruism that calls for sacrificing oneself to attain the ends of the People. In this view, society rather than the individual passes moral judgment. Social policies are measured by their consequences instead of by abstract principles of what is right or just. There are no facts, no set rules of logic, no objectivity, and no certainty. There are only policies and proposals for social actions that must be treated as working hypotheses. The experience of consequences will indicate the need to keep or alter the original hypotheses.

Knowledge of the world is impossible apart from actions on it. There is no reality out there—both facts and values are products of men interacting with an environment and shaping it to their wills. Society for Dewey is something free men create out of their intellects and imaginations. An advocate of social malleability, he speaks of men reconstructing what they have experienced in order to impose a particular character on it, thereby bringing an explicit reality into being. Men are free to choose their own way of thinking and to create whatever reality they want to embrace. However, a man's mind is conditioned by the collective thinking of other people. The mind is thus a social phenomenon—truth is what works for the group.

It is participation in the common life of democratic society that realizes the freedom of the individual and produces growth in him and in society. Democracy expresses the consensus of the collective—society is a moral organism with a "general will." Each man is to do his duty by adapting himself to the ever-changing views of the group.

Men simply act. They usually do not and need not reflect before acting. The goal of thought is merely to reconstruct the situation in order to solve the problem. If the proposal when implemented resolves the issue then the idea is pragmatically true. Truth cannot be known in advance of action. One must first act and then think. Only then can reality be determined.

Value judgments are to be made according to desires based on feelings. The test of one's desire is its congruity with the majority of other men's wishes, feelings, and values at that time. These, of course, can be examined and abandoned in a future situation. Value judgments are instrumental, never completed, and therefore are corrigible. In the end it is feeling for the pragmatist that is paramount.

Dewey was primarily concerned with the democratic ideal and its realization in every sphere of life. He advocates education as a way to reconstruct children according to the pragmatist vision of man. Child-centered, rather than subject-centered, education treats the student as an acting being and therefore is focused on discrete, experiential projects. Dewey dismisses as irrelevant the teaching of fundamental knowledge such as reading, writing, math, and science. Both the educator and the students are to be flexible and tentative. The purpose of a school is to foster social consciousness. The child is to be taught to transcend the assimilation of truths and facts by learning to serve and adapt to others and to comply with the directives of their representatives. A disdain for reason and knowledge is thus combined with the practice of altruism (otherism) and collectivism.

Like Marx, Dewey comprehended and appreciated the conflictual essence of the Hegelelian dialectic. Dewey stressed the clash in the education process between the child and the curriculum and between the potential and talent of the student and the structure of an outmoded school system. The traditional curriculum, loaded down with formal subjects, was unsuited to the child's active and immediate experience. Dewey saw children as alienated from their academic work because of a contradiction between the interests of the school and the real interests of the students. There was an incongruity between the values, goals, and means embodied in the experience of a mature adult and those of an undeveloped, immature being. The teaching of abstract, general principles, and eternal and external truths was beyond a child's understanding and a barrier to the authentic growth and development of the child.

Dewey's new school would become a vehicle for the dealienation and socialization of the child. The school would be an embryonic socialist community in which the progress of the student could only be justified by his relation to the group. Dewey's activity method and manual training could produce a collective occupational spirit in the school.

Dewey, like Marx, was convinced that thought is a collective activity in which the individual simply acts as a cell in the social body. For Dewey, the individual is only a conduit conveying the group's influence with a person's beliefs deriving from others through tradition, education, and the environment. Dewey's notion that thought is collective, along with his enmity toward human reason and individual responsibility, led to his advocacy of collectivist economic planning. For Dewey, cognition is an activity of the group or society as a whole and innovations are the products of collective science and technology rather than the creation of individual thinkers and doers.

Rekindling the Philosophy of Freedom

There has been a steady erosion of the ideas upon which our nation was founded. The thoughts of the philosophers discussed earlier led the revolt against the ideas of negative freedom, natural rights, a knowable reality, the power of man's intellect, the limited state, individualism, and the good life as one of personal self-fulfillment. These ideas have been replaced in the minds of many academicians (mainly in the arts, humanities, and social sciences), politicians, economists, novelists, journalists, media people, labor leaders, and others with the ideas of positive freedom, welfare rights, skepticism, relativism, pragmatism, the welfare state, collectivism, and the virtuous life as one of self-sacrifice. An ironic double message of this new worldview is that: (1) an individual cannot be certain of anything; and (2) society knows (at least as far as "knowledge" is possible), thus requiring the individual to conform to its beliefs. We are told not to worry about this apparent contradiction—as Hegel explained, contradictions provide the means for attaining the truth!

There is a desperate need to return to the thought of the rational philosophers who provided the theoretical basis for our country—Aristotle, Aquinas, Locke, Smith, etc. In addition, the writings of more contemporary thinkers such as Hayek, Mises, Rand, Rothbard, Nozick, Friedman, Hazlitt, and others also exhibit the premises of a proreason, reality-based view of life. We need citizens who will insist on the principles underlying a free society as explained by these thinkers. We need to change public opinion through education and persuasion.

Encourage professors to proclaim a rational profreedom philosophy in their college courses. Support private enterprise, privatization, collegiate entrepreneurship programs, and school choice. Come back to teach classes yourself. Join free-market oriented organizations. Donate freedom-oriented books to community and university libraries. Support solely academic programs that are consistent with the freedom philosophy. Reach out to politicians, economists, writers and other media people, the entertainment community, clergymen, professionals in a variety of fields, and the general public by explaining and teaching by example the worth and meaning of values and ideas such as the free market, limited government, private property, honesty, integrity, self-reliance, and responsibility.

History is made by men and their ideas. The Industrial Revolution, America, and capitalism were the result of the ideas of individual rights, private property, religious freedom, and limited government. Similarly, collectivist ideas produced the totalitarian states, the world wars of the twentieth century, the New Deal, Hitler's national socialism, and today's welfare state.

Despite the downfall of socialism in Eastern Europe and the U.S.S.R., its doctrines and values live on in the minds of many Americans. The philosophy of collectivism still dominates the world today. Consequently, there is a need for us to be able to recognize and refute the fallacies and errors of the basic premises of collectivism so thoroughly that even the collective leaders themselves will understand and acknowledge their errors. If we can reach and convert these intellectual leaders, they in turn can help us convince the masses and future intellectual leaders of the superiority of a free society. By awakening public interest in sound philosophical ideas, we can rekindle the freedom philosophy.

Recommended Reading

Boorstin, Daniel J. *The Seekers*. New York: Random House, 1998.

Copleston, Frederick. *A History of Philosophy*. New York: Doubleday, 1985.

Ebenstein, William, and Alan O. Ebenstein. *Great Political Thinkers: Plato to the Present*. New York: Harcourt, 2000.

Flew, Anthony. *Introduction to Western Philosophy*. London: Thames and Hudson, 1989.

Hayek, Friedrich A. *Individualism and Economic Order*. Chicago: University of Chicago Press, 1948.

Höffding, Harold. *History of Modern Philosophy*. New York: Dover Publications, 1924.

Hohlander, Paul. *Political Pilgrims: Western Intellectuals in Search of the Good Society*. New Brunswick, N.J.: Transaction Publishers, 1998.

Jones, W. T. *A History of Western Philosophy*. New York: Harcourt, Brace, & World, 1962.

Kenny, Anthony. *A Brief History of Western Philosophy*. Oxford: Blackwell, 1998.

Levin, Yuval. *Tyranny of Reason*. Lanham, Md.: University Press of America, 2001.

Mises, Ludwig von. *Theory and History*. Westport, Conn.: Arlington, 1969.

Peikoff, Leonard. *The Ominous Parallels*. New York: Stein & Day, 1982.

Popper, Karl. *The Open Society and Its Enemies*. Princeton, N.J.: Princeton University Press, 1971.

Rosen, Stanley, ed. *The Examined Life: Readings in Western Philosophy from Plato to Kant*. New York: Random House, 2000.

Sabine, George H. *A History of Political Theory*. New York: Holt, Rinehart, &

Winston, 1961.

Schneider, H. W. *A History of American Philosophy*. New York: Columbia University Press, 1963.

Strauss, Leo, and Joseph Cropsey, eds. *History of Political Philosophy*. Chicago: University of Chicago Press, 1987.

Stumpf, Samuel. *Socrates to Sartre*. New York: McGraw-Hill, 1993.

Thornton, Bruce S. *Plagues of the Mind*. Wilmington, Del.: ISI Books, 1997.

Windelband, Wilhelm. *History of Philosophy*. New York: Harper and Row, 1958.

19

Cultural Relativism

The promoters of multiculturalism in America are unhappy with their country's culture. They are alienated from its capitalistic Eurocentric values, a culture that has given its people—including those who despise it—more prosperity, creature comforts, freedom, rights, and opportunity than any other culture in the world, past or present. Having lavishly benefited from the abundant fruits of this culture . . . they evidently see no challenge left for them. . . . Thus meaning and satisfaction lie in championing the cultures of other peoples' and minority groups, who are "oppressed" by the Euro-American culture.

—Alvin J. Schmidt

Relativism, the idea that truth is a historically conditioned notion that does not transcend cultural boundaries, has existed since the Greek era, some 2400 years ago. Relativism contends that all truth is relative except for the claim that "truth is relative."

Cultural relativism wrongly claims that each culture has its own distinct but equally valid mode of perception, thought, and choice. Cultural relativism, the opposite of the idea that moral truth is universal and objective, contends there is no such thing as absolute right and wrong. There is only right and wrong as specified by the moral code of each society. Within a particular society, a standard of right and wrong can be inviolate. Cultural relativism maintains that man's opinion within a given culture defines what is right and wrong.

Cultural relativism is the mistaken idea that there are no objective standards by which our society can be judged because each culture is entitled to its own beliefs and accepted practices. No one can object to any society's intolerance that reflects its indigenous worldview. Because there is no objective moral truth that pertains to all people and for all times, one moral code is no better or no worse than any other (i.e., the moral equivalence doctrine). Thus, we should not impose our values on other societies. It follows that, according to cultural relativism, we cannot object to Hitler and Naziism, Mayan infant sacrifice, China's massacre of students in Tiananmen Square, South Africa's apartheid, genital mutilation (i.e., female circumcision) of young girls in Africa, and so on, because each of these practices is justified by the worldview within which it exists. Nor could we contend that one culture is superior to another culture. In addition, we would also be prevented from criticizing our own culture's practices such as slavery. Furthermore, within the perspective of cultural relativism, there would be no need for, or argument for, social progress. Toward what objective goal would we progress?

Multiculturalism, racism, postmodernism, deconstructionism, political correctness, and social engineering are among cultural relativism's "intellectual" descendents. The remainder of the chapter addresses the philosophical underpinnings of these movements, analyzes each of them, and explains why Western culture is objectively superior to other cultures.

Philosophical Roots and Development of Cultural Relativism and Its Descendents

Relativism, the view that truth is different for each individual, social group, or historic period, had its beginnings during the ancient Greek period. However, it was David Hume (1711-1776) whose clear and rigorous formulation of this worldview made it an important idea in the Modern period. Hume argued for moral relativism because no one can know anything for certain. Consequently, a person is unable to pass judgment on alternative moral systems. Hume's skepticism claims that neither reason nor the senses can supply reliable knowledge and that, consequently, man is a helpless being in an unintelligible universe.

Hume attempted to destroy the concept of causality in the objective world. He argued that because all of our knowledge comes from experience, we couldn't have any knowledge of causality because we do not experience causality. According to Hume, what we refer to as causality is simply our habit of associating events because of experiencing them together, but this does not mean that the events have any necessary connection. Experiences of contiguity, priority, and constant conjunction do not imply a necessary connection between objects.

Immanuel Kant (1724-1804) agreed with Hume regarding the inability to see or prove causality in the objective (i.e., noumenal) world, but said that people will always experience the world in causal networks because causality is a feature of the subjective (i.e., phenomenal) world. Kant believed that men are cut off from the objective world and can never know the world in itself (i.e., as it is). However, the human mind has fundamental concepts, categories, or filters built into it through which man cognizes the world. Men structure the world that they experience so that it conforms to the human mind. Therefore, men never know things in themselves (i.e., as they really are) only as they appear given the method of man's cognitive operations. Reality as perceived by man's mind is distorted according to the nature of man's conceptual faculty.

Man's basic concepts (e.g., causality, time, space, entity, quality, quantity, etc.) do not stem from experience or reality but from an automatic system of concepts, categories, and filters in his consciousness which impose their own design on his perceptions of external reality and render him unable of perceiving it in any way other than the way in which he does perceive it.

Imagine that every human is born with red organic lenses in his eyes through which he sees the world. The world would appear red even though red is not a feature of the objective world in itself. Red is a feature of the subjective world. The functions of the mind's filters are analogous to that of such lenses.

Kant said that we see the world in terms of entities because we have an entity category built into our minds. For that same reason, we experience the world in terms of a system of causal networks. We can't know what is really out there in the objective world.

Kant's epistemological dualism states that there is an object in itself and the same object as it appears to us (i.e., as filtered through our epistemological apparatus). Kant holds that the mind is concurrently both helpless and creatively powerful. It is helpless with respect to knowing the objective world but it is omnipotent regarding the social world (i.e., the world as created by the human mind). Reality becomes social because people create reality.

According to Kant, there is only one type of human mind that is universally the same (except for individual idiosyncrasies that occur because of our humanity and hence imperfection). Each person has the same categories and thus constructs the world in the same way. As members of the same species, we each have the same processing apparatus.

Kant contended that reality (as far as we can know it) depends on the cognitive functioning of the human mind in total. Society sets the norms of truth and falsity and right and wrong. This is the essence of Kant's social primacy of consciousness theory in metaphysics. Man's ideas are essentially a collective delusion from which no person has the power to escape. If a man sees things differently than the majority, then he must be mistaken due to some defect in his own information processing mechanism. Since and because of Kant, "objectivity" is generally thought to mean collective subjectivism. Truth, to the extent that it can be known in the phenomenal world, is to be determined by means of public polls.

Kant believed that man's categories were unchangeable. Contrariwise, Hegel (1770-1831) argued that they evolve and change and that evolution is essential to understanding consciousness, history, and mankind. Marx (1818-1883) claimed that they changed differentially according to economic subgroups. This fragmentation or pluralization of Kant's social subjectivism has ultimately developed to the point where today's multiculturalists claim that groups create their own reality based on race, ethnicity, gender, sexual preference, etc.

Each multicultural subgroup has its own reality, its own logic, its own truth and falsity, and its own right and wrong. It is therefore impossible to discuss, argue, or judge any one group's truth as better than any other. With no way to reason among the groups, the only alternatives are either isolationism or group warfare through which political power is used to slug out group differences.

Rousseau (1712-1778) held that reason had its opportunity but had failed, claiming that the act of reflection is contrary to nature. Rousseau asserts that man's natural goodness has been depraved by the progress he has made and the knowledge he has acquired. He proceeded to attack the Age of Reason by emphasizing feeling, the opposite of reason, as the key to reality and the future. His thought thereby foreshadowed and gave impetus to the Romantic Movement.

Following Kant and Rousseau, the romanticists believed that reason is limited to the surface world of appearance, and that man's true source of knowledge is feeling, intuition, passion, or faith. In their view, man is essentially an emotional being and therefore must seek the truth and act accordingly. The virtuous individual was a "man of feeling" who was sensitive to the plights of others and who spontaneously exhibited sympathy, pity, and benevolence to them.

Godwin (1756-1836) had a profound sense of egalitarianism. He believed that it was desirable and just for the output of society, to which all contribute, to be shared among all with some degree of equalization. He viewed the differences among individuals as being the product of different social circumstances, not in inherent differences in people's abilities. Although he realized that some differences were the results of inheritance, he firmly believed that proper environmental structuring could overcome any inherent inequalities.

Nietzsche (1844-1900) contended that feeling and intuition are actually forms of reason and viewed the universe as a realm of colliding wills and violent conflict. He also held the view that a few superbeings (supermen or overmen) who were "beyond good and evil" had the right to rule the masses for their own higher purposes. These exceptional individuals, possessing the highest level of development of intellectual, physical, and emotional strength, would possess the courage to revalue all values and act with freedom to their internal Will to Power. As a result, the lowest levels of society would believe themselves to be exploited and oppressed and would experience a deep-rooted resentment. The result would be a negative psychic attitude, a will to the denial of life, and revenge in the form of translating the virtues of the superior into vices.

Kierkegaard (1813-1855) said that truth is subjectivity and that authentic existence is a matter of faith and commitment. In turn, Heidegger (1899-1976) maintained that (1) man is "thrown into the world"; (2) existence is unintelligible; (3) reason is invalid; (4) man is a creature in fear of the primary fact of his life—death; and (5) man is destined by his nature to "angst," estrangement, and futility. Heidegger's oftentimes-unintelligible writings can be described as the intellectual counterpart of modern art.

This brief review of philosophy has identified the roots of many of today's prevalent concepts, including relativism, social subjectivism, collectivism, determinism, pluralism, economic egalitarianism, irrationalism, elitism, and the will to power, resentment, and historical victimization. These are the concepts that underlie, in varying proportions, the various intellectual descendents of cultural relativism.

Multiculturalism

The main idea of multiculturalism is the equal value of all cultures (i.e., cultural relativism). However, multiculturalism does not mean cultures as normally understood but rather as biologically defined (i.e., ethnically, racially, or sexually defined) groups. Multiculturalism, a politicized form of cultural relativism, rejects the idea that there are general truths, norms, or rules with respect to both knowledge and morals. Gone are the Enlightenment beliefs in objectivity, reason and evidence, and principles of freedom and justice that apply equally to all individuals. Unlike cultural relativism, multiculturalism excludes one worldview from the realm of equally valid worldviews—the Eurocentric Western perspective based on the contributions of dead white males. Multiculturalists dismiss the significance of Western civilization by claiming that Western traditions of elitism, racism, and sexism are the cause of most of our current problems. They accept a Romantic view of human nature as beneficent and benign until it was corrupted by flawed Western ideology and culture.

Multiculturalism implies that race, ethnicity, and sex (or sexual preference) have an inescapable effect on the way people think and/or the values they hold or are capable of holding. There are many closed systems of perception, thought, and feeling each affiliated with some biologically defined group. Rational dialogue among individuals from different groups is precluded because each group has its own "truth" and standards for its attainment. The multiculturalist maintains that each person is simply a representative of a particular biologically defined perspective who must agree with his own group's worldview (unless he wants to be ostracized) and thus be unable to rationally discuss and meaningfully evaluate and critique ideas with representatives of other groups. Multiculturalism thus destroys an individual's confidence in his own mind—this occurs when a person allows his group to tell him what to believe.

At one time, truth was viewed as transcendent, fixed, and unchanging. Epistemological egalitarianism has accompanied the loss of transcendence. Each group of persons now is thought to have an equal right to make truth claims. Think of the absurdity in which unreflected upon opinions are weighted equally with well-thought-out opinions in today's numerous opinion polls that tend to be tabulated according to biologically defined categories. Truth is now thought to be a constructed cultural product that is immanent in each individual culture or subgroup. For the multiculturalist, truth only exists by consensus within each biologically defined group.

Multiculturalism is anti-individualistic in the sense that it expects each person to agree with the perceptions, thoughts, and judgments of his group in order for his own perceptions, thoughts, and judgments to be legitimate. The multiculturalist believes that a person's thoughts are either the collectively constructed thoughts of his racial, ethnic, or sexual group or are the thoughts foisted upon him by the dominant white male worldview. A ruling premise of multiculturalism is that ethnic origin carries with it irrevocable attributes—if a person has a certain name and physical features, then he must have a particular perspective on life and the world. Multiculturalists assign each rational and autonomous individual into a group based on the group's specific, absolute, and nondebatable dissemblances from other groups.

Multiculturalism attempts to replace individual rights with collectivism by assuming that a man's identity and value are derived solely from biology, and that what is important is not what a person does as an individual, but rather what some members of his biological group currently do or did years ago. It follows that collective guilt replaces individual responsibility—a person must assume the responsibility for acts committed by his ancestors and pay for these acts ad infinitum.

The victim mentality is both a cause and effect of multiculturalism. Multiculturalism promotes a culture of victims who have a perpetual claim on society and the government. The result is the division of society into political interest groups with conflicting demands that cannot all be met.

Educational proposals from multiculturalists attempt to inculcate in students the idea that Western classical liberal order is, in fact, the most oppressive order of all times. As a result, people are taught to view themselves as victims. This perspective is based on the relativistic assumption that because all cultures are inherently equal, differences in wealth, power, and accomplishments between cultures are, for the most part, due to oppression. Thus, in order to establish cultural equality, multiculturalists emphasizing non-Western virtues and Western oppression dismiss the illiberal traditions of other cultures and attack the ideas of a common culture based on an intellectual, moral, and artistic legacy derived from the Greeks and the Bible.

There would be no harm in multiculturalism if the term simply meant that we should acknowledge and teach truths about many cultures. It is admirable to teach students both the noblest aspects of various cultures and of their failings. Unfortunately, multiculturalism's pluralism and relativism has engendered a reluctance to acknowledge anything positive about Western culture while concurrently maintaining a nonreflective and approving position toward non-Western and minority ideas. Students are taught that no "properly educated" person would be willing to pass judgment on another culture. If a student should deny the equality of all cultures he would be told he was guilty of "ethnocentrism."

Multicultural educational policies are based on the mistaken notion that cultures consist of mostly benign characteristics. In actual fact, there are both laudable and condemnable aspects of all cultures. Once it is recognized that different cultures exhibit varying degrees of good and evil, it becomes appropriate to inquire which culture exhibits the best characteristics on an overall basis. Some cultures are better than others: reason is better than force; a free society is superior to slavery; and productivity is better than stagnation.

Multiculturalists argue that education can build the self-esteem of minority students by presenting non-Western cultures in a favorable light in order to compensate for historical and curricular injustices, thereby restoring cultural parity between ethnic groups. Replacing education with therapy, the multiculturalist attempts to enhance self-esteem by teaching the students of oppressed cultures to be proud of their particular ancestry or race. This will only work if there are laudable truths that can be taught about a student's ethnic heritage. When education is turned into therapy, the likely result is to teach history not to ascertain truth but to empower (i.e., enhance the self-esteem) of various factions. The result is the introduction of distortions, half-truths, fabrications, and myths into the curriculum in order to make students from certain groups feel good. In addition, multiculturalists denounce the emphasis in American schools on American history and culture and western civilization. Some even portray western civilization and Americans as evil and ideas such as reason and objective truth as Eurocentric (and patriarchal for the feminist) biases with the purpose of exploiting oppressed cultures.

Academic standards of excellence are of no use to the multiculturalist because they are simply means through which the dominant culture oppresses minority cultures. Not only are objective tests denounced as racist, multiculturalists demand that students be graded only within their cultural or racial group and/or that tests be redesigned so that minority students perform on the average as well as those in the dominant cultural group.

Students are instructed that there are no objective merits or failings of theories, arguments, policies, works of art, and literature, etc. Instead, they are only valorizations of power that require deconstruction in order to reveal their true nature as devices of repression. It is Marxism that has provided multiculturalism with its rationale and concepts (e.g., oppression, imperialism, inequality, revolutionary change) that are used to devalue and destroy American culture.

The goal of the multiculturalist is to change the United States from a culturally assimilated society to an unassimilated multicultural society with a wide range of cultures and subcultures accorded equal status. Multiculturalism promotes quotas rather than competition, allocating resources rather than earning them, and a cabinet that looks like America instead of one that has an adequate background to do the required job. Multiculturalists fail to see that the diversity methods they use to find and create diversity will, in fact, divide the country. The result will be a widespread, societal tendency toward hatred, revenge, or belief in the innate superiority of one's group and a feeling of solidarity and self-righteousness.

Racism

Racism, a type of multiculturalism, is the erroneous idea that a person's race determines his identity. It is the belief that one's values, beliefs, and character are determined by one's ancestry rather than by the judgments of one's mind. In the name of diversity and multiculturalism many Americans are taught to base their sense of self in their racial or ethnic identity. In fact, "critical race theory" contends that there is no reality independent of a person's ethnicity, no universal rules of logic, and no objective facts. Accordingly, each person is destined to interpret events according to the sentiments of his racial group. Such an attack on reason creates a herd mentality by which people thoughtlessly follow those who proclaim themselves to be the leaders.

Racial preference is the common ingredient of the diversity movement (i.e., diversity awareness, training, hiring, admissions, accommodations, etc.). Proponents do not realize that racism cannot be cured with more racism. When people are taught to think in racial terms instead of according to individual merit and character, and groups are identified as having special status (e.g., affirmative action programs), the logical result is likely to be warranted resentment and indignation.

Obviously, the rational and proper approach is to evaluate candidates based on individual merit. This simply means appraising candidates based on their possession of relevant knowledge and skills, their willingness to exert the requisite effort, and their possession of a good moral character.

The diversity movement states that its purpose is to eradicate racism and produce tolerance of differences. This is a pretense. A person cannot teach that identity is determined by race and then expect people to view each other as individuals. The idea of deriving one's identity from one's race is depraved. People have competent minds, efficacious intellects, and free wills that enable them to be judged as individuals.

A person cannot inherit moral virtue or moral vice. Think of the absurdity of recent proposals for apologies and compensation on behalf of America and the U.S. government to Afro-Americans whose ancestors suffered as slaves. This proposal assumes that whites today, who have never owned slaves, are almost universally against racism, and who bear no individual responsibility for slavery, somehow hold a "collective responsibility" solely by being members of the same race as the slave owners of the Old South. A person who is a member of a certain race cannot legitimately be blamed for the deeds of other members of that race unless people are simply interchangeable cogs within a racial collective. Compensation for slavery means randomly chastising today's whites by taxing them and denying them jobs, promotions, and admissions to schools through welfare and affirmative action programs, in order to reward chance blacks. Individuals should be judged based on their own actions. They should be rewarded on their own merits and should not be compelled to apologize or pay for acts committed by others, simply because those others are of the same race.

Individualism is the only acceptable alternative to racism. It is essential to recognize that each person is a sovereign entity with the power of independent judgment and choice.

Political Correctness

Multiculturalism leads to politically correct language. Such language must be consistent with multiculturalist principles. This means that language should: (1) not favor one group over another; (2) not infringe on any group's right to sovereignty; (3) not interfere with the peaceful relationship of any minority group with those from other groups; (4) not hinder society (i.e., the state) in its attempts to protect cultural groups (i.e., social, economic, and ethnic minorities) whose views are declared to be equally valid and who have the "right" to equal opportunity, integrity, and point of view; and (5) not promote stereotypes of any kind.

The obsession of the morally superior, sensitive, and conspicuously compassionate elite with the subjective feelings of people is part of today's prevailing therapeutic vision of man. This infatuation with sensitivity has spread throughout the media and academia, leading to the creation of feel-good euphemisms which part with accuracy and unambiguity in the interest of feeling and sympathy. Unfortunately, these "linguistic smile buttons" simply camouflage reality rather than change it.

Advocates of political correctness attempt to homogenize our language and thought not only to enhance the self-esteem of minorities, women, and beneficiaries of the welfare state but also to preserve the moral image of the welfare state itself. One approach to reaching this goal is to eliminate disparaging, discriminatory, or offensive words and phrases and the substitutions of harmless vocabulary at the expense of economy, clarity, and logic. Another approach is to deconstruct a word or phrase into its component parts, treat the component parts as wholes, and focus on secondary meanings of the component parts. For example, the term *mankind* is said to be exclusive, misleading, and biased when it is employed to refer to both men and women.

The politically correct fail to understand that language is the result of an evolved social process that results in a systemic order achieved without the use of a deliberate overall plan. Language simply arises out of accidents, experiences, and historical borrowings and corruptions of other languages. No one intended to exclude women when generic terms like *he* or *mankind* were used. With respect to human beings, the male gender was used to denote the species. On the other hand, both countries and ships are referred to as *she*. Using *he* or *she* or *him* or *her* simply clutters the language and conveys no further information. However, such use does imply that those who use the masculine terms hold hostile or exclusionary thoughts toward women! This leads people to believe that every use of generic male terms is evidence of male antagonism toward women when, in fact, such usage merely avoids awkward phrases and cluttered language.

Political correctness supplies a language through which it is easy to be a victim and always someone or something that can be blamed. Think of terms like *culturally deprived, developmentally challenged*, etc. Political correctness involves a lot of people attempting to explain the reasons for their lack of great success. These victim-type explanations or excuses generally include the idea that a person is having a rough time because of his particular race or gender. Essentially, political correctness is a way to rationalize who you are and why you are not better than what or who you are.

Victims are taught that their failures and suffering are invariably the result of some unfair and rectifiable condition that social engineers could remedy if the insensitive would simply let them. This reinforces the erroneous views that human life is perfectible and that all suffering is a deviation that can be corrected. People are led to believe that the world should be a place where they never suffer disappointment or failure. Of course, the tragic truth is that people can fail and that individuals are unequal in talents and achievements.

On some campuses seeking higher standards of human accomplishments is no longer valued as highly as politically correct thinking. Academic freedom through free speech is accompanied by high social costs on campuses, where truth is viewed as nothing more than different perspectives being offered by different groups in order to promote their own interests. Education-imposed biases restrict students' thinking when curricula are developed to be nonsexist, peace centered, antibiased, and politically correct.

Political correctness (and multiculturalism) threatens free speech in both the academic sphere and the nonacademic workplace and ultimately the very foundation of American society. The government has, in essence, eliminated most free speech protection in the workplace. Free speech, which is an economic good to academics through which they make their living, has fared somewhat better in the educational world.

Broadly conceived, political correctness includes a number of initiatives such as: altering vocabularies in order not to offend particular groups, affirmative action in admissions and hiring, multicultural education, and broadening the scope of classical texts to include those written by minority authors and women. Then there are the workshops in which people are taught by "experts" how to be attuned to others' feelings and how to avoid being found guilty of "sexual harassment," "racial insensitivity," and so on.

Deconstructionism

Deconstruction denotes a political practice of trying to devalue and dismantle the logic by which a specific system of thought preserves its integrity. Deconstructionists claim that words are inadequate for defining reality. They argue that language, particularly in written form, intercedes between the reader and the ideas.

According to deconstructionists, everything is simply perspectival appearance and there is not a fixed way of discerning linguistic meaning. It follows that when critics analyze a work of literature, they do not analyze what the writer originally meant but rather what the reader interprets from the work.

Deconstructionists, as critics of text and language, try to understand how the media and vocabulary used to represent ideas fail to mean the same thing to all people. As the idea of author has lost its significance, there is no longer a need to determine what the meaning was in its original context. Instead, the reader's context becomes paramount.

After the idea of objective and attainable truth has been discredited as myth, there is no longer confidence in truth that is obtainable through reason. Deconstructionists argue that reason is simply an attempt at "metanarrative" (i.e., an attempt to control societal values). Literature and language become means of promoting ideology as each group represents its own worldview. They become means for enforcing a specific ideology on others for the purpose of exploitation.

Postmodernism

According to postmodernism, reality is socially constructed and pluralism is a fact of life. Postmodernists exhibit disbelief in metanarratives in a myriad of areas such as literary criticism, political theory, music, architecture, etc. They display disdain for the modern ideas of rationality, linear progress, and one right way to do things. Postmodernists find fault with systems of thought that try to explain the world, its social and natural laws, its true morality, the path of history, and the nature of the human person, in universal terms that apply equally to all people in all times and places.

Postmodernism tends to revolve around the following themes: (1) the attainment of universal truth is impossible; (2) no ideas or truths are transcendent; (3) all ideas are culturally or socially constructed; (4) historical facts are unimportant and irrelevant; and (5) ideas are true only if they benefit the oppressed. Postmodernists generally use Marxist rationale and concepts (e.g., oppression, inequality, revolution, and imperialism) to attack and discredit American culture.

Postmodernism brings metaphysics, ontology, epistemology, and ethics to an end because these types of study assume a fixed, universal reality. Postmodernism denies the basis for knowing anything except itself. Consequently, postmodernists proclaim a universal tolerance of all ideas. Ironically, the result is a philosophy that accepts only local truths (rather than universal truths), thereby dividing people according to race, gender, locality, etc. The result of this division is an intolerance that is exhibited in racism, sexism, nationalism, etc. When various peoples' truths are different depending upon the differences between them, then the differences between them cannot be overlooked—they are too important.

Postmodernism encompasses the idea that people tell stories in order to explain the world. None of these stories is reality but are simply representations of reality based on incomplete and often inaccurate information. There are a variety of socially constructed realities, belief systems, and stories that attempt to explain the world. People construct stories that seem to fit the information at their disposal. This is analogous to Thomas Kuhn's idea of paradigm shifts in science. When experiments yield evidence that does not fit the reigning paradigm, then eventually a new paradigm that better explains the evidence at hand is adopted.

Postmodernism can be evidenced in the following instances. Some scientists believe that there is no one self; rather the self is a changing socially constructed reality. Other scientists now contend that one of the brain's functions is to tell stories (even with only few facts and frequently without the use of logic) in an effort to make sense of the world. Literary criticism is thought by many to find meaning in the reader's experience—the reader creates the book's reality. In turn, literary deconstructionists debate the idea of representing anything with words. Postmodernists tend to view the world as theater in which we are all competing spin-meisters. For example, political leaders try to get their story told by the media and believed by the people. In law, many scholars dismiss the idea of permanent legal principles. In psychology, a method for treating people involves the creation of a new life story for them (i.e., putting a different spin on their circumstances).

Postmodernists are unified in their repudiation of universal truths. They then depart from their commonality to join various factions in order to participate in the debate. The deconstructionists were discussed earlier in this chapter. Constructionists, realizing that we can't universally know objective reality, contend that we can construct or define it in any manner we choose. Then there are the pragmatists who contend that the lack of universal truths is sufficient reason to retreat to one's own local community—people should stay with the beliefs and concepts that they are capable of knowing, those natural to their own cultural group.

Postmodernists are constantly redefining themselves and are searching for new meaning. As problem finders and problem solvers, they tend to reduce life (and especially political and social issues) to problems and solutions. They also like to engage in zero-base thinking, dismissing the systemically evolved knowledge of the ages.

The Philosophy of Social Engineering: A Recent Descendent of Cultural Relativism

The philosophy of social engineering, as reflected in contemporary civil rights policies and agendas, is primarily based on five concepts: collectivism, determinism, economic egalitarianism, elitism, and historical victimization. Multiculturalism, a merger of collectivism and determinism, asserts that no person can avoid the forces imposed by race, ethnicity, gender, etc. Fortunately, according to the proponents of social engineering, there exists an elite able to remedy historical victimization. Undergirding the philosophy of social engineering is the idea that all individuals should be economically equal. When equality does not exist, it must be due to exploitation and discriminatory exclusion. Consequently, the elite needs to act through the legal and educational systems in order to establish the economic equality that would have existed in the absence of exploitation and domination.

The elite includes individuals and groups who far exceed the general population in intellect, morality, and dedication to the "common good." Their general superiority enables them to use their articulated rationality to function as surrogate decision makers in governmental economic and social planning. Their special wisdom, knowledge, virtue, compassion, commitment, and intentions qualify them to guide the actions of the many either through articulation or force. Because the elite tend to assume that human nature is infinitely malleable, they attempt to mold the nature of the people according to their superior judgments and advanced views.

Unfortunately for its advocates, the philosophy of social engineering is irrational and inconsistent. Collectivism represents nothing that exists in reality. Only individuals, with countless differences and experiences, can think and act. Although persons can share biological characteristics, they will differ in numerous other ways that are necessary to their identities as individual persons. If determinism is valid, then elitism is infeasible because elites would be affected by causal factors just like everyone else. To propose that they would be exempt from such control would contradict the idea of determinism. In addition, economic egalitarianism is inconsistent with determinism. If determinism is true, then the nonegalitarian status of today's world is simply unavoidable. It is purely the consequence of historical determinants whose effects could not be different from what they are. Egalitarianism is also denied by the notion of elitism that acknowledges the existence of a caste of individuals who are more intelligent and possesses superior moral understanding. Finally, the idea of victimization loses its plausibility if both collectivism and determinism have been dismissed as irrational.

In his *Tyranny of Reason*, Yuval Levin explains that the social scientific outlook holds that society and man can be understood through scientific study and that truth in the social world is essentially no different than truth found by science in nature. This failure to recognize that human beings are fundamentally different from the physical objects examined by science and the inappropriate application of scientific reasoning by arrogant social engineers and technocrats can have devastating consequences, including the limitation of man's freedom in thought and action and the devaluation of a man's search for meaning in his life.

Confused students of politics and society have attempted to apply the same rules and standards to both the natural world and the social world and have searched for a precise rational formula behind the social behavior of men. So-called experts fail to realize that scientific thinking seeks meaning in causes existing in the past, whereas human beings make decisions based on purposes reaching toward the future. Because the world of science is a world of causes, not of purposes, it cannot answer the "why" question. The human world cannot be adequately described in terms of causes without purposes and means without ends.

Approaching the human world from the perspective of scientific certainty constrains man's freedom, robs people of a sense of control, and encourages people to hand over their fates to social engineers who believe in the inevitable progress of mankind and in their own superior ability to discover, comprehend, and predict the proper arrangement of society and the underlying truths of the human world. Of course, the knowledge needed by these social architects and constructivists is unattainable—the best we can achieve is partial knowledge of the human world.

Determinism arises naturally from the social scientific outlook. The belief in determinism leads people to think that they have no active role to play in controlling their own futures. Utopian social scientists tend to have contempt for deliberative politics and participatory democracy and to prefer the neutral scientific manager, central planning, social engineering, and government control of the economy.

Western Culture Is Objectively Superior

Today, many intellectuals claim that Western culture is not any better (some say it is worse) than other cultures. In addition, they argue that there are no objective standards that can be used to evaluate the moral merit or demerit of various cultures.

In reality, the superiority of Western culture can be objectively demonstrated when cultures are appraised based on the only befitting standard for judging a society or culture—the extent to which its core values are life affirming or antilife. Prolife culture recognizes and honors man's nature as a rational being who needs to discern and produce the circumstances that his survival and flourishing require. Such a culture would promote reason, man's natural rights, productivity, science, and technology. Western culture, the prime example of this type of culture, exhibits levels of freedom, opportunity, health, wealth, productivity, innovation, satisfaction, comfort, and life expectancy unprecedented in history.

Western civilization represents man at his best. It embodies the values that make life as a man possible—freedom, reason, individualism, and man's natural rights; capitalism, self-reliance, and self-responsibility based on free will and achievement; the need for limited, republican representative government and the rule of law; language, art, and literature depicting man as efficacious in the world; and science and technology, the rules of logic, and the idea of causality in a universe governed by natural laws intelligible to man. These values, the values of Western civilization, are values for all men cutting across ethnicity, geography, and gender.

Recommended Reading

Aronowitz, Stanley, and Henry Giroux. *Postmodern Education.* Minneapolis: University of Minnesota Press, 1991.

Bernstein, Richard. *Dictatorship of Virtue: Multiculturalism and the Battle for America's Future.* New York: Alfred A. Knopf, 1994.

Caputo, John D. *Deconstruction in a Nutshell: A Conversation with Jacques Derrida.* New York: Fordham University Press, 1996.

Collier, Peter, ed. *The Race Card: White Guilt, Black Resentment, and the Assault on Truth and Justice.* Rocklin, Calif.: Prima Publishing, 1997.

Doll, William. *A Postmodern Perspective on Curriculum.* New York: Teachers College Press, 1993.

D'Souza, Dinesh. *Illiberal Education: The Politics of Race and Sex on Campus.* New York: Macmillan, 1991.

———. *The End of Racism.* New York: Free Press, 1996.

Duignan, Peter, and L. H. Gann. *Political Correctness: A Critique.* Stanford, Calif.: Hoover Institution Press, 1995.

Eastland, Terry. *Ending Affirmative Action: The Case for Colorblind Justice.* New York: Basic Books, 1996.

Ellis, John. *Against Deconstruction.* Princeton, N.J.: Princeton University Press, 1990.

Ellis, John M. *Literature Lost: Social Agendas and the Corruption of the Humanities.* New Haven, Conn.: Yale University Press, 1997.

Gitlin, Todd. *The Twilight of Common Dreams: Why America Is Wracked by Cultural Wars.* New York: H. Holt, 1995.

Glazer, Nathan. *We Are All Multiculturalists Now.* Boston: Harvard University Press, 1997.

Grenz, Stanley J. *A Primer on Postmodernism.* Grand Rapids, Mich.: Eerdmans, 1996.

Horowitz, David, and Peter Collier, eds. *The Heterodoxy Handbook: How to Survive the PC Campus.* New York: Regnery, 1994.

Hutcheon, Linda. *The Politics of Postmodernism.* London: Routledge, 1989.

Jay, Gregory S. *American Literature and the Culture Wars.* Ithaca, N.Y.: Cornell University Press, 1997.

Kimball, Roger. *Tenured Radicals: How Politics Has Corrupted Our Higher Education.* Chicago: Ivan R. Dee, 1998.

Leo, John. *Five Steps Ahead of the Thought Police.* New York: Simon & Schuster, 1994.

Levin, Yuval. *The Tyranny of Reason.* Lanham, Md.: University Press of America, 2000.

Loury, Glenn C. *One by One from the Inside Out: Essays and Reviews on Race and Responsibility in America.* New York: Free Press, 1995.

McGowan, John. *Postmodernism and Its Critics.* Ithaca, N.Y.: Cornell University Press, 1991.

Miller, John J. *The Unmaking of Americans: How Multiculturalism Has Undermined the Assimilation Ethics.* New York: Simon & Schuster, 1998.

Mouffo, Chantal, ed. *Deconstruction and Pragmatism.* London: Routledge, 1996.

Nolan, James L. *The Therapeutic State.* New York: New York University Press, 1998.

Okin, Susan Moller. *Is Multiculturalism Bad for Women?* Princeton, N.J.: Princeton University Press, 1999.

Podgórecki, Adam, Jon Alexander, and Rob Shields, eds. *Social Engineering.* Ottawa, Canada: Carleton University Press, 1996.

Rothbard, Murray N. *Egalitarianism as a Revolt against Nature and Other Essays.* Washington, D.C.: Libertarian Review Press, 1974.

Sachs, David O., and Peter A. Thiel. *The Diversity Myth.* Oakland, Calif.: Independent Institute, 1998.

Schmidt, Alvin J. *The Menace of Multiculturalism: Trojan Horse in America.* Westport, Conn.: Praeger, 1997.

Skrentny, John David. *The Ironies of Affirmative Action: Politics, Culture, and Justice in America*. Chicago: University of Chicago Press, 1996.

Steele, Shelby. *A Dream Deferred: The Second Betrayal of Black Freedom in America*. New York: Harper Collins, 1998.

Sykes, Charles. *A Nation of Victims*. New York: St. Martin's Press, 1993.

Taylor, Charles. *Multiculturalism, Examining the Politics of Recognition*. Princeton, N.J.: Princeton University Press, 1994.

Thermstrom, Stephen, and Abigail M. Thermstrom. *America in Black and White: One Nation, Indivisible*. New York: Simon & Schuster, 1997.

Thibodaux , David. *Political Correctness*. Las Vegas, Nev.: Huntington, 1992.

Windschuttle, Keith. *The Killing of History: How Literary Critics and Social Theorists Are Murdering Our Past*. New York: Free Press, 1997.

20

Communitarianism

I want everyone to keep the property that he has acquired for himself according to the principle: benefit to the community precedes benefit to the individual. But the state should retain supervision and each property owner should consider himself appointed by the state. It is his duty not to use his property against the interests of others among his own people. This is the crucial matter. The Third Reich will always retain its right to control the owners of property.

—Adolf Hitler

Communitarians are a diverse group of philosophers and social and political activists who believe that the purpose of society is to uphold and sustain community life. If there is any unity in communitarian thought, it comes from its opposition to classical liberalism's claim that attaining and maintaining freedom and justice should be the central and primary concern of the political order. Communitarians oppose the strict application of abstract and universal rules to persons who vary widely in their personal and social characteristics and circumstances in favor of personal justice and a legal framework that consists of particular laws and outcome-based justice being applied to specific persons or groups.

Communitarians argue that man basically is not a rights-bearing, property-seeking, individual, but rather is a social being who can only thrive in stable associations and communities. They state that the individual is a construction or invention that appeared late in human history, preceded by the community, without which he cannot exist. They are convinced that liberal public philosophy is destroying the social underpinnings of the "good society" and lament that most modern men fail to acknowledge the existence of, and the obligation to seek, a comprehensive common good that transcends one's personal interests. They are united by their common fear that the realization that we are bound by shared purposes, values, traditions, and obligations is being replaced with an atomistic, Hobbesian individualism that upholds individual rights at the expense of camaraderie, social cohesion, and the pursuit of the common good. Communitarians complain that modern society has become a place of uncaring individualism, social disintegration, and amoral relativism where men elevate their personal interests above the common good.

Their conclusion tends to be that a return to past forms of community is both possible and morally desirable. Preferring to look backward, they reason that if we can find virtue in the past, then its attainment in the future would then be deemed possible. Heartened by this possibility, they enthusiastically promote an effort to restore the notion of responsibility and to establish a balance between both rights and responsibility and individual and community.

Foundations of Communitarianism

Communitarians draw inspiration from a variety of thinkers. From Plato comes the idea that the political community ranks highest among all communities in this world. For Plato, political community is man's associative reality and, in its most perfect condition, the mode of community most natural to man. Like Plato, Rousseau makes his main objective the emancipation of man from the conflicts, corruption, and uncertainties of society. He too sees the political community as the best means for effecting such liberation. Rousseau's community is indistinguishable from the state. His idea of the "general will" is not synonymous with the "will of all"—it is the will of the political organism, which he construes as an entity with a life of its own, and apart from the individual members of which it is constructed. Rousseau's general will demand the unqualified obedience of every person in the community. For Rousseau, the state is the most exalted of all forms of community.

Hegel viewed the state as but one of a number of institutions essential to man with its power over individuals channeled through other associations. He viewed society as plural with several natural centers of authority. He therefore recognized the importance of communities and institutions existing between the individual and the state.

Hegel, like present-day communitarians, viewed the free, rational, autonomous, person as a figment of the philosophical imagination. Today's communitarians, in the tradition of Hegel, promulgate a view of rights and responsibilities that diverges sharply from that of Locke, Jefferson, and Madison. Their perspective is that the community or the state is seen as more real than the individual and that the individual who deviates from the social norms is deemed to be objectively irrational. Hegel's thought made possible the attribution of a superior value to collective entities over and above the value of the individuals who comprise them.

The communitarian emphasis on positive responsibilities to others, instead of on negative rights and the negative responsibility not to impose costs on others, draws from the traditional Kantian emphasis on duty. Because of Kant, the virtue of attending to one's own well-being has been stripped of its moral value. Instead, Kantian morality rests on one's disinterested intuitions that tend to be both altruistic and egalitarian.

Nietzsche would agree with today's communitarian theorists in arguing that democratic political life is based on prerational moral commitments to shared concerns and opinions. Nietzsche, however, did not endorse the communitarian perspective. A critic of democratic community, Nietzsche stated that the morality of such a community depends upon a herd animal mentality. He explained that mere devotion to community has no moral superiority to the instinctive behavior of herd animals.

In the tradition of John Dewey, political communitarians argue for community that is constructed and sustained through participation in public life. Dewey, who believed that shared existence is the essence of community life, argued that public life requires public action and public choice. Following Dewey, political communitarians search for communities built in democratic, pluralistic, spheres. It follows that citizens are bound together not simply because of what they believe in common, but also because of what they do together (e.g., public discourse, shared experiences, mutual sympathy, etc.). For political communitarians, symbolic meanings, attained through ritual and habit, are as powerful as rational dialogues. Dewey, and his descendent political communitarians, call for active participation in democratic decision making through attending public assemblies, joining in debates over public policy, and choosing positions in which they set the common good over their private interests. Dewey went so far as to explain that the individual act of thinking is a collective phenomenon. He taught that the primary source of social control in schools is the group, rather than the teacher. As such, the student was to be guided by relativism rather than principle and by the changing feelings of the collective of his contemporaries instead of by standards of knowledge and reason. Students would be taught "life adjustment," social values, and to submit to the tribe rather than to develop their minds.

Essentially, communitarianism most closely resembles Tönnies' preindustrial Gemeinschaft model in which social relationships were characterized by smallness, long duration, cohesion, emotional intensity, primary and face-to-face relationships, stable values, freely shared norms, respect for standards, and a low incidence of deviance. On the other hand, Gesellschaft, a product of modernization, referred to a social system in which change prevails—its social relationships were said to be large scale, impersonal, formal, typically antagonistic, uncertain, and subject to change. According to Tönnies, Gesellschaft would lead to ill-defined roles and to anomie, atomization, and alienation. Tönnies and other classical communitarians thus perceive the impact of change as social disaster.

There are a number of prominent contemporary communitarian thinkers, including Charles Taylor, Alasdair MacIntyre, Michael Sandel, Michael Walzer, Roberto Unger, and Amitai Etzioni, the movement's leading spokesman. The following section takes a look at Etzioni's fundamental teachings.

Amitai Etzioni's Responsive Community

Amitai Etzioni is the founding father and leading voice of contemporary communitarianism. His goal is to catalyze a national moral revitalization and preserve civil society. Consequently, he barely discusses communitarianism within its philosophical traditions. Instead, his sprawling, inconsistent, and intellectually deficient writings are pragmatic and aimed at an audience of activists and policymakers rather than intellectuals. Etzioni wants to do for society what the environmental movement seeks to do for nature.

Etzioni states that there are not now, and never were, freestanding individuals. Rather, he explains that people are socially constituted and continually penetrated by culture, social and moral influences, and one another. Etzioni focuses on community as the basis for determining and affirming people's basic values and as the center of their responsibilities. He argues that people who claim rights must be willing to balance them with responsibilities to help others—people must all sacrifice, take care of their responsibilities, and do their share. According to Etzioni, what we need is a revival of the idea that small sacrifices by individuals can create large benefits for all of us.

Etzioni's agenda for the Communitarian Movement includes: (1) a moratorium on the minting of most new rights; (2) reestablishing the link between rights and responsibilities; (3) recognizing that some responsibilities do not entail rights; and (4) carefully adjusting some rights to changed circumstances. This agenda indicates that Etzioni is primarily an advocate of "positive" state-made rights rather than negative rights.

He states that we require a set of social virtues that we as a community endorse and actively affirm. Etzioni explains that growth in virtue is mainly achieved by instilling the proper values in children by the family, schools, and other character-building agents. Etzioni tries to give a normative justification for values by referring to the criteria of (1) consensus-building within and across communities and societies, and (2) the manner in which values promote the basic social virtues that he claims are self-evident. He advocates relying on some traditional values, reformulating others, and creating new ones.

According to Etzioni, the basic shared core values of communitarianism include: (1) democracy; (2) acceptance and respect for the Constitution and Bill of Rights; (3) layered loyalties to the many communities that make up our polity; (4) a sense of voluntariness to membership in any given community; (5) tolerance, neutrality, and mutual respect for the beliefs of other subgroups; (6) a limited practice of identity politics in political movements; (7) fair treatment for all without prejudice or discrimination; (8) reconciliation with those estranged from us; (9) teaching the common heritage and values we share in America; and (10) small and large dialogues within and among communities. Etzioni believes that members of a community must feel that they have some core beliefs and values in common that are worth sacrificing for—otherwise, they will not look beyond their narrow partisan interests.

Etzioni promotes the idea of a supracommunity or "community of communities" in which citizens would engage in "megalogues" to determine their shared values and discuss national issues. He is searching for a secular Utopia to be constructed through (1) megalogues circumscribed by "rules of engagement" designed so as to avoid debate about metaphysical fundamentals and through (2) indoctrination, beginning in childhood, in shared values. These rules and values are apparently to be determined by a self-appointed elite of communitarians. As a result, Etzioni's communitarianism is an example of secular intellectuals' ongoing will to power.

Etzioni endorses a variety of social structures to inculcate values and virtues, including families, schools, communities (such as voluntary associations, churches, and public spaces), and the "community of communities." These represent the social basis for the moral voice. Although small size characterizes three of his four social formations, Etzioni focuses an inordinate amount of his attention on the fourth—the community of communities.

He is inconsistent and ambivalent about wanting to turn the clock back to an imagined past. On the one hand, Etzioni finds some types of community as more valid than others—he especially prefers families and neighborhoods to the voluntary forms of community. On the other hand, he states that he does not want to return to traditional communities with their authoritarian power structures, rigid stratification, and discriminatory practices against women and minorities. He also says that he wants to create new, nongeographical communities to fulfill many of the moral and social functions of traditional communities. Etzioni is open to recognize virtual communities, feminist communities, and gay and lesbian communities. However, displaying his bias against economic institutions, he does not include corporations as communities.

Etzioni says that he is reluctant to write morality into the law because autonomy is basic to communitarianism. For example, instead of censorship, he favors informal social mechanisms to curb inflammatory or obscene speech. Those who say things communitarians don't like or agree with will be kept in line by means of ostracism and intimidation (i.e., the tyranny of the majority). Etzioni has a difficult task in explaining how miscreants are to be made to conform if their behavior is simply antisocial and not illegal. This is especially touchy in light of his espoused core value of tolerance, neutrality, and mutual respect for the beliefs of others.

Revealing a belief in the nonabsolute nature of a person's negative rights, Etzioni says that the common good of the United States is the relevant community limiting individual autonomy. He argues that some persons may be inconvenienced by some measures, but the greater good of the community will be served. In his communitarian view, people must feel they are part of something larger than themselves—they must be willing to sacrifice for the welfare of others and for society as a whole. In his opinion, only with such a feeling will people respond to the "gentle prodding" he so frequently refers to.

Etzioni is willing to engage in debate with respect to virtually any domestic policy issue, including the right, usefulness, and constitutionality of police to conduct random checks of motorists' sobriety; the free speech/hate speech debate; nonelective monitoring of HIV; drug testing; mandatory national service for high school graduates; child-rearing methods; the influence of political action committees, etc.

He personally would want moderate restraints on privacy like sobriety checkpoints and greater testing for HIV. To combat hate speech, he encourages more speech rather than censorship. Etzioni also wants policies that strengthen childcare, discourage divorce, promote moral education in the schools, and require high school graduates to perform national service involving participation in agencies such as the Peace Corps and Vista. In addition, he would like to see nationally standardized public school curricula, community courts as an alternative to the official judicial system, public financing of elections, a ban on political action committees, and free broadcast time for candidates. With respect to drugs, he states that they should not be legalized because laws communicate and symbolize the values that the community holds dear.

Etzioni would reject the right of the motorcycle or automobile rider to decide for himself whether or not to wear a helmet or a seat belt. He reasons that if they are injured, the public may have to defray the cost of their injuries. It follows that the riders have a duty to protect themselves so as not to inflict a burden on society through their injuries. Etzioni's repudiation of the right of the rider to choose with respect to helmets and seat belts is predicated on the supposed existence of another right—that the injured person has the positive right to be cared for at the expense of the public. Etzioni's claim of that right is thus employed to deny the negative right of the rider to choose for himself. Here, and in other cases, Etzioni and other communitarians want to deny particular negative rights in favor of other positive rights. In other words, he wants to reject negative liberties and assign to society the power to regulate the behavior of individuals in order to lessen society's potential liability.

Etzioni claims that excesses of economic freedom constitute society's largest problem. He advocates legal remedies to reform campaign financing, slow down or stop the removal of tariffs and other trade barriers, and create community jobs. He also wants people to agree to work sharing and to live a simpler lifestyle. Etzioni also believes that the privatization of social security would erode the spirit of community and solidarity expressed in social security and replace it with a sense of atomistic individualism.

Etzioni believes that society has legal and legitimate authority to determine who will own, control, and benefit from the corporations that it creates. He declares that the right to participate in the governance of a corporation should be shared by all stakeholder groups, rather than only by stockholders. He argues that the corporation should be treated as property of those who invest in it, including stockholders; employees (especially those who worked loyally for it for a great many years); the local community (to the extent that it provides special treatment to a corporation); creditors who provide start-up, working, and expansion capital; and clients who continue to purchase a company's products and services when it could either purchase them at better prices or on better terms or buy products of better quality from other businesses.

Etzioni's communitarianism does not reveal a coherent system of substantive principles. As can be seen, case after case is settled through a combination of common sense observation and pragmatic techniques. His "I vs. We" paradigm is deeply flawed at best.

Communitarian Flaws

We should be suspicious of calls for "community" because historically such calls have been accompanied by oppressive sentiments such as nationalism, militarism, racism, and religious and other intolerances. In addition, there have always been potential leaders who claim superior intelligence, insight, and ability to recognize, understand, and articulate the common good and who seek to impose their idea of a good society on others.

By and large, communitarians fail to understand that a community is best viewed as an instrument for helping individuals achieve their chosen goals—it is something that people can freely contract into and withdraw from. Communitarians tend to view it as a good in itself—as a source of value that can make demands upon people.

Perhaps a community can gain allegiance and command sacrifices when it is homogenous, place-bounded, and governed by traditional structures of authority. However, modern society is too complex, dynamic, and diverse to succumb to the idea of such an all-encompassing community. A golden-age vision of shared communities of fate is inapplicable to the problems of contemporary society based on uncertainty and risk. Typically, traditional communities were reluctant to accept innovation and change, inward directed, and hostile to outsiders. People in such communities were bound together by isolation, unremitting labor, rigid status hierarchies, and patriarchal domination.

Many communitarians suggest that we need to look to the past in order to solve today's problems. Social reformers tend to blame the current ills of Western society on the loss of community. They frequently refer to an ideal past in which societies were characterized by respect for tradition, shared values, and commitment to the common good. They argue that community needs to reclaim its former role in order to counter the negative effects of individualism.

Derek Phillips provides compelling evidence that the good old days were not as good as portrayed by communitarians whether in ancient Athens, medieval Europe, or in eighteenth- and nineteenth-century America. Phillips thoroughly illustrates the lack of public virtue and common interest in traditional communities. There were many types of citizens who did not share a sense of common purpose, attachment to the community, and civic involvement. Phillips argues that what was thought to be community was likely to be discrimination in practice as groups would exclude or marginalize individuals who would destroy consensus regarding the common good. Community life in the past was largely imposed on people and was very often based on involuntary relationships. Today, people choose their associates.

Robert Owen's 1825 utopian New Harmony community excluded persons of color and "troublemakers" and forbade women from being part of the managing community. Even then the community failed to unify—its members were just not like-minded enough!

Edward Bellamy, in his 1888 novel *Looking Backward*, writes longingly of a society where the emphasis is on we rather on me and not on individual rights but on the common good of the community. Ironically, his ideal community is America in the year 2000!

Communitarians say that if we lose the traditions of family, locality, and religion, then we lose the identities and civic values that they provide. They argue that individual lives only make sense when they are involved in joint ventures and that; as a result, community often takes precedence over individual choices. They fail to see the harm in community remedies that oftentimes involve coercion (e.g., divorce reforms and curfews).

Communitarians not only proclaim that the self is socially constructed, they also demand a moral homogeneity that endangers the human spirit. A morally homogeneous society would bypass the dialectic of moral development that is fostered by a society of multiple perspectives that educate the person through rewards, punishments, praise, shame, joy, and pain.

It is not entirely evident that the bonds of civic life have eroded to the extent that many communitarians charge. Although many traditional institutions of civic life have declined or disappeared, many new ones have arisen to succeed them.

Today's voluntary communities recognize the open-ended character of human sociality. Communities of choice based on work, friendship, or some other common interest are certainly preferable to the bondage of old-fashioned community. A true community is not a geographically or socially fixed one. Rather, it is what is formed through the collection of relationships in which people live and work out their individual identities. In a free society people are permitted to recognize the subtleties of all types of social exchange and are able to question the desirability of all kinds of traditional affiliations. The ability to form and participate in freely chosen communities is a manifestation and celebration of human agency.

Many communitarians dislike and distrust voluntary communities. Some even believe that the only true community is one created and controlled by democratic political processes. Such communitarians are not proponents of true community, but are collectivists and statists or want people to serve society or humanity.

In practice, serving society or humanity translates into serving institutions such as the state. We need to fight the idea that it is praiseworthy and appropriate to serve society and its institutions. The excellence and goodness of man's life lies in its own integrity and quality rather than in services performed for society. Individual human beings should not be sacrificed for the sake of an abstract concept such as the public interest or the common good. In actual communities, these tend to be the interests or goods of persons in power or majorities of their members.

Communitarians blame the loss of community they perceive on the market and its voluntary institutions such as the corporation—they do not even count the corporation as a form of community! People participate in organizations such as the corporation for a variety of reasons. They join in shared organizational practices and activities in order to serve their diverse and oftentimes conflicting ends. When the overall good of the survival and profitability of the corporation is met then the stockholders obtain profits, employees get wages, customers receive goods and services, etc.

Voluntary communities and associations occupy the space of civil society that should be framed but not dominated by the state. In a free society, people look to civil society rather than to political society to solve problems such as poverty and unemployment. The legitimate role of the state is juridical in nature and involves the establishment and maintenance of an institutional and legal framework of abstract, evolved rules of conduct that are essential to an ordering process through which people pursue their own aims.

Communitarians prefer a society where laws take into account the particular characteristics and circumstances of each person. They believe that a society governed by general, impersonal, and universal rules are unjust. They fail to see that their desire for personal justice is the antithesis of the rule of law, irreconcilable with a free society's complex spontaneous order, and destructive of the legal foundations of a free society. They simply do not understand the consequences of abandoning abstract, universal justice and replacing it with specific and personalized laws.

Many communitarians highly value political participation and believe that the common good can be attained through the process of debating its meaning. Such dialogue does not help in determining the rules needed for the functioning of a free society. In a free society, realizing the common good requires the rule of law and the abandonment of the desire for personal justice. All we need to have in common in a free society are certain shared abstract rules that allow for the peaceful reconciliation of mutually conflicting purposes. The result is an ethical individualism through which people follow their chosen goals as long as they do not infringe on natural rights of others.

The proper role of law is to forbid and punish wrongs of violence, fraud, or negligence and protect rights of person, property, and contract. The law should not be used to send messages regarding the shared moral values that have emerged from communitarian dialogues. The absence of a law regarding a given behavior does not mean that the behavior is endorsed or promoted. Such laws would reflect moralistic views imposed by the tyranny of the majority. Disapproval of state attempts to forbid self-destructive or imprudent behavior does not mean approval of that behavior. It is preferable for a legal framework to be based on more inclusive and impartial values such as metanormative justice and natural rights that support the interests and goals of all citizens.

Recommended Reading

Alvineri, Shlomo, and Avner de-Shalit, eds. *Communitarianism and Individualism.* Oxford: Oxford University Press, 1993.

Bell, Daniel. *Communitarianism and Its Critics.* Oxford: Clarendon Press, 1993.

Bellamy, Edward. *Looking Backward, 2000-1887.* New York: Penguin, 1982; Original, 1888.

Coughlin, Richard M. "Whose Morality? Which Community? What Interests? Socio-Economic and Communitarian Perspectives." *Journal of Socio-Economics* 25, 1996.

Daley, Markate, ed. *Communitarianism: A New Public Ethics*. Belmont, Calif.: Wadsworth Publishing Co., 1994.

Delaney, C. F., ed. *The Liberalism-Communitarianism Debate*. Lanham, Md.: Rowman & Littlefield, 1994.

Etzioni, Amitai. *The Moral Dimension: Towards a New Economics*. New York: Free Press, 1991.

———. *Rights and the Common Good: The Communitarian Perspective*. New York: St. Martin's Press, 1994.

———. *The Spirit of Community*. New York: Touchstone, 1995.

———. *The New Communitarian Thinking: Persons, Virtues, Institutions, and Commuunities*. Charlottesville: University of Virginia Press, 1995.

———. *The New Golden Rule: Community and Morality in a Democratic Society*. New York: Basic Books, 1997.

———. *The Essential Communitarian Reader*. New York: Rowman & Littlefield, 1998.

Frazer, Elizabeth. *The Problems of Communitarian Politics: Unity and Conflict*. Oxford: Oxford University Press, 1999.

Friedman, Jeffrey. "The Politics of Communitarianism." *Critical Review* 8, 1994.

Fowler, Robert Booth. *The Dance with Community*. Lawrence: University Press of Kansas, 1993.

Frohnen, Bruce. *The New Communitarians and the Crisis of Modern Liberalism*. Lawrence: University Press of Kansas, 1996.

Guttman, Amy. "Communitarian Critics of Liberalism." *Philosophy and Public Affairs* 14, 1985.

Holmes, Stephen. *The Anatomy of Antiliberalism*. Boston: Harvard University Press, 1993.

Kautz, Steven. *Liberalism and Community*. Ithaca, N.Y.: Cornell University Press, 1995.

Lichterman, Paul. *The Search for Political Community*. Cambridge: Cambridge University Press, 1996.

Lukes, Steven. *Individualism*. Oxford: Basil Blackwell, 1973.

MacIntyre, Alasdair. *After Virtue*. Notre Dame, Ind.: Notre Dame University, 1984.

MacIntyre, Alasdair. *Who's Justice? Who's Rationality?* Notre Dame, Ind.: Notre Dame University Press, 1988.

Mulhall, Stephen, and Adam Swift, eds. *Liberals and Communitarians*. Oxford: Blackwell, 1992.

Paul, Ellen Frankel, and Fred D. Miller Jr. *The Commumitarian Challenge to Liberalism*. Cambridge: Cambridge University Press, 1996.

Paul, Jeffrey, and Fred D. Miller Jr. "Communitarian and Liberal Theories of the Good." *The Review of Metaphysics* (June 1990).

Phillips, Derek L. *Looking Backward: A Critical Appraisal of Communitarian Thought*. Princeton, N.J.: Princeton University Press, 1993.

Rasmussen, David B., ed. *Universalism and Communitarianism*. Cambridge, Mass.: MIT Press, 1990.

Sandel, Michael J. *Liberalism and the Limits of Justice.* Cambridge, Mass.: Cambridge University Press, 1982.

———. *Liberalism and Its Critics.* Oxford: Blackwell, 1984.

Tam, Harry Benedict. *Communitarianism: A New Agenda for Politics and Citizenship.* New York: New York University Press, 1998.

Taylor, Charles. *Sources of the Self.* Cambridge, Mass.: Harvard University Press, 1989.

Walzer, Michael. *Spheres of Justice.* New York: Basic Books, 1983.

21

Environmentalism

Man is created to praise, reverence, and seize God our Lord, and by this means to save his soul. The other things on the face of the earth are created for man to help him in attaining the end for which he is created. Hence, man is to make use of them in as far as they help him in the attainment of this end. . . .

—St. Ignatius of Loyola

Many environmentalists argue that the individual cannot be left free because the result will be global warming, destruction of the ozone layer, and other environmental calamities. They believe that threats of ecological crises are so enormous that people must drastically change their lifestyles and reduce their standards of living and that government must sacrifice individual liberties by taking control of private property and natural resources.

The earth is actually not on the brink of environmental devastation. The public is being barraged with biased and misleading information about environmental issues in order to support a political agenda. Some environmentalists paint a darker picture in order to rally individuals and institutions to action.

There are some well-founded environmental problems, but these tend to be concerned with human health concerns in developing countries. These real environmental problems include diseases arising from inadequate sanitation; the use of primitive biomass fuels such as wood and dung; primitive agricultural and industrial practices; improper disposal of hazardous wastes; soil erosion; loss of soil nutrients due to lack of fertilizer; lack of sewage disposal facilities; water contamination due to human bodily waste; lack of refrigeration; and insufficient facilities for the treatment of drinking water. These environmental problems result in high infant mortality, a low average human life in years, and low human productivity and standards of living. Such problems are proven, understood, frequently local in nature, highly risky to human life and health, and solvable through economic growth that accompanies private property and free markets. Economic growth and environmental protection are intimately and positively related.

Affluence enables people to contemplate more than just survival. People living in a subsistence state cannot afford the luxury of worrying about environmental issues that are speculative, said to be cataclysmic and global in scope, of extremely low and largely hypothetical risk, and have "solutions" that cost many times more than the predicted benefits.

Foundations of Environmentalism

The perspective of many of today's environmentalists can be traced back to Jean Jacques Rousseau who believed that the more men deviated from the state of nature, the worse off they would be. Espousing the belief that all degenerates in men's hands, Rousseau taught that men would be free, wise, and good in the state of nature and that instinct and emotion, when not distorted by the unnatural limitations of civilization, are nature's voices and instructions to the good life. Rousseau's "noble savage" stands in direct opposition to the man of culture.

Rousseau's ideas filtered through Marx, Hegel, and the German ecologist, Ernst Haeckel, who invented the term *ecology*. Haeckel urged self-sacrifice and central planning for ecological purposes.

Today's environmentalists maintain the innate goodness of pristine nature; the contaminating influences of reason, civilization, and culture; the unerring authority of the collective will; egalitarianism; and the sacrifice of the individual to the group. They believe that the earth is inherently fragile, that man's activities threaten the earth, that a world at risk demands common sacrifice, and that men must join together if they want the world to survive.

The romantic belief that the earth, untouched by human hands, is the ideal, has led many to deify nature and oppose human dominion over creation. It follows that nature is not to be exploited, but is something sacrosanct or even sacred. *Gaia* or Mother Nature is often viewed as a megaorganism. These deep ecologists have thus turned ecology into a religion by adopting paganism. From this perspective, men are nothing special and, due to their destructiveness, are often depicted as a form of pollution. Man's status has thereby been downgraded to the same (or even lower) level as animals. The goal of such environmentalists is not clean water or clean air or a safe environment for men but instead to protect sacred Mother Earth from man. To do this, many environmentalists appear to be ready to reduce human population so that we can return to a simpler, purportedly better past.

Environmentalists reject technology and civilization for a mythological time when man and nature lived harmoniously, when a bountiful earth provided all that was needed for people to survive without work or effort, and when the curses of war, private property, and slavery did not exist. Most environmentalists assume that men are natural creatures who have been alienated from their true identity because of progress and civil society. Technological society has separated humans from themselves, from each other, and from the rest of the natural world.

Such environmentalists see people as simply part of the larger ecological whole and oppose the view that men are the rational masters of nature. For them, nature has a spiritual standing, an intrinsic value, and rights. They are certainly opposed to the Judeo-Christian tradition of God making humans in His own image and allowing them dominion over the earth and all things in it.

Many environmentalists claim that a redistributionist state is nature's proper steward and only hope. They want to use state power to force social changes. This requires a centrally planned system based on governmental command and control regulations. Environmental protection has even been hailed as the best central organizing principle of the state.

The Greens and their allies, the leaders of the environmental movements, are political and social activists whose solutions always depend on political force or coercion. Power is thereby placed in the hands of those who believe that they are the only ones with the ability to properly direct human affairs.

The Flawed Doctrine of Nature's Intrinsic Value

Many environmentalists contend that nature has an intrinsic value, in and of itself, apart from its contributions to human well-being. They maintain that all created things are equal and should be respected as ends in themselves having rights to their own actualization without human interference. Ecological egalitarians defend biodiversity for its own sake and assign the rest of nature ethical status at least equal to that of human beings. Some even say that the collective needs of nonhuman species and inanimate objects must take precedence over man's needs and desires. Animals, plants, rocks, land, water, and so forth, are all said to possess intrinsic value by their mere existence without regard to their relationship to individual human beings.

Environmentalists erroneously assign human values and concern to an amoral material sphere. When environmentalists talk about the nonhuman natural world, they commonly attribute human values to it, which, of course, are completely irrelevant to the nonhuman realm. For example, "nature" is incapable of being concerned with the possible extinction of any particular ephemeral species. Over 99 percent of all species of life that have ever existed on earth have been estimated to be extinct with the great majority of these perishing because of nonhuman factors. Nature cannot care about "biodiversity." Humans happen to value biodiversity because it reflects the state of the natural world in which they currently live. Without humans, the beauty and spectacle of nature would not exist—such ideas can only exist in the mind of a rational valuer.

These environmentalists fail to realize that value means having value to some valuer. To be a value some aspect of nature must be a value to some human being. People have the capacity to assign and to create value with respect to nonhuman existents. Nature, in the form of natural resources, does not exist independently of man. Men, choosing to act on their ideas, transform nature for human purposes. All resources are man-made. It is the application of human valuation to natural substances that makes them resources. Resources thus can be viewed as a function of human knowledge and action. By using their rationality and ingenuity, men affect nature, thereby enabling them to achieve progress.

Man's survival and flourishing depend upon the study of nature that includes all things, even man himself. Human beings are the highest level of nature in the known universe. Men are a distinct natural phenomenon as are fish, birds, rocks, etc. Their proper place in the hierarchical order of nature needs to be recognized. Unlike plants and animals, human beings have a conceptual faculty, free will, and a moral nature. Because morality involves the ability to choose, it follows that moral worth is related to human choice and action and that the agents of moral worth can also be said to have moral value. By rationally using his conceptual faculty, man can create values as judged by the standard of enhancing human life. The highest priority must be assigned to actions that enhance the lives of individual human beings. It is therefore morally fitting to make use of nature.

Man's environment includes all of his surroundings. When he creatively arranges his external material conditions, he is improving his environment to make it more useful to himself. Neither fixed nor finite, resources are, in essence, a product of the human mind through the application of science and technology. Our resources have been expanding over time as a result of our ever-increasing knowledge.

Unlike plants and animals, human beings do much more than simply respond to environmental stimuli. Humans are free from nature's determinism and thus are capable of choosing. Whereas plants and animals survive by adapting to nature, men sustain their lives by employing reason to adapt nature to them. People make valuations and judgments. Of all the created order, only the human person is capable of developing other resources, thereby enriching creation. The earth is a dynamic and developing system that we are not obliged to preserve forever as we have found it. Human inventiveness, a natural dimension of the world, has enabled us to do more with less.

Those who proclaim the intrinsic value of nature view man as a destroyer of the intrinsically good. Because it is man's rationality in the form of science and technology that permits him to transform nature, he is despised for his ability to reason that is portrayed as a corrupting influence. The power of reason offends radical environmentalists because it leads to abstract knowledge, science, technology, wealth, and capitalism. This antipathy for human achievements and aspirations involves the negation of human values and betrays an underlying nihilism of the environmental movement.

Many environmentalists and scientists do not believe in free will or the possibility of knowledge (i.e., that there is such a thing as objectivity). If forces beyond his power of choice determine man's actions, and if man's mind is unable to apprehend truth, it follows that there are no grounds for recognizing a profound difference between man and animals.

Only Humans Can Have Rights

A proper theory of rights presupposes creatures capable of defining, understanding respecting, and violating the moral boundary lines necessary for peaceful interaction within society. As moral agents, human beings have rights to choose to act in their own personal interest. Because animals are not moral agents, there is no justification to recognize rights in the nonhuman realm. Man is the only entity with the ability to recognize and respect moral boundaries. In addition to rights, human beings have reciprocal duties to respect the rights of others.

Animal rights activists fail to recognize the gulf that exists between man and the rest of the natural world. Sentience is the only attribute that is common to both men and animals. Animals cannot think, are not aware of their own existence and finitude, are unable to stand outside themselves to consider their own actions, and are not capable of fulfilling duties to honor the rights of others.

If the notion of animal rights were accepted as valid, the result would be that animals would have the right to live as their nature requires but that men would not have the same right. It is worth noting that as the idea of animal rights has gained more proponents, the act of abortion has become more accepted. Both ideas involve a radical reassessment of the value that is placed on human beings in the order of creation.

Facts vs. Rhetoric

Most Americans believe that the world's natural resources are being used up, that the ozone layer is depleting, that global warming is fast approaching, that hundreds of species are becoming extinct each year, that our forests are being destroyed by loggers, and that there will eventually be too many people for the planet to support. The resulting public perception is that environmental problems are of such magnitude that an all-embracing government can only solve them.

There are environmental problems, but claims of imminent disasters are not supported by facts. Exaggeration, false claims, unsupported conjectures, invalid inferences, and media manipulation are employed to inflame fear to attain ideological ends. Simplified dramatic statements and doomsday scenarios are used to capture the public imagination.

Good science is characterized by sufficient evidence, an understanding of the past, technical competence, careful use of scientific methods, rational analysis, and integration of data from a wide array of seemingly disparate phenomena. We need the very best science as we go about the environmental task. Weak or bad science is being used to blame pollution for global warming and ozone depletion, pesticides for cancer, etc. Let's look at a few examples.

The greenhouse effect is real, is a natural phenomenon, and involves gases acting like glass in a greenhouse trapping heat around the earth. Without the greenhouse effect, the earth would be cold, desolate, and unlivable.

During the last hundred years global average temperature has increased by almost one degree Fahrenheit. Over half of the warming occurred before 1945 when emissions of greenhouse gasses such as CO_2 started to rise dramatically. In addition, there has actually been a slight cooling over the last two decades. It may be that temperature changes over the last century may simply be due to natural climate fluctuations. The earth has experienced major weather changes over time, ranging from ice ages to periods of hot temperatures. There is apparently no one right temperature.

The fear of global warming is largely based on computer models that are so lacking that their predictions simply amount to speculation. These simplistic computer models have predicted that increased human-generated emissions should have already caused the earth to warm much more than it has due to the buildup of CO_2 and other greenhouse gases. In fact, global satellite and weather balloon measurements have been unable to discern any warming trend at all. It is safe to say that there is no consensus among climatologists that human-induced warming endangers the earth.

Perhaps a slight increase in temperature may even be desirable. People in colder climates would certainly benefit. If the earth would get warmer, most of the warming would take place in the winter and during nights. Fewer people would die because of the cold, growing seasons would last longer, and people would spend less on energy.

Human actions probably do have some effect on global temperature, but the temperature changes are most likely so small and so mild that they are inadequate to justify restrictive policies and global warming treaty commitments. Controversial data, limited knowledge of the effects, divided scientific opinion, the uncertain prospects for drastic climate changes, and the probable high costs of aggressive emissions-abatement policies, make the responsible course of action to be reasonable concern and continual study of the phenomenon. This would permit time for the development of reasonably priced substitutes for high-carbon-emitting fossil fuels.

Clearly, draconian energy restrictions are currently not needed to avoid global warming. If convincing evidence ever indicates the likelihood of destructive human-induced global warming, then scientists should first explore less drastic measures such as reforestation and distributing trace amounts of iron throughout the oceans.

Another exaggerated claim by environmentalists is that famine and resource depletion from overpopulation is an imminent danger. We are told that we are running out of living space and that because of population growth, we are rapidly depleting our resource base with devastating consequences awaiting us in the future.

Alarmists fail to mention that population increases have coincided with increases in production, science, medicine, food, information, communication abilities, etc. Because of productivity increases, the earth is actually relatively less populated even though there are many more people in the world.

We are told that we should save resources for unborn future generations who have a right to these resources. It is interesting to note that people have rights to resources before 'they are born but somehow lose their rights to resources after they are in the world. Every generation is some earlier generation's future generation. Apparently, the only present generation that has the right to consume resources is the last generation before the earth's extinction.

Environmentalists also overlook the fact that using what are considered to be natural resources today do not mean that we are consuming what people in the future will consider to be natural resources. They also ignore the reality that the relative abundance of natural resources can change radically with scientific and technological advances. As particular resources become scarcer, incentives will lead scientists and entrepreneurs to develop new technologies requiring substitute or perhaps dissimilar resources, thereby re-creating the resource base. Physical resources, in themselves, are irrelevant. It is the interaction of man, science, and nature that brings resources into being. What can be, and is, used creatively by man changes with time, technology, and consumer tastes and demands.

It is often pointed out that Americans use more of many resources per capita than people in most countries and than those in the past. Again, critics fail to point out that Americans also produce more resources per capita than people in most countries and those people in the past. They also neglect to mention that Americans do not consume more than they produce.

Modern Americans are more risk intolerant than people in other countries and in the past. It is natural for wealthy and healthy people to be more concerned with risks. As a result, the United States government has expanded its number of fear-inducing agencies. For example, there are the Environmental Protection Agency (EPA), Food and Drug Administration (FDA), Federal Trade Commission (FTC), Occupational Safety and Health Agency (OSHA), among others. These agencies are typically biased against change and fail to consider the costs of technological and economic stagnation in comparison to the cost of the risk of the technology and process itself.

Because life is risky, hazards must be assessed and choices must be made. Government intrusion into the risk assessment process has resulted in numerous and costly endeavors to rectify health and safety threats that are not very hazardous.

For instance, we are told to be wary of the harmful effects of man-made chemicals. Yet, most of us have not been made aware that 99 percent of chemicals labeled as toxic are natural rather than man-made. Poisons, radiation, and carcinogens exist in nature. Half of chemicals found in nature are carcinogenic when given to laboratory animals in large quantities. The same goes for man-made chemicals when administered in massive doses.

In fact, all chemicals are toxic when a large enough dose has been received. Keeping in mind that the world is comprised of nothing but chemical elements, it follows that everything can be considered to be a poison. What is needed is information about the levels of human tolerance for the toxic substance in question.

High-dose tests for cancer on animals cannot tell us the significant cancer risk for humans. Rather than the chemical itself, it is more likely to be the dose itself that is the major risk factor for cancer. Chronic cell division occurs as a result of chronic tissue wounding. Humans have a number of natural defenses against exposure to both natural and synthetic toxins at the low exposure levels normally encountered via synthetic pesticide residue, water pollution, contact with toxin-producing plants, etc.

Schools Encourage Environmental Activism

Misinformation is also being used to turn children into environmental activists. They are being taught that human beings are evil, that acid rain is destroying our forests, that overpopulation will exhaust our resources, that global warming will lead to drastic climate change, that the ozone layer is being ripped apart, that ecosystems are collapsing, that deserts are expanding, and that topsoil is rapidly being depleted. All of these topics are currently being debated or have been refuted by scientists.

Schools frequently espouse political advocacy to serve the environmental movement's goals and encourage students to join an environmental group. Educators tend to emphasize growth limits, technophobia, and government action as the only way that environmental problems can be solved.

Students are not told that there are controversies regarding global warming, population growth, declining food supplies, etc. Recycling is almost universally advocated. Students are not told that it costs local governments and residents more in their time and money than can be recovered by selling the recycled items. They are also not told that recycling paper frequently results in increased water pollution and higher energy use and discourages the planting of trees.

It is certainly not wrong to teach environmental issues. Children should be taught to respect natural resources and the environment. However, students should be taught scientific facts and findings and the complexities of the various issues. It is wrong to use misleading or biased information in order to support a political agenda. Many science educators are being unscientific by pretending that things are worse than they are in order to further some personal environmental cause. Educators often uncritically present false knowledge about the environment as scientific fact. These presentations frequently include a dose of anti-Western ideology. "Ecorealism" is the best tool for safeguarding nature.

Free-Market Environmentalism

Without free markets, nature would be left to the mercy of the state. Central planning is made impossible by the nature of the universe. Government just does not have the means to acquire the detailed information dispersed throughout the world that is essential for efficiency, technological change, and care of the environment. The socialist world suffers from the worst pollution on earth. Natural resources fare much worse in the hands of the government than they do under private control.

Environmental plundering in the socialist world is a prime example of the tragedy of the commons. When property is governmentally or communally owned and treated as a free resource, resources will be overused with little or no regard for future consequences.

The American government also has a record of environmental mismanagement. In its efforts to protect ecology, government has prohibited development along seashores, limited the use of private property that is home to allegedly endangered species such as the spotted owl, prevented the development of land because of potential damage to a government-designated wetlands, etc. In addition, it has been government's violation of property rights through subsidies, regulation, zoning, and eminent domain that has resulted in misuse of the environment.

Certainly, pollution and toxic waste disposal, overuse of some resources, and so on, are legitimate concerns. However, we need to recognize that resources that have been privately protected have fared better than their politically managed counterparts. Private property and free markets create powerful incentives that lead to more effective and more efficient environmental protection and stewardship. People have natural incentives to care for their own property. This eliminates or reduces the need for collective ownership and control of resources.

Free-market environmentalism seeks ways of placing resources in the hands of individuals or groups concerned about the well-being of the resources and of themselves. In a free market, entrepreneurs compete to develop effective low-cost ways to solve environmental problems. Their incentives flow from their estimates of future potential profits and the freedom to pursue their ideas. The free market permits individuals to discover new opportunities for improving environmental quality and to produce it in the private sector. Creativity is encouraged if individuals are free to use their minds and have adequate incentives to do so. Entrepreneurs care about the future because they care about their short-term and long-term profits. A person who owns resources will earn the rewards of good stewardship and bear the consequences of poor stewardship. When an owner cares for and protects his resources, their value tends to increase or at least be maintained.

Entrepreneurs can use business tools to save endangered species, develop wildlife habitat, preserve open space, etc. For example, there is a large demand for quality recreation, hunting, and fishing experiences by consumers willing to pay user fees for such experiences. The income earned would justify the costs of improving conditions for wildlife, monitoring land use, limiting hunting pressure on various species, leasing water to increase instream flows, etc.

Arbitrary destruction of animals takes place mainly because no one owns wildlife. There would be accountability if wildlife were private property. Some entrepreneurs might believe that the value of certain endangered species in the future would be greater than the cost of preserving land instead of cultivating it. Others who predict that forests will have greater value in the future have incentives to protect them.

Then there is the fact that the free market discourages waste. Given that air pollution is frequently made up of unburnt fuel, profit-making companies have an incentive to save fuel by reducing pollution. Likewise, firms can save money by conserving costly chemicals or metals instead of losing them in the waste stream. Free markets, science, and technology can lead to processes that minimize pollution at the lowest cost. Economic prosperity does not conflict with a healthful environment.

Private Property and Common Law

Environmental problems are due to the tragedy of the commons rather than to the privatization of resources and the adoption of principles that prohibit dumping and other forms of trespass. These principles include privately owned property, personal liability, and court enforcement of private property rights. The goal is to define property rights in all natural resources in order to avoid the tragedy of the commons. Without a doubt, it will be challenging to extend property rights to all such resources. For example, creative and unique legal arrangements will be required to protect air sheds and oceans.

A system based on private property rights would encourage people to limit pollution. The common law, along with the doctrines of trespass, wrongful bodily invasion, and public and private nuisance would supply protection through damages or injunctions. If rights have been trespassed, the polluter must find ways to keep the emissions from traveling onto others' land or airspace. If operations are impossible without pollution that is harmful to others, then the firm will have to cease operations. As a result, private property owners will have incentives to negotiate among themselves with respect to the market value of pollution. In addition, private owners will be motivated to develop and protect property rights by means of technological advances.

Waste, a by-product of human activity, becomes pollution when it is deposited where another property owner does not want it. The imposition of harmful waste product or emissions onto the person or property of another without that person's consent is considered trespass under the common law which provides a framework in which victims of smoke, chemicals, noise, and so on, can seek redress.

Unfortunately, today's law has divided nuisances into public and private types. Public nuisances are those deemed to interfere with interests common to the general public. In turn, a private nuisance is said to interfere only with a private person's use of his land. The law holds that pollution that offends all the neighbors in a given area is considered to be subject to redress only by a public authority. In other words, a private individual is not permitted to sue in such a case.

The English common law tradition of private property rights includes the right to be free from pollution. This tradition must be revived. Sound liability laws are needed to hold people responsible for their actions. Each owner is accountable for what any object under his control does to injure others. Carefully defined property rights will help to reduce social conflicts.

Damaged parties should have their day in court to seek relief from the harmful effects of another's property through the collection of damages or the issuance of injunctions. A just legal system would prohibit all environmental assaults such as seepage, transmitting toxic substances, and polluting the public realm. The idea is that beyond an innocuous level of waste disposal, no pollution would be permitted. Of course, there are technological problems to be addressed when considering how much exposure constitutes reaching the threshold for injury. Life can absorb some measure of potentially injurious pollution without harm.

Automobile exhaust fumes should be internalized or prohibited when they exceed a certain threshold. Technology is available to measure automobile emissions of traveling vehicles. Fixed emissions checkpoints along the road can measure how much exhaust a car emits. If the car exceeds the threshold, a picture of the license can be taken and the person fined. This approach would be especially attractive if highways were privatized. The highway owner, using emissions measurement devices, could charge user's fees to persons whose vehicles exceeded certain pollution limits. Furthermore, if homeowners associations were designated as the owners of the airspace in which they live, the highway owner could then pay the association to be permitted to pollute.

We need to ensure that polluters pay for the costs of the harm they inflict upon others. This is best done by decentralizing environmental policy and relying on private solutions and common law remedies. Free and rational men in voluntary actions are the best conservationists.

Recommended Reading

Bailey, Ronald. *Eco-Scam: The False Prophets of Ecological Apocalypse*. New York: St. Martin's Press, 1993.

Bailey, Ronald, ed. *The True State of the Planet*. New York: Free Press, 1995.

———. *Earth Report 2000: Revisiting the True State of the Planet*. Introduction by Michael Novak. New York: McGraw-Hill, 1999.

Bandow, Doug, ed. *Protecting the Environment: A Free Market Strategy*. Washington, D.C.: Heritage Foundation, 1986.

Beckerman, Wilfred. *Through Green-Colored Glasses: Environmentalism Reconsidered*. Washington, D.C.: Cato Institute, 1996.

Bernstam, M. S. *The Wealth of Nations and the Environment*. London: Institute of Economic Affairs, 1991.

Easterbrook, Gregg. *A Moment on the Earth: The Coming Age of Environmental Optimism*. New York: Penguin, 1996.

Huber, Peter. W. *Hard Green: Saving the Environment from the Environmentalists*. New York: Basic Books, 2000.

Lewis, Martin. *Green Delusions*. Durham, N.C.: Duke University Press, 1994.

Lichter, S. Robert, and Stanley Rothman. *Environmental Cancer: A Political Disease?* New Haven, Conn.: Yale University Press, 1999.

Michaels, Patrick J. *Sound and Fury: The Science and Politics of Global*

Warming. Washington, D.C.: Cato Institute, 1992.

Michaels, Patrick J., and Robert C. Balling. *The Satanic Gases*. Washington, D.C.: Cato Institute, 2000.

Pepper, David. *The Roots of Modern Environmentalism*. London: Routledge, 1984.

Ray, Dixie Lee, and Louis R. Guzzo. *Trashing the Planet: How Science Can Help Us Deal with Acid Rain, Depletion of the Ozone and Nuclear Waste (among Other Things)*. Washington, D.C.: Regnery Gateway, 1990.

———. *Environmental Overkill: Whatever Happened to Common Sense?* Washington, D.C.: Regnery Gateway, 1993.

Rubin, Charles T. *The Green Crusade*. Lanham, Md.: Rowman & Littlefield, 1998.

Simon, Julian L. *The Ultimate Resource*. Princeton, N.J.: Princeton University Press, 1981.

———. *The Ultimate Resource 2*. Princeton, N.J.: Princeton University Press, 1998.

———. *Population Matters: People, Resources, Environment, and Immigration*. New Brunswick, N.J.: Transaction Publishers, 1990.

———. *Hoodworking the Nation*. New Brunswick, N.J.: Transaction Publishers, 1999.

Simon, Julian L., ed. *The State of Humanity*. Oxford: Blackwell Publishers, 1996.

Singer, S. Fred, and Frederick Seitz. *Hot Talk Cold Science: Global Warmings Unfinished Debate*. Oakland, Calif.: Independent Institute, 1998.

Whelan, Robert, Joseph Kirwan, and Paul Hoffner. *The Cross and the Rain Forest*. Grand Rapids, Mich.: Actor Institute and Wm. B. Eerdmans, 1996.

Wildavsky, Arron. *But Is It True?: A Citizen's Guide to Environmental Health and Safety Issues*. Boston: Harvard University Press, 1997.

22

Public Education

Every politically controlled educational system will inculcate the doctrine of state supremacy sooner or later. . . . Once that doctrine has been accepted, it becomes an almost superhuman task to break the stranglehold of the political power over the life of the citizen. It has had his body, property, and mind in its clutches from infancy. An octopus would sooner release its prey. A tax-supported, compulsory educational system is the complete model of the totalitarian state.

—Isabel Paterson

American students have been experiencing lower math, science, and literary skills and less knowledge in social studies, history, and other subjects. Proposed solutions have included greater funding, a longer academic year, national standards, measures to reduce school violence, and educational vouchers. The only proper solution is to completely separate state and school, thereby permitting education to be purchased and sold through the free-market system. Consumer-financed education must replace tax-based funding of education. We need to dissolve public schools and replace them with educational businesses. By de-monopolizing public schools, we would raise standards, better motivate teachers and students, allow greater innovation, bring costs down, and meet the particularized needs of our children.

Public education is inconsistent with freedom and responsibility. Public education erodes personal freedom and thus should be replaced with parental choice, competition, and market solutions. Parents are responsible for the education of their children. Under a free market, families would decide which are the best educational vehicles for each of their children.

State schools are based on the assumptions that the government is sovereign in education that people are morally and legally obligated to fund the public school system, and that state schools can, and should, teach neutral values. Government policy imposes strict rules and regulations and a directive to use education to engineer political and social outcomes. Public education is a collectivist welfare program in which people are coerced to participate. Not only is political consensus substituted for private individual decisions, the benefits of public education are not commensurate with its costs and its subsidized prices distort individual decision making.

In the past, families, religious groups, and private schools dominated education, but today the state is in charge. We need to eliminate state involvement in education. A person should be free to pay for a child's education if he wanted to. Today, people are forced to pay for schools' imparting ideas that they would not voluntarily support. Freed of their educational tax burden, individuals would have the funds to pay for private education. In addition, competition would raise school quality and would make private education more affordable and available.

Totally separating education from the state means abolishing school taxes and compulsory school attendance. By divorcing education from political power, parents and their children will be free to pursue education that best serves their needs.

History and Philosophy of Public Education

Rousseau, like Plato before him and Mann and Dewey after him, believed in the perfectibility of man provided that he was educated so that he could not want to do evil. According to Rousseau, there exists a "general will," over and above wills of individuals. He taught that there is intellectual elite who is able to discern the commands of the general will and, because of that knowledge, have the authority to implement those commands. The existence and authority of the general will is the cornerstone of Rousseau's philosophy of education.

In *Emile*, Rousseau portrays the ideal education in the story of a child, who, free from the restrictions of an adult's will, is able to study nature and thus learn what he needs to know. However, Emile has an enlightened tutor, whose purpose is to secretly manufacture the conditions under which nature will teach the student what the tutor wants the student to learn. Through the tutor's disguised intentions, the student, by equating his own will with the will of his tutor, is conditioned to identify his own will with the general will.

German thinkers from Luther to Fichte to the Prussian monarchs developed theories of compulsory state education. Hegel viewed the state, through which the general will found expression, as the supreme earthly manifestation of the Absolute and as the embodiment of ethics. People found freedom when they recognized the state's exalted status and accepted the state's objectives as their own objectives. This view ultimately gave rise to American nationalism and the movement toward universal education.

For the first two hundred years in America, from the early 1600s to the early 1800s, public schools were virtually nonexistent. Before the 1830s, education was primarily an informal local activity. Private education in early America included the home, church, Catholic and Protestant schools, charity schools for the poor, apprenticeships, private study, and circulating libraries. With the variety of educational systems available to our forefathers, tax-financed schools did not receive much support. For many years, the only strong advocates of state schools in the United States were Boston Unitarians who denied Christian teachings and accepted Rousseau's ideas that negative behavior was the result of miseducation rather than due to man's fallen nature.

Although tax-financed common schools existed by the 1830s, most parents continued to send their children to private schools. However, the public school agenda of the Unitarians and other elites began to advance with urgency as Catholic immigration, especially from Ireland and Germany, soared in the 1840s and 1850s. Protestants began to fear that Catholic immigrants and the poor would become an unassimilated mass.

Horace Mann, a Unitarian lawyer and legislator, had been appointed secretary of the newly created Massachusetts Board of Education in 1837, the first state board of education in the United States. During his twelve years as its head, Mann created a unified system of common schools including teacher-training initiatives and dedication to a utopian vision of perfecting the moral character of the nation's youths. Mann was a die-hard Unitarian moralist who perceived the public school as the cure for social ills and exhibited faith in human goodness given the right education and environment. Mann, an admirer of the Prussian approach to public education, said that closing down prisons would be possible, given a generation of schools according to his prescriptions.

Mann's goal was to establish mechanisms of social control. He advocated a standard curriculum, centralization of public funds, a strongly moral character of instruction, and state leadership in training teachers dedicated to the common school agenda. Mann and his fellow reformers sought to use the state's authority and resources to impose a single ethos on every school in the name of enlightenment and social unity.

Originally, many Protestants criticized the peculiar religious character of the common public school. Mann's religion without salvation was attractive to an elite who was confident of its own success and of the country's inevitable progress. Protestant critics feared that the schools' espoused nondenominational neutrality was the same as the institution of secularism through the public schools.

However, the large influx of Catholic immigrants who tended to establish their own schools was thought by many to be a threat to Protestantism. Encouraged by the Unitarians, many Protestants began to embrace the state school concept. Because the establishment of Protestantism as the American national church was impossible due to the nation's emphasis on religious tolerance, it was thought the public school could perhaps become an acceptable substitute mechanism to control religion. Protestants thus saw the public school as a potential mechanism for instilling the true faith.

Mann's nondenominational approach did incorporate Bible reading (the King James version), daily prayer, and hymns into its activities. Of course, as America became more secularized, so did the public schools. Public education in America really began to boom after the Civil War, as government-controlled and funded schools replaced the earlier private education system. The biggest boost for state schools came when states began to enact laws of compulsory attendance.

Catholics felt left out of the public school system. As a consequence, the Catholic parochial school system was established in 1874. Catholics, like the Protestants, Unitarians, and others realized that whoever controls the schools controls the upcoming generation.

By altering and connecting Rousseau's ideas of an independently existing general will with the principle of majority rule, nineteenth-century American intellectuals thought that the "will of the majority," as interpreted by themselves, provided a unique source of beneficence and wisdom. Education controlled by that "will" would foster the public good.

John Dewey's progressive model of active learning or pragmatism promoted a revolt against abstract learning and attempted to make education an effective tool for integrating culture and vocation. Dewey was responsible for developing a philosophical approach to education called "experimentalism" which saw education as the basis for democracy. His goal was to turn public schools into indoctrination centers to develop a socialized population that could adapt to an egalitarian state operated by an intellectual elite.

Thinking for Dewey was a collective phenomenon. Disavowing the role of the individual mind in achieving technological and social progress, Dewey promoted the group, rather than the teacher, as the main source of social control in the schools. Denying the ideas of universal principles, natural law, and natural rights, Dewey emphasized social values and taught that life adjustment is more important than academic skills.

Dewey explained that the subject matter and moral lessons in the traditional curricula were meant to teach and inspire but were irrelevant to the students' immediate action experiences. The contradiction between the students' real interests and those of the traditional school alienated students from their schoolwork. School-age children were caught between the opposing forces of immature, undeveloped beings and the values, meanings, and aims of subject matter constructed by a mature adult. Dewey believed that students' energy, talent, and potential could not be realized within the structure of an archaic school system.

Dewey and other members of the Progressive movement wanted a predictable method for providing a common culture and of instilling Americans with democratic values. As a result, by the end of the nineteenth century, a centrally controlled, monopolistic, comprehensive, and bureaucratic public education system was deemed to be essential for America's future.

During the twentieth century, the job of public education was expanded to inculcating moral values, providing nutrition and health, protecting children from psychological and physical abuse, and combating crime and delinquency. Later, additional social and political goals such as racial integration, democratic participation, environmental awareness and activism, and social tolerance were added.

The Nature of Public Education

Public schools are coercive political monopolies that are funded through compulsory taxation and that have a captive audience of pupils through mandatory attendance laws. People must pay for the school system even if they do not use public schools or are not satisfied with them. The state uses its coercive taxing power to take money from some, even individuals who do not have children, to fund the education of others. Because most people cannot afford to pay private tuition after bearing their school tax burden, the market for private schools is artificially restrained. There would be many more, and a larger variety, of private schools in the absence of a tax-supported system. In fact, the bankruptcy of some private schools can be attributed to unfair competition from the public system.

Decisions are made from the top down. Small groups of elected or appointed state officials ignore market forces and make decisions regarding teaching methods, curricula, textbooks, class size, teacher qualifications, etc. Public education is designed to serve the state and their ruling elite who endeavors to create a one size fits all education for a population of diverse children.

Public education views children as property of the state, undermines parents' moral authority and responsibility, and stifles the entrepreneurial spirit. A system of force and compulsion replaces education with indoctrination. Students learn officially approved state doctrine from state-approved teachers using state-approved texts. Public schools promote agendas that conflict with parents' rights to shape the values and beliefs of their children.

Opponents of free-market education believe that only public education can impart the skills, values, knowledge, and attitudes needed for good citizenship. Political correctness and outcome-based education result from public educators' attempts to socialize the young to make society in their own egalitarian image through the use of compulsory state education. Public education thus tends to be more formative and indoctrinating than it is informative.

Parents have been denied the right to choose the type of education they want for their children. Children do not learn in the same way, at the same rate, by the same methods, or under the same conditions. Parents are in the best position to take into account the relevant differences in their individual children and should be permitted to select the appropriate education for each of them. Not all parents want their children educated in the same way. The superior performance of home-schooled children testifies to the ability of parents compared to that of state-certified teachers.

Public educators want uniformity in the schools, because in their minds there would be social inequality if everyone did not have the same education. However, specialized schools that vary in their methods, goals, materials, and assessment methods would better cater to the diversity of human beings.

Public schools do impart values, but they are the values of conformity and docility. Public schooling suppresses the individuality, initiative, and creativity of students. In its efforts to stay ideologically independent, public education is likely to sacrifice intellectual and character development.

The idea has caught on that every individual has a right and a duty to be educated and that society through the government has the obligation to fund the education of its citizens. Supporters of public schooling have maintained that many children will go uneducated if education were not compulsory and if the state did not deliver it. The state assumes that parents are irresponsible and must be forced to do what they should do. Parents are not free to ignore school attendance by their children and are not free to ignore tuition payments through taxation. By avowing the legitimacy of public education, voters try to transfer their responsibility for educating their children to the state. However, parental moral responsibility for his or her child's education cannot be shifted to anyone else.

Public schools get their customers through compulsory attendance laws. Public education is based on the prison concept. Tax-funded schools have coercion as part of their culture. As wards of the state, children are jailed with a mandatory sentence until they are 16. The state removes children from parents assumed to be incompetent in order to keep them from being antisocial and to make them into complacent workers and citizens.

When law mandates schooling, the sense of opportunity that accompanies free choice, is missing. If education is not compulsory, then students perceive education as an opportunity rather than as a requirement. In the absence of compulsory education, students would no longer be captive to ideological and political brainwashing on the part of teachers and administrators.

Most Americans accept the propriety of forcibly taking some people's money in order to educate other people's children. Students are thus taught by example that they are entitled to government "gifts" and that it is proper to obtain an end through organized force. State education teaches that there are a multitude of good ends that can be attained by the state taking wealth to pay for them in the same manner as it pays for students' educations. If children are led to believe that they are owed benefits from the government without any work or its product being exchanged, they tend to think that it is not necessary for them to perform work to obtain any of their desired possessions.

Compulsion negatively affects attitudes, and poor attitudes obstruct education. Compulsory education has drawn some children into classes who do not want to be there, thereby lowering the quality of education as standards are reduced to meet the lowest common denominator. Some students just don't belong in school, but the government not only forces their attendance, it also compels those who do belong and want to be there to associate with delinquents and the uneducable. Of course, due to self-interest, only a few would go uneducated if education were noncompulsory. Attendees would have a financial incentive to get the most out of their education.

When the state provides a "free education" the value of the education is decreased in the minds of parents as well as in the minds of students. Parents will not be as interested in ensuring their children's attendance when schools are free. In addition, parents will not demand much from their children or the schools when education does not cost them anything. Quality declines when the connection between service and payments is severed. Public education breaks the link between consumers' demands for education and their ability to control their own resources in voicing that demand.

Public education continues because it is funded through compulsory tax payments. Because public schools are guaranteed revenue, there is no incentive to strive for excellence. When a school has monopoly control over students, the motivation to produce successful students is lacking. Public education deprives parents of their right to select the kind of schooling that is best for their children. The state taxes away parents' income and permits public bureaucrats to run the school system as they see fit.

Public schools are insulated from failure and protected from competition. Consequently, it is safe for them to ignore their customers. Public educators have little incentive to provide quality, to respect and please their customers, to pursue innovations, to produce results, to be efficient, or to control their costs.

Politicians push for higher taxes to foster their political images by exhibiting their concern for improving public schools. In addition, school administrators do not try to be efficient or cut cost because such behavior would lead to a reduced budget. This helps to explain why the United States spends more per student per year than any other major nation. At the same time, student performance has not kept par with the increase in resources devoted to public schooling.

Public school systems lack the entrepreneurial ingredient. The educational bureaucracy is unable to calculate net income or net loss, has no way of using cost-benefit analysis to see if expenditures were appropriately applied, and do not know if they are using taxpayers' money to accurately respond to consumer demand.

Public education uses taxation to evade market prices. There is an immense difference between government paying for education and the parent paying for it in a free-market situation. When public education is financed by the state, the real price to taxpayers is much greater than the price perceived by the consumers. The family of a student only pays part of the cost of a state-financed education with the rest of the cost being transferred to taxpayers with no or fewer children than the particular family has.

Vouchers and Other Pseudoreforms

Proponents of educational choice have proposed educational vouchers, charter schools, and tax deductions for private educational expenditures. The fundamental problem, public funding of education, remains under each of these alternatives. There are always strings attached when state funds are provided. Government intrusion always follows government funding.

With respect to educational vouchers, publicly funded vouchers would be issued to parents of school-age children to spend at the government-approved school of their choice. Parents would be given a voucher worth a precise amount of public tax money. The parent would have the state-granted right to choose from among the local schools that meet the state's standards. Vouchers are based on the assumption that the states, rather than the parents, are sovereign over education. Controlling school eligibility for reimbursement through vouchers will restrict parents' choices. The state, the source of educational funding, retains its sanctioning authority under the voucher system.

Every private school that accepts a voucher payment is subject to local, state, and/or federal rules and regulations. Private enterprises cease to be private with the introduction of public funds. Because state funds support private schools in a voucher system, it follows that private schools will be accountable to the government if they are to succeed. For example, public educational officials could require open admissions; insist that a private school's student population reflect the community it serves, including proper quotas of minority students; require that vouchers must be accepted as full payment even if they are of less value than the school's tuition; demand that voucher money not be used to finance religious education, etc. A voucher system could also be used to exclude schools that teach "politically incorrect" ideas or that employ teaching methods contrary to the prevailing orthodox methods championed by public education bureaucrats.

As long as an education is publicly funded, decisions regarding educational policy will be politically made. Under the voucher system, voucher supported private schools become part of the state's monopoly on education. The voucher system creates an illusion of parental authority without the substance of such authority. A voucher program violates the principle that parents are morally and financially responsible for their children's education. In a voucher system, coercive taxation remains the source of education funding. A cosmetic change at best, a voucher program gives the appearance that parents are exercising choice, while, at the same time, transferring the evils of the public system to private schools.

Vouchers will lure students back into publicly financed education. Currently, many parents remove their children from public education as a matter of principle. The voucher system will entice parents because its benefits will only be received if parents enroll their children in state-approved schools. Vouchers will lessen the demand for private education that is outside the taxpayer financed education system. Parents who want to keep their children out of government-run schools will have to say no to free education in a state school, turn down vouchers for government licensed schools, and then pay additional funds to send their children to an authentically independent school! In essence, these parents will be paying for education three times while their children only receive one education each.

A charter school is a partially autonomous publicly financed school that is operated by a group of community members, teachers, and/or parents. It operates under a charter with a local school district board of education or sometimes with an outside agency such as an institution of higher learning. Charter schools are free to a certain degree, but, like the voucher system, charters will corrupt such schools. Restrictions confronting charter schools include the source of its funding, regulations stemming from government control, and such schools' lack of market feedback and accountability.

Some advocate private educational expense deductions for federal income tax purposes. Pretax dollars would be used to finance children's education under this approval. Less beneficial than a tax credit, such a deduction would only ameliorate one's tax penalty. In addition the main problem will still be that the educational "benefit" originates in the political order and must be utilized within the political framework.

True Educational Freedom

The best school choice plan is the free market. Education should be bought and sold through free-market processes. The separation of state and education would restore intellectual freedom, academic integrity, and individual achievement. The private market can best provide high-quality and efficient education services. Private educational institutions can supply a superior educational product but currently, because of subsidized tuition at public schools, most students select the lower-priced option. When a child attends a private school, the family must pay taxes to subsidize the cost of students in public education and pay the whole cost of education at a private school.

Education is an economic commodity to be purchased in the marketplace according to the preferences and valuations of education consumers. In a free education market parents and students would decide based on the perceived costs and benefits of each option. In essence, the procurement of an educational service does not differ from the acquisition of any other private good.

Outcomes in a consumer-funded education market would be the result of voluntary purchases by educational consumers. The best schools would earn the most income. Profit calculations would permit schools to gauge their performance according to customer evaluations. Parents would choose schools based on performance and reputation. Paying customers value and select competent schools and teachers. Thus, it follows that the consumers of education should be the payers.

Market-based schools have incentives to furnish quality education at a competitive price. Competition would drive poor schools from the market. Market mechanisms would provide the most efficient allocation of resources. Schools would compete for the best students and students would compete for the best teachers and schools. Teachers' salaries would be determined by market competition. Schools would provide instruction at a variety of locations with varying philosophies, specialization areas, and costs. Schools would arise to meet the demands of various students' abilities and needs. Where the demand for a specific type of education arises, an entrepreneur would form the desired institution of learning. With the diversity that exists among individuals, a variety of schools would appear to meet individual educational needs.

It is critical that parents purchase education directly, when, and only for as long as, they believe their children require it. Only the total separation of state and school can reinstitute parental responsibility, protect parents' rights, and allow students, schools, and teachers to flourish in a free educational environment. Parents have moral authority over, and responsibility for, their own children.

If school taxes are abolished, parents will benefit by keeping their own money. The money belongs to the parents, not the government. They would then be free to choose their own children's schools. For example, if parents want their children to have prayer, then they would send them to a school that has prayers. If they don't want their children to have prayer, then they would send them to a school that has no prayer. Parents should be free to send their children to religious schools, progressive schools, trade schools, home school, or even no school at all. Of course, it is likely that the pursuit of happiness will supply enough incentive for people to want their children to improve educationally. Schools privately funded and freely selected would be mediating associations like churches, corporations, and unions, and would foster a true sense of belonging and identity.

In private schools in a free market, failure to provide the promised results would lead to declining enrollments and financial losses. Competition breeds quality. For example, the free market would encourage teachers to improve their skills and would attract others into the teaching profession. Good teachers would be rewarded and poor teachers would be forced to select other careers. The market would also indicate which teaching approaches worked best in given situations and would stimulate creative individuals to produce and market learning materials. True educational businesses would evaluate teachers and their instructional operations to determine whether or not the customers are satisfied and getting their money's worth of education.

Educational competition would result in the lowering of costs. Competition would make private education more affordable and widely available. This means that poor families would be more able to afford the cost of financing their children's educations. In addition, if the poor were excused from the numerous education taxes that currently exist, then they would have the funds to pay for private education. It is also likely that private scholarships and charitable assistance will be available for lower income families, especially when the person or organization funding the scholarship knows that he is paying for a superior educational product.

In a free market, consumer demand and choice would determine which schools survive and prosper. A private, noncompulsory educational system would be better able to provide for diverse student needs, backgrounds, interests, goals, and preferences. A system of voluntary, unsubsidized education means rescinding government-compelled financing, attendance, credentialing, accreditation, and curriculum. It means the full separation of school and state.

Recommended Reading

Arons, Stephen. *Compelling Belief: The Culture of American Schooling.* New York: McGraw-Hill, 1983.

Blumenfeld, Samuel. *Is Public Education Necessary?* Boise, Idaho: Paradigm Company, 1985.

Boaz, David, ed. *Liberating Schools: Education in the Inner City.* Washington, D.C.: Cato Institute, 1991.

Chubb, John E., and Terry M. Moe. *Politics, Markets and American Schools.* Washington, D.C.: Brookings Institute, 1990.

Coulson, Andrew. *Market Education.* Somerset, N.J.: Transaction Publishing, 1999.

Flew, Antony. *Power to the Parents: Reversing Educational Decline.* London: Sherwood Press, 1987.

Gatto, John Taylor. *Dumbing Us Down: The Hidden Curriculum of Compulsory Schooling.* Philadelphia: New Society Publishers, 1992.

Harmer, David. *School Choice: Why You Need It—How You Get It.* Washington, D.C.: Cato Institute, 1994.

House, H. Wayne, ed. *Schooling Choices.* Portland, Ore.: Multomak Press, 1988.

Illich, Ivan. *Deschooling Society.* New York: Harper and Row, 1970.

Kirkpatrick, David W. *Choice in Schooling: A Case for Tuition Vouchers.* Chicago: Loyola University Press, 1990.

Lieberman, Myron. *Privatization and Educational Choice.* New York: St. Martins Press, 1989.

———. *Public School Choice: Current Issues/Future Prospects.* Lancaster, Pa.: Technomic, 1990.

———. *Public Education: An Autopsy.* Cambridge, Mass.: Harvard University Press, 1993.

Love, Robert. *How to Start Your Own School.* Ottawa, Ill.: Green Hill Publishers, 1973.

Murphy, Joseph. *Pathways to Privatization in Education.* Stamford, Conn.: Ablex Publishing Corporation, 1998.

Randall, E. Vance. *Private Schools and Public Power: A Case for Pluralism.* New York: Teachers College Press, 1994.

Richman, Sheldon. *Separating School and State: How to Liberate America's Families.* Fairfax, Va.: Future of Freedom Foundation, 1994.

Rickenbacher, William, ed. *The Twelve-Year Sentence.* LaSalle, Ill.: Open Court, 1974.

Rinehart, James R., and Jackson F. Lee, Jr. *American Education and the Dynamics of Choice.* New York: Praeger, 1991.

Sowell, Thomas. *Inside American Education: The Decline, the Deception, The Dogmas.* New York: Free Press, 1992.

Viteritti, Joseph P. *Choosing Equality: School Choice, the Constitution, and Civil Society.* Washington, D.C.: Brookings Institute, 1999.

West, Edwin G. *Education and the State: A Study in Political Economy.* Indianapolis, Ind.: Liberty Fund, 1994.

Whitehead, John W., and Alexis Irene Crow. *Home Education: Rights and Reasons.* Wheaton, Ill.: Crossway Books, 1993.

Wyness, Michael G. *Schooling, Welfare and Parental Responsibility.* Washington, D.C.: Falmer Press, 1996.

23

Taxation

Your federal government needs your money so that it can perform vital services for you that you would not think up yourself in a million years.

—Dave Barry

Income taxation in the United States began as an emergency means to be exacted only during times of war or drastic revenue needs. Its growth during the last century was caused by increased federal revenue demands and the growing willingness to use the tax law as an instrument of social and economic change.

The idea of taxes raises questions of justice and morality regarding the nature of government, its proper objectives, its use of force in obtaining its revenues, and the distribution of the tax burden. Taxes can be used by government to control citizens. Throughout the ages and around the world, taxation has had enormous influence on the structuring of society and the status of the individual within society. Today, in America, income taxation presents one of the greatest potential threats to individuals and their rights to life, liberty, and pursuit of their own happiness.

The Nature of Taxation

Taxation is the price we pay for government services. A tax is a compulsory payment by individuals to government. Taxes are always coercive—the idea of voluntary taxation is oxymoronic. If taxes were voluntary contributions, then many persons would quite likely not want to pay their share unless they knew that everyone else would pay their share. Then too, voluntary taxes would be subject to the possibility that government might only protect those who contributed to its operations. Voluntary taxation would encourage plutocracy with those paying giving the orders.

Legitimate government activity consists of defense and protection of life, liberty, and property. Every dollar of taxes must provide an equivalent legitimate benefit, or else taxes become an even greater form of theft. Taxes raised for purposes other than defense and protection become a way for government to control citizens. Taxation can, and has, become a tool of fiscal and monetary management and a means for redistributing wealth. The purpose of reallocating money via taxation is to distribute it differently than free-market transactions would. Taxation thereby becomes a means to thwart individuals' minds by using their money contrary to their judgment. When taxes are used to redistribute wealth and support social programs, they not only divert resources from other useful purposes, they also become a power contest between organized interest groups. Special interest groups and lobbyists pressure Congress to pass tax laws conducive to their own self-interests. Various special treatments make economic decisions dependent upon arbitrary tax rules instead of on economic factors. Business decisions are made with an eye toward tax advantages.

Disguised and Hidden Taxes

Disguised taxes are not labeled taxes but have the same effects that taxes have. For example, inflation is a tax against savings. When government increases the money supply through deficit spending and the abandonment of the gold standard, it reduces the economic value of money that thrifty people accumulate as savings. Inflation thus encourages people to spend rather than to save.

In addition, social security insurance payments retard capital accumulation when people are forced to pay into a "fund" but are forbidden to make any creative use of their contributions. In reality, social security is not insurance and it is not funded.

Then there is the insidious practice of requiring taxes to be withheld by employers from the wages of the employees. Not only are these monies taken out of the hands of the earner earlier than they need be, the practice of having the employers automatically deduct and remit the tax collection to the government makes the payment of taxes seem less painful to the employees.

Also, there are cases in which taxes are incorporated into the price of things to make them less noticeable. This practice can be found in cigarettes, liquor, gasoline, etc. And, of course, the effect of government regulation is the same as that of taxation—earnings are used to enforce government policies.

Tax Effects

Taxes are destructive—they tend to destroy the power of individuals to create and keep what they have created. In particular, progressive taxation dampens incentives to produce goods and services and deters capital accumulation. The graduated income tax discourages excellence through the periodic (i.e., yearly) retraction of rewards. Progressive taxation thus burdens society's most productive members.

By reducing the opportunity cost of consumption relative to investment, the government causes consumption activities to be favored over saving and investment activities—acts of investment can be traced back to acts of saving.

Taxes reduce citizens' levels of living. For every dollar spent by the government, individuals have one less dollar to spend for themselves. Taxes, especially those that are progressive and/or that are spent for illegitimate activities, contradict the principles of freedom and justice that America was built upon.

In addition, tax increases reduce the price of leisure. It follows that many people will decide to work less and spend more time in leisure activities. Furthermore, as the government collects and redistributes more funds, there is an increased incentive to attempt to become a recipient of government transfer payments.

Also, the more government benefits one group at the expense of others, the less respect citizens have for tax laws and the less likely they are to feel obligated to pay their share of taxes. Then too, a tax and spend program tends to undermine the spirit of helpfulness and voluntary charity on the part of citizens. The more functions assumed by the government, the weaker the belief that helping one's neighbor is a proper voluntary action of the individual.

Taxes in a Free Society

What, if any, tax structure can be said to be compatible with the philosophy of freedom? The purpose of the state is to provide only those benefits necessary to prevent harm and keep peace that apply equally to all members of the community. More specifically, a free and orderly society requires state force to deal with aggression and fraud and a court of final resort to settle disputes that were insoluble through private means. Private judicial arrangements of conciliation, mediation, and arbitration and private defense agencies can accomplish a great deal. However, there still remains the need for a coercive court of final appeal to enforce judgments and protect individual rights.

The legitimate functions of the state require funding. These include defense, peacekeeping, preventing and protecting individuals from force and fraud, and maintaining a just, common, and equal system of administering justice and settling disputes. In other words, the state should provide a stable system of governance that protects life, liberty, and property while maintaining due process of law for its citizens.

Tax laws and/or user fees should only raise the revenues necessary to fund the legitimate purposes of the government. In addition, the amount of taxes or user fees one pays should only equal the cost of providing the service a person uses. Voluntary associations should perform nonessential functions. Tax law should not be used as a tool for implementing social policy.

The objective of the government's financing policy should be limited to obtaining sufficient revenues to run legitimate government programs. Unfortunately, during the twentieth century, there has been an increased willingness to use the tax law to affect a variety of economic and social changes through the addition of a number of secondary tax objectives such as: (1) encouraging growth (or slow down) in the U.S. economy; (2) promoting short run stabilization of the economy and controlling the price level; (3) providing social justice through the redistribution of wealth; (4)

preserving the competitive position of small firms; (5) encouraging the growth of certain industries and certain segments of the economy and discouraging the growth of others; (6) promoting employment; (7) promoting (or discouraging) the investment of risk capital; and (8) helping to serve ever-changing national priorities. Taxation should not be used as a tool for effecting economic changes by altering consumption patterns, redistributing income and wealth, providing jobs for the unemployed, stimulating business spending, etc.

The Search for a Just Tax

Equity signifies equal treatment of equals. Horizontal equity in taxation means that persons under similar circumstances should bear equal tax burdens. It follows that individuals with the same income or the same increases in income or wealth should be taxed equally.

A tenable case can be made that each individual and entity (e.g., corporation, foundation, etc.) receives an equal value from government protection and thus should pay an equal flat amount. But do persons and entities with higher incomes or greater wealth benefit more from legitimate government expenditures (i.e., defense and property protection)? Are these activities more proportionate to income? Does the wealth creator benefit more from the proper function of government than does the nonproducer? If greater benefits were received, then tax justice would call for larger tax payments.

A reasoned and practicable case can be argued that an individual or entity with more to protect may require legitimate government services more frequently and in greater amounts than persons or entities with less at stake. It follows that all persons, or persons operating in voluntary association as entities, should pay a flat percentage of funds received from every source with no exceptions.

There would be no preferential treatment for various sources of income—labor, investment, entrepreneurship, gifts, prizes, scholarships, inheritances, etc. Favoring certain types of income (or outlays for that matter) would lead to discrimination. There would no longer be incentives for pressure groups to work for the enactment of provisions favorable to income sources of different kinds and natures.

A flat (i.e., universal, proportional, or single) tax rate meets the requirement of higher taxes on higher incomes. A flat tax rate is consistent with the rule of law and with the principle of nondiscrimination. The idea of ability to pay, in its original traditional meaning, supports a tax proportionate to income. Under the proportional theory of tax justice, a wealthy person would pay more taxes than would a poor person. Every dollar of income or assessed property value would be taxed at a flat percentage rate.

Advocates of progressive taxation have modified the meaning of ability to pay to support the idea that those with greater tax paying ability should pay a larger portion of total taxes in order to distribute tax collection equitably among taxpayers. Those in favor of graduated tax rates thus found a new norm of vertical equity to replace the older, established standard of horizontal equity. The idea of vertical equity is virtually synonymous with the revised meaning of ability to pay.

One theory of justice that ostensibly underpins progressive taxation is the idea that it imposes equality of sacrifice. Individuals with larger incomes are said to place a lower value on additional dollars earned (or that would be paid on taxes) than do persons with lower incomes. Proponents of progressive taxation use marginal utility theory to argue that as incomes increase, the importance of an additional dollar decreases and, therefore, taxing higher income involves a lesser sacrifice per dollar than obtaining the equivalent revenue at lower levels of the income scale. A wealthy man's last dollar of income is judged to mean less to him than what the last dollar of a poorer man's income means to him. The contention is made that taking more of what the wealthier values less attains tax justice. The espoused goal of sacrifice theorists is to minimize the aggregate sacrifice of all taxpayers.

However, sacrifice theory can be criticized. Both the pain of taxes and the value of money are immeasurable psychological experiences that vary across individuals. Men differ by their circumstances, motivation, philosophical premises, psychological characteristics, preferences, education, etc. It follows that no one can know the proper amount of justice or fairness based on the doctrine of vertical equity. There is no objective method to measure whether or not one person obtains more or less value from an additional dollar of income compared with other individuals.

Progressive taxation has also been "supported" by the doctrine of the desirability of economic equality. Many hold that heavier taxes on higher incomes are justified by the belief that inequalities are immoral and that taxation is an appropriate means of reducing them. The imposition of graduated tax rates is seen as a way of achieving greater equality in the distribution of after-tax income. Egalitarians want to pull the successful back into the pack via the income tax.

The attempt to attain equality through tax policy is a product of envy. Government use of progressive taxation leads people to believe that they have a legitimate claim to the country's overall wealth and to the wealth of any person earning more than they earn. Egalitarians view income as a common resource pool, believe that no one deserves greater income than anyone else, and work to deprive people the right to the income that they earned.

Progressive taxation abandons any attempt to connect the usage of government services with tax payments. Services are distributed according to need while receipts are extracted according to ability to pay. A progressive tax system permits a majority of individuals to impose tax rates upon a select minority who, for the most part, have earned their position because they have provided a good or service that others value highly. In other words, the majority is allowed to vote a rate of tax for the minority to which the majority itself is not subject. The majority is able to vote on the degree to which it wants to reduce economic inequalities between itself and a wealthier minority.

Today, the idea of welfare implies an income transfer through taxation from people who have earned it to members of a subgroup adjudged to need income but who have not been able to earn it through their own productive efforts in the marketplace. Today's domestic welfare and foreign aid programs redirect tax money to others.

To the founders of our country, welfare meant providing the necessary common conditions for people to fare well on their own by seeking their own happiness, prosperity, and success. They did not mean providing benefits to some particular group or locale.

Today, progressive taxation is seen as means to achieve "social justice." The inherent assumption of progressive taxation is that the rights of the wealthy minority are not as inviolate as the needs and wants of the poor majority. Under such a system, there always exists the temptation to raise tax rates on the more productive in order to pay for new social programs that transfer funds to the poor. The result is a growing tendency for state supervision of welfare and prosperity to be substituted for personal responsibility.

A Consumption Tax: Some Advantages but Still Coercive

If a flat tax rate was applied to consumption instead of income, then the current bias against savings would vanish and economic growth would increase. Replacing progressive income taxation with a tax on consumption would increase national savings rates. Under a system of consumption taxes, the federal tax would be separately listed and imbedded in the price of what we purchase. Taxes would be levied on what is sold, not on individuals and corporations.

By exempting investments or savings from taxation, consumption taxes would encourage savings and stimulate capital formation. In essence, individuals would be taxed on what they remove from the economy (i.e., when they spend to consume), rather than when they produce via work, saving, or investing.

Various types of consumption tax systems exist and have their advocates. A cash flow expenditure tax is based on one's total income minus his savings. A value-added tax (VAT) is levied on goods and services at each production stage through the retail level. The seller collects it with a percentage rate applied to the difference between a company's sales and its purchases. This amount is incorporated in the price of the product or service. Finally, in the national sales tax approach, a sales tax is levied on the sales of goods and services and is collected from the consumer by the seller.

The confiscatory income tax was originally supposed to replace the tariff. Today we have income taxes and both tariff and nontariff trade restrictions. Currently, there is talk of "replacing" the income tax with consumption or national sales taxes. If history repeats itself, we could end up with both an income tax and a consumption tax and with higher taxes in total. Of course, there may be a chance, most likely a slim one, that the creation of the new, more painless, consumption tax would displace the old income tax with net gains (i.e., lower total taxes) for society. Perhaps it would be more prudent to call for reductions or an end to incomes taxes (along with severe spending cuts) and to insist that the cut taxes not be replaced with another tax. The amount of the total taxes collected is more important than the method used to collect the taxes. Although some taxes are worse than others, there is no such thing as a good tax.

Funding Government without Taxation

Is it possible to fund the functions of a government of a free society without taxation? Even in a minimal state, police, military members, judges, and others have to be paid. Are there any feasible alternatives to taxation? Perhaps it is possible for government to act like any other service provider through the offering of services and allowing individuals to decide for themselves which services they want to use and pay for.

A person is paying a user fee when he chooses to use a government service and pays for it. User fees differ from taxes in that user fees are voluntary and the amount paid is directly tied to what is being used. The greater the extent that government is financed through user fees, rather than through taxes, the more it approximates private companies operating in free markets. The user-fee approach is evident in today's mixed economy with respect to toll roads, parks and other recreational facilities, waterways and harbors, and so on. A user-fee approach for government services permits people to make a rational decision regarding the purchase or non-purchase of the service.

In his various writings, Tibor Machan has made a well-reasoned case that a libertarian legal order or government could provide critical yet exclusive private as well as public goods for fees thus making it possible to obtain the financing of government voluntarily. The supplying of the private goods can be linked to the citizen-consumer, who would pay for these goods. Given that each of these private goods is also a uniquely political good, it would produce the occasion to raise funds for the public good that is also necessary.

Machan explains that contract protection is a private good that government supplies at some level of the adjudicatory process. This service has the essential public feature of due process because even if a controversy is handled by a private arbitration board, the governmental legal structure must exist as a last resort or ultimate protector to ensure due process in concerns such as arrest, trial, seizure of property, and imprisonment, should the arbitrators' decision be refused by one of the parties.

The classical public good that government would provide is the national military defense. Machan details how the government would both protect contracts and provide for the national defense with payments for the contract services being used to also fund the defense of the nation. He posits that having one's freedom protected and maintained with respect to contractual relationships would be one of the most popular services sought in a free society. A system of contract fees, collected when contracts are registered or signed, with provisions for additional payments in the event of special services needed throughout the period of the contract, would supply funding for the legal system and its administrators required to interpret and enforce contracts and to settle disputes if they should arise.

Fees for other governmental services deliverable to individuals could be established in much the same manner as for contract protection. In addition, if criminal actions are involved, fees could be assessed and distributed according to the determination of legal responsibility. Court costs could be charged to guilty parties and criminals could be made to defray other costs such as police services.

Machan expands his case by observing that the government has overhead costs, including those needed to provide for the defense of the system of laws itself. Foreign aggression is a clear threat to the system. It follows that government charges for providing its various services could reasonably include some component to offset the cost of defense against foreign aggression. Private goods, obtainable from the government, such as the protection of voluntary contractual agreements, could thus be legitimately used to support the public good of national defense.

Machan's fee-for-services-plus-overhead approach is one possible way to finance government in a free society—one in which the scope of government would be confined to protecting and preserving individuals' Lockean natural rights. Given the soundness of this idea, it should be conceded that it is not only feasible, but also desirable, to give up taxation for some other noncoercive arrangement.

Toward a Less-Taxing Future

Our long-term optimal but ambitious goal is to eliminate income taxes, privatize nonessential government functions, and finance legitimate government operations through user fees. In the meantime, at the very least, America's progressive income taxation system could be repealed and replaced with either a proportional (flat) tax on all sources of income or with a tax on consumption expenditures. All individuals would stand equally before the tax law and would be subject to the same rate of taxation. Either of these major changes would eliminate the power of special interests, simplify the taxation process, improve individuals' incentives, and reduce compliance costs.

In addition, and even more importantly, government spending should be limited to that necessary for maintaining the peace and providing only these services for which the use of force is necessary and proper. Taxes should never be levied for any objective other than raising revenue for legitimate government operations. There should be no transfer payments between income groups and between generations, no regulatory agencies, and no funding of the humanities, arts, and sciences.

Many public enterprises will have to be privatized. Until then, taxes should be tied as closely as possible to the objective for which the money is to be used. The amount of tax one would pay should equal the cost of providing the service he is using. Those who benefit from a government service ought to pay for its provision. User fees (e.g., roads through tolls and gasoline taxes) should fund such operations as much as possible until the inappropriate government operation can be privatized. After all illegitimate government activities have been privatized, the country could then establish a proportional income tax, a consumption tax, or the much preferable mechanism of user fees that would only raise enough money to finance functions that the state should properly perform. Taxation is actually a form of tyranny. The compulsory nature of taxation makes it indistinguishable from theft.

Recommended Reading

Adams, Charles. *For Good or Evil: The Impact of Taxes on the Course of Civilization*. Lanham, Md.: Madison Books, 1994.

Brownlee, W. Elliott. *Federal Taxation in America: A Short History*. Cambridge: Cambridge University Press, 1996.

Graetz, Michael J. *The Decline (and Fall?) of the Income Tax*. New York: W. W. Norton, 1997.

———. *The U.S. Income Tax: What It Is, How It Got That Way, and Where Do We Go from Here*. New York: W. W. Norton, 1999.

Holmes, Stephen, and Cass R. Sunstein. *The Cost of Rights: Why Liberty Depends on Taxes*. New York: W. W. Norton, 2000.

Kelman, Mark. *Strategy or Principle?: The Choice between Regulation and Taxation*. Ann Arbor: University of Michigan Press, 1999.

Kemp, Jack, and Ken Blackwell, eds. *The IRS v. the People*. Washington, D.C.: Heritage Foundation, 1999.

Leef, George C. "Some Thoughts on Taxation," *The Freeman* (September 1978).

Machan, Tibor R. "Dissolving the Problem of Public Goods, Financing Government without Coercive Means." *The Liberatarian Reader*. Edited by T. R. Machan. Lanham, Md.: Rowman & Littlefield, 1982.

Pasquariello, Ronald D. *Tax Justice: Social and Moral Aspects of American Tax Policy*. Lanham, Md.: University Press of America, 1985.

Pollack, Sheldon D. *The Failure of U.S. Tax Policy: Revenue and Politics*. State College: Pennsylvania State University Press, 1996.

Rockwell, Lewellyn, ed. *Taxation: An Austrian View*. Boston: Dordrecht, 1992.

Roth, William V. Jr., and William H. Nixon. *The Power to Destroy*. Boston: Atlantic Monthly Press, 1999.

Richman, Sheldon. *Your Money or Your Life: Why We Must Abolish the Income Tax*. Fairfax, Va.: Future of Freedom Foundation, 1999.

Shlaes, Amity. *The Greedy Hand: How Taxes Drive Americans Crazy and What to Do about It*. New York: Random House, 1999.

Slemroad, Joel, and Jon M. Bakija. *Taxing Ourselves: A Citizen's Guide to the Great Debate over Tax Reform*. Boston: MIT Press, 1998.

Utz, Stephen. *Tax Policy: An Introduction and Survey of the Principle Debate*. Egan, Minn.: West Group, 1993.

Weston, Stephen F. *Principles of Justice in Taxation*. Waltham, Mass.: AMS Press, 1968.

24

Protectionism

Perhaps the removal of trade restrictions throughout the world would do more for the cause of universal peace than can any political union of peoples separated by trade barriers.

—Frank Chodorov

Free trade recognizes the right of individuals to engage in voluntary transactions in goods and services across international borders. In addition, free trade creates jobs by reducing prices. With more money left in the hands of consumers, their additional spending will stimulate production and employment. Furthermore, free trade shifts jobs from high relative cost sectors that cannot compete to low relative cost sectors that may be able to compete. When individuals voluntarily purchase an imported article they get a superior product and/or a better price. Free international trade imparts benefits to all countries, firms, and individuals who participate by permitting, on an international basis, the specialization that occur in a free economy.

Protectionists overlook the benefits of specialization and comparative advantage. A tariff diverts production from countries where output per unit is higher to countries in which output per unit is lower. In addition, a restrictive trade policy reduces person to person contact and social harmony, increases provincialism, invites retaliation, and stifles innovation (by reducing competitive pressures). Furthermore, and most importantly, import restrictions violate individuals' freedom to exchange.

The Law of Comparative Advantage

Specialization is made possible and desirable by comparative advantage. It is always beneficial for a country to specialize in what it can produce best with the resources available to it and to trade with others to obtain other products.

The law of comparative advantage declares that every nation can improve its economic position by specializing in the most efficient product lines available to them. These product lines are those in which its productivity relative to other product lines is greatest. It follows that even the country that is least efficient in producing every product will benefit from free trade. It does this by specializing in what it is only somewhat inefficient in producing.

Total economic well-being is thus furthered as each person, region, and country specializes in providing those goods and services that it can produce, in relative terms, most efficiently. International trade is a positive-sum activity that increases the wealth and employment opportunities of all countries by permitting them to capitalize on their comparative advantages in production.

Trade benefits are based on relative production costs rather than on the level of production costs. Every nation has a relative cost advantage in some pursuit. A country such as the United States has lower relative total production costs in some endeavors because of its high labor productivity and low capital costs. Another less industrialized country's comparative advantage with respect to another product is likely to be due to its lower labor costs. Free trade allows one country to benefit from the comparative advantages and specialization in production found the world over. It is through the price mechanism that individuals and nations discover their comparative advantages.

Trade Barriers

At root, the issue of tariffs and other trade barriers is a moral concern. To place such restrictions on the exchange of property is an infringement on the natural right to own and exchange property. Protectionism threatens the consumers' rights to choose from among goods and services. Protectionism is the policy of using coercion to restrict imports of foreign goods.

To argue for tariffs and other trade restrictions is the same as arguing against technological change and human progress. Trade barriers decrease the advantages gained through the international division of labor. The argument for protectionism is the argument for higher prices, lower quality goods, economic stagnation, and coercive monopoly.

Protectionists maintain that permitting consumers to purchase foreign made products causes unemployment at home. We are told that jobs are lost when we are invaded by cheap foreign goods. Protectionists argue that tariffs and quotas keep domestic wages from being reduced to the wage levels in countries from which we import. When firms within certain industries call for protection to allegedly protect consumers from poor quality products and to ensure their employees' jobs, their real goal is to gain security through the removal of competition.

The real effects of protectionism are to reduce consumer choice, to raise the price of protected foreign products and domestic goods, to misallocate resources, and to lower worldwide production. Protectionists' policies may "save" some jobs in a specific industry, but only at the expense of the overall welfare of the country. Tariffs promote the production of items in which a nation is inefficient and deter other production lines in which the country has a comparative advantage. By repealing tariffs, things that could be produced more efficiently in one country would be made there and items that could be purchased less expensively abroad would be imported.

Protectionism temporarily helps some producers, but it cannot do this without harming others. Who is hurt by tariffs? First there are those who buy a product upon which the tariff has been levied. Consumers of the tariffed foreign good and consumers who buy an American-made product at a high price that is protected by the tariff both bear the cost of the tariff. Both foreign and domestic producers can raise their prices as the result of the tariff. Purchasers would have less wealth to spend elsewhere. Further, there are the nonconsumers who would have entered the market if the lower price had been in effect. Also injured are domestic firms that now sell fewer goods because Americans have to spend more to purchase the tariffed products. In addition, American companies would necessarily export fewer goods because foreigners have made fewer dollars in America to pay for American exports. Trade restrictions on imports are also restrictions on exports. When we purchase foreign products, we actually create American jobs as dollars come back to the United States as payments for American-made goods, as investments in America that beget domestic job opportunities, or to pay off debt burdens.

Also harmed by a tariff is the foreign importer who earns fewer profits. Oftentimes, the consequence is retaliatory tariffs imposed by foreign governments on our products going abroad.

If a foreign country imposes a tariff on our products, our best response is not to retaliate at all. In fact, we should drop all tariffs and increase imports of the products of the offending nation. Foreigners in that country would then have a lot of paper dollars that they could use to purchase our products. We would have real foreign-made consumer goods in our possession, but would only be giving up paper currency. Imports are our gain from trade—the more goods, the better. When a country chooses not to retaliate, it provides its citizens with the benefits of free choice. Any country would benefit from eliminating tariffs and import quotas, even if other nations do not reciprocate. A country should not misallocate its resources and give up the benefits of specialization just because another nation does that to its inhabitants.

Certainly, if a tariff is removed, some workers in the protected industry may lose their jobs and some or all of the firms in the protected industry may be forced to close by the foreign competition. Workers will have to look for employment elsewhere. However, other job opportunities will be made available because the money that consumers previously had to pay for tariffs could be used to buy or produce new products or services or more of already existing products and services. Employment is created in other sectors because free trade permits resources to flow to areas that consumers consider being of highest value to them.

Protectionism benefits a relatively small group of special interests. There would be more people employed in protected activities, but at the expense of fewer people employed elsewhere in the economy. For example, trade barriers in the steel industry may save jobs in that industry for a short time period, but at the cost of destroying even more jobs elsewhere. American automakers would pay more for steel. This would lead to higher prices for American cars, thus reducing sales and ultimately causing layoffs of employees. Higher steel prices raise the costs of building cars in Detroit and promote the American sales of Japanese automakers whose final products embody the tariffed material, steel.

Contrary to protectionists' claims, cheap foreign labor does not constitute an unfair advantage. As long as the productivity of American workers is greater, they are not at a disadvantage. The reason that labor is less expensive in some countries is because their workers have lower productivity. High wages are found in nations in which workers' productivity in high and low wages are found in nations where productivity is low. American wages are higher because the marginal productivity of U.S. workers is higher. U.S. workers have greater productivity primarily because of the capital equipment with which they work. In terms of labor cost per unit of production, the average American worker is the lowest paid worker in the world. Due to the use of tools and equipment, his productivity-to-wages ratio is far greater than the productivity-to-wages ratio of workers in other countries. Because of the plentitude of capital equipment, U.S. workers relatively provide the least expensive labor in the world.

What dictates a country's comparative advantage in international trade is the relative total amount of resources used to produce a product, not solely the labor utilized. Low-wage nations import American goods because the United States has a comparative advantage in producing some goods, regardless of our seemingly higher wages. Whereas one country may have a comparative advantage in one product area due to its lower labor cost, another country may have a comparative advantage in another product area because of its low capital costs and high labor productivity. Whatever the particular scenario, low-wage countries must ultimately do something with the dollars they gain from the sales they make to Americans.

A tariff levied against "cheap labor" products would economically hold back foreign workers and keep domestic consumers from purchasing less-expensive products. Such a tariff would also maintain American workers in industries where they have no comparative advantage and keep them out of areas in which they would be most productively employed. Free trade shifts jobs from high relative cost sectors that cannot compete to low relative cost sectors that can compete. The case for free trade is the case for lower prices, higher-quality goods, economic growth, and competition.

Trade Deficits Should Be Welcomed

Many people believe that a trade surplus is good while a trade deficit is bad, that imports decrease profits and eliminate jobs, that being a debtor nation is unhealthy, and that a nation's economy is better when it exports more than it imports. People refer to a trade deficit as exporting American jobs. Actually, being a debtor nation and having a trade deficit are not bad situations for a country to be in.

Part of the problem may be due to the arcane definitions used in "balance of payments" accounting. To begin with, the balance of trade is the difference between the money value of a nation's merchandise imports and the money value of its merchandise exports. A more inclusive measure, the balance of payments includes merchandise transactions, credit transactions, and government payments (e.g., foreign aid) abroad. The balance of payments portrays trade patterns. Whereas the current account measures flows of goods and services, the capital account measures flows of funds and financial assets. There is no real balance of payments predicament. By definition, the balance of payments always is in balance. For example, if there is a current account deficit then there has to be a reciprocal capital account surplus. A current account goods and services trade deficit is balanced by a favorable investment surplus. Foreign private individuals, companies, or governments must be acquiring more real or financial American assets than American individuals, companies, or governments are amassing foreign assets.

The balance of trade idea has its roots in the mercantilist period of the sixteenth to eighteenth centuries. Mercantilism is based on the notion that a country gains wealth only by exporting its goods. According to mercantilist writers, a nation should never import more from foreigners than it exports to them. If it did, the country would have to pay the difference in gold (i.e., specie). The nation could thus accumulate specie by exporting more goods than it imported. Mercantilists taught that the gold flow into the country would encourage the nation's economic power and productivity.

However, as gold flows in, money would become more abundant and goods would become scarcer. As a result, prices would rise and foreigners would reduce their imports so that they could purchase less-expensive goods at home. Consumers in the home market would then import cheaper foreign goods and export gold. In other words, gold inflows would increase domestic prices and consequently discourage exports while encouraging imports.

Today, in the absence of such gold flows, foreigners must have a supply of the exporting country's domestic currency if they want to buy the exporting country's domestic goods. The supply of obtainable currency dwindles as the demand for goods persists. The price of the exporting domestic nation's currency rises, making it more expensive to acquire the currency necessary to purchase the goods. Sensibly, foreign buyers will shift to their own or other markets.

Supply and demand for various currencies regulates exchange rates. Exchange rate adjustments balance the supply and demand for respective currencies to correspond to the supply and demand for goods, services, and investments that could be acquired with the different currencies.

Trade is a two-way street. The dollars Americans pay for foreign-made products ultimately are respent in America, thereby creating domestic jobs in the exporting sector. Foreigners must either spend dollars in our country or sell them to someone who will spend them here. We can trade dollars for products only as long as foreigners want dollars or U.S. goods. If they do not want American dollars or goods then adjustments will be made in the value of the dollar.

In a trade deficit, one nation is giving up dollars and the other nation is giving up products. It is a matter of taste, preference, and choice regarding which is more valuable—the dollars or the goods. How can nations be hurt by a trade deficit if individuals are not? A nation is not an entity to which economic principles apply. There is nothing unfavorable about voluntary trade from the perspective of the individuals involved in the trade. They would not have made the trade if they judged it to be unfavorable. Nations do not trade—only individuals do. If each individual gains in every trade, then how can the entire nation be harmed by a trade deficit?

A trade deficit consists of a net transfer of dollar claims from American individuals to foreign individuals. The dollars received by foreigners will either be spent on American real goods and services or invested in American capital and equities markets. When dollars are returned for real American goods and services, they directly stimulate our domestic employment. On the other hand, if the dollars are invested in U.S. capital and equities markets, then foreigners may actually be helping to build new facilities in America, thereby stimulating the creation of new American jobs. Of course, they could choose to buy an existing business rather than start a new one. Foreigners could also leave their money in a U.S. bank account. The bank, in turn, would lend the money to American citizens to build homes or for other purposes and to American companies to build new facilities, develop new product lines, etc. Finally, foreigners could use their dollars to purchase U.S. Treasury notes, thus liberating and allowing Americans' savings to be available for capital investment.

When a trade deficit increases, net foreign investment in the United States also necessarily increases. These occurrences are simply two sides of the same coin. Being a "debtor nation," like America since 1985, means that foreigners invest more in the United States than U.S. citizens invest abroad. The influx of foreign capital into our economy is beneficial and should be welcomed. Foreign investment in the United States provides jobs and stimulates economic growth. Or, put another way, trade deficits actually bring economic health. It is a myth that trade deficits cost American jobs.

Finally, it is interesting to note that protectionists are impossible to satisfy with respect to foreign trade. On one hand, they grumble when money leaves the country (i.e., when imports exceed exports). Then, when dollars return to America in the guise of foreign investment, they bemoan that an excessive amount of foreign money is entering the country and that America is being taken over by foreigners!

Dumping: Evil or Opportunity?

Protectionists have used the term *dumping* as a vague negative refrain. Dumping has been defined as selling abroad below cost or at a lower price than that prevailing in the home market of the exporter. A problem with the "below cost" type of definition is that costs can be computed in many ways. A single cost just does not exist.

No matter which definition is being employed, we can safely say that dumping refers to the existence of extremely inexpensive imports. Dumping results in the dumper losing money while the purchaser has saved money that can be used elsewhere. When goods are dumped into the American market, U.S. consumers enjoy lower prices and increased purchasing power.

Temporarily lowering prices is a common business practice. There are many sound business reasons for lowering prices (i.e., dumping) in foreign markets. For example, firms finding themselves with excess inventories may decide to sell below the normal retail price. Some products may just no longer be in great demand in one's home market. In addition, a producer may want to continue a certain production level during an economic downturn at home. In such a case, it may be better to sell products abroad at a lower price than to shut down production for the duration of the economic downswing. Also, foreign monopolists, unable to attain more domestic sales, may be able to increase their profits by expanding sales in foreign markets. As long as production costs are met by foreign sales, the decrease in per unit production costs will increase earnings in the domestic market. This can occur when a company is experiencing increasing returns to scale in production. The foreign market enhances the home market giving rise to economics of scale.

Then there is so-called predatory dumping in which foreign firms are alleged to dump their products in an attempt to drive their competition out of business with low prices. Protectionists say that the foreign dumper will then raise his prices. Such a dominant position will be difficult to achieve and maintain. Efforts to later raise the product's price above the competitive price would attract others into the market and force the prices down. In addition, given that predatory dumping is perceived as such, all domestic competing firms would need to do to spoil the dumper's plans is to cut production during the dumping period and keep capacity available for production subsequent to the dumping period.

We should not only permit but also encourage foreign firms to sell their goods below cost or below the home price. We can improve our standard of living by consuming their final goods and utilizing their intermediate goods to reduce our production costs.

Of course, the domestic firms competing with the foreign dumper will confront a challenge. They will need to cut costs, at least temporarily shift production to other goods, differentiate their products, etc.

Free Trade Promotes Peace and Prosperity

Each person has a natural right to be free from arbitrary interference. Trade barriers disrupt voluntary and mutually beneficial activities. Isolationism promotes the belief that the outsider is different and of lower stature. Protectionist policies reduce social harmony.

Free trade breaks down barriers and the narrowness of provincialism, increases tolerance, and encourages friendly relations. Voluntary exchange counteracts nationalistic tendencies and replaces parochial attitudes with a global perspective. Trade requires one to understand the customs of the people he is trading with.

Free trade is about peace. As has often been said, "If goods don't cross borders, armies will." The removal of trade barriers would help the cause of universal peace and minimize conflicts around the world.

When trade is free, consumers gain from the products of other countries and friendships and trust develop. Third World nations are helped through free trade. By removing our import barriers, we can give private firms in Third World nations easier access to our markets. If our government restricted foreigners' opportunities to acquire dollars by selling goods in America, then they would not be able to buy as much from us. Not only will the residents of these nations have the chance to develop new industries and expand their existing ones, their contract with people from free nations will promote the recognition of human rights and workers' rights all over the world.

In addition, when we invest in underdeveloped countries, we make it possible for them to experience greater material abundance. American firms supply superior tools, which were made possible through the capital accumulation process, to local foreign laborers to use in the processing of previously unused and unrecognized resources.

Recommended Reading

Bovard, James. *The Fair Trade Fraud*. New York: St. Martin's Press, 1991.

Curtiss, W. M. *The Tariff Idea*. Irvington-on-Hudson, N.Y.: Foundation for Economic Education, 1953.

Ebeling, Richard M., and Jacob G. Hornberger, eds. *The Case for Free Trade and Open Immigration*. Fairfax, Va.: Future of Freedom Foundation, 1995.

Friedman, Thomas L. *The Lexus and the Olive Tree*. New York: Farrar, Strauss & Giroux, 1999.

Hayek, Friedrich A. *Monetary Nationalism and International Stability*. New York: Augustus M. Kelley, 1971.

Hazlitt, Henry. *Economics in One Lesson*. New York: Crown Publishers, 1979.

Krauss, Melvyn B. *The New Protectionism: The Welfare State and International Trade*. New York: New York University Press, 1978.

———. *Development without Aid*. New York: McGraw-Hill, 1983.

Lavoie, Don, and Emily Chamlee-Wright, eds. *Culture and Enterprise: The Development, Representation, and Morality of Business*. London: Routledge, 2001.

McCord, Norman, ed. *Free Trade: Theory and Practice from Adam Smith to Keynes*. Newton Abbot, U.K.: David and Charles, 1970.

McGee, Robert W. "Business in the Global Economy." *The Freeman* (July 1994).

Micklethwait, John, and Adrian Wooldridge. *A Future Perfect: The Challenge and Hidden Promise of Globalization*. New York: Times Books, 2000.

Robbins, Lionel. *Economic Planning and International Order*. New York: Macmillan, 1937.

Rowley, Charles K., Willem Thorbecke, and Richard E. Wagner. *Trade Protection in the United States*. Brookfield, Vt.: Edward Elgar, 1995.

Sumner, William Graham. *Lectures on the History of Protection in the United States*. New York: G. P. Putnam's Sons, 1888.

West, John, ed. *Trade, Investment and Development: Reaping the Full Benefits of Open Markets*. Paris, France: Organization for Economic Cooperation and Development, 1999.

Yeager, Leland B., and David G. Tuerck. *Foreign Trade and U.S. Policy: The Case for Free International Trade*. New York: Praeger, 1976.

25

Antitrust Laws

All antitrust laws should be repealed. The most important argument against antitrust is that laws designed ostensibly to restrict monopolization have been repeatedly employed by the government to restrict and restrain the competitive process. Businesses that innovate, market aggressively, and increase production while lowering prices have been a primary focus of antitrust enforcement. . . . The essence of the monopoly problem is the existence of government legal impediments to rivalry or cooperation. Legal barriers to entry and prohibitions on inter-firm cooperation prevent the market from generating, disseminating, and using the information that the traders require for efficient plan coordination.

—Dominick T. Armentano

Antitrust laws purport to prevent monopolies and encourage competition. However, since their advent in 1890, history has shown that they do not prevent monopoly, but, in fact, foster it by limiting competition. These laws permit the federal government to regulate and restrict business activities, including pricing, production, product lines, and mergers, ostensibly in order to prevent monopolies and stimulate competition. In actual fact, government has been the source of monopoly through its grants of legal privilege to special interests in the economy. The social cure for such "coercive" monopoly is deregulation and repeal of the antitrust laws. This chapter surveys and analyzes the history of antitrust law, its questionable enforcement in a variety of cases, and the irrational and problematic theory on which it is based. The conclusion reached will be to advocate a strict separation of business and government by abolishing antitrust laws and agencies.

A Brief Chronology of Antitrust Law

The alleged purpose of the antitrust laws has been to protect and benefit consumers by fostering competition. This is based on the theory that firms in concentrated markets could lessen competition, restrict output, raise prices, and misallocate economic resources. However, a case can be made that concentration and market share are related to economic efficiency rather than to monopoly power. In addition, it can be argued that antitrust laws have been enacted to protect less efficient competitors.

The thesis of two books written by Gabriel Kolko was that market outputs were increasing and prices falling relative to other sectors of the economy in many of the trust industries in the period preceding 1890—the year the Sherman Antitrust Act was passed. Kolko argues that certain businesses that were experiencing falling profits and intense competition turned to the federal government to regulate the market on their behalf. Kolko explains that, contrary to popular belief, the antitrust laws were not sparked by public indignation, but rather by competition-fearing firms that worked for legislation to provide a political and economic framework through which competition would be restricted. For example, the railroads sought regulation, rate setting, and so on, in order to eliminate price competition, guarantee exclusive markets, etc.

According to this theory, the purpose of antitrust regulation was not the existence of power over markets but the absence of it! It follows that antitrust laws (and cases) can be more accurately viewed as special interest legislation intended to protect less-efficient firms and redistribute income.

The Sherman Act (1890) makes every contract or combination in restraint of trade and every conspiracy to monopolize the trade or commerce of the United States a misdemeanor. This act was passed despite the fact that congressmen had admitted that the trusts had caused lower prices, thus benefiting consumers. What these legislators were actually objecting to was that a number of firms (many of which were their political supporters) had been driven out of business or had experienced a decreased market share. This law, as well as the other antitrust laws, actually protects less-efficient companies from their competitors and increases the political standing of members of Congress and enhances the careers of administrative bureaucrats. For example, at the time of the Sherman Act, less efficient petroleum companies lobbied for a federal law to regulate the activities of the so-called petroleum trust.

The Clayton Act of 1914 outlawed four specific practices, and added a general rule against unfair methods of competition. The particular devices outlawed were price discrimination, exclusive dealing and tying contracts, intercorporate stockholdings, and interlocking directorates.

The Federal Trade Commission Act of 1914 created the Federal Trade Commission and gave it similar powers to those given to the Department of Justice under the Sherman Act. The two agencies operate in harmony and often one agency takes up a matter that the other has declined.

The Robinson-Patman Act (1936) was passed as an amendment to Section Two of the Clayton Act. This act provides that the price for goods of like grade and quality must be the same to all purchases subject to these qualifications: (1) The price discrimination is not illegal if it can be shown that it has no tendency to lessen competition or create a monopoly; (2) It is allowable if it is undertaken in order to meet competition "in good faith"; (3) Price discrimination may be adjudged to be legal if the seller can demonstrate that his selling costs are lower to one buyer than to another; and (4) The discrimination may be permitted if its undertaken in order to dispose of goods that might otherwise deteriorate or become obsolete.

Significant Antitrust Cases

Although the Sherman Act had forbidden all monopolies, whether good or bad, Chief Justice White's opinion is Standard Oil (1911) added the "Rule of Reason," which permitted the parties involved to make their case as to the reasonableness of their actions. Despite the institution of this rule, the fact that Standard Oil's market share had fallen from 88 percent to 68 percent by the time the government instituted antitrust action, and the fact that the courts conducted no economic analysis of its conduct and performance, Standard Oil was convicted of violating the antitrust laws. In addition, Standard Oil's lower prices, rather than being due to predatory pricing could be attributed to efficiencies obtained through the integration of its refining, marketing, pipeline operations. The American Tobacco case, also in 1911, reinforced the Standard Oil decision. Both companies were dissolved into smaller firms despite the fact that neither firm monopolized or restrained trade—both expanded outputs, innovated, and lowered prices.

In 1920 the Court applied the "Rule of Reason" to acquit U.S. Steel, saying that it was a "good trust." International Harvester (1927) was acquitted on similar grounds.

Then in the Alcoa case (1945), Judge Learned Hand rejected the "Rule of Reason" saying that the Sherman Act forbade all monopolies, not just bad ones. Companies like Alcoa and later Brown Shoe (1962), were found guilty of monopolistic practices, not because they raised prices, but because they took advantage of opportunities to expand capacity and meet customers' demands. Facing invisible competition (i.e., the idea that if a monopoly ever tries to take advantage of its position, then another firm may move into the market and go into direct competition by offering lower prices), Alcoa behaved as if it had competition by stressing cost cutting, embracing new opportunities, and capitalizing on its experience, trade connections, and elite personnel. As a result, the price of Alcoa's aluminum dropped from $8.00 per pound in 1888 to $.20 per pound by the 1930s. The government, being more concerned with protecting non-competitive firms, argued that efficiency was no defense. During 1939-1946 the Court moved to define conscious parallelism (i.e., tacit collusion) as being equivalent to explicit collusion, where the effect was the same. The landmark case was American Tobacco (1946), in which the three leading cigarette firms were convicted of being in restraint of trade because of their coordinated activities. A few years later, the Court and the FTC changed direction and generally rejected parallelism as proof of conspiracy. A notable 1976 exception resulted in an agreement between General Electric and Westinghouse to drop their common approach to pricing generating equipment. Parallel behavior is now usually permitted as long as it is in accordance with sound business behavior (i.e., the

"Rule of Reason") and is not accomplished by means of an expressed agreement or coercion.

In the A & P case (1946), the company was found to have gained discriminatory advantages through its wholesale produce subsidiary. The company's experience demonstrates that vertical integration can confer real economies in transferring goods from one stage to another. Although the company reduced its costs and consumer prices because of its vertical integration, it was found to be in violation of the antitrust laws because of the effect it would have on its competitors. Not only had consumers benefited from the purchasing methods pioneered by A & P, the company's conduct did not go beyond what one would expect of a vigorous rival seeking to minimize costs and to maintain its market position. A & P's success created incentives for others to imitate its methods and introduce their own innovations (e.g., the supermarket). A & P, like Alcoa earlier, was found guilty of competing too vigorously and successfully.

United Shoe Machinery was convicted in 1954 because of its high market share and systematic use of price discrimination. Two years later in the Du Pont "Cellophane" case, the "Rule of Reason" was applied to acquit the defendant whose behavior was judged to be good.

In the Brown Shoe case (1962), the Supreme Court found different markets to be relevant in considering the probable effects of horizontal combinations and vertical integration. Brown, a supplier of medium-priced (mostly men's) shoes wanted to merge with Kinney Shoe Company, a retailer and small producer of lower-priced (mostly women's) shoes. The Department of Justice sued to halt the merger on the grounds that competition would be reduced. The companies contended that they did not compete with each other because they served different markets. The merger was not allowed although it would have resulted in a firm that controlled just 5 percent of the national shoe market. The merger was prohibited, partly on horizontal grounds, because Brown retailed shoes in competition with Kinney. Vertical grounds were also cited because the merger would give Brown the opportunity to tip Kinney's purchases toward Brown shoes to the exclusion of other shoemakers. The Court, stressing that tendencies toward concentration are to be curbed in their incipiency, ruled that such vertical foreclosure could prevent other companies from obtaining retail sales. In effect, the merger was struck down even though there would be benefits to consumers.

When Procter and Gamble bought Clorox in 1958, P & G was the largest household products firm and a candidate to enter the bleach business itself. Clorox, the dominant bleach firm, had a long-established 55 percent market share. P & G was forced to divest itself of this company in 1968. The FTC argued, and the Supreme Court agreed, that P & G's advertising power was transferable and would aid Clorox and thus reduce competition.

During the 1970s, the FTC argued that four cereal producers (Kellogg, General Mills, General Foods, and Quaker Oats) that controlled about 90 percent of the sales in the ready-to-eat breakfast cereals market were participants in a "shared monopoly." The contention was that large advertising expenditures and excessive product differentiation effectively excluded competitors from the market and resulted in higher prices and excess profits. The FTC, in effect, charged the firms with brand proliferation (i.e., giving the consumers what they want). Rather than behaving like monopolies, which theoretically would restrict output and restrain trade, they competed to expand trade and output. An administrative law judge handed down an opinion in favor of the companies in 1981 because the FTC staff had failed to prove conspiracy in the case.

In 1974, the Department of Justice filed a suit contending that AT & T had (1) prevented competing long-distance carriers from connecting to local exchanges and (2) obstructed other equipment manufacturers from selling telecommunications equipment to subscribers or to Bell operating companies. The government's argument was that Bell had used its regulated natural monopoly in the local telephone market to create monopoly power in the long-distance and telephone equipment markets. In defense, Bell argued that the size and scope of its system promoted rapid technological change and made its monopoly a reasonable and efficient way to conduct the telephone business. Bell's management surprisingly settled with the government in a consent decree that essentially met every point of the state's proposed remedy. Bell's local telephone operating companies was divested from AT & T and, in 1984, was regrouped into seven large regional telephone holding companies.

In 1969, the government charged that IBM had attempted to monopolize and had monopolized general-purpose digital computers. Alleged anticompetitive steps included tie-in pricing, excessively low prices to discourage entry, and introduction of new products that tended to reduce the attractiveness of other companies' products. IBM's defense was that the government was penalizing success rather than anticompetitive behavior. In 1982, the case was dismissed as "without merit." The government's reasoning was that the industry was subject to the full force of the market and that state attempts to restructure the computer market would be more likely to harm than promote economic efficiency.

Microsoft is currently being accused of integrating Windows with Internet Explorer and bundling them together as one product in order to "force" customers to have all of Microsoft's products. It is alleged that Microsoft is violating antitrust laws because it prevents people from breaking down Windows into its component parts and installing some, but not all, of the parts. Microsoft supporters contend that customers are happy to receive an extra product at no additional cost and that Microsoft's opponents are simply envious of Microsoft's success. Consumers and PC manufacturers like integration—tying can be a helpful way to economize on resources. In addition, clicking an icon on Windows desktop is only one of many ways to access the Internet. Customers can even use Microsoft's own browser to download a competing browser for future use. From a free-market perspective, the situation simply appears to be competition between rivals vying for leadership in sales and innovation. Microsoft, like Standard Oil, is a victim of a political assault because it has innovated, expanded output, and reduced prices. Both attacks were initiated by less-efficient rivals who wanted to accomplish through the political process what they could not accomplish in the competitive marketplace. Because Windows and Internet Explorer are Microsoft's property, the company logically has the right to sell them how they choose and to tell PC makers the terms under which they should be sold.

A Look at Some Antitrust Targets

The alleged purpose of antitrust laws is to protect competition based on the idea that a free unregulated market will inevitably lead to the establishment of coercive monopolies. However, a coercive monopoly cannot be established in a free economy—the necessary precondition of a coercive monopoly is closed entry that can only be achieved by an act of government intervention in the form of special regulations, subsidies, or franchises. There is no invulnerable monopoly unless it is protected by the state. As long as the possibility of substitution exists, there should be no fear of coercion by monopolists. Rival firms can develop substitutes for the monopolized good or service. In the absence of force, others are free to enter the field and offer similar goods or services. As long as others are free to enter any business of their choice, no firm can get away with whatever it wants to do without facing the prospect of a would-be competitor entering the market. Industrial concentration is most often caused by superior efficiency on the part of one or a few firms in a given industry. It follows that a reduction in the number of competitors is not necessarily in restraint of trade unless it was accomplished through force or fraud.

The term *shared monopoly* connotes a conspiracy among firms to monopolize a market. What it actually refers to is a few firms who conduct a large portion of the business in some product or service line. These firms are not monopolists—they are in fact competing with one another. The concept of "shared monopoly" is therefore logically deficient.

In addition, there is nothing wrong with output restriction. Owners of property have the moral right to use and allocate their resources in what they perceive the most efficient and profitable manner over time in accordance with existing and expected future market scarcities.

Pricing has been a particularly popular area for antitrust action. If a company charges a price higher than its competition and it continues to attract customers, it is deemed to have a monopoly per se (e.g., drug companies). If a firm charges a lower price then it is attempting to monopolize (e.g., Wal Mart). And if several firms charge the same or similar prices they are guilty of price-fixing (e.g., airlines). In the first case, if the prices are set high, then new competitors could be expected to enter. In the second case, the firm is likely to simply be competing, although it is often charged with "predatory pricing"—pricing products below costs temporarily in order to drive competition out of the market and then raising the price in a market devoid of competition. In the long run, predatory pricing cannot work because firms cannot suffer losses for long periods of time and the fact that if the prices are subsequently raised then the prospect of profits will attract new entrants, including beaten companies that could reopen. In regard to the third case, there is nothing sinister about price coordination or other forms of collusion for that matter. Companies cooperating to increase their profits are no different from any joint venture, partnership, or joint stock company. In addition, it is well known that cartels are inherently unstable because of the tendency for members to cheat. Then there is the possibility that price coordination may actually improve the efficiency of the market because the reduction of price variability could reduce search costs on the part of the consumers.

Antitrust restrictions on mergers and acquisitions have had the effect of protecting incumbent managers and corporate assets from the prospect of efficient reorganization. There is nothing wrong with buying out competitors because no coercion is involved. Vertical mergers are often disallowed on the grounds that purchasing a raw materials supplier forecloses rivals of the manufacturer with respect to the raw materials. In addition, it is often alleged that it is wrong for a supplier to merge with a retailer because this supposedly cuts off competition of the supplier regarding channels of distribution. The assumption that increased purchases of a raw material by one firm means that there will be less for others is illogical. As long as there is a demand for a raw material someone will step up to supply it. With respect to suppliers supposedly cut off from channels of distribution, nothing is stopping them from integrating or from finding other retailers to deal with.

Prevention of exclusive distribution agreements not only impede the development of the most efficient arrangements for distributing goods and services, an individual's right to voluntarily negotiate the most profitable contracts would also be denied. Exclusive deals are perfectly acceptable—there may be some other firms that would then create competing products. Also attacked are tying contracts—agreements between buyer and seller that bind the buyer to purchase one or more products in addition to the product in which he is mainly interested. Forbidding the legitimate marketing strategy of the entire package or none of it denies the owner of a product to offer it for sale in the form that he desires.

As can be seen from the above, the very practices most threatened by antitrust are the core elements of the competitive process. The effect of antitrust restrictions is to protect inefficient competitors and harm consumers.

Pure and Perfect Competition: An Unrealistic Ideal

Antitrust regulation is based on an unrealistic economic model that compares the structure of existing markets with an arbitrary abstract ideal of pure and perfect competition that can never be attained in the real world. This model, which is used as a benchmark to judge monopoly and for resource misallocation analysis, includes the following conditions: (1) homogenous and unchanging products offered by all the sellers in the same industry; (2) numerous sellers who individually have insignificant impacts on prices; (3) the possession by all market participants of perfect knowledge with respect to all relevant information; (4) no barriers to entry or departure to and from the market (i.e., ease of investment and disinvestment through equal and costless entry and departure); (5) firms do not cooperate (i.e., collude); (6) no fear of retaliation by competitors in response to a firm's actions; (7) no need for advertising; and (8) economic profits tend toward zero.

The traditional antitrust model teaches that competitive markets tend toward equilibrium where price, marginal cost, and minimum average cost are all equal and where consumer welfare is maximized. According to this perspective, consumer welfare could not be maximized if companies advertised, products were differentiated, some firms could achieve economies of scale that are unobtainable by their competitors, or if collusion or high market share could lead to a degree of control over market prices.

The traditional antitrust model is irrelevant in a dynamic business world involving imperfect information. True competition is a process, not a structure, in which a profit-seeking company, operating with limited information, attempts to coordinate production and distribution with the desires of potential customers.

Real-world divergences from pure and perfect competition are not necessarily indicative of market failures. Companies should advertise and attempt to differentiate their products. Competition in a free market includes the process of observing and adjustment under conditions of uncertainty involving both cooperation and rivalry. An innovative firm's lower costs should keep high-cost firms out of the market. When price exceeds cost, information and incentives are provided to entrepreneurs to invest resources in a particular line of business.

Antitrust regulation undermines the discovery process. Regulators, judges, politicians, and economists cannot know the most efficient organization of an industry, including the number of firms it should include, what prices they should charge, and what kinds of contractual agreements they should make with retailers, consumers, and each other. Such knowledge can only emerge through a trial and error discovery process in the marketplace. The essence of a free market is not pure and perfect competition but rather the freedom to compete.

According to George Reisman, the Platonic ideal of pure and perfect competition has been derived from an ideology that is based on the collectivist view that the individual human person is subservient to a greater entity—Society, the State, or Mankind. It follows that private property is not truly private—it is merely held as a trustee for the real owner, Society. The reasoning is that Society has a preemptive right to the property of every producer and permits him to continue in business only for the time and to the extent that Society considers to be in the maximum interest of all.

It follows that acceptance of the altruist ideal of unrewarded service to others is behind the antitrust model of pure and perfect competition. According to altruist morality, the conduct the model requires is pure and perfect. It portrays a world in which no one can succeed at the same time that others fail. Consequently, all firms participate in a process that yields equal benefits to all. The traditional economic theory of antitrust is based on the following philosophical premises: (1) Selfishness is immoral; (2) Capitalism is based on selfishness; (3) Capitalism is therefore immoral and leads to immoral consequences; and (4) Social (i.e., distributive) justice is the moral basis for judging business behavior.

Even advocates of capitalism such as the economists of the Chicago school rely on neoclassical price theory, cost-benefit analysis, and the model of pure and perfect competition as the consumer welfare standard for a firm's real-world performance. These economists' use of tools such as concentration ratios, consumer surplus analysis, market share analysis, Herfindahl indices, Gini coefficients, and others, evidences their underlying altruist premises. Any market that does not meet the economists' altruistic Platonic standard is deemed to be a threat to competition and is censured. Successful businesses are thus punished for not being passive, altruistic servants of society.

Antitrust Laws Should Be Repealed

A review of antitrust laws, cases, and targets, and the economic model upon which they are based indicates that antitrust is largely a failed and discredited policy. Laws allegedly passed to protect customers have been used to punish efficient companies that have increased output and lowered prices. Governments to restrain and restrict the competitive process have used laws ostensibly designed to restrict monopoly. Rather than protect consumers, it is possible that antitrust laws are enacted to subsidize and protect less-efficient firms from the rigors of the competitive process. Antitrust enforcement can be used as a war against the competitive practices that businessmen can employ to better serve customers. Antitrust laws thus discourage abler firms from operating to the best of their abilities. In essence, the effects of antitrust laws are like those of a cartel—maintaining the status quo by stabilizing prices and assuring each firm that its profits and market position are secure.

Antitrust proponents may be confusing the concepts of competition and monopoly power. When a firm advertises, is it competing or being anti-competitive? If a company innovates or spends money on research and development is competing or creating a "barrier to entry"? If a firm lowers its price, is it competing or trying to gain a monopoly? Competition, rightly understood, is a dynamic, rivalrous, process of discovery. It is not monopoly, but the prevention of competition that is to be feared—monopoly that results from superior performance should be welcomed. The idea of barriers to entry confuses coercive legal barriers with legitimately earned performance and cost advantages that are likely to benefit, rather than harm, customers. Competition simply refers to a situation where the basic rules of a free society are followed—freedom of contract, private property, etc. The essence of a free market is not pure and perfect competition but freedom of competition.

In essence, there are two types of monopoly—efficiency and coercive. An efficiency monopoly earns a high market share because it does good work. Such a monopoly has no legal power to force people to do business with it. On the other hand a coercive monopoly results from a state grant of exclusive privilege. The government may: ban competition, grant privileges, immunities, or subsidies to one company; or impose costly requirements on others. What really bothers individuals about monopoly is not that one firm has economic dominance over a product or service, but that compulsion, force, or special privilege is used to prevent other firms from entering the market. There is no social harm in a monopoly if others have an equal right to enter the field of business. There is a large difference between monopoly in the sense of being the sole firm in a market, and in the exploitative sense of using state help or force to keep competitors out. The real robber barons are firms that look to privileges. Only a coercive monopoly hurts people because force, rather than ability, is used to keep others out of the market. The only way that a firm can gain a monopoly without having to fear the threat of competition is through the force of the government.

The essence of the monopoly problem is the existence of legal barriers to competition or rivalry. These keep the market from producing, disseminating, and utilizing the information that people need for planning and decision making. Legal restrictions cause monopoly power and prices. Repealing antitrust laws and ending government-sponsored monopoly will handle the monopoly problem handled more efficiently through the market process.

It is interesting to note that real monopoly power has essentially been immune from antitrust regulation—government-created monopolies are not made the target of antitrust investigations. Cable TV and local telephone services are monopolies by law. Government licensing and tariff and quota protection restrict competition and produce monopoly profits for privileged private interests. Government-supported cartels (e.g., agriculture, oil production, transportation) result in long-run monopoly profits.

Antitrust law is a collection of vague, inconsistent, complex, and non-objective laws that can make virtually any business practice appear to be illegal. These laws are so vague that businessmen have no way of knowing until after the fact if a given action will be declared illegal. Often this system of "retroactive" law punishes a firm or individual for an action that was not legally defined as a crime at time of its commission. Vagueness is inherent in terms such as *intent to monopolize* and *restraint of trade*—there exists no exact definition for these and other such terms.

Antitrust laws are selectively applied. The antitrust bureaucracy chooses cases to prosecute based on their potential to further their own private interests and careers. Antitrust is used to transfer wealth from large unorganized groups of individuals to the narrow, organized interests of other groups of individuals. These antitrust benefits accruing to some (i.e., by limiting competition from their rivals) involve costs that are usually not apparent because they are spread over so many other firms and individuals.

Antitrust laws also involve large economic costs. Not only do these include the expenses involved in defending one's firm in antitrust actions, but also in the innovations not undertaken, the competitive strategies not employed, and the mergers that are foregone due to the legal uncertainty associated with antitrust statutes and bureaucrats.

Recommended Reading

Armentano, Dominick. *Antitrust and Monopoly: Anatomy of a Policy Failure.* New York: Wiley, 1982.

———. *Antitrust Policy: The Case for Repeal.* Washington, D.C.: Cato Institute, 1986.

Baldwin, William L., and David McFarland. "Tying Arrangements in Law and Economics." *Antitrust Bulletin* 8, nos. 5-6 (September-December 1963).

Bork, Robert. *The Antitrust Paradox: A Policy at War with Itself.* New York:

Basic Books, 1978.

Brozen, Yale. *Concentration, Mergers and Public Policy.* New York: Macmillan, 1982.

DiLorenzo, Thomas J. "The Origins of Antitrust: An Interest-Group Perspective." *International Review of Law and Economics* 5 (June 1985).

DiLorenzo, Thomas J. and Donald Boudreaux. "The Protectionist Roots of Antitrust." *Review of Austrian Economics* vol., 6 no. 2 (1993).

DiLorenzo, Thomas J., and Jack C. High. "Antitrust and Competition, Historically Considered." *Economic Inquiry* 26 (July 1988).

Flynn, John J. "Monopolization under the Sherman Act: The Third Wave and Beyond." *Antitrust Bulletin* 26, no. 1 (spring 1981).

Folsom, Burton W. Jr. *The Myth of the Robber Barons.* Herndon, Va.: Young America's Foundation, 1991.

Huber, Peter William. *Law and Disorder in Cyberspace.* London: Oxford University Press, 1997.

Kolko, Gabriel. *The Triumph of Conservatism.* New York: Macmillan, 1963.

———. *Railroads and Regulation.* Princeton, N.J.: Princeton University Press, 1965.

Letwin, William. *Law and Economic Policy in America: The Evolution of the Sherman Antitrust Act.* New York: Random House, 1965.

Levy, Robert A. "Microsoft and the Browser Wars." *Policy Analysis, Cato Policy Analysis* no. 296 (February 19 1998).

Liebowitz, Stanley J., Stephen E. Margolis, and Jack Hirshleifer. *Winners, Losers, and Microsoft.* Oakland, Calif.: Independent Institute, 2001.

Manne, Henry G. "Mergers and the Market for Corporation Control." *Journal of Political Economy* 73, no. 2 (April 1965).

Marvel, Howard P. "Exclusive Dealing." *Journal of Law and Economics* 25, no. 1 (April 1982).

McChesney, Fred S., and William F. Shugart. *The Causes and Consequences of Antitrust: The Public Choice Perspective.* Chicago: University of Chicago Press, 1994.

McGee, John S. "Predatory Price Cutting: The Standard Oil Case." *Journal of Law and Economics* 1 (October 1958).

Posner, Richard A. *Antitrust Law: An Economic Perspective.* Chicago: University of Chicago Press, 1976.

Reisman, George. "Platonic Competition." *The Objectivist* (August-September 1968).

Ridpath, John B. "The Philosophical Origins of Antitrust." *The Objecitivist Forum* (June 1980).

Shenfield, Arthur. *Myth and Reality in Anti-Trust.* London: IEA, 1983.

Stigler, George. "Perfect Competition, Historically Contemplated." *Journal of Political Economy* 65 (February 1957).

Tarbell, Ida M. *The History of Standard Oil Company* (2 vols). New York: Peter Smith, 1950.

Thorelli, Hans B. *The Federal Antitrust Policy: Origination of an American Tradition.* Winchester, Mass.: Allen & Unwin, 1954.

26

Government Regulation

The argument that regulations are needed to protect people from their own bad decisions is an argument for protecting them from their own minds. It assumes not only that free men will too often make wrong decisions but—even more preposterously—that government will somehow make the right ones!

—Edmund Contoski

America was founded on the basis of an explicit philosophy of individual rights. The Founding Fathers held the view that government, while deriving from the consent of the governed, must be limited by the rights of the individual. The purpose of government was to maintain a framework within which individuals can pursue their own self-interest, controlled by the competitive marketplace. Until the early 1900s, the United States had a very limited government; however, since the Great Depression, both attitudes toward government and the interpretation of the Constitution changed, resulting in an increasingly large government that has spread its functions to now include: maintaining national defense and internal law and order; protecting property rights; enforcing contracts and adjudicating disputes; promoting exchange by providing a stable monetary system; handling market defects and promoting competition by regulating the American product, labor, and financial markets; providing public goods; maintaining transportation and postal systems; using fiscal and monetary policy to promote a high level of employment, economic growth, and price stability; protecting people from unintended by-products of business activities, including the degradation of the environment, unsafe products and workplaces, and the exclusion of minorities; and redistributing income through the impact of taxes, inheritance laws, and transfer payments (i.e., social security, aid to families with dependent children, and unemployment compensation). A substantial proportion of the above functions deal with the area of government regulation.

An Overview of Regulation

The Constitution provides for certain government interventions. However, it stresses minimum intervention. Regulation, a mechanism for implementing social choices, is based on the following constitutional powers: (1) the power to regulate interstate and foreign commerce; (2) the power to tax and spend; (3) the power to borrow; and (4) the power to promote the general welfare.

Regulations are promulgated by agencies in response to laws passed by Congress to remedy a perceived "market failure" or to attain a social goal. When the government regulates business it sets legally enforceable standards for conducting what are considered to be legitimate business activities. Within their range of jurisdiction, federal, state, or municipal agencies set standards by which goods and services must be produced, marketed, transported, financed, sold, or disposed of.

By legally requiring that people behave in certain ways not in their best interests in carrying out their professional tasks, regulation can distort firms' behavior and choices. By forcing the terms of exchange, regulation requires people to transfer value directly to other people. Because the terms of a regulated exchange are coerced, they are against the judgment of at least one of the participants in the transaction. The purpose of regulation is having government intervene in order to force an exchange that would not be agreed upon in free market.

Government regulation occurs when: (1) undesirable market structures are said to exist (i.e., fewness of firms); (2) there is a perceived need to conserve and efficiently use a natural resource; (3) significant negative economic externalities (e.g., pollution) are associated with a firm's activities; (4) the market or other conduct of a firm is judged to be socially undesirable (e.g., price discrimination); and (5) there is a desire to control or dilute large power blocks in the economy (e.g., the strategic position of utility companies). These reasons primarily involve perceived or actual market failures.

The term *market failure* implies that the market is a means to certain desired ends. If these ends are not attained, a deficiency is said to exist in the market system. Many proponents of market failure theory argue that certain public goods such as electricity or water would be provided inefficiently in a market setting. Others take the market failure concept even further by calling for government to correct the inability or unwillingness of private firms to provide certain values. The idea of a market failure has been extended to include the failure of a free market to produce specific goods and services at a cost or in quantities judged to be desirable or reasonable. The political process is thus used to lobby the government to interfere and correct the market failure by requiring firms to produce certain goods or services or at a given price. This revised and expanded concept of economist's idea of market failure not only claims that what is produced should be produced efficiently, but also that the market should supply additional goods and services in quantities and prices not in the firm's own perceived best interests.

The enhanced version of market failure theory can be traced to the ideas of democracy and positive rights. According to democratic theory, a demand by the majority ought to be met even if that means government intervention into the economic sector. However, a law can still be a violation of natural rights, no matter how popular it may be. In addition, people do not possess positive rights and are not owed involuntary servitude by their fellowmen. Examples of recent claims to positive rights include the right to a job, the right to job safety, the right to education, and the right not be discriminated against.

Many types of perceived market failures turn out to be caused by non-market institutions or political failures such as the influence or capture of the regulatory process by vested interests and industry experts. The idea of political failure includes the notion that there is a tendency for government to do more harm then good when it intervenes in economic activities. Even in cases of true market failure there is no compelling reason to believe that the situation will not worsen through government intervention. The costs of market failure versus the cost of government failure need to be compared. Regarding the values that the market system does not provide, it is wrong to assume that government can bring about their supply in the right amounts efficiently and without great costs elsewhere.

A new type of regulation, social regulation, gained in importance during the post-World War II period. Unlike economic regulation (which focuses on market or economic variables, entry to or exit from markets, and types of services that can be offered), social regulation focuses on firms' impacts on people as employees, consumers, and citizens. Social regulations attempt: to provide protection from discrimination in employment practices; to ensure safe and healthful workplaces; to protect consumers against risks from unsafe products; and to protect citizens from environmental pollution. In contrast to economic regulations, social regulations are usually rather lengthy and specific and are normally aimed at business practices affecting all industries—only occasionally are there social regulations that are industry specific. The Environmental Protection Agency, for example, sets precise pollution reduction goals and timetables for all firms and, as a result, is less likely to identify with, and have sympathy for, those regulated than an agency like the Federal Communications Commission, which is related to a specific industry. The growth in social regulation has signaled an increasing role for government in the affairs of businesses of all sizes. This power shift from managers to government regulators has led to a blurring of the distinction between private power and public power.

While economic regulation has decreased over the last few decades, social regulation has been on the rise. The inspectors, reviewers, and other staff of social regulatory agencies outnumber the staffs of federal economic regulatory agencies. The government uses regulatory power to attain all types of "socially desirable" ends in areas such as the reduction of pollution, improved areas for the handicapped, workplace safety, product safety, etc. The function of social regulation has not been to control entry, exit, prices, or profit, but to address such market failures as externalities and information inadequacies.

Costs and Consequences of Regulation

Government intervention into private markets produces costs and unintended consequences more harmful than the targeted problem itself. Government actions create obstacles to prosperity and economic growth. Initially, the impacts of government regulation are to increase firms' costs, slow down their decision-making processes, and reduce the resources available to produce goods and services. Ultimately, it the consumer who is at the receiving end of the repercussions generated by regulation. It is imperative to look at the effects on all groups and in the long run.

One adverse effect of regulation is the administrative, on-budget costs to taxpayers for running and maintaining federal regulatory agencies. Bureaucrats have vested interests in creating increased demands for their own regulatory skills (and for more resources) by producing a broad, complex, maze of rules through which firms and individuals must pass. Businessmen and other citizens, in turn, seek to expand the scope of the regulatory process because each envisions a way of gaining from it—people are motivated to create ways of also qualifying for the benefits to those favored by various regulations.

Direct compliance expenditures include the costs of processing paperwork, accountant and attorney fees, staff time needed to understand and comply with the web of federal regulations, specific equipment requirements, the time lost waiting in lines for permits and inspections, etc. Not only are such costs passed on to customers in the form of higher prices, compliance costs also produce a lag in the introduction of new products because firms must get permission from an array of agencies at each level of government and oftentimes from the courts.

Opportunity costs, hidden or indirect costs of regulation, are the benefits that would have occurred if resources had not been devoted to some regulatory activity. By focusing on what opportunity is foregone by spending the money on particular regulations, we can estimate the lost benefits of alternative public or private uses of taxpayers' wealth. Those foregone benefits can be viewed as deadweight losses.

When regulators ask if people are in favor of safer products, they are asking for a comparison between something and its absence. The benefits gained through regulation should be compared with what could be obtained with the same resources in the absence of regulation. Employing resources can only produce the benefits of government regulation that citizens may prefer to use in other ways. Whereas the effects of government regulation can be pointed to, the costs of the preferred choices of individuals are unseen.

Many regulations increase the cost of employing workers and thus act like a hidden tax on job creation. The minimum wage law and federal labor laws increase the cost of employing workers and decrease wages and/or employment. Government-mandated costs such as unemployment and disability insurance, retirement benefits, childcare, government paperwork requirements, and the cost of lawyers and accountants raise the cost to employers above the rewards received by the worker. This can lead to layoffs, or at a minimum, to a slowdown in the creation of new jobs.

The intended purpose of minimum wage laws is to help the lowest wage earners at the expense of their employers. The actual result is to increase unemployment among the poor and unskilled. Such a law does not increase the worth of any employee; it merely makes unemployable any worker whose service potential is worth less than the minimum wage. If such a restriction did not exist everyone looking for employment would find some type of job.

Federal labor laws restrict the flexibility of companies to hire and dismiss workers. Such laws also require the firm to engage in costly and time-consuming negotiations with labor unions. In addition, compulsory union dues reduce the net benefit received by workers, thereby decreasing the supply of labor.

Proponents of government regulation make the case that while regulations may cut jobs in some companies, it increases them in other firms. Although it is true that jobs are created in companies that help firms to comply with rules (e.g., with Treasury or environmental regulations), the truth is that regulation diverts employment from productive (i.e., value-added) to unproductive (i.e., non-value-added) activities.

Costs of regulation to the economy and society include the loss of enterprises that cannot afford to meet the hundreds of government regulations, the reduced flow of new and improved products, and a less rapid rise in the standard of living. Some firms are forced to close their businesses or to carry them overseas. For surviving domestic firms, regulatory costs are a hidden tax reducing the competitiveness of domestic companies in a global marketplace.

Not only do rent controls violate the rights of both landlords and tenants to freely and jointly decide the price of a rental unit, rent controls create shortages and decrease the quality of housing. Tenants desire the best apartment for lowest possible rent and landlords want the highest rent they can get. Rent controls have produced notorious housing shortages and have encouraged the wasteful use of space. There is no incentive to build new housing under rent control. Landlords have no incentive and little capital to invest in new construction or to keep low-income housing in good repair. In turn, tenants are encouraged to use space wastefully because of low fixed rents and legal protection against rent increases.

Duties, import quotas, and other restrictions on free trade can only benefit any domestic industry at the expense of consumers who must buy higher priced (or lower quality) goods. Tariffs, like price supports, shift higher costs and inferior quality goods onto consumers.

The nature of price controls (i.e., maximum or minimum prices) is to control and force people to do what the government wants them to do. In a free society, a government does not have the right to interfere with the choices of people to do business with each other at terms mutually agreed upon.

Without the benefit of feedback market signals, regulators have no basis of knowing which actions are "correct" and which are mistaken. Prices maintained by artificial mechanisms necessarily contain misinformation. Regulatory measures such as price fixing obscure the true cost of one course of action compared with its alternatives, inhibit the feedback that permits transactors to communicate, and create market distortions that ultimately harm consumers.

Prices are mechanisms for carrying out the rationing function and are fast, efficient conveyors of information through a society in which fragmented knowledge must be coordinated. Accurate prices resulting from voluntary exchanges allow the economy to achieve optimal performance in terms of satisfying each person as much as possible by his own standards without sacrificing others' rights to act according to their own standards.

Regulation impairs economic growth, retards the innovation process, and delays the adoption of new technologies. For example, Americans are frequently deprived of superior medicines because the United States is one of the last countries to allow the introduction of new and better pharmaceutical products. Slowness in drug approval prevents Americans from obtaining drugs that might save their lives and/or increase the quality of their lives.

Automobile safety requirements for seat belts, air bags, auto inspections, and so on, may not necessarily reduce highway accidents, injuries, and fatalities. Drivers may be willing to accept a certain level of risk and therefore might compensate for "safer" vehicles through reckless driving.

Regulated firms whose profit is limited to a stipulated percentage multiplied by the sum of the allowable expenses and assets in its "rate base" have every incentive to permit costs to rise and to become too capital intensive, given that the regulatory agency accepts these expenditures as valid for inclusion in the rate base. There is little incentive for regulated firms to keep costs down and great incentive to see them rise.

Traditional economic theory postulates the following reasons for excluding competitors: (1) external effects (e.g., broadcast interference which renders unrestricted competition infeasible) and (2) industries (usually natural monopolies such as electricity, gas, or telephone) that require huge investments in fixed costs in which cost per unit of output is constantly declining and, therefore, in which one producer can supply the market more cheaply than multiple producers. Regulatory agencies have thus been assigned the valuable legal right to exclude firms from entering the industry they regulate. Although inconsistent with the "public interest," a rational response of members of regulatory commissions is to protect and favor incumbents who can possibly reward them in the future (e.g., by employing them in firms they currently regulate).

Similarly, the government can restrict entry into a given market by requiring occupational licenses, certifications, and business permits. Here there is also a strong bias towards incumbents. Existing practitioners in a licensed occupation are almost always exempted from escalating qualification standards such as educational requirements, apprenticeship requirements, and tougher qualifying examinations. The change in qualification standards is often accompanied by rules forbidding either price undercutting or price advertising. A good case may be made that the espoused public interest benefit of weeding out unqualified practitioners may be less than the related costs.

Deregulation

Deregulation is based on an ethical base that recognizes the primacy of conscious and informed individual choice and responsibility for one's actions. Since the 1970s, there have been major efforts to lessen or eliminate economic regulations where competition sufficiently serves the public interest. During the last few decades, the United States has deregulated airlines, trucking, taxi fleets, utility rates, interest rates, broker rates, etc.

Before 1978, for nearly 50 years, the airlines had been run as a highly regulated quasi-utility, with each carrier allowed to fly only those routes, and charge only those prices, approved by the Civil Aeronautics Board (CAB). The CAB began to deregulate in 1977 by granting increased freedom in pricing and easier admittance to routes not previously served. As a result, fares were lowered, passenger load factors were improved, the cost per seat was decreased, profits soared, and customers received better service. Then, in 1978 Congress passed laws that phased out the CAB, abolishing its authority to control prices and entry. Lawmakers began to recognize that airline regulation tended to increase risk and decrease safety—not only did such regulation increase carrier costs, it made routing more circuitous, required people to spend more time in the air, and caused planes to make more takeoffs and landings.

An unanticipated benefit from airline deregulation was a decrease in auto accidents. Lower airfares shifted more travelers to airlines from other modes of transportation such as the automobile. The deregulation of airlines thus saved lives because travel by automobile is riskier and more likely to result in injuries and fatalities.

Congress passed the Motor Carriers Act of 1980 that permitted more pricing freedom to individual carriers, made entrance to the market less burdensome, and removed many costly Interstate Commerce Commission (ICC) restrictions. Before such deregulation, the ICC created inefficiencies and artificial demand for trucking services through regulations such as: (1) forcing many trucks to come back empty instead of returning home carrying another load, and (2) forbidding a truck carrying one product or a product in a specified stage of completion to haul another product or the same product in a different completion phase. Deregulation in the trucking industry resulted in lower prices per truckload shipment, fewer complaints, and better service.

Also, in 1980, Congress allowed railroads more flexibility in rate setting, and in 1986 the ICC was abolished. The results were similar to those attained in the trucking industry. There was a reduction in the cost per mile of freight shipped, lower rates for customers, and more money available to spend on deferred maintenance and on better equipment.

Deregulation in the petroleum industry has reduced gas prices. Furthermore, beneficial but less complete patterns of deregulation have taken place in telecommunications, banking, and other financial services.

Instead of Government Regulation

Proponents of a free society uphold individual freedom as the primary principle for the state to protect and therefore do not recognize the moral legitimacy of government regulation. Individuals have natural rights to be free from having others interfere with their lives, liberty, and property. Governments are much too willing to formulate and adopt "solutions" to problems that would be better left for the free market to deal with.

Many regulations involve men voluntarily dealing with other men. It is through the regulatory process that the state forces the terms of exchange in such transactions. Protection is the purported reason for many regulations. However, the government often fails to recognize that any transaction is voluntary in the absence of coercion and that, therefore, protection is only appropriate when force is involved.

Some paternalistic defenders of regulation contend that regulation is necessary to protect people from their own faulty judgments and wrong decisions. Essentially, this is an argument for safeguarding people from their own rational minds. Most people do not have to be forced to do what they believe to be in their own best interest. Certainly, some individuals are less able than others at discerning what is to their own best advantage. That is no legitimate reason for others to be denied their rights, through regulation, to act according to their own judgments.

Anti-individualism underlies the tendency of government to regulate behavior. This concept includes the notion that selfish men must be forced to serve a higher purpose such as the "common good," others' needs, the majority's desires, or the goals of political authorities which ostensibly are in the public interest.

The public interest viewpoint mistakenly assumes that government officials have both sufficient knowledge and the proper incentives necessary to rationally affect private markets. In a democracy, government bestows benefits in anticipation of receiving votes. Regulators react to payoffs and pressures from special interest groups. As government intervention increases, so does the motivation for private individuals and firms to invest less in the quest for profits and more into the pursuit of government protection and favors. Whenever a new law is passed, citizens wonder if it applies to their own situations. They seek to expand the applicability of the law because each envisions a way of prospering from it. People have the incentive to find ways of also qualifying for the benefits. Whenever the government has special benefits to give, there will be companies and individuals lobbying for handouts.

Certainly, markets are the best means for achieving the most efficient distribution of goods and services. When a business abides by the rules of the free market, it has not been granted any special privileges by the government and therefore has no legislative advantages over its competitors and is unable to charge artificially high prices to customers.

Much of what government regulation attempts to do can be dealt with by the courts. Judicial means can be utilized to remedy many injustices. The law of torts may be able to cope with much of what is now handled through government regulation.

In addition, regulation does not necessarily have to include the government. A great deal of regulation is currently privately produced and administered by trade associations and other independent bodies. These private associations oversee members' actions through monitoring, standard setting, product testing, inspection, warranty approval, certification, arbitration, etc. The federal government should seriously look into transferring most (if not all) regulatory functions to independent, private third parties. Including these private associations in the regulatory process will downsize and perhaps ultimately eliminate the current command-and-control system and replace it with a more responsive and adaptable process.

Recommended Reading

Barnam, Michael S. *Alternatives to Regulation.* Lexington, Mass.: Lexington Books, 1981.

Derthick, Martha, and Paul J. Quirk. *The Politics of Deregulation.* Washington, D.C.: Brookings Institute, 1985.

Gart, Alan. *Regulation, Deregulation, and Reregulation.* New York: John Wiley & Sons, 1993.

Higgins, Richard S., and Paul H. Rubin, eds. *Deregulating Telecommunications.* New York: John Wiley & Sons, 1996.

Kirkpatrick, Jeane J. "Global Paternalism: The U.N. and the New International Regulatory Order." *Regulation* (January-February 1983).

Kohlmeier, Louis M. Jr. *The Regulators.* New York: Harper and Row, 1969.

Kristol, Irving. "A Regulated Society." *Regulation* (July-August 1977).

Lilly, William, and James C.Miller. "The New 'Social Regulation.'" *The Public Internet* (spring 1977).

Machan, Tibor R., and M. Bruce Johnson, eds. *Rights and Regulation.* Cambridge, Mass.: Ballinger Publishing Co., 1983.

McKenzie, Richard B. *Airline Deregulation and Air Travel Safety.* St. Louis, Mo.: Washington University, Center for the Study of American Business, 1991.

Mitnick, Barry M. *The Political Economy of Regulation.* New York: Columbia University Press, 1972.

Peltzman, Sam. *Political Participation and Government Regulation.* Chicago: University of Chicago Press, 1998.

Poole, Robert W. Jr., ed. *Instead of Regulation.* Lexington, Mass.: Lexington Books, 1981.

Reisman, George. *Government against the Economy.* Ottawa, Ill.: Jameson Books, 1979.

Robyn, Dorothy L. *Braking the Special Interests: Trucking Deregulation and the Politics of Policy Reform.* Chicago: University of Chicago Press, 1987.

Shleifer, Andrei, and Robert Vichny. *The Grabbing Hand: Government Pathologies and Their Cures.* Boston: Harvard University Press, 1999.

Spangler, Mark. *Clichés of Politics.* Irvington-on-Hudson, N.Y.: Foundation for Economic Education, 1994.

Teske, Paul. *Deregulating Freight Transportation: Delivering the Goods.* Contributions by Samuel Bert and Michael Mintrom. Washington, D.C.: American Enterprise Institute Press, 1995.

Weidenbaum, Murray L. *Business and Government.* Upper Saddle River, N.J.: Prentice-Hall, 1999.

27

Inflation and Money

This is what "money management" really means. In practice it is merely a high-sounding euphemism for continuous currency debasement. It consists of constant lying in order to support constant swindling. Instead of automatic currencies based on gold, people are forced to take managed currencies based on guile. Instead of precious metals they hold paper promises whose value falls with every bureaucratic whim. And they are suavely assured that only hopelessly antiquated minds dream of returning to truth and honesty and solvency and gold.

—Henry Hazlitt

Money is the lifeblood of commerce. In order to permit the market to operate, we need to ensure a stable, noninflationary currency. Inflation invariably distorts the market. There are always different groups in the population being affected dissimilarly by inflation. Inflation leads to a misdirection of production and employment, resulting in a misallocation of resources. Money that loses its value through inflation circumvents the mind by destroying the means of economic calculation and planning.

Printing more money causes inflation. The government's monetary policies are responsible for this. Keynesian spending policies and ideology and the abolishment of the gold standard have permitted the government to depreciate our currency.

The answer is to eradicate state control of the money supply. We need to divest government of its power to arbitrarily increase or decrease the money supply. In addition, we must build in pressures toward fiscal responsibility by the government with respect to the production of balanced budgets and reduction of debt. The federal government must learn to live within its means—government deficits must be prevented. The establishment of the gold standard will stifle the hidden and deceptive tax of inflation. Inflation could be controlled if government were not able to monetize debt or manipulate reserve requirements.

Defining Inflation

Money is a commodity the value of which stems from its usefulness as a medium of exchange. The best money is the one developed through the market system. Because barter has obvious limitations, one commodity (e.g., gold) arises as easier to trade and more useful as a medium of exchange. Exchange rates (i.e., prices) are established between this one commodity and each of the other goods. Historically and pragmatically, a commodity's ability to function as money has been transferred to money substitutes (e.g., the dollar). Honest money is fully backed by commodities like gold.

Inflation, a monetary phenomenon, is an increase in money and credit. Its major consequence is rising prices. Inflation consists of expanding a nation's money supply by adding something other than real money (e.g., gold). Such fiat money, backed only by government decree, produces general price increases. If the quantity of money is increased, the purchasing power of the monetary unit declines and the quantity of goods and services that can be purchased for one unit of this money also decreases. When government expands the quantity of paper money, the purchasing power of the monetary unit drops and prices rise. After the new money has been added to the economy, the total wealth produced is not any greater than it was previously. With added money now being spent, but with no additional goods and services to spend it on, prices will rise. In the United States, it is only the federal government and government-recognized banks that can print money and/or create new dollar credit.

Why Does the Government Inflate?

Inflation is a dishonest and deliberate policy and tool of politicians who do not wish to reduce their spending. The government "creates" new money in order to cover what it spends in excess of its income. The existence of an unbalanced budget is a frequent reason for the government to print more money. When more is spent than is raised by taxes, the government makes up the difference with fiat money. The basic cause of inflation is the government's unwillingness to cut its spending plans or to raise the funds it desires by increasing taxation or by borrowing from the public.

Politicians want to spend but they do not want to raise taxes. Because higher taxes are unpopular, inflation commonly becomes the answer to deficit financing. When the government prints more money, people don't have to pay additional taxes, but ultimately they realize that dollars are not worth what they were previously. Monetary debasement is a scheme in which government force is used to take wealth from people and spend it. When the government makes new money and spends it, the effect on prices and the supply of goods and services is no different than when a private counterfeiter does so.

Exorbitant government expenditures are often the result of government efforts to redistribute income and wealth. Inflation can be connected to the appearance of the welfare state. Political leaders, confident in their own abilities, rationality, ability to control nature and society, and to produce continual progress, use government force to redistribute wealth in their compassionate efforts to achieve economic equality. Additional dollars, created through the printing press and credit expansion, enable the government to spend more and support more "deserving" nonproducers than it could otherwise.

Inflation transfers wealth from creditors to debtors of which the federal government is the largest. Debtors make payment with currency that is worth less than when the debt was assumed. Inflation repudiates government debt at the same time that it depreciates the purchasing power of the debt.

How the Government Inflates

The government has several ways of increasing the money supply. Expansion of the money stock is carried out by monetizing federal debt, by Federal Reserve "open market operations," and by credit expansion through commercial bank loans to private borrowers.

In America, the Federal Reserve System currently has control of the issuance of unbacked currency. The government's demonetization of gold established government-sanctioned paper as the exclusive medium of exchange. The government blocked holders of paper money from protecting themselves from the ravages of inflation when it denied American citizens the freedom to select gold in preference to inflatable fractional reserve money. Essentially, all the government has to do when it wants to spend more money than has been collected in taxes is to borrow nonexistent money from the Federal Reserve through the issuance of government securities. This new money is spent and deposited in banks, thereby becoming the fractional reserve for even more unbacked money. New money creation builds on itself and snowballs. The only limits to the money supply are arbitrary reserve requirements on banks (i.e., the reserves in cash that a commercial bank holds against deposits) and debt limits established by Congress.

The Treasury seldom sells government bonds directly to the Federal Reserve. Rather, the Federal Reserve purchases bonds on the open market thus giving the Treasury room to sell its bonds on the market. The result is the same even though the mechanics make the process a bit less obvious.

When the Federal Reserve buys government securities on the open market it expands the supply of money and credit. Using a cashier's check, the Federal Reserve pays for the securities with its private holdings. The seller, in turn, deposits the check in a commercial bank. This increases the bank's reserve balance of cash thus enabling it to lend out several times the amount of the deposit. Production of fractional reserve money merely requires a journal entry crediting a borrower with a sum of money and issuing a deposit receipt in this amount. Commercial banks thus can increase the quantity of money by lending several times as much as the amounts deposited by their customers in their accounts. The use of fractional reserves clearly demonstrates the fraudulent nature of lending claims to mythical property.

Money should be backed by a 100 percent reserve of what is used to back it. If the government were unable to monetize its debt or manipulate reserve requirements, then obstacles to inflation would be in place. Under a 100 percent gold reserve standard or system, there would be little or no inflation because prices would depend on the existing supply of gold. With the inability to expand the volume of money and credit at will, the political evil of inflation would no longer be able to be perpetrated by agents of the U.S. Treasury and officials of the Federal Reserve System.

The Consequences of Inflation

Inflation is a type of tax that falls on each citizen in the form of higher prices for what he purchases. It is analogous to a sales tax on all goods and services. Inflation levies a tax on all who have money or have money owed to them. Like taxes, inflation distorts prices, changes production patterns, transfers wealth from savers to spenders, discourages saving and investment, and stifles individual initiative.

A particularly evil form of taxation, inflation does not affect people in proportion to their income or wealth. Its incidence depends on the business or industry in which one works, the elasticity of demand for different commodities, the specific forms in which a person holds his assets and debts, etc. There is no way for the government to create new dollars or bank credit so that each person will benefit equally and simultaneously.

Inflation starts with government expansion of the money supply that immediately creates benefits for some persons while producing losses for others. Commonly, individuals on fixed incomes and owners of bonds, loans, and savings accounts suffer losses while borrowers and property owners enjoy gains.

Some individuals have the advantage of receiving the newly created currency and bank credit sooner than others. Such persons are able to buy more than they could previously or to offer higher prices for goods and services they desire. People who receive the new money and credit first receive a temporary benefit at the expense of others who receive the new money or credit later. Those receiving the new money or credit first have greater income and thus can purchase many goods and services at prices that existed at the beginning of the inflation. The first groups spend their money when prices have gone up least (or not at all) and the last groups consume and pay when prices have increased the most.

When the first recipients of the new dollar offer higher prices, prices tend to be raised by the suppliers of the goods and services for which higher prices had been offered. The increased number of dollars generates shifts in income and wealth. Those who receive unexpectedly high prices for their commodities benefit from the inflation. They experience "windfall" profits at the expense of holders of monetary assets (i.e., dollars and assets fixed in number of dollars).

The influx of new fiat money permits people who gain access to it early to buy at yesterday's prices. However, there are others to whom the new money arrives much later. They are forced to pay higher prices than they did previously for some or nearly all of the goods and services they desire to buy. The last recipients of the new money pay higher prices while their incomes remain constant or do not go up proportionately with prices.

Inflation tends to initially create more employment. It is likely to at first increase sales and selling prices at a faster rate than it increases expenses. Nevertheless, this effect is fleeting and occurs only when and if inflation is unanticipated. When individuals begin to expect inflation, they will make compensating adjustments and demands thus causing costs to catch up with selling prices. Wages, interest, and raw materials prices increase as fast (if not faster) than a product's retail price, profit margins narrow, and the businessman realizes that his profits have been illusory.

At each stage of the sequence of transactions by which the new money works its way through the economy, the advantage of receiving additional dollars declines. Those who receive it much later must adapt to a situation in which the items they want are increasingly more expensive.

Inflation falsifies economic calculations and accounting profits and leads businessmen to make errors. Inflation misdirects production so that scarce resources are dedicated to inappropriate projects. Illusory profits deceive producers, invite malproduction and malinvestments and make planning a nightmare. The initial aura of prosperity dissipates as prices go up, wages lag, and business decisions brought about by false market signals produce bad results.

Inflation dampens producers' incentives to save and invest in production facilities. As a result, less is produced. Furthermore, because there has been less production, there is less to consume, save, and invest. What's more, with less saved and invested currently, there will be less produced in the future for individuals to consume, save, and invest. The increasing uncertainty of profits discourages new investment to a greater degree than what the overall increase in profits due to inflation does to encourage investments. Investment, employment, and production are misdirected by inflation, and ultimately they are all discouraged by it.

When the government expands the money supply to finance its debts or to create economic prosperity, the result is higher prices. People have more dollars but the dollar loses its purchasing power. Inflation reduces the value of the currency, and to pay its debts the government uses the amount of that reduction. When monetary authorities inflate and depreciate money, people are forced to accept it at face value and in full payment. The federal government, as a huge debtor, benefits greatly from monetary depreciation. When monetary value declines, lenders suffer losses in purchasing power while borrowers (like the government) gain a like amount. Creditors are defrauded when debtors discharge their debts by exchanging inferior money.

When progressive tax rates are unadjusted for inflation, the increase in the nominal value of wages places individuals in progressively higher tax brackets, thus permitting the government to collect a larger proportion of income and assets. By denying inflation adjustments, the state can also exact more taxes from businesses. Higher taxes are paid when depreciation and other production costs are understated and profits are overstated.

Oftentimes, when the government wants to stimulate the economy, it gets the Federal Reserve System to reduce interest rates. To do this, it must create more spendable money. Increasing the supply of loanable funds decreases interest rates. This can be done by getting the central bank to purchase government securities or by directly monetizing debt (i.e., by simply printing more money). When monetary authorities expand the quantity of money and credit, they cause interest rates to initially fall. Businesses are lured into expanding by the lower interest rates. As a result land, labor, and capital are bid up. After a while, lenders will catch on and want a real return. After the new money has flowed through the economy, rates will return to normal and mistakes will be evident.

Inflation deters saving and investment and promotes a search for alternatives to saving during the inflation. Why work hard, save, and invest if the purchasing power of dollars saved is expected to fall? People attempt to identify and acquire a real store of value in the form of nonmonetary or hard assets such as precious metals, diamonds, real estate, machinery and equipment, and rare items such as stamps, antique furniture, art works, books, coins, firearms, etc. People will save and invest little, if any, unless they are confident that their property will be safe and that their savings and money will retain its purchasing power.

Not recognizing the government's own responsibility for inflation, politicians assign the blame to the private sector and advocate the use of price controls to fight inflation. They fail to understand that price controls cannot stop or even slow down inflation. All these controls can do is reduce profit margins, discourage production, and create shortages. Furthermore, and most importantly, they do not understand that price controls represent the antithesis of economic freedom.

Real Monetary Reform

Traditionally, the gold standard has been used to tie the value of money to something more constant and stable than the capricious desires of government officials. Such an impersonal protection is needed to restrain the actions of those who hold a legal monopoly on the creation of money. Under the gold standard, the quantity of the money supply is independent of the policies of government bureaucrats and politicians. Gold represents value uncontrolled by government. The gold standard takes decisions regarding the quantity of money out of the hands of politicians.

Making paper money redeemable in gold keeps the government from arbitrarily increasing the money supply. Not only does full redeemability of the currency unit restrict government power, it also supports public confidence in money, allows market forces to work, and protects citizens from disguised taxation through monetary inflation.

The gold standard provides a market-based medium of exchange and stable monetary system through which men can exchange and save the results of their labor. This monetary stability will force the government to abstain from monetary depreciation. Not only would the government have to stop inflating, it would also be forced to balance its budget and eliminate many welfare programs. Under a gold standard, politicians cannot spend more unless they raise taxes.

Under the gold standard, all claims to gold (i.e., dollars) are receipts for gold and are fully convertible into a specific amount of gold. Money and credit expansion is brought to a sudden halt when government and banks have to redeem their notes in gold. Redemptions would be a chief obstacle to government's unlimited money creation and spending.

Under the gold standard, banks and individuals would be able to make loans, but they would be limited to the amounts savers had accumulated and were making available for lending purposes. The gold standard's requirement of fully convertible money would keep more than one claim to the same money from occurring.

Because of its natural attributes and relative scarcity, gold has long served as a dependable medium of exchange. The quantity of gold changes very slowly over time. Consequently, currencies fully backed by gold are susceptible to only a negligible rate of inflation. There has been a gradual increase in the store of gold with the annual increase in the world stock of gold usually amounting to between 1.5 and 3 percent. Over time, the total gold stockpile held by central banks and individuals has always increased and has never decreased.

If gold was money, there would be a negligible price level increase when more gold is mined, refined, and processed and an even slighter decrease as some gold is removed from the monetary realm to be used in industry, dentistry, jewelry, etc.

Some are concerned that new annual supplies of gold will be insufficient to carry on the growing amounts and value of world trade. Gold, a hard currency, may have a new production rate that may not keep pace with economic growth. This really presents no problem. The existing quantity of money is always enough to conduct the existing volume of trade. Some deflation may be inevitable, but this simply means that overall prices will be lower.

Recommended Reading

Boskin, Michael J. *Inflation and Its Discontents*. Stanford, Calif.: Hoover Institution Press, 1997.

Dowd, Kevin. *The State and the Monetary System*. New York: St. Martin's Press, 1989.

Garrett, Garet, and Murray N. Rothbard. *The Great Depression and New Deal Monetary Policy*. San Francisco, Calif.: Cato Institute, 1980.

Greaves, Bettina Bien. "The Tragedy of Inflation More than High Prices." *The Freeman* (October 1981).

Hahn, Frank. *Money and Inflation*. Boston, Mass.: MIT Press, 1985.

Hazlitt, Henry. *What You Should Know about Inflation*. New York: Funk and Wagnalls, 1968.

————. *The Inflation Crisis and How to Resolve It*. New Rochelle, N.Y.: Arlington House, 1978.

————. *Economics in One Lesson*. New York: Crown Publishers, 1979.

Heilperin, Michael A. "Aspects of the Pathology of Money." *Monetary Essays from Four Decades*. London: Michael Joseph, 1968.

Humphrey, Thomas M. *Money, Banking and Inflation: Essays in the History of Monetary Thought*. Miami, Fla.: Edward Elgar, 1993.

Mises, Ludwig von. *The Theory of Money and Credit*. Indianapolis, Ind.: Liberty Classics, 1981.

Patterson, Robert T., ed. *Why Gold?* Great Barrington, Mass.: American Institute for Economic Research, 1964.

Rockwell, Llewellyn H., ed. *The Gold Standard: An Austrian Perspective*. Lexington, Mass.: Lexington Books, 1985.

Rothbard, Murray N. *What Has Government Done to Our Money?* Santa Ana, Calif.: Rampart College, 1974.

Skousen, Mark. *Economics of a Pure Gold Standard*. Auburn, Ala.: Ludwig von Mises Institute, 1988.

White, Lawrence H. *Competition and Currency: Essays on Free Banking and Money*. New York: New York University Press, 1989.

PART VI

IN RETROSPECT AND PROSPECT

28

Conceptual Foundations Revisited

There is power only in principles: they alone are a beacon light for men's minds, a rallying point for convictions gone astray.

—Frederic Bastiat

The power of ideas is great. If we are to educate, persuade, and convert others to free-market thinking, we need to articulate, in structured form, the conceptual and moral foundations of free enterprise. We are obliged to expound a coherent and consistent body of principles that are in accord with reality and that properly reflect and explain capitalism. In other words, we must approach the idea of free enterprise from a philosophical point of view. The survival of free enterprise may be in jeopardy unless people understand its conceptual and moral foundations.

Classical liberalism is a rational doctrine based on a clear understanding of man and society in which economics, politics, and morality (all parts of one inseparable truth) are found to be in harmony with one another. Classical liberalism's search for truth has provided us with a systematic theory consistent with the nature of man and the world.

From a deductive perspective, philosophy precedes and determines politics, which, in turn, precedes and determines economics. On the other hand, the philosopher must begin by inductively studying the fundamental nature of existence, of man, and of man's relationship to existence. This is the point at which we will begin our review of the conceptual foundations of a free society.

The Nature of Man and the World

In developing a conceptual framework for free enterprise, it is necessary to focus our attention on the enduring characteristics of reality. Men live in a universe with a definite nature and exist within nature as part of the natural order. Using their minds, men have the ability to discover the permanent features of the world. A unified theoretical perspective and potent intellectual framework for analyzing the social order must be based on the constraining realities of the human condition. Reality is not optional.

We live in a systematic universe with an underlying natural order that makes it so. There are discernible regularities pervading all of creation. There is an underlying order that gives circumscription, predictability, and their character to all things. Through the use of the mind, men can discover the nature of things, the laws that regulate or apply to them, the way they now exist, and the ways they can potentially be. The hypothetical concept of the state of nature can be employed to uncover the nature of things. To determine the nature of anything, it is necessary to remove all that is unique and exclusive (i.e., all of the accidental attributes) to a thing and examine it in terms of the common characteristics it shares with all others of its type. This is done in order to study the fundamental nature of existence, of man, and of man's relationship to existence. Our goal is to discover the natural order as it applies to man and his affairs. There exists a natural law that reigns over the affairs of human conduct. Natural law theory holds that there is a law prior to man, society, and government. It is a law that must be abided by if each of these is to attain its true character and fulfillment. When a person rightly regards the nature of things, he is employing right reason.

To ascertain man's nature, we must, through a process of abstraction, remove all that is accidental to any specific man. What is left must be man's distinctive features and potentialities. It is man's ability to reason that separates him from other vital organisms. Man's rational faculty distinguishes him from all other living species. Conceptualization (i.e., reason) is man's unique and only proper way of dealing with the rest of the natural world. It is in man's nature to use his rational powers, to form concepts, to integrate them, to evaluate alternatives, to make choices, and so on. In order to survive and flourish, men must come to terms with the requirements of reality.

The ability to control one's actions (i.e., natural liberty) is an inborn condition of man. In the nature of things no person can use the mind, senses, or appendages of another. Man is free to use his faculties provided that he does not harm others in his use of them. All thinking and acting is done by individual persons in their own spatiotemporal localities—a society cannot think nor act although men can choose to act in a coordinated manner with one another. Men have the ability to cooperate and achieve through voluntary action.

Natural Law Doctrines

Natural law doctrines include, but are not limited to, the state of nature, natural rights, the social contract, and the rule of law. Because natural law can be inferred from what is innate in the nature of man and the world, it would be compelling even if God did not exist. Natural law can be deduced with or without a religious framework. Natural law doctrines are discovered through the use of reason.

The state of nature includes the suppositional circumstances that are assumed to have existed before the institution of a civil government. Because all persons are free and equal in the state of nature, it follows that no one person has the natural right to reign over any of the others.

Society is natural to man as an associative being. It is within society that man can make voluntary exchanges that please and fulfill him. Furthermore, government is essential to enable each man to keep what is his and to live peacefully while having mutually beneficial voluntary relations with others. The state is not society. It is simply the entity charged with the function of protecting society that overflows the boundaries of the state. If a society was synonymous with the state, it would not be free because all human activity would be prescribed and governed by law.

The ideas of social cooperation, spontaneous order, and progressive evolution of the social order are included within natural law. That which is appropriate for society is appropriate for human nature, and thus, according to natural law. If the law emerges and evolves spontaneously, then it has its roots in human nature and human intelligence.

The natural law insists that everything stands under the test of reason grounded in reality. The particular nature of entities requires particular actions if the desired ends are to be attained. Natural laws of human action, discoverable through the use of reason, necessitate specific means and arrangements to affect the desired ends. The laws of nature determine the consequences. The free society works because it is in accord with nature. Natural law provides for reasoning and verification about what is good and what is not good.

Natural law underpins the inalienable rights of life, liberty, and the pursuit of happiness. Negative liberty, the absence of constraints and restraints imposed upon a person by other persons, can be arrived at by studying the distinctive faculties and abilities of human beings and abstracting away the particular levels or amounts that specific individuals possess with respect to their faculties and abilities. What remains is the ability of each man to think his own thoughts and control his own energies in his attempts to act according to those thoughts. Negative freedom is thus a natural requirement of human existence.

Freedom from man-made constraints and obstacles is a necessary condition to fulfill the potentialities of one's nature. This does not mean freedom from obstacles in general. Not having the abilities or resources is not coercion and therefore does not constitute a lack of freedom.

According to the precepts of natural law, a person should not be forced into acting or using his resources in a way in which he has not given his voluntary consent. It follows that man has certain natural rights to life, to the use of one's faculties as one wills for one's own ends, and to the fruits of one's labor. These rights inhere in man's nature and predate government, constitutions, and courts. Natural rights are derived from the facts of human nature and are respected because they are promotive of individuals' well-being.

The social contact is the tacit agreement of all which is essential, in the nature of things, to the existence of society. It is the implicit and concurrent covenant not to use violence, to fulfill agreements, not to trespass, not to deny others the use of their property, etc. The social contract is the understood, timeless, and universal contract that necessarily must exist if people are to live peacefully within society.

Social interactions and associations offer great benefits to individuals, including friendships, more information, specialization and the division of labor, greater productivity, a larger variety of goods and services, etc. Throughout history, economic activities have been the main type of social interaction and cooperation among people. Government thus became increasingly necessary as the range and complexity of market transactions grew.

Government is needed in order to enable people to live well in society. It is needed to prohibit and punish the private violation of the natural rights of those who peacefully use their energies and resources, to punish fraud and deception, and to settle disputes that may arise.

Of course, the existence of a natural order prior to government means that government's role should be limited and restrained. Natural law theory limits government to its proper sphere, sets bounds to its actions, and subjects the government itself to the law. It follows that to circumscribe government to its proper role, power must be separated into its different functions and power must be counterbalanced to keep those who govern from exceeding their legitimate bounds. This is important because when those who govern act outside the law, they do so with the full coercive power of the government.

Under the rule of law, everyone, including the government, is bound by rules. The idea that the government is under the law is a condition of the liberty of the people. The rule of law requires law to be general and abstract, known and certain, and equally applicable to all persons in any unknown number of future instances.

A constitution is a law for governments. Constitutional governments are characterized by specific restraints and enumerations of their powers. The force behind constitutional governments is the idea of a higher natural law restricting the operations of the government.

The notion of metanormative justice, an idea in harmony with natural law, is concerned only with the peaceful and orderly coordination of activities of any possible human being with any other in a social setting. This type of justice refers to equal treatment under social and legal conditions that include a collection of known rules regarding allowable and nonallowable actions that will lead to unequal positions with no one knowing in advance the particular result this arrangement will have for any specific person.

Similarly, the state can properly be said to be ensuring the common good when it protects man's natural right to seek his own happiness. Only protected liberty (or self-directedness) can be said to be good for, and able to be possessed by, all persons simultaneously. No other definition of the common good can be in harmony with an ordered universe and the natural law. The common good properly understood is protected freedom that permits persons to pursue happiness or the good that each defines for himself. The government achieves the common good when its functions are limited to protecting the natural right to liberty and preserving peace and order.

There is a critical distinction between the legitimacy of a right and the morality of exercising that right. The government should only be concerned with questions such as the domain of rights, the proper role of violence, and the definitions of aggression and criminality. The government should not be concerned with all personal moral principles. There is a huge difference between establishing the permissibility of an action and the goodness or morality of it. The state should be concerned with the rights of men and not with the oughts of men.

It follows that because religion is a private matter, the government has no right to enter the field of religious beliefs on the side of theism or on the side of atheism. People are free to hold any religious or nonreligious view they choose. Religion is a matter of personal conviction.

A healthy, differentiated social order relies on a separation of political, economic, and moral-cultural-religious systems. The power of the state should not be enhanced by the identification with religion. Churches need to be free from state power. The Constitution and Bill of Rights correctly state that neither a state nor a federal government can set up a religion nor can they pass laws that aid one religion, aid all religions, or prefer one religion over another. Neither can they neither force nor influence a person to go to or remain away from church against his will or force him to profess a belief or disbelief in any religion. The state is properly required to be neutral in its relations with groups of religious believers and nonbelievers.

On the other hand, the concrete human being is not compartmentalized. Religious people, as well as nonreligious people must be free to express their arguments in the public square and to hold public offices. It is not wrong for political players to cite their personal religious views as a factor in their stand on political issues. Likewise, it is not a violation of the principle of separation of church and state for like-minded members of a church, synagogue, mosque, or an atheistic organization to argue for political ends. It is legitimate to discuss the moral dimensions of public issues. What we want is freedom of religion, not freedom from religion. The Constitution and Bill of Rights speak to the separation of institutions and not to a commingling of political and religious ideologies or thought. The same values that underpin one's political beliefs also underlie one's religious beliefs.

Imperfect Man in a Finite World

Human nature is essentially unchanging and unchangeable. Men have always been imperfect in their knowledge, in their integrity, and in their ability to love and respect their fellowmen. Men possess all of the frailties of a finite nature. Accept them as they are and don't expect human behavior to improve much over the long run. Men are essentially self-centered but conditions can be improved within that constraint by relying primarily on incentives (i.e., rewards and punishments) rather than on dispositions. Because of human limitations and imperfections, man's ability to improve society is restricted.

Social outcomes are mainly a function of incentives presented to individuals and of the conditions under which they interact in response to them. Given man's moral and intellectual limitations and egocentricity, the fundamental challenge is to make the best of the possibilities within the constraints of man's nature.

In addition, resources are always inadequate to fulfill all the desires of all of the people. There are no solutions, only trade-offs that leave man's desires unfulfilled. We must accept the reality of economic constraints and the trade-offs they imply. We need to realize that human limitations are moral as well as intellectual and that resources are taken from other uses. Men choose between alternatives, regulate their behavior deliberately, and act purposively to attain their chosen ends.

It is imperative to have the right processes for making trade-offs and correcting inevitable errors. We need to maximize individuals' ability to use scattered fragments of knowledge and to correct mistakes as quickly as possible. Societal progress is most effectively and equally attained through systemic social processes (e.g., moral tradition, the market, the law, and families) rather than through solutions proposed by government officials. Society is a spontaneous order not under anyone's design or control. It cannot be a field of problems awaiting solutions because no one knows enough to successfully engage in comprehensive social and political experiments.

Human beings cannot flourish unless they direct their own actions. Each man is ultimately responsible for what happens to him and has the potential to rise above influences of environment, heredity, and chance to alter and determine his own future. The task of human persons is to do well in their own lives. Men, by virtue of being human, possess the capacity to exercise free will and have the inalienable right to do so. The natural order can be altered by men using their reason and free will, but who can also choose to treat others rightly or wrongly. Natural law grounds the propriety of human actions and values in the facts of reality and human nature. There is a natural order, which would result in the consonance of everyone's interests, if all people would participate in life fairly and justly.

Whereas potential natural resources are the given, the variable is human action. Human beings are unique individuals as well as members of a distinct species. It follows that each singular person's self-enhancement is a matter of what suits him best. Human variability in abilities and tastes is a source of comparative advantage that results in specialization, division of labor, and exchange. Similarly, the uneven distribution of natural resources, climate variability, and the diversity of human abilities lead to the ideas of the comparative advantage of nations and free trade. Variation leads to differential attainment in all areas of human endeavor and the dissimilar acquisition of income and wealth. Because the natural order of human society is variety, diversity, and inequality, virtue, charity, and compassion can only exist in a world of free and unequal individuals. In a free society, in accord with the natural order, natural differences among people would result in some being better off than others, but there would be no political inequality—everyone would be equal before the law and possess equal rights, freedom to choose, and equality of opportunity.

Although environmental factors can mitigate or intensify mental and physical differences, nonequality will continue to be the natural order. Differences in individual talents, motivations, and resources that each of us has are not inherently unjust—there will always be inequalities among people. The idea of justice does not apply to the metaphysically given. It is not unjust for some people to be born with less ability or resources than others.

Economic and social equality can only be attained at the cost of political equality, if it is possible to attain it all. Because people differ in intelligence, physical abilities, and drive, it follows that, given freedom; people will also vary in achievement, income, wealth, and status. People are unequal in reality. In fact, to say that persons are equal simply means that they are equal in one or more respects—not in all respects.

Once freedom has been achieved, a man is free to do and act according to his plans and decisions. Of course, having the capacity to choose does not exempt him from the law of cause and effect. A man can choose to act in agreement or disagreement with natural law. However, once a choice has been made, the inviolate and inexorable workings of natural law and cause and effect come into play by supplying a reward or a penalty as a result of the choice made. A person cannot manifest real freedom unless he is willing to accept the natural consequences of his freely made choices.

Personal Flourishing and Happiness

Personal flourishing requires the rational use of one's talents, abilities, and virtues in the pursuit of one's freely chosen goals. Happiness is the positive experience that accompanies or flows from the use of one's individual human potentialities in the pursuit of one's values and goals. In other words, personal flourishing leads to happiness.

The right of private property is a precondition for making the pursuit of one's flourishing and happiness possible. No more fundamental human right exists than the right to use and control one's things, thoughts, and actions so as to manage one's life as one sees fit. If one has the right to sustain his life, then he has the right to whatever he is able to produce with his own time and means. Each person has the right to do whatever he wants with his justly held property as long as in so doing he does not violate the rights of another. Without private ownership, voluntary free trade and competition would be impossible.

As men found specialization desirable, an exchange mechanism evolved through which one person, who could produce an item more efficiently than others, could exchange it for an article that he could not make as efficiently as another person could make it. As trade and commerce developed, this giving-and-getting arrangement became more and more protected by formal contract. The idea of sanctity of contract is essential to a market economy and one of the most important elements that hold a civilized society together.

A market economy is a voluntary association of property owners for the purpose of trading to their mutual advantage. The market accommodates people who seek to improve their circumstances by trading goods and services in a non-coercive setting. Markets are efficient and effective mechanisms for ensuring that society is arranged to maximize individuals' ability to act on their best vision of their well-being. The market process reflects both social cooperation and voluntarism in human affairs. A market economy is a necessary condition for a free society.

Private markets encourage people to interact, cooperate, learn, and prosper from their diversity. The market economy inspires people to seek out others who are different from them, treat their differences as opportunities, and garner mutual gains through their cooperative interaction. When two people make a deal, each one expects to gain from it. Each person has a different scale of values and a different frame of reference. The market mechanism permits people to maximize their results while economizing their efforts.

The value of any good or service is whatever others willingly give in voluntary exchange in particular circumstances. The judgments of all parties are continually and everlastingly changing. There is no one optimal product or service specification. Not only do consumer tastes vary among prospective purchasers at any one point in time, they also change over time and situationally so that experimentation and research in product and service specifications is a continuous process.

The market is an effective communicator of data. With its continuing flow of positive and negative feedback, the market allows decision makers to review a constantly changing mix of options and resulting trade-offs and to respond with precision by continually making incremental adjustments. The role of prices as transmitters of knowledge economizes the amount of information required to produce a given economic result. No one person need have complete information in order for the economy to convey relevant information through prices and achieve the same adjustments that would obtain if everyone had that knowledge. Prices are a mechanism for carrying out the rationing function and are a fast, efficient conveyor of information through a society in which fragmented knowledge must be coordinated. Accurate prices, resulting from voluntary exchanges, allow the economy to achieve optimal performance in terms of satisfying each person as much as possible by his own standards without sacrificing others' rights to act according to their own standards.

Work is built into the human condition. Men have to work in order to sustain themselves. The things by which people live do not exist until someone creates them. Man survives by using his reason and other faculties to adjust his environment to himself. Productive work is also a means through which people attain purpose in their lives. Work is at the heart of a meaningful life and is essential for personal survival and flourishing. Work is necessary not only to obtain wealth but also to one's purpose and self-esteem. There are integrated links between reality, reason, self-interest, productive work, goal attainment, personal flourishing, and happiness.

There is an inextricable association between purposeful work and individual freedom. Both employees and employers are parties to a voluntary agreement, the terms of which both parties are legally and morally obliged to honor. Both seek to gain from the arrangement. As independent moral agents, the employee and employer agree to terms in a matter that affects their lives, their values, and their futures. A freely chosen job can be a source of one's happiness and self-respect.

Unlike the state, which is based on coercion, civil society is based on voluntary participation. Civil society consists of natural and voluntary associations such as families, private businesses, unions, churches, clubs, charities, etc. Civil society, a spontaneous order, consists of a network of associations built on the freedom of the individual to associate or not to associate. The voluntary communities and associations of civil society are valuable because human beings need to associate with others in order to flourish and achieve happiness. For example, freely given charity may be considered as an embodiment of one's struggle for self-perfection. In this context, charitable activities may be viewed as fulfillment of one's potential for cooperation and as a specific demonstration of that capacity—not as an obligation owed to others.

Business is the way a free society arranges its economic activities. Business deals with the natural phenomena of scarcity, insatiability, and cost in a valuable and efficient manner. The business system creates equality of opportunity and rewards businessmen who take advantage of opportunities by anticipating consumer preferences and efficiently using resources to satisfy those preferences. Through his thought and action, the businessman enables other people to obtain what they want.

The corporation occupies an important position within civil society. The corporation is a social invention with the purpose of providing goods and services in order to make profits for its owners, with fiduciary care for shareholders' invested capital. Corporate managers thus have the duty to use the stockholders' money for expressly authorized purposes that can run from the pursuit of profit to the use of resources for social purposes. Managers have a contractual and moral responsibility to fulfill the wishes of the shareholders and, therefore, do not have the right to spend the owners' money in ways that have not been approved by the stockholders, no matter what social benefits may accrue by doing so.

Unionism currently consists of both voluntary and coercive elements. Voluntary unions restrict themselves to activities such as mass walkouts and boycotts. They do nothing to violate the rights of others by using violence against them. Coercive unions use physical force (e.g., picketing when its purpose is to coerce and physically prevent others from crossing the picket line and from dealing with the struck employer) aimed at nonaggressing individuals. Mass picketing that obstructs entrance or exit is invasive of the employer's property rights as are sit-down strikes and sit-ins that coercively occupy the property of the employer. People who are willing to work for a struck employer have a legitimate right (but currently not a legal right in many states) to do so. In addition, the struck employer has a legitimate right to engage in voluntary exchanges with customers, suppliers, and other workers.

Coercive unions achieve their goals through the coercive power of the state. Most states' legislation excludes nonunion workers when a majority of the workers choose a particular union to be their exclusive bargaining agent. The state should not be concerned with a private citizen's agreement to work with a particular firm. In a free society, one based on natural law principles, each person would be free to take the best offer that he gets. In a free society, unions could merely be voluntary groups trying to advance their members' interests without the benefit of special privileges. In such a society, some workers would join one union, some would join other unions, and some would choose to deal with the employer directly and individually.

Obstacles and Threats to a Free Society

There are a great many coercive challenges, encroachments, and constraints that have inhibited the establishment of a society based on the natural liberty of the individual and the realities of the human condition. By nature, these barriers tend to be philosophical, economic, and political. Some of the strongest attacks on, and impediments to, a free society include: collectivist philosophies, cultural relativism, communitarianism, environmentalism, public education, taxation, protectionism, antitrust laws, government regulation, and monetary inflation. These bureaucratic and socialistic ideologies and schemes tend to stem from various sources such as true human compassion, envy, the insecurity of people who want protection from life's uncertainties, categorical "solutions" proposed to solve problems, idealism, and the tendency to think only of intended, primary, and immediate results while ignoring unintended, ancillary, and long-term ones.

The paradigm of statism has failed in solving men's difficulties and, in endeavoring to do so, has generated anomalies and further and more complicated problems and crises. Historically, statism has been causally related to most of the problems faced by men. Statism is life negating, destructive of people's control over their own lives, and subversive of the natural fact of people's basic responsibility for their individual existences. Statism's public policies cause specific problems such as poorly educated children, impeded free trade, balance of payments problems, malinvestments and misallocations of resources, monopolies, depressions and recessions, wars, citizen dependence on the state, inflation, and so forth.

We need to be able and willing to convincingly combat proposals for larger social security and Medicare benefits, higher tariffs, import quotas, price and wage controls, public housing, farm and other subsidies, higher taxes, and so on. We have to do all in our power to convince and convert the mass of people who are being victimized by state power and collectivist ideas. We must repeat and repeat the truth that individual freedom, private property, free markets, and a limited government produce a civil society that best meets the needs and preferences of, and is in accord with the nature of, imperfect but rational beings in a finite world.

Recommended Reading

Boaz, David. *Libertarianism: A Primer*. New York: Free Press, 1997.

Buckle, Stephen. *Natural Law and the Theory of Property*. Oxford: Oxford University Press, 1991.

Conway, David. *Classical Liberalism: The Unvanquished Ideal*. London: MacMillan, 1997.

Finnis, John. *Natural Law and Natural Rights*. Oxford: Oxford University Press, 1980.

Friedman, Milton. *Capitalism and Freedom*. Chicago: University of Chicago Press, 1962.

Gierke, Otto von. *Natural Law and the Theory of Society*. Translated by Ernest Barker. Boston: Beacon Press, 1957.

Hayek, Friedrick A. *The Road to Serfdom*. Chicago: University of Chicago Press, 1944.

———. *The Constitution of Liberty*. Chicago: University of Chicago Press, 1960.

Hazlitt, Henry. *The Foundations of Morality*. Los Angeles: Nash Publishing, 1972.

LeFevre, Robert. *The Fundamentals of Liberty*. Santa Ana, Calif.: Rampart Institute, 1988.

Locke, John. *Essays on the Law of Nature*. Edited by W. von Leydon. Oxford: Clarendon Press, 1952.

Machan, Tibor R. *Classical Individualism*. London: Routledge, 1998.

Mises, Ludwig von. *Human Action: A Treatise on Economics*. New Haven, Conn.: Yale University Press, 1949.

Narveson, Jan. *The Libertarian Idea*. Philadelphia: Temple University Press, 1988.

Novak, Michael. *Three in One: Essays on Democratic Capitalism 1976-2000*. Edited by Edward W. Younkins. Lanham, Md.: Rowman & Littlefield, 2001.

Nozick, Robert. *Anarchy, State, and Utopia*. New York: Basic Books, 1974.

Rand, Ayn. *Capitalism: The Unknown Ideal*. New York: Signet, 1967.

Rasmussen, Douglas B., and Douglas J. Den Uyl. *Liberty and Nature*. La Salle, Ill.: Open Court, 1991.

———. *Liberalism Defended*. Cheltenham, U.K.: Edward Elgar, 1997.

Read, Leonard. *Anything That's Peaceful*. Irvington-on-Hudson, N.Y.: Foundation for Economic Education, 1964.

Revel, Jean-François. *The Flight from Truth: The Reign of Deceit in the Age of Information*. New York: Random House, 1991.

Rothbard, Murray N. *Man, Economy, and State*. Mission, Kans.: Sheed, Andrews & McMeel, 1962.

————. *For a New Liberty: The Libertarian Manifesto*. New York: Collier, 1978.

————. *The Ethics of Liberty*. Atlantic Highlands, N.J.: Humanities Press, 1982.

Rowley, Charles Kershaw, ed. *Classical Liberalism and Civil Society*. Cheltenham, U.K.: Edward Elgar, 1998.

Sowell, Thomas. *Knowledge and Decisions*. New York: Basic Books, 1980.

————. *A Conflict of Visions*. New York: William Morrow & Co., 1987.

Strauss, Leo. *Natural Right and History*. Chicago: University of Chicago Press, 1953.

Sturgis, Amy H., ed. *Great Thinkers in Classical Liberalism*. Nashville, Tenn.: Lockesmith Institute, 1994.

Wild, John Daniel. *Plato's Modern Enemies and the Theory of Natural Law*. Chicago: University of Chicago Press, 1953.

29

The Future

We must make the building of a free society once more an intellectual adventure, a deed of courage. . . . We need intellectual leaders who are prepared to resist the blandishments of power and influence and are willing to work for an ideal, however small may be the prospects of its early realization. They must be men who are willing to stick to principles and to fight for their full realization, however remote.

—Friedrich A. Hayek

Ideas rule the world. Especially important are the philosophical ideas that determine conceptions of the human person in relation to the world in which he lives. Throughout history, the philosophy of individualism has played a critical role in man's progress. Each individual is a discrete being with a unique mind and a distinctive set of abilities, desires, and motivations. Each person is a self-responsible causal agent who has the capacity to pursue his well-being through his intellectual and physical actions. By nature, each person has the right to have the opportunity to develop his potential as a free, individual human being. People are happier when their lives are lived in freedom. When people exercise their freedom they enter the arena of morality as responsible free agents.

For centuries the philosophy of freedom and individualism has underpinned the political and economic order that characterized the American way of life. Unfortunately, beginning in the 1930s, American society has become more and more collectivized. Special interest groups have increasingly persuaded the government to grant them special privileges. People form political coalitions in order to be better at obtaining government favors. People implore the government for assistance. As government has become more dominant and has produced programs to meet our needs, it has also corrupted people's values and made them dependent on government. There has been a growing tendency for government to expand and undermine personal freedom and responsibility. The doctrine of statism has been driven into the minds of children throughout the twentieth century through public education and the media. The idea of security itself has changed over time. The classical idea of security of the person, of possession, and of exchange has been broadened to provide for people's "positive" rights to publicly provided health care, retirement funds, unemployment insurance, and other welfare programs. In addition, the regulatory arena has become a market in which politicians obtain political and financial support in exchange for regulation that benefits some of those being regulated. As a result, many citizens and firms prefer to buy favors from government officials rather than invest their time and effort in productive endeavors in the private sector.

Many Americans today do not realize they are not free and do not have a real understanding of what it means to live in a free society. They do not perceive that we have adopted various forms of the welfare state and the planned economy. They do not comprehend that these embody the rejection of the philosophy of freedom that flourished in America during the eighteenth and nineteenth centuries.

Most Americans alive today have never witnessed an unencumbered market economy. They tend to think that freedom encompasses income taxation, public schools, welfare programs, protectionism, government-provided medical care, regulatory agencies, rent controls, subsidies, business-government partnerships, minimum wage laws, etc. Yet, people are taught that they are living under "capitalism" and that capitalism is somehow compatible with an intrusive, activist state. They are even led to believe that the interventionist state is a prerequisite for supporting a market economy. The existence of this misunderstanding and ignorance is explainable once we realize that most people are products of the government's schools that teach people to embrace socialism. They teach that free enterprise exists when the government owns enterprises and redirects wealth and that when the state takes money via taxation it is permissible because it is for the general welfare.

How do we go from our current interventionist political and economic system to a society of laissez-faire capitalism? We cannot just wait for the state to wither away. On the other hand, prospects for one monumental step to a free-market society are not realistic. Many intermediate, transitional, and incremental steps are more likely to take us to our destination. We must disseminate the principles and theories of the freedom philosophy and promote the values of the free enterprise system in understandable, nontechnical terms. We need to achieve a revolutionary shift of conventional wisdom. We need to point out the theoretical and systemic errors of statism and the growing anomalies in reality where the welfare-state model just does not work. We must explain how the state does not provide a free ride and how almost everything done by the government is done inefficiently. We must have a fierce commitment to reality and work individually and in concert with others in order to battle apathy and affection for the state, capture people's imaginations, convince and convert people to the freedom philosophy, defeat statism, and reestablish freedom as the foundation for our political and economic systems.

Where We Are

Individuals have a natural right to security according to its meaning at the time America was founded. The original idea was to have state protection against external aggression without regard to the level of wealth of respective individuals. This type of security forms the foundation of the concept of personal autonomy and includes security of possession, freedom of contract, and security of exchange. This notion of security has been expanded and transformed over time, especially during the twentieth century.

Modern expansions and redefinitions of "security" have led to the downplaying of the classical conception of negative liberty and to an upgrading of the idea of positive liberty. Security, in the minds of many, now means protection from physical privation; the assurance of a minimum level of sustenance, standard of life, and income; the right to useful and renumerative work; the right to earn enough to provide sufficient food, clothing, and housing; the right to adequate health care; the right to a good education; protection from the economic risks rising from sickness, accidents, unemployment, and old age; and so on.

The new meaning of security renounces the old one. When a nation undertakes the protection of individual citizens' minimum standard of living, then certain people receive priority, thus increasing the risks for others. Providing economic security for some special interest groups increases the overall economic insecurity for the general population. The provision of security includes both cash transfers and various types of regulation. The extent of government action increases when different types of failures are chosen for special protection.

Some call for the redistribution of wealth in the name of economic justice. Others believe that the government can and should step in to solve society's problems. The underlying premise of both is that the world is perfectible and that man has the means to perfect it through the institution of government and the reason of its leaders. Of course, we know that the world is not perfectible and that the free market has the fundamentally proper view of human nature.

We live in a world of risk and uncertainty. People want and lobby for security. In our democratic society, the demand for security has expanded immeasurably. Many people fear freedom and the burden of responsibility. Government programs have undermined people's personal responsibility. As government has taxed people more in order to take care of them, people's ability to take care of themselves has diminished.

Scarcity always establishes constraints on what individuals can possess. It is not possible for all legitimate human desires to be satisfied. It is also not possible to eliminate all risks. There is no way to legislate risk out of existence.

In addition, there is an innate inequality of men with respect to their mental and physical abilities. People are individuals with regard to their minds and bodies. Each member of the human community possesses inborn differences. It follows that, because every person is unique, they gravitate in different directions in their pursuit of happiness. It is also obvious that individuals can only flourish and realize their individual potentialities if they are permitted to control their own lives free of outside coercion. Capitalism and democracy have emerged as means for creating the conditions required for personal flourishing.

Unfortunately, during the twentieth century, the government has increasingly controlled people's daily lives. Individual freedom has been sacrificed for a system of rules through which politicians impose their views on what is best for us. The result has been more and more people placing less and less value on liberty and increasingly endorsing the state's regulation of their lives.

Risk-averse people are likely to prefer the assurance, certainty, and protection offered by our government-sponsored welfare programs, including publicly administered health care, retirement, and unemployment insurance arrangements. Citizens in democracies tend to be unwilling to forfeit the protections offered to them even when those protections are of low quality and produced inefficiently and at high cost.

Certainly, the preservation of security is one of the major goals of a social order. However, we need to return to the more narrow classical definition that universally respects security of person, possession, and exchange. The use of state coercion against force and fraud promotes these three securities. Conversely, when the state promotes positive freedom and positive economic rights, it fosters the type of insecurity and public force that a legitimate political and legal system forbids. Practically, everything done by our current interventionist government violates someone's natural rights.

It is a fact of reality that people want protection from nature's uncertainties. People long for security against the vicissitudes of life. The legitimate purpose of government is not to rectify all of the insecurities experienced by citizens. The only conceptually and morally justifiable security that a proper state can provide is security of the person, of possession, and of exchange. It is thus essential to strip government down to its essential functions and restore the individual liberty that has withered away in the name of democracy. The freedom that accompanies a proper government cannot guarantee anything except the right to try to achieve one's dreams. The system most conducive to the flourishing of the human person is the one that governs least.

Not only do we have to make the conceptual and moral case for the classical conception of liberty, we also need to identify the concrete types of security people crave in both the classical and modern senses and explain how most of them will be more available and better provided in a free market. We need to demonstrate how private insurance markets can do a better job at handling insurable risks than can a welfare state system. Risk-averse people need to be convinced that they will fare better in a society governed by a minimal state. People need to be persuaded that private insurance markets can supply protection that is superior to that provided by the Social Security system, government-sponsored welfare programs, and other state-run insurance arrangements. The case must be made that the private sector can do a better job in addressing uncertainty and risk. People need to be assured that the private sector has greater incentives and more flexibility than the public sector and that it should be permitted to increase its efforts to supplant the state's social welfare programs such as health care, disability benefits, old-age benefits, etc.

People ought to be free to use their own resources as they see fit for their own perceived current and future needs and desires. Ending social security would permit individuals total freedom regarding the planning and management of their own futures. Because we are all different and distinct in our situations and value determinations, it follows that no other person or group of persons can do a better job planning an individual's future than the person himself. Not only is America's traditional, government-managed Social Security system a legacy of a failed socialist ideology, it attempts to aggregate and homogenize individuals into wide composite categories of requirements and needs. Social Security and other government social insurance and welfare programs undermine the operation of voluntary market-based solutions to social problems.

Currently, the state impedes citizens' concern for others that is crucial to personal maturation and flourishing by substituting for personal charity. The state gives people an excuse to avoid charity, thus placing an obstacle to individuals' actualization with respect to their potentialities that are other directed. All of us are social in the sense that our flourishing requires a life with others.

In addition, the state assures people that they will be helped if they become needy. Presently, there is a tendency for people not to trust private charity. As a result, in order to attain the certainty of aid, they are willing to accept the inefficiencies of the public welfare system. A convincing case needs to be made that the state is an inappropriate avenue for people's redistributive impulses and that private charity will fill the gap when private insurance arrangements do not adequately cope with life's probabilistic aberrations.

We need to paint an appealing portrait of what life would be like in a free society—one in which participation in markets and other voluntary associations are encouraged. We need to demonstrate how the moral-cultural system, buttressed by the mediating structures of family, church, private charities, schools, and other voluntary associations, provides a preferable outlet for people's desires to take part in civil society. Things can be done publicly without being done governmentally. What is required is a free market that is circumscribed by a set of ideas and values provided by institutions such as churches, schools, the family, the media, and so on. When left free, people tend to be social, helpful, and compassionate. Civil society offers much greater and better chances for meaningful self-expression and participation than does the political sphere.

Time for Change

We need to return to the political and economic foundation upon which our nation was born. We must strengthen our commitment to individual freedom, free markets, and private property rather than to statist regulatory government. We must rid society of the statist notion that politics and the political process best address people's needs and problems. We must discredit the idea that the state exists to give citizens what they want. We must refute the statists' claim that there is a right to education, health care, etc. The role of the state should be confined to protecting the freedom that allows individuals to pursue happiness or the good that each defines for himself. Step by step we must eliminate government agencies and cabinet departments except for defense, justice, state, and treasury. What would remain would be the executive, legislative, and judicial branches but with greatly reduced powers.

The egalitarian belief that people must be identical throughout society is wrong. Those life forms that are most alike are the lowest life forms. Man, the highest form of life, displays the most diversity and the widest individual differences. A legitimate political and economic system must be firmly based on human nature. A limited "night watchman" government is consistent with man's diversity, rationality, and need for personal freedom. A limited government is consistent with the nature of man and the world, recognizes the variety and diversity of man and his talents, and gives that diversity the opportunity for full expression. A society of free and responsible individuals includes a diversity of tastes, values, desires, and visions of happiness. People should have the maximum chance to select their own way of life, within the constraints of resource scarcity, according to each person's structure of desires and without value judgments regarding the decisions made by each individual, as long as a person does not encroach on the freedom of others to make their own life choices.

Today, our freedoms are invaded by external government controls. The less economic policy, the better. We must reduce as much as possible the weight of the state and increase the jurisdiction of the market. It is not regulation but individual action, private property rights, competition, and fluctuating prices that force adaptation to changing conditions and that promote efficient resource utilization.

A capitalist system is not egalitarian. You cannot achieve excellence and progress unless you have inequality and diversity. Division of labor and specialization are natural outcomes of the multiplicity of natural conditions. Economic progress requires the freedom of individuals to use the diverse talents and localized information that only they can possess. Our material abundance and opportunities for fulfilling work are largely the result of the productivity and creativity of our competitive economic system despite the existence of many bureaucratic barriers.

Progress is difference and change. If individuals were not free to try new things, then we would never have any improvements. In order to have progress, there must be freedom to attempt new advances. Progress is impossible unless people are free to be different. Regulation and controls stifle innovation and experimentation. Bureaucracy gets in the way of change. Capitalism has made advances possible, not solely in providing life's necessities, but in science, technology, and knowledge of all types upon which human society depends. Freedom attracts innovators and explorers and gives life to their ideas. Freedom for people to act in their own self-interest is the mainspring for a diversity of ideas, innovations, and experiments that lead to the discovery of new products, services, and other means of production.

Progress requires the use of information that exists only as widely dispersed knowledge that each person has with respect to his own circumstances, conditions, and preferences. Such tacit, locationally specific knowledge is only useful if people are free to act upon it. A free market permits prices to emerge from the use of people's localized knowledge. These prices contain more and better information and result in better decisions than what can achieved under a regime of central planners. Limited government and decentralized markets permit more freedom and foster more prosperity than do state-dominated and centralized bureaucracies.

The free market is superior to central planning regarding the uses of localized information and in combining those uses into an efficient system of production and consumption. Markets spread ideas, encourage the constant search for improvements, and evolve through trial and error, experimentation, and feedback. Markets produce a positive, emergent order.

Technological progress has reduced the ability of the state to control productive processes. Production systems are now smaller, more flexible, and more mobile than they were in the past. By accelerating change and disaggregating the distribution of knowledge, technological advances increase the preeminence of market-based economies. There is an inextricable connection between freedom and technology. Information empowers people. The information age and information technology are the enemies of centralized bureaucracies and totalitarian states. As information, technological progress, and businesses move faster, it will be increasingly more difficulty for the state to keep pace. Without doubt, cyberspace and the Internet will permit a more open, participatory economy, thus furthering and enhancing the importance of the free market. Nations based on political control and a centralized economy will be undermined by the free market and the microchip. By giving people access to information, the Internet empowers people and disempowers government.

Cyberspace permits limitless opportunities and empowers the individual. The Internet is making existing forms of commerce more efficient and is fostering the emergence of self-organizing supranational communities. These new virtual communities are bound by common interests rather than by physical borders. The Internet provides immeasurable "space," allows people to choose their own communities, transcends national and cultural boundaries, enhances personal freedom by facilitating the spread of information and ideas, and provides access to a whole new world of goods and services.

The Internet is a medium that can transmit a person's ideas to the rest of the world without revealing his physical location. People are able to erect walls of cryptography in their efforts to create new social experiments. Cyberspace privacy, stemming from the science of cryptology in the private sector, will ultimately take too much effort and cost for the government to break. Widely available, low-cost encryption devices will make it difficult, if not impossible, to keep track of individual knowledge workers who offer their trades on the Internet. Networking tools, such as reforwarders will make undesired identification and location more and more difficult. People will be able to create and exchange wealth without being watched by some sovereign power. Technological progress will alter the production of wealth in fundamental ways and reduce the threat that governments pose to people's liberty and prosperity.

The products of men's minds can be communicated via the Internet, which provides the power to access and to distribute information and ideas. People will be able to take a large part of their productive work and use it to participate in unconstrained commerce within an economic system essentially immune from government surveillance. Of course, the goods most readily traded in cyberspace are an individual's skills and knowledge. Although there will always be products with physical attributes such as steel and automobiles, the majority of the new wealth in the economy will be created in the information industries. Much of the wealth produced in this parallel economy may never exist in the physical world and may not have to be exchanged for government currency in order to be useful in commercial transactions. Wealth can be transferred electronically in the substance of the products and services sold over the Internet and in the form of newly developed monetary instruments.

Internet currency or payment systems could be specifically developed to the requirements of cyberspace. After all, money is merely an agreement within a community of people to use something as a medium of exchange. In essence, a medium of exchange is an abstract concept. Traders simply agree to buy and sell in terms of an abstract value unit. When people form such an agreement, a money system is established and money is created whenever people pay for a purchase. Trade requires a standard of value relativity. Any number of different commodities could be chosen as the initial standard (i.e., the number 1). Once adopted, the unit forfeits its identity with the community with which it was originally identified and value relativity occurs automatically as commercial transactions take place. In other words, the unit is extricated from the concrete to become an abstract concept.

It is thus conceivable that a connection to external physical objects may not invariably be required to ground the value of money in cyberspace. It may be feasible to establish an independent electronic currency as the share of the world's wealth generated in the cybereconomy increases. The success of any such new monetary unit must necessarily and inherently depend on the consent of the participants in the community. One or more Internet currencies could prosper alongside traditional national currencies. In essence, nontraditional currencies exist today. For example, frequent flyer miles can be used to pay for air travel, hotels, taxis, long-distance phone calls, and so on. We can certainly imagine someone paying us for a service that we provide over the Internet, which we then, in turn, spend on another person's cyberproducts or services.

Technology is the enemy of bureaucrats and dictators. By freeing people from centralized control, technology gives them power over their own lives. Totalitarian governments cannot keep pace with the rewards of freedom in an open society. Free markets always defeat industrial policy.

We need to demonstrate to the world that a free society is good for people. To do this, we need to adopt policies for freer trade and greater international investment. We need to eliminate restrictions on trade and capital flows and to encourage the free flow of information around the world. Globalization can be a liberating process for human beings everywhere.

Of course, there is also still much to be done in the United States that is currently under the influence of an interventionist and regulatory government. The time is ripe to reestablish the philosophy of freedom as the foundation for the American economic system. People are becoming less antagonistic toward business. There is now less confidence in welfare state programs. More and more, people are talking about tax and budget cuts, privatization of some government functions, and spending reductions with respect to Social Security, Medicare, and other government programs. It is time to take steps toward the establishment of a laissez-faire society.

What Must Be Done

In the twentieth century, under the influence of interventionist ideas, American business has been increasingly controlled and regulated by government. The competitive process does not function effectively or efficiently if it is burdened with controls, regulations, and taxes. We need to get government out of the way. We need to roll back the size of government. We need to cut government spending and continue to balance the federal budget. We need to move from an encumbered market economy and intrusive government to a free-market economy and limited government. Although we would like to achieve our goal as rapidly as possible, establishing a fully capitalistic society is a tremendous challenge that will likely take generations to form.

Many practical steps must be undertaken, including, but not limited to, the following: (1) privatizing government property, programs, and functions such as education; (2) reducing and ultimately abolishing income and inheritance taxes; (3) establishing freedom of production and trade by abolishing labor, licensure, antitrust, zoning, and other laws and regulations; (4) instituting gold as money; (5) eliminating Social Security, Medicare, public welfare, and public hospitals; (6) separating government and sciences because force and the mind are not compatible; (7) ending business subsidies; (8) allowing free trade by eliminating tariffs, quotas, and other protectionist measures; (9) ceasing to be the world's policemen while maintaining a strong defensive military; and (10) eliminating government agencies and most cabinet departments, leaving a minimal state sufficient to protect contractual and property rights and provide for America's defense.

Let's take a look at a few of the above measures, beginning with privatization, which involves the transfer, divestiture, or contracting out of assets or services from the tax-supported public sector to the competitive markets of the private sector. Methods of privatization abound. Commercialization, getting out of a type of business altogether, is one type of privatization. An example of this is cities getting out of the garbage collection business. Governments can contract out to private firms. Governments can also make an outright gift or sell physical assets to a private entity. In fact, it would be best if most government-owned land, natural resources, and tangible assets (except for military bases, courthouses, police stations, and other assets related to government's essential functions) were sold or given away. The government could sell public schools and universities, public hospitals, national parks, the post office, etc. It is interesting to note that the U.S. Post Office is presently experiencing a type of involuntary, market-driven and unintended privatization because of the growing popularity of private mail services, e-mail, and fax machines. Another approach to privatization would be the sale of stock in a newly privatized firm that was primarily state owned. Then there is the issuance of vouchers that can be redeemed in the marketplace thus giving people choices. For example, educational vouchers could be an intermediate step that moves us toward our real goal of totally free-market education.

Recommending and supporting optimal, feasible, imperfect, and partial measures for getting closer to our destination of a free market and a free society can be justified. A compromise such as funding education through vouchers may be acceptable if it facilitates rather than complicates an additional move toward free-market education. Of course, we should always support the ultimate goal of real freedom as the desired end of any such transitional process. For example, a voucher system for education could be "advocated" by free-market proponents if they voiced their support of such a measure as merely an incremental step toward the actual goal of replacing the current system of compulsory statist education with a totally market-based approach to education.

Privatization can be undertaken at all levels of the government. Social Security, the U.S. Post Office, the air traffic control system, Amtrak, electric utilities, electromagnetic frequencies, surplus military bases, and commodity lands are obvious candidates at the national level. At the state level, utilities and prison management are good examples. In addition, there are numerous candidates at the local level, including fire and police protection, waste treatment, parking structures, jails, snow removal, etc. No matter what level, it holds true that the private sector introduces competition, motivation, and accountability and imposes a penalty for poor performance. A state-run enterprise that is assured of its existence regardless of its results leads to mediocre performance at best.

High taxes on income, savings, and investments have hampered business activities and productivity. People and firms should keep more of what they earn. Intermediate steps toward the eradication of income and inheritance taxes could include: (1) the reduction of marginal tax rates and capital gains tax rates; (2) the elimination of double taxation; (3) the expansion of tax credits for research and development spending; and (4) perhaps the replacement of progressive income and inheritance taxes with a flat tax or a consumption tax provided that the amounts raised would be substantially lower than what is currently collected. The tax structure could also be revised to encourage, rather than penalize, capital accumulation. Current laws encourage consumption instead of savings and investment. Capital accumulation is needed to build new facilities, expand and upgrade existing ones, and take on new research and development activity.

We should certainly push for the repeal or reduction of the income tax. We should call for immediate abolition even though the result may be gradual elimination in the end. Some free-market proponents maintain that we should never call for the abrogation or lessening of the income tax while at the same time supporting its replacement with a sales tax or other form of tax, because a sales tax, like any other tax, involves the initiation of force against persons. They believe that it is immoral to support any form of taxation because, by doing so, a person is acting as if the replacement tax is a moral tax. Unfortunately, income taxation currently exists and we must begin with that fact of reality in our efforts to correct this situation. If the coercive state gives us a choice of ending income taxation if we replace it with a sales or other tax that will extract less money from its citizens, then it should not be regarded as immoral to make use of our restricted choice to cut back taxes and reduce state power.

Not only does regulation drain capital and discourage innovation, it is morally wrong and ought to be abolished. We must accelerate the trend toward deregulation. Innovation and change depend on freedom. Often, requests for state-mandated licensing requirements, tariffs, quotas, and other regulations come from business leaders. What they are looking for is not freedom but security for their own interests. The freedom they seek is freedom from the uncertainty of competition while saying that it is competition that they want to protect. Many interventions are government responses to disguised pleas that result in the forced transfer of wealth to those lobbying for the regulation. Competition does not have to be protected or created. It is built-in to the nature of man. Antitrust laws attack the activities by which the businessman attains his profit, market share, and other goals. To secure profits, businesses typically innovate in ways that temporarily lead to monopoly power. In a proper and moral free-market system, business must be permitted to enjoy their profits as long as they did not result through the use of force or fraud. We must keep government from stepping in at the first indication of monopoly power.

Our country must have real money, a sound currency. If we are to have freedom, we must abolish inflation. When additional money is pumped into the economy, inflation results, malinvestments distort the economy, and the value of money is gradually eroded. We must end the deceptive inflation that has destroyed economic stability. A 100 percent gold reserve standard will end inflation by taking the power to inflate away from the government and the banking system.

One of our greatest threats is government control over money. The legal authority to print unlimited amounts of money provides government with the power to confiscate wealth through the hidden tax of inflation. Through the central banking mechanism, the government achieves monopoly control and management of the supply of money. A central bank and central monetary planning are currently widely accepted as indispensable monetary institutions to attain economic stability. When government controls the money supply, it has the capability to create inflation, redistribute wealth, produce misallocations of capital and labor, distort the structure of relative prices, and so on.

The government controls the banking system through its power to determine the amount of loanable funds to which financial institutions have access. There is no feasible way that the Board of Governors of the Federal Reserve System know what the value of money ought to be, what the effect of money supply changes will be on market interest rates, or what impacts their actions will have the savings and investment decisions in the economy.

It is no wonder that many free-market supporters are calling for an end to the government's monopoly control over money. This could be accomplished through the repeal of legal tender laws and the Federal Reserve Act and by abolishing the Federal Reserve System. As a result, monetary and banking institutions in the United States would be totally privatized and liberated from government regulation and control. The denationalization of monetary would depolitcize the process of money creation and eradicate the state's manipulation of interest rates and savings and investment decisions in the private sector. In essence, private individuals would establish the commodities to be used as money and the type of financial institutions utilized in the savings and investment process.

The private sector must be permitted to expand its efforts to replace the government's social welfare programs. It cannot be disputed that the private sector has stronger incentives and more flexibility than the public sector with respect to the provision of arrangements for people to achieve personal security. Such programs would not only exist, but would flourish, in private markets.

Science delineates the conditions under which men must act and explains the effects of man's courses of action. Science is the process of reason, the opposite and enemy of force. Force is the province of government. Opponents of freedom argue that if scientific research is to be done, it must be done by the state because the vast resources and capital required could best be obtained by the government. However, all aspects of man's existence should be subject to the study and judgment of the intellect, man's distinctive attributes that can only operate apart from the coercion of others. By nature it is morally wrong for the scientist to surrender his mind to the wielders of coercion. In addition, the private sector is capable of funding and conducting scientific research. The private sector has been responsible for many of men's most important scientific advances such as smallpox vaccination, polio vaccine, the discovery of the structure of DNA, the discovery of penicillin, and so on. The cost of science may be high, but so are the rewards.

By now the reader has probably observed that the above discussion is concerned with the procedural or practical steps that need to be taken in order to move toward a society of laissez-faire capitalism. However, we must realize that the institutions of any society stem from the ideas of the majority of the influential people in that society. If we are to attain our goal of a capitalistic society, we must get influential people to change their ideas. These ideas will then filter throughout society. By reaching people interested in ideas we can help spread the philosophy of freedom. Ideas are the forces that shape our lives and the world we live in.

Education, Persuasion, and Conversion

Ideas are the most powerful forces in the world and the motive power of human progress. There already exists a body of well-articulated, theoretically consistent, systematic, and intellectually sound defenses of capitalism which expound the principles of traditional liberalism, voluntary cooperation, and individual freedom and which expose the errors of collectivism and coercionism. As moral warriors for capitalism, it is our aim to disseminate the conceptual and moral foundations of a free society. To do this we must express the ideas underlying the free market and limited government in the clear, cogent, and non-technical language of the layman. We must introduce people to the idea of the free market as a moral institution and not solely as a means for efficient production. Effective freedom education not only imparts knowledge of economic principles, but also seeks to develop a sense of rightness, self-reliance, and responsibility.

We need to market our ideas. To do this, we need accessible, interesting, and exciting works presenting the case for freedom and against collectivism. Our goals are to strengthen and hearten those who already accept the freedom philosophy, to convert collectivists and advocates of interventionism (who apparently hold mixed premises) to the principles of individual freedom, and to teach the intellectual and moral principles underlying a free society to those in upcoming generations who will become our future intellectual leaders and masses.

As change agents, we must convert people's political and economic philosophies to the philosophy of freedom. Movement toward a free society must be preceded by an educational campaign. To recruit others to the philosophy of freedom, we must educate, persuade, and convert. We need to convince a sufficient number of people of the rightness of our ideas. When we are communicating our ideas to others, we must be able to apply abstract principles to concrete situations, to recognize principles in particular cases, and to apply and support consistent courses of actions across various issues.

Building a free society is an intellectual adventure requiring a great deal of courage. We must be dedicated to preserving and strengthening the ideological and moral foundations of a free society. We must engage a large number of people who understand that free enterprise must be defended on moral and conceptual grounds and who are dedicated to doing so. We need to be willing to work for an ideal, adhere to the principles of a free society, and fight for their full realization. Capitalism needs its teachers, defenders, champions, and exemplars.

What can we do to move toward our destination? First of all, each of us has to order and integrate his own thoughts and make certain that they are consistent to the best of our ability and intelligence. We must be able to explain what capitalism is and the reasons why any rational person should respect it and support it. We must fight apathy and affection for the state. In addition, we must be able to recognize and refute collectivist errors so thoroughly that even collectivists themselves are able to recognize and acknowledge them, and perhaps even abandon their beliefs. We must also be able to assault intellectual obstacles to a free society such as public education, antitrust laws, regulations, social security, the welfare state, communitarianism, cultural relativism, environmentalism, and so on. And certainly, we must not take actions to seek out government protection and subsidies for our own businesses and industries nor spend time and effort in order to obtain personal favors from the government.

The effective marketing of the freedom philosophy involves the positive case for choice and individual responsibility. It requires the power of attraction and cannot depend on coercion. While making a lucid and compelling case for liberty, one must maintain a respectful tolerance for the contrary beliefs and opinions of others. In a free society, the only appropriate means of attempting to change other people's minds and actions are reason, persuasion, and example. One cannot force his subjective value structure upon a resistant recipient without taking away that person's freedom of choice and action.

Each of us needs to be an unceasing student who never stops learning about the philosophy and practice of freedom. This will enable us to improve our abilities to communicate ideas and to persuade others. Because a free society will not exist unless a sufficient number of people believe in a free society, we must learn both theory and facts and attempt to convince others of the correctness of the freedom philosophy. We need to make libertarianism relevant to people in the real world. We must be able to convincingly make the case for liberty and motivate people to embrace it. The first priority of each friend of freedom is thus the educate himself.

To foster freedom, each of us must read and study in order to be prepared when we find the occasion to defend liberty verbally or in writing. By refining our ideas and arguments, we will be able to argue honestly and convincingly for a system that both works and that is appropriate for human beings. It is personally rewarding to improve one's understanding of free enterprise and his ability to explain its principles to others. Seriously advancing the cause of liberty can be a great source of joy and self-fulfillment.

We have numerous interactions with individuals during our everyday lives. It is especially through these interactions that we can transmit the freedom philosophy to the general public. In this way, we can make progress toward changing the fundamental beliefs that are held by members of our society. Foundational ideas usually change slowly, but the fact remains that they can and do change. Our goal is to bring about an evolution (or preferably a revolution) in the way people view the proper role of government.

When we engage in discussions regarding the ideas of liberty with friends, colleagues, and acquaintances, we must use precise language and communicate our ideas persuasively and effectively. We must be able to predict the objections and reactions of others and must not attribute sinister motives to those who disagree with us. Most are reasonable and civil people who are simply mistaken in their beliefs. Consequently, we should approach them with a good will, explain our ideas calmly and without exaggeration, avoid the use of offensive or forceful exposition, refrain from the use of personal attacks, and never be antagonistic.

Those of us who are educators can teach libertarianism implicitly by communicating and defending the preeminence of reason and the fundamentality of natural law with our students. We can teach them that if the foundation is not solid, then neither will anything else be. We can emphasize the essential role of abstract principles and systematic theory. If we can get students to apply their reason to the real world, then they will have the ability to perceive the moral bankruptcy of collectivism and to discover and espouse the intellectual and moral foundations of freedom.

It is of no use fighting other libertarians when trying to spread the philosophy of freedom. Theoretical attacks and nit-picking should be avoided in our efforts to popularize libertarianism. Although genuine theoretical differences may exist between various brands of Austrians, classical liberals, Objectivists, anarchists, and so on, these disputes are certainly of little or no relevance to potential converts and newcomers to libertarianism. We need to be knowledgeable, dedicated, and nonparochial in our efforts to spread our message.

We must call people's attention to the conceptual and moral principles of a free society and convince individuals to support these principles. We can talk to our friends and associates, write articles and books, take part in conferences and seminars, give lectures, organize campus youth, donate free-market books to public and college libraries, arrange nonviolent demonstrations against governmental injustices, write book reviews, write letters to the editor, and take part in other peaceful activities that have a libertarian society as their ultimate goal.

We can teach through our actions when we consistently practice the principles we advocate and defend. It takes moral courage to apply principles consistently. Because discernment is necessary for a moral life, each of us needs to use our rationality to distinguish between measures we should take and those we should not take and government products that are appropriate for us to use and those that are not proper for us to use. To do this, we must apply general principles to highly diverse, concrete contexts. We must do our best to adhere to consistent tenets of liberty. We must attempt to live our lives consistently with the principles and beliefs we profess. By doing so, we can positively attract people interested in our actions and in the rationale underlying our actions. Through our conduct and our ability to explain our conduct and how it is based on the philosophy of freedom, we can become persuasive for freedom both in word and in deed. We can thereby encourage others to "do freedom."

The particular actions chosen by any one of us to advance the idea of freedom depends upon each individual's circumstances, value structure, perception of reality, and rationality. Most of us will certainly choose to drive on state-funded roads. Of course, we are free to concurrently offer our preference and perspective on the desirability and practicality of the adoption of a system of private roads in the future. We can certainly articulate our preferences regarding prevailing norms. What about the state's postal services? Perhaps we should use E-mail, fax machines, and private mail services, whenever practicable, instead of submitting to the governmental system. Should we vacation at a national park, go to a concert or sporting event at a tax-subsidized auditorium or arena, or attend (or teach at) a state university? With respect to positive actions we might decide to home school, buy over the Internet or at garage sales, thus avoiding sales taxes, and so on. Whatever our specific choices, we need to commit to doing specific things. When we practice the freedom philosophy, we will help to spread the concept to liberty to others.

As long as there are people interested in truth, we will be able to make a difference. There is great reward in seeking and expressing truth and principle. Our goal of a durable free society is realistic and could be achieved if enough people supported the freedom philosophy. Every believer and practitioner of this life-promoting theory is a marketer for that system of beliefs. We must work in and through other people in order to get them excited about and dedicated to furthering the prospects of a free society. We have tremendous opportunities because each of us simultaneously participates in numerous associations with others. We can master and clearly present abstract systematic free-market theory in a readily accessible manner, advocate specific measures moving America in the right direction, discern ways in our daily lives in which we can practice the freedom philosophy, and create attention-creating devices such as slogans through which we can attract potential new believers. We must each use our rationality to select the actions that will consistently and constantly bring us toward the future free society in which we would want to live. In a sense, if we fight for that future, we live in that future.

The dissemination of knowledge to a wide audience is essential for the success of the free-market movement. Today, there are numerous high-quality free-market-oriented organizations and think tanks that encourage people to embrace the ideas of liberty and that deserve our support. Included in this group are the Acton Institute, Advocates for Self-Government, American Enterprise Institute, Ayn Rand Institute, CATO Institute, Center for Libertarian Studies, Center for Market Processes, Competitive Enterprise Institute, Foundation for Economic Education, Future of Freedom Foundation, Henry Hazlitt Foundation, Independent Institute, Institute for Humane Studies, Libertarian Alliance, Liberty Fund, Ludwig von Mises Institute, Objectivist Center, Reason Foundation, Smith Center for Private Enterprise Studies, and Students in Free Enterprise. Many more comparable organizations appear in the appendix to this book.

In addition to the availability of a great number of libertarian books, there is also a large selection of outstanding free-market journals and magazines such as *The Cato Journal, Critical Review, The Free Market, The Free Radical, Ideas on Liberty,* (formerly *The Freeman*), *The Independent Review, Journal of Libertarian Studies, Journal of Markets and Morality, Liberty, The Mises Review, National Review,* and *Reason.* Again, please see the end of this work for a more complete list. On top of these, we have several world-class libertarian newspaper columnists such as Walter Williams and Thomas Sowell. On television, however, we currently have only one reporter who objectively, consistently, and convincingly defends capitalism—ABC's John Stossel. There is a clear need for a new generation of television reporters who champion free enterprise or who, at least, are not prejudiced toward business.

Perhaps the real future of libertarianism is in cyberspace. Web publications suit the freedom philosophy. When a person publishes on the Internet anyone in the world can read his ideas. Not only is it easy to link from one Web page to another, each of us can communicate directly with our targeted audience through email, chat rooms, and so on. The unregulated Internet permits a diversity of views and cannot be easily controlled by politicians and governments. The electronic environment does not lend itself to the purposes and methods of the state. Web sites are accessible to the general public and can be used by dedicated and knowledgeable libertarians to spread their message. The Internet can be an excellent tool to diffuse libertarian ideas throughout society, both among opinion leaders and average citizens alike. Many freedom-oriented organizations and individuals have their own Web sites. Some publications appear both in tangible and Internet versions. Other journals and magazines exist solely in the electronic frontier. In addition, large numbers of new libertarian communities and nations are being developed in cyberspace.

We must work to create a culture of liberty that would serve as the foundation for a free society. Attitudinal and behavioral changes are a function of culture. Because the required cultural changes cannot be legislated, we need to study the cultural and nonrational factors that affect people's attitudes toward political, economic, and moral-cultural freedom. It is essential for us to be culturally aware, acknowledge the importance of culture, and appreciate insights from a diversity of disciplines.

There is a crucial need for cultural intellectuals who can help spread the philosophy of freedom to the general public. There are currently very few libertarians in the media and academia who we can depend upon to advocate a free society. We must work to lessen the prevalent bias against capitalism in newspapers, magazines, novels, plays, television programs, philosophy and history books, and so on. For years, the media have consistently and persistently attacked capitalism, commerce, and the premises of classical liberalism. We must cultivate a new generation of artists and reporters who will help to disseminate the ideas of liberty. Currently ABC reporter, John Stossel, stands above all others as an objective and staunch defender of the free market and critic of the failings of government. His specials, *Greed* and *Mr. Stossel Goes to Washington*, are excellent vehicles for evangelizing people to believe in freedom. His works present the essential case for political and economic liberty in an interesting and highly accessible form.

In *Total Freedom*, Chris Matthew Sciabarra cautions us not to reduce the study and defense of freedom to economics or politics with an inadequate understanding of the interconnections between the philosophical, the historical, the personal, and so forth. Sciabarra's message is that libertarians need an effective strategy that recognizes the dynamic relationships between the personal, political, historical, psychological, ethical, cultural, economic, and so on, if they are to be successful in their quest for a free society. He explains that attempts to define and defend a nonaggression axiom in the absence of a broader philosophical and cultural context are doomed to fail. Typical libertarian opposition to state intervention is not enough. Libertarians must pay greater attention to the broader context within which their goals and values can be realized. The battle against statism is simultaneously structural (political and economic), cultural (with implications for education, race, sex, language, and art) and personal (with connections to individuals' tacit moral beliefs, and to their psychoepistemological processes). The crusade for freedom is multidimensional and takes place on a variety of levels with each level influencing and having reciprocal effects on the other levels.

It is possible to analyze society from different vantage points and on different levels of generality in order to develop an enriched picture of the many relationships between the various areas involved. Change must occur on many different levels and in many different areas. It cannot just be dictated from the political realm, but must filter through all of the various levels and areas. Any attempt to understand or change society must entail an analysis of its interrelations from the perspective of any single aspect.

People need to understand both the necessity for objective conceptual foundations and the need for cultural prerequisites in the fight for the free society because some cultures promote, and others undermine, freedom. Freedom cannot be defended successfully when severed from its broader requisite conditions. We must attempt to grasp and address all of freedom's prerequisites and implications.

Although we need to always keep our ultimate goal in mind, realism is required. Even though we should urge the immediate eradication of most government activities, their gradual elimination is more likely. Short-run or intermediate goals (e.g., tax cuts or tax reforms such as a flat or sales tax that reduces tax revenue) that have a good chance of near-term adoption are acceptable as long as we realize that they are only transitional steps toward our final goal. A compromise such as funding schooling through vouchers or tax credits would at least be an incremental step away from totally publicly run schools. Likewise, we should welcome the piecemeal privatization of any of the government's operating activities except, of course, for defense against both external and internal aggression.

The gradual breakdown and crises of the reigning welfare-state paradigm enhance our future prospects for a free society. Only a free society is compatible with the true nature of man and the world. Capitalism works because it is in accordance with reality. Capitalism is the only moral social system because it protects a man's mind, his primary means of survival and flourishing. Truth and morality are on our side. Our battle is intellectual, moral, and cultural. Our message should appeal to all individuals and groups across the public spectrum. Let us hasten the demise of statism and the establishment of a free society by working individually and in concert with others to educate, persuade, and convert people to a just and proper political and economic order that is a true reflection of the nature of man and the world properly understood.

Recommended Reading

Anderson, Annelise, and Dennis L. Bark, eds. *Thinking about America: The United States in the 1990s.* Stanford, Calif.: Hoover Institution, 1988.
Anderson, Martin. *The Unfinished Agenda.* London: Institute of Economic Affairs, 1986.

——. *Revolution*. New York: Harcourt Brace Jovanovich, 1988.

Boaz, David. *Libertarianism: A Primer*. New York: Free Press, 1997.

Boaz, David, and Edward H. Crane, eds. *Market Liberalism: A Paradigm for the 21st Century*. Washington, D.C.: Cato Institute, 1993.

Chamberlin, Neil. *The Place of Business in America's Future*. New York: Basic Books, 1973.

Dahlberg, Arthur Olaus. *How to Save Free Enterprise*. Greenwich, Conn.: Devin-Adair, 1975.

Ebeling Richard M., ed. *Austrian Economics: Perspectives on the Past and Prospects for the Future*. Hillsdale, Mich.: Hillsdale College Press, 1991.

——. *The Future of American Business*. Hillsdale, Mich.: Hillsdale College Press, 1996.

Epstein, Richard A. "Imitations of Libertarian Thought." *Social Philosophy and Policy* (summer 1998).

Fulda, Joseph S. *Eight Steps towards Libertarianism*. Bellevue, Wash.: Free Enterprise Press, 1997.

Harper, F. A. *Liberty: A Path to Its Recover*. Irvington-on-Hudson, N.Y.: Foundation for Economic Education, 1949.

Henderson, David R. *The Joy of Freedom*. New York: Financial Times, 2001.

Hospers, John. *Libertarianism: A Political Philosophy for Tomorrow*. Los Angeles, Calif.: Nash Publishing, 1971.

Johnson, Paul. *Will Capitalism Survive?* Washington, D.C.: Ethics and Public Policy Center, 1979.

Kelley, John L. *Bringing the Market Back In*. New York: New York University Press, 1997.

Lepage, Henri. *Tomorrow Capitalism*. LaSalle, Ill.: Open Court, 1978.

Lester, J. C. *Escape from Leviathan*. New York: Palgrave, 2000.

Macey, Jonathan R. "On the Failure of Liberatarianism to Capture the Popular Imagination." *Social Philosophy and Policy* (summer 1998).

Machan, Tibor R., ed. *Libertarian Alternative*. Chicago: Nelson Hall, 1974.

Reed, Lawrence W., ed. *Private Cures for Public Ills: The Promise of Privatization*. Irvington-on-Hudson, N.Y.: Foundation for Economic Education, 1996.

McKenzie, Richard B. *Bound to Be Free*. Stanford, Calif.: Hoover Institution Press, 1982.

——. *Competing Visions: The Political Conflict over America's Economic Future*. Washington, D.C.: Cato Institute, 1985.

——. *The Paradox of Progress: Can Americans Regain Their Confidence in a Prosperous Future?* Oxford: Oxford University Press, 1997.

Micklethwait, John, and Adrian Wooldridge. *A Future Perfect: The Challenge and Hidden Promise of Globalization*. New York: Crown Publishers, 2000.

Postrel, Virginia. *The Future and Its Enemies*. New York: Free Press, 1998.

Reisman, George. *Capitalism*. Ottawa, Ill.: Jameson Books, 1996.

Rogge, Benjamin A. *Can Capitalism Survive?* Indianapolis, Ind.: Liberty Press, 1979.

Sciabarra, Chris Matthew. *Total Freedom: Toward a Dialectical Libertarianism.* University Park: Pennsylvania State University Press, 2000.

Tanner, Michael. *The End of Welfare: Fighting Poverty in Civil Society.* Washington, D.C.: Cato Institute, 1997.

Walton, Clarence C. *Business and Social Progress.* New York: Praeger, 1970.

Williams, Walter E. *More Liberty Means Less Government.* Stanford, Calif.: Hoover Institution Press, 1999.

Williamson, Marianne. *Imagine: What America Could Be in the 21st Century.* Emmaus, Pa.: Rodale Press, 2000.

Wolfram, Gary. *Towards a Free Society.* New York: McGraw-Hill, 1993.

Appendix

A Reader's Guide to

Free-Market Organizations and Periodicals

Organizations

Acton Institute for the Study of Religion and Liberty
161 Ottawa, NW, Suite 301
Grand Rapids, MI 49503
616-454-3080
Email: *info@action.org*
Web Page: *http://www.acton.org*

Adam Smith Institute (USA)
305 9th St., SE
Washington, D.C. 20003
202-544-8071

Adam Smith Institute
23 Great Smith Street
London SW1P3BL, England
011-44-20-7222-4995
Email: *madsen@adamsmith.org.uk*
Web Page: *http://www.adamsmith.org.uk*

Adam Smith Research Centre
Bednarska Street 16
Warsaw Ma 00-321
Poland
48-22-828-47-07
Email: *adam.smith@adam-smith.pl*
Web Page: *http://www.smith.pl*

Advocates for Self-Government
1202 N. Tennessee St., Suite 202
Cartersville, GA 30120
770-386-8372, 800-932-1776
Email: *Advocates@self-gov.org*
Web Page: *http://www.self-gov.org*

Agorist Institute
236 E. 3rd Street, Suite 201
Long Beach, CA 90802
213-590-0488
Email: *Agorist@newlibertarian.com*
Web Page: *http://www.Agorist.com*

Alexis de Tocqueville Institution
1611 N. Kent Street, Suite 901
Arlington, VA 22209
703-351-0090
Email: *Kenbrown@erols.com*
Web Page: *http://www.adti.net*

America's Future Foundation
1508 21st Street, NW
Washington, D.C. 20036
202-544-7707
Email: *jsbarry@americasfuture.org*
Web Site: *http://www.americasfuture.org*

American Enterprise Institute
1150 17th St., NW
Washington, D.C. 20036
202-862-5800
Email: *Aei@aei.org*
Web Page: *http://www.aei.org*

American Institute for Economic Research (AIER)
P.O. Box 1000
Great Barrington, MA 01230
413-528-1216
Email: *aierpubs@aier.org*
Web Page: *http://www.aier.org*

Americans for Tax Reform Foundation
1920 L Street, NW, Suite 200
Washington, D.C. 20036
202-785-0266
Email: *gnorquist@atr.org*
Web Page: *http://www.Atr.org*

Annecy Institute for the Study of Virtue and Liberty
429 N. St., SW, Suite 109 South
Washington, D.C. 20024
202-863-0756
Email: *jmbeers@earthlink.com*

The Association of Private Enterprise Education
The University of Tennessee at Chattanooga
313 Fletcher Hall
615 McCallie Avenue
423-755-4118
Email: *J-Clark@utc.edu*
Web Page: *http://www.Apee.org*

Atlantic Institute for Market Studies
1657 Barrington Street, Suite 521
Halifax, NS B3J 2A1
Canada
902-429-1134
Email: *brianleecrowley@aims.ca*
Web Page: *http://www.aims.ca*

Atlas Economic Research Foundation
4084 University Drive, Suite 103
Fairfax, VA 22030
703-934-6969
Email: *Atlas@AtlasUSA.org*
Web Page: *http://www.his.com/~atlas*

Ayn Rand Book Store
Email: *website@ayarandbookstore.com*
Web Page: *http://www.ayarandbookstore.com*

Ayn Rand Institute
The Center for the Advancement of Objectivism
4640 Admiralty Way, Suite 406
Marina del Rey, CA 90292
Email: *mail@aynrand.org*
Web Page: *http://www.aynrand.org*

Carl Menger Institute
Montigasse la/3
Vienna, A-1170
Austria
43-1-462-176
Email: *mail@menger.org*
Web Page: *http://www.menger.org*

Cascade Policy Institute
813 SW Alder, Suite 707
Portland, OR 97205
503-242-0900
Email: *info@CascadePolicy.org*
Web Page: *http://www.cascadepolicy.org*

CATO Institute
1000 Massachusetts Avenue, NW
Washington, D.C. 20001-5403
202-842-0200
Email: *cato@cato.org*
Web Page: *http://www.cato.org*

Center of the American Experiment
1024 Plymouth Building 12 South 6th Street
Minneapolis, MN 55402
612-338-3605
Email: *amexp@amexp.org*
Web Page: http://www.amexp.org

The Center for the Defense of Free Enterprise
12500 N.E. Tenth Place
Bellevue, WA 98005
425-455-5038
Web Page: *http://www.cdfe.org*

Center for Free Enterprise
Do-Won Bldg. 292-20 Dowha-dong Mapo-ku
Seoul,'121-728
Korea
82-2-6730-3000
Email: *kch@cfe.org*
Web Page: *http://www.cfe.org*

The Center for Independent Studies
P.O. Box 92
St. Leonards, NSW 1590
Australia
02-9438-4377
Email: *cis@cis.org.au*
Web Page: *http://www.cis.org.au*

Center for Individual Rights
1233 20th Street, NW, Suite 300
Washington, D.C. 20036
202-833-8400
Email: *cir@mail.wdn.com*
Web Page: *http://www.cir-usa.org*

Center for Libertarian Studies (CLS)
P.O. Box 4091
Burlingame, CA 94011
800-325-7257; 415-692-8456

Center for Market Processes
George Mason University
4084 University Drive, Suite 208
Fairfax, VA 22030
703-993-1142
Email: *jbe@gmu.edu*
Web Page: *http://www.gmu.edu*

Center for the Study of Market Alternatives
2399 S. Orchard
Boise, ID 83715
208-368-7811

Center for the Study for Public Choice
George Mason University
4400 University Drive
Fairfax, VA 22030
703-993-2330

Citizens for a Sound Economy
1250 H Street, NW, #700
Washington, DC 20005-3908
202-783-3870
Email: *cse@cse.org*
Web Page: *http://www.cse.org/cse*

Civitas: Institute for the Study of Civil Society
The Mezzanine Elizabeth House 39, York Road
London, SE1 7NQ
United Kingdom
44020-7401-5470
Email: *robert.whelan@civitas.org.uk*
Web Page: *http://www.civitas.org.uk*

Claremont Institute
250 West First Street, Suite 330
Claremont, CA 91711
909-621-6825
Email: *info@claremont.org*
Web Site: *http://www.claremont.org*

Competitive Enterprise Institute
1001 Connecticut Ave., NW, Suite 1250
Washington, D.C. 20036
202-331-1010
Email: *info@cei.org*
Web Page: *http://www.cei.org*

Conservative Bookstore
Web Page: *http://www.conservativebookstore.com*

Defenders of Property Rights
1350 Connecticut Avenue, NW, Suite 410
Washington, D.C. 20036
202-822-6770
Email: *mail@yourpropertyrights.org*
Web Site: *http://www.yourpropertyrights.org*

Discovery Institute
1402 Third Avenue, Suite 400
Seattle, WA 98101
206-292-0401
Email: *discovery@discovery.org*
Web Page: *http://www.discovery.org*

Dumont Institute for Public Policy Research
71 S. Orange Avenue, Box 260
South Orange, NJ 07079-1715
201-387-0744
Email: *bob@dumontinst.com*
Web Page: *http://www.angelfire.com/nj/dumontinstitute*

Edmund Burke Institute
11 Churchfield Lawns Skerries
Dublin
Ireland
353-1-849-1376
Email: *edmundburke@eircom.net*
Web Page: *http://www.edmundburke-institute.com*

Ethics and Public Policy Center
1015 15th Street, NW, Suite 900
Washington, D.C. 20005
202-682-1200
Email: *ethics@eppc.org*
Web Page: *http://www.eppc.org*

Evergreen Freedom Foundation
P.O. Box 552
Olympia, WA 98507
360-956-3482
Email: *effwa@effwa.org*
Web Page: *http://www.effwa.org*

Foundation for Economic Education (FEE)
Irvington-On-Hudson, NY 10533
30 South Broadway
914-591-7230
Email: *iol@fee.org*
Web Page: *http://www.fee.org*

Foundation Francisco Marroquin
P.O. Box 1806
Santa Monica, CA 90406-1806
310-395-5047
Email: *pvhffm@ix.netcom.com*
Web Page: *http://www.ffmnet.org*

Foundation for Free Enterprise
South 61 Paramus Road, P.O. Box 768
Paramus, NJ 07653-0768
201-368-2100
Email: *jgalandak@fee.org*
Web Page: *http://www.cianj.org*

Fraser Institute
626 Bute Street
Vancouver, BC, Canada V6E 3M1
604-714-4545
Email: *info@fraserinstitute.ca*
Web Page: *http://www.fraserinstitute.ca*

Free Congress Foundation
717 Second Street, NE
Washington, D.C. 20002
202-546-3004
Email: *paulwey@freecongress.org*
Web Page: *http://www.freecongress.org*

Free Market Foundation
903 East 18th Street, Suite 230
Plano, TX 75074
972-423-8889
Email: *freemrkt@flash.net*

Free Market Foundation of Southern Africa
P. O. Box 785121
Maude Streets
Sandton, GA 2146
South Africa
27-11-884-0270
Email: *fmf@mweb.co.za*
Web Page: *http://www.freemarketfoundation.com*

Future of Freedom Foundation
11350 Random Hills Road, Suite 800
Fairfax, VA 22030
703-934-6101
Email: *info@fff.org*
Web Page: *http://www.fff.org*

Goldwater Institute
500 East Coronado Road
Phoenix, AZ 85004
602-462-5000
Email: *dolsen@goldwaterinstitute.org*
Web Page: *http://www.goldwaterinstitute.org*

The Gus A. Stavros Center for Free Enterprise and Economic Education
4202 East Fowler Avenue, CEE 101
Tampa, FL 33620
813-974-2175
Email: *StavrosCenter@tempest.coedu.usf.edu*

Henry Hazlitt Foundation
401 North Franklin, Suite 3E
Chicago, IL 60610
312-494-9440
Email: *Chris@free-market.net*
Web page: *http://www.free-market.net*

Heartland Institute
800 East Northwest Hwy, Suite 1080
Palatine, IL 60067
708-202-3060
Email: *think@heartland.org*
Web Page: *http://www.heartland.org*

Heritage Foundation
214 Massachusetts Avenue, NE
Washington, D.C. 20002-4999
202-546-4400
Email: *info@heritage.org*
Web Page: *http://www.heritage.org*

Hoover Institution on War, Revolution and Peace
Stanford University
Stanford, CA 94305-6010
650-723-0603
Web Page: *http://www.hoover.stanford.edu*

Hudson Institute
5395 Emerson Way
Indianapolis, IN 46226
317-545-1000
Email: *info@hudson.org*
Web Page: *http://www.hudson.org*

Independence Institute
14142 Denver West Pkwy, Suite 185
Golden, CO 80401
303-279-6536
Email: *webmngr@i2i.org*
Web Page: *http://www.independenceinstitute.net*

The Independent Institute
100 Swan Way
Oakland, CA 94621-1428
800-927-8733 (U.S. only); 510-568-6047 (outside U.S.)
Email: David J. Theroux, President, *info@independent.org*
Web Page: *http://www.independent.org*

Independent Institute of Socio-Economic and Political Study
P.O. Box 219 Republic of Belarus
Minsk, 220030
Belarus
017-222-80-49
Email: *iisep@user.unibel.by*
Web Page: *http://www.iiseps.by*

Individual Rights Foundation
601 West 5th Street, 8th Floor
Los Angeles, CA 90071
213-680-9940
Web Page: *http://www.cspc.org/irf*

Individual Rights Foundation
9911 West Pico Blvd, #1290
Los Angeles, CA 90035
310-843-3699

Institute for Economic Affairs
2 Lord North Street
London SW1T3LB, England
0114471-799-3745
Email: *enquiries@iea.org.uk*
Web Page: *http://www.iea.org.uk*

Institute for Free Enterprise
Meridian at Ballston 900 N. Stuart St., #1416
Arlington, VA 22203
703-312-6008
Email: *o_knipping@yahoo.com*
Web Page: *http://www.unternehmerische-freiheit.de*

Institute for Humane Society (IHS)
George Mason University
3401 North Fairfax Dr., Suite 440
Arlington, VA 22201-4432
703-993-4880, 800-697-8799
Email: *ihs@gmu.edu*
Web Page: *http://www.TheIHS.org*

Institute for Humane Studies
4084 University Drive, #101
Fairfax, VA 22030-6812
703-934-6920
Web Page: *http://osf1.gmu.edu/~ihs*

Institute of Political Economy
Utah State University
Logan, UT 84322-0725
801-797-2064

Intercollegiate Studies Institute
3901 Centerville Road, P.O. Box 4431
Wilmington, DE 19807
302-652-4600
Email: *isi@isi.org*
Web Page: *http:// www.isi@isi.org*

International Society for Individual Liberty (ISIL)
836-B Southampton Road, #299
Benicia, CA 94510
707-746-8796
Email: *isil@isil.org*
Web Page: *http://www.isil.org*

James M. Buchanan Center
George Mason University MSN 1D3
Fairfax, VA 22030
703-993-2330
Email: *crobert@gmu.edu*
Web Page: *http://www.gmu.edu*

The James Madison Institute
P.O. Box 37460
Tallahassee, FL 32315
850-386-3131
Email: *jmi@jamesmadison.org*
Web Page: *http://www.jamesmadison.org*

The Jefferson School
P.O. Box 2934
Laguna Hills, CA 92653
Web Page: *http://www.capitalism.net*

John Locke Foundation
200 West Morgan Street, Suite 200
Raleigh, NC 27601
919-828-3876
Web Page: *http://www.johnlocke.org*

John Locke Institute
4084 University Drive, Suite 102
Fairfax, VA 22030

Laissez Faire Books
938 Howard Street, Suite 202
San Francisco, CA 94103-4114
Email: *custsvc@laissezfaire.org*
Web Page: *http://www.laissezfairebooks.com*

Libertarian Nation Foundation
335 Mulberry Street
Raleigh, NC 27604
Email: *info@libertarian.org*
Web Page: *http://www.libertariannation.org*

Libertarian Party of U.S.A.
2600 Virginia Avenue, NW, Suite 100
Washington, D.C. 20037
202-333-0008, 800-682-1776
Email: *hq@lp.org*
Web Page: *http://www.lp.org*

Liberty Fund
8335 Allison Pointe Trail, Suite 300
Indianapolis, IN 46250-1684
317-842-0880
Email: *dhart@libertyfund.org*
Web Page: *http://www.libertyfund.org*

Liberty Tree Network
100 Swan Way
Oakland, CA 94621-1428
Email: *LibertyTree@insependent.org*
Web Page: *http://www.liberty-tree.org*

The Libertarian Alliance
25 Chapter Chambers, Esterbrooke Street
London SW1P 4NN, England
44-020-7-821-5502
Email: *Chris@rand.demon.co.uk*
Web Page: *http://www.libertarian.co.uk*

Ludwig von Mises Institute
518 W. Magnolia Avenue
Auburn, AL 36832-4528
334-844-2500
Email: *mail@mises.org*
Web Page: *http://www.mises.org*

Mackinac Center for Public Policy
119 Ashman St., P.O. Box 568
Midland, MI 48640
517-613-0900
Email: *mcpp@mackinac.org*
Web Page: *http://www.mackinac.org*

Manhattan Institute
52 Vanderbilt Avenue
New York, NY 10017
212-599-7000
Email: *mi@manhattan-institute.org*
Web Page: *http://www.manhattan-institute.org*

Mercatus Center
3301 N. Fairfax Drive, Suite 450
Fairfax, VA 22201-4433
703-993-4910
Email: *tcowen@gmu.edu*
Web Site: *http://www.mercatus.org*

National Center for Policy Analysis
12655 N. Central Expwy., Suite 720
Dallas, TX 75243-1739
972-386-6272
Email: *ncpa@public-policy.org*
Web Page: *http://www.ncpa.org*

The Objectivist Center
11 Raymond Avenue, Suite 31
Poughkeepsie, NY 12603
Email: *toc@objectivistcenter.org*
Web Page: *http://www.objectivistcenter.org*

Pacific Legal Foundation
2151 River Plaza Drive, Suite 305
Sacramento, CA 95833
916-641-8888

Pacific Research Institute for Public Policy
755 Sansome Street, #450
San Francisco, CA 94111
415-989-0833
Email: *pripp@pacificresearch.org*
Web Page: *http://www.pripp@pacificresearch.org*

Pioneer Institute
85 Davonshire Street, 8th Floor
Boston, MA 02109
617-723-2277
Email: *pioneer@pioneerinstitute.org*
Web Page: *http://www.PioneerInstitiute.org*

Political Economy Research Center
502 South 19th Ave., #211
Bozeman, MT 59715
406-587-9591
Email: *perc@perc.org*
Web Page: *http://www.perc.org*

Privatization Center
3415 S. Sepulveda Blvd, #400
Los Angeles, CA 90034
310-391-6525

Progress and Freedom Foundation
1301 K Street, NW, Suite 550 East
Washington, D.C. 20005
202-289-8928
Email: *pff@aol.com*
Web Page: *http://www.pff.org*

Property Rights Foundation of America, Inc.
P.O. Box 75
Stoney Creek, NY 12878
518-696-5748

The Radical Academy
The Center for Applied Philosophy
Port Orford, Oregon
Web Page: *http://www.radicalacademy.com*

Reason Foundation
3415 S. Sepulveda Blvd., Suite 400
Los Angeles, CA 90034
310-391-2245
Email: *gpassantino@reason.org*
Web Page: *http://www.reason.org*

Smith Center for Private Enterprise Studies
California State University, Hayward
Hayward, CA 94542
510-885-2640
Email: *cbaird@csuhayward.edu*
Web Page: *http://www.sbe.csuhayward.edu/sbesc*

Social Philosophy and Policy Center
Bowling Green State University
Bowling Green, OH 43403
419-372-2536
Web Page: *http://www.sppc@listproc_bgsu.edu/offices/sppc*

St. Lawrence Institute
P.O. Box 307, NDG Station
Montreal, QC H4A 3P6
Canada
514-233-8321
Email: *sid@stlawrenceinstitute.org*
Web Page: *http://www.stlawrenceinstitute.org*

Students in Free Enterprise (SIFE)
1959 East Kerr Street
Springfield, MO 65803-4775
417-831-9505
Email: *sifehq@sife.org*
Web Page: *http://www.sifehq@sife.org*

Young America's Foundation
110 Elden Street
Herndon, VA 20170
800-292-9231
Email: *yaf@yaf.org*
Web Page: *http://www.yaf.org*

Periodicals

Ama Gi
United States
Email: *submit@amagi.net*
Web Page: *http://amagi.net*

The American Enterprise
American Enterprise Institute
Washington, D.C.
United States
Email: *eli@aei.org*
Web Page: *http://theamericanenterprise.org*

American Experiment Quarterly
1024 Plymouth Building
12 South 6th Street
Minneapolis, MN 55402
612-338-3605
Email: *amexp@amexp.org*
Web Page: *http://www.amexp.org*

American Outlook
Hudson Institute
5395 Everson Way
Indianapolis, IN 46226
317-545-1000
Web Page: *http://www.hudson.org*

American Purpose
Ethics and Public Policy Center
1015 15th Street, NW, Suite 900
Washington, D.C. 20005
202-682-1200
Web Page: *http://www.eppc.org*

The American Spectator
2020 North 14th Street, Suite 750
Arlington, VA 22216
703-243-3733
Web Page: *http://www.spectator.org*

Campus: Intercollegiate Studies Institute
3901 Centerville Road, P.O. Box 4431
Wilmington, DE 19807-0431
302-652-4600
Web Page: *http://www.isi.org*

Capitalism Magazine
Web Page: *http://www.capitalismmagazine.com*

The Cato Journal
1000 Massachusetts Avenue, NW
Washington, D.C. 20001
Email: *cato@self-gov.org*
Web Page: *http://www.cato.org*

City Journal
Manhattan Institute
52 Vanderbilt Avenue
New York, NY 10017
212-599-7000
Web Page: *http://www.manhattan-institute.org*

Consent
Canada
Email: *feedback@freedomparty.org/consent*
Web Page: *http://www.freedomparty.org/consent*

Critical Review
P.O. Box 1254, Dept. W
Danbury, CT 06813
203-794-1312
Email: *critrev@aol.com*
Web Page: *http://www.criticalreview.com*

FFF en Español
Future of Freedom Foundation
United States
Email: *info@fff.org*
Web Page: *http://www.fff.org/spanish*

Forbes
28 West 23rd Street
New York, NY 10010
212-366-8900
212-620-2200
Web Page: *http://www.forbes.com*

Formulations
Libertarian Nation Foundation
335 Mulberry Street
Raleigh, NC 27604
Email: *info@libertariannation.org*
Web Page: *http://www.libertariannation.org*

Free Life
25 Chapter Chambers
Easterbrooke Street
London, SWIP 4NN
07956 472 199
Email: *sean@libertarian.co.uk*
Web Page: *http://btinternet.com/~oldwhig/freelife*

The Free Market
Ludwig von Mises Institute
518 W. Magnolia Ave.
Auburn, Alabama 36832-4528
Email: *mail@mises.org*

The Free-Marketer
United States
Web Page: *http://free-market.net*

The Free Radical
New Zealand
Email: *editor@freeradical.co.nz*
Web Page: *http://www.freeradical.co.nz*

Freedom Daily Essays
Future of Freedom Foundation
11350 Random Hills Road, Suite 800
Fairfax, VA 22030
703-934-6101
Email: *Info@fff.org*
Web Page: *http://www.fff.org/freedom*

Full Context
1175-D Kirts Blvd.
Troy, MI 48084
Email: *editor@fullcontext.org*
Web Page: *http://www.fullcontext.org*

Hoover Digest
Hoover Institution
Stanford University
Stanford, CA 94305
800-935-2882
Email: *digest@hoover.stanford.edu*
Web Page: *http://www.hoover.stanford.edu/publications/digest*

Humane Studies Review
Institute for Humane Studies
George Mason University
3301 North Fairfax Drive
Arlington, VA 22201-4432
Email: *ahsturgis@mindspring.com*
Web Page: *http://www.humanestudiesreview.org*

Ideas en Acción
Fundación Atlas para una Sociedad Libre
Argentina
Email: *atlas@free-market.net*

Ideas on Liberty
Foundation for Economic Education
30 South Broadway
Irvington-on-Hudson, NY 10533
914-591-7230
Email: *iol@fee.org*
Web Page: *http://www.fee.org*

Imprimis
Hillsdale College
Hillsdale, MI 49242
Email: *web@hillsdale.edu*
Web Page: *http://www.hillsdale.edu*

The Independent Review
The Independent Institute
413 West 14th Avenue
Covington, LA 70433
Email: *Independent@free-market.net*
Web Page: *http://www.independent.org/review*

The Individual: Magazine of the Society for Individual Freedom
104 Drive Mansions
London, SW6 5JH
0171-371-7530

Jefferson Review
P.O. Box 37460
Louisville, KY 40253-0610
Email: *editor@jeffersoonreview.com*
Web Page: *http://www.jeffersonreview.com*

Journal of Entrepreneurship Education
Email: *info@alliedacademies.org*
Web Page: *http://www.alliedacademies.org/sife*

The Journal of the James Madison Institute
P.O. Box 37460
Tallahassee, FL 32315
850-386-3131
Email: *info@jamesmadison.org*
Web Page: *http://www.jamesmadison.org*

Journal of Libertarian Studies
Center for Libertarian Studies
P.O. Box 4091
Burlingame, CA 94011
800-325-7257
Email: *info@libertarianstudies.org*

Journal of Markets and Morality
Center for Economic Personalism
Action Institute for the Study of Religion and Liberty
Email: *info@acton.org*
Web Page: *http://www.acton.org*

The Journal of Private Enterprise
Trinity College
300 Summit Street
Hartford, CT 06106-3100
Email: *GeraldGunderson@mail.trincoll.edu*
Web Page: *http://www.apee.org/journal*

Le Québécois Libre
Montreal, PQ
Canada
Email: *ql@quebecoislibre.org*
Web Page: *http://www.quebecoislibre.org*

Left and Right
Ludwig von Mises Institute
518 Magnolia Ave.
Auburn, AL 36832-4528
334-321-2100
Email: *mail@mises.org*
Web Page: *http://www.mises.org*

Lew Rockwell.com
Center For Libertarian Studies
P.O. Box 4091
Burlingame, CA 94011
800-325-7257
415-692-8456
Email: *lew@lewrockwell.com*
Web Page: *http://www.lewrockwell.com*

Liberalia
Email: *cmichel@cmichel.com*
Web Page: *http://www.liberalia.com*

Libertas Journal
ESEADE
Buenos Aires, Argentina

The Libertarian Communicator
1202 N. Tennessee Street, Suite 202
Cartersville, GA 30120
800-932-1776
Email: *Advocates@self-gov.org*
Web Page: *http://www.thelibertariancommunicator.com*

The Libertarian Enterprise
Liberty Information Network
Fort Collins, CO
Email: *TLE@johntaylor.org*
Web Page: *http://www.webleyweb.com*

Liberty Free Press
Canada
Email: *editor@libertyfreepress.com*
Web Page: *http://www.libertyfreepress.com*

Liberty Haven
Web Page: *http://www.libertyhaven.com*

Liberty Story
Email: *powellj@libertystory.net*
Web Page: *http://www.libertystory.net*

Liberzine.com
Email: *webmsta@liberzine.com*
Web Page: *http://www.liberzine.com*

The Mises Review
Ludwig von Mises Institute
518 W. Magnolia
Auburn, AL 36832-4528
334-321-2100
Email: *mail@mises.org*
Web Page: *http://www.mises.org*

Miss Liberty's Film and TV World
Email: *oz@missliberty.com*
Web Page: *http://www.missliberty.com*

National Review
National Review, Inc.
150 East 35th Street
New York, NY 10016
Web Page: *http://www.nationalreview.com*

National Review Online
215 Lexington Avenue
New York, NY 10011
212-679-7336
Web Page: *http://nationalreview.com*

The New Australian
Melbourne, Victoria
Australia
Web Page: *http://newaus.com.au*

New Libertarian
Email: *info@newlibertarian.com*
Web Page: *http://www.newlibertarian.com/nlzine*

Policy Review
The Heritage Foundation
214 Massachusetts Avenue, NE
Washington, D.C. 20002
202-546-4400
Web Page: *http://www.hertiage.org*/policyreview

Quarterly Journal of Austrian Economics
Ludwig von Mises Institute
Auburn, AL 36849-5301
334-321-2100
Email: *qjae@mises.org*
Web Page: *http://www.qjae.org*

The Radical Capitalist
The Promethean Theatre Co.
701 7th Avenue, Suite 9W
New York, NY 10036
212-719-9812
Email: *editors@prometh.com*
Web Page: *http://www.prometh.com/radcxp*

Reason Online
Reason Magazine
Los Angeles, CA
Email: *Reason@free-market.net*
Web Page: *http://www.reason.com*

Reason Papers
Tibor R. Machan
Department of Philosophy
Auburn University
Auburn, AL 36849

Regulation
Cato Institute
1000 Massachusetts Avenue, NW
Washington, D.C. 20001
202-842-0200
Web Page: *http://www.cato.org*

Review of Austrian Economics
Ludwig von Mises Institute
578 W. Magnolia Avenue
Auburn, AL 36832-4528
334-321-2100
Email: *mail@mises.org*
Web Page: *http://www.mises.org*

Social Philosophy and Policy
Social Philosophy and Polly Center
Bowling Green State University
Bowling Green, OH 43403
Web Page: *http://www.bgsu.edu/offices/spcc/journal*

Spintech Magazine
Michael R. Allen
United States
Email: *mrallen@spintechmag.com*
Web Page: *http://www.spintechmag.com*

Tocqueville Magazine
France
Email: *ecolibre@mail.com.fr*
Web Page: *http://www.ecolibre.com/magazine*

The Voluntaryist
P.O. Box 1275
Gramling, SC 29348
Email: *vlntryst@aol.com*
Web Page: *http://www.members.aol.com/vlntryst*

The Weekly Standard
1150 17th Street NW Suite 505
Washington, D.C. 20036-4617
Web Page: *http://www.weeklystandard.com*

Index

Index

About the Author

Edward W. Younkins is Professor of Accountancy and Business Administration in the Department of Business and Technology at Wheeling Jesuit University and the founder of the university's undergraduate degree program in Political and Economic Philosophy. He is also the founding director of the university's Master of Business Administration (M.B.A.) and Master of Science in Accountancy (M.S.A.) programs. In addition to earning state and national honors for his performances on the Certified Public Accountant (CPA) and Certified Management Accountant (CMA) exams, respectively, Dr. Younkins also received the Outstanding Educator Award for 1997 from the West Virginia Society of Certified Public Accountants. The author of numerous articles in accounting and business journals, his free-market-oriented articles and reviews have appeared in *Ideas on Liberty* (formerly *The Freeman*), *The Journal of Markets and Morality, The Social Critic, Le Québécois Libre, Liberty Free Press, The Free Radical, Free Life, The Individual,* and many other publications. He recently edited a collection of Michael Novak's articles and essays entitled *Three in One: Essays on Democratic Capitalism, 1976-2000.*